Global Finance in Emerging Market Economies

Emerging market economies have accounted for three quarters of world economic growth and more than half of world output over the last decade. But the energy and ideas inherent in emerging economies cannot generate growth by themselves without resources to support them—and first among these resources is money which is needed to purchase the capital and know-how that turn ideas and initiative into income. How do emerging economies rich in resources other than money *get* money? This question encapsulates what emerging market finance is all about, and why finance is absolutely crucial to economic development.

In emerging countries, most of the population does not have access to bank accounts or financial markets to save or borrow. The result is that many firms cannot get access to financial resources to grow, while households cannot borrow and save in ways that could reduce the riskiness and poverty of their lives. Even those that do have access to formal finance find that credit is unreliable and expensive. These financial failures limit growth and also increase the frequency of costly financial crises.

These issues, and many more like them, mean that finance in emerging economies is different and often more complex than the view presented in most textbooks, where finance is only considered from the perspective of wealthy, developed economies. This book addresses this failure by focusing on the important characteristics of financial systems in emerging market economies and their differences from those in developed countries. This book surveys both theoretical and empirical research on finance in emerging economies, as well as reviewing numerous case studies. The final chapters describe and compare financial systems within the four different regions that encompass most emerging economies: Sub-Saharan Africa, the Middle East, Asia, and South America.

Todd A. Knoop is Richard and Norma Small Professor of Economics and Business at Cornell College, USA.

Routledge international studies in money and banking

Global Finance in Emerging Market Economies

Todd A. Knoop

Routledge
Taylor & Francis Group

LONDON AND NEW YORK

First published 2013
by Routledge
2 Park Square, Milton Park, Abingdon, Oxfordshire OX14 4RN

Simultaneously published in the USA and Canada
by Routledge
711 Third Avenue, New York, NY 10017

First issued in paperback 2014

Routledge is an imprint of the Taylor and Francis Group, an informa business

British Library Cataloguing in Publication Data
A catalogue record for this book is available from the British Library

Library of Congress Cataloging in Publication Data
Knoop, Todd A.
Global finance in emerging market economies/by Todd A. Knoop.
  p. cm.
  Includes bibliographical references and index.
  1. Finance–Developing countries. 2. Banks and banking–Developing
countries. 3. Investments, Foreign–Developing countries. 4. Economic
development–Developing countries. I. Title.
  HG195.K66 2013
  332′042091724–dc23

                                                          2012030934

ISBN 978-0-415-50121-7 (hbk)
ISBN 978-1-138-90135-3 (pbk)
ISBN 978-0-203-06822-9 (ebk)

Typeset in Times New Roman
by Wearset Ltd, Boldon, Tyne and Wear

Contents

Figures

Tables

Preface

Given that you have bothered to crack open this book, you most likely do not have to be convinced that growth in emerging market economies is an important issue in understanding modern global economics.[1] But it is worth convincing you anyway. Emerging economies have always been important economically, if only because emerging countries constitute 85 percent of the world's population and 75 percent of the world's landmass. However, over the last two decades emerging economies have begun to build economic weight that is quickly becoming proportional to their large demographic frames. In 2005, for the first time total output in the emerging world exceeded that of the developed world (measured at purchasing power parity), while the GDP of the seven largest emerging economies (China, India, Brazil, Russia, Indonesia, Mexico, and Turkey) had reached nearly 70 percent of the output levels of the seven largest developed countries (the G7: United States, Japan, Germany, United Kingdom, France, Italy, and Canada).[2] Today emerging market economies also constitute more than 50 percent of the world's exports and investment and consume 60 percent of the world's energy.

The importance of emerging economies will continue to increase in the future given their recent history of extremely rapid growth. Emerging market economies have accounted for three-fourths of world economic growth over the last decade. While projections of the future are always hazardous for economists' public reputations, if emerging economies can continue to grow at similar levels, forecasts are that by 2050 the emerging world will constitute roughly 60 percent of global output and the seven largest emerging economies will have reached output levels that are 75 percent larger than the G7 economies.[3] According to such projections, only two countries which are today considered to be developed—the United States and Japan—will be among the ten largest economies in the world.

Behind all of this growth among emerging countries has been, and will continue to be, financial intermediation. Today emerging economies account for 25 percent of global financial assets (doubling since 2000), which includes 35 percent of stock market capitalization (tripling in size since 2000) and 81 percent of foreign exchange reserves. In 2011, 22 percent of total bank assets were located in emerging economies as well as seven of the 20 largest banks in the world.[4]

Developed and efficient financial systems are absolutely crucial to economic development (for reasons that will be elaborated upon in Chapter 1). However, while most economists would quickly agree with the proposition that economies in the emerging world have different characteristics from those in the developed world, there is relatively little recognition (or understanding) that the financial systems in emerging economies are particularly dissimilar from the financial systems in rich countries. For example, in emerging market economies firms must often rely on informal loans from individuals, their suppliers, or their customers and not from banks or financial markets. Loans are usually small in size and short in length of time. For those firms that do have access to loans through the formal financial system, short-term bank loans are typically the only option. Bond markets, which allow for long-term lending, are largely non-existent and stock markets are only available to the very largest corporations. Because of this lack of access (and the increased cost of finance for those who do have access to finance), there is no mechanism to ensure that those firms with the most productive uses for financial resources can get access to them.

The constraints on individual households in emerging market economies can be even more limiting and costly. For these households, not only is borrowing in the formal sector difficult, but even saving in the formal sector can be hard. Nearly 2.4 billion people in emerging market countries, or 62 percent of the population, do not have a deposit account in a bank.[5] This is true of only 12 percent of those living in developed countries. Without access to bank accounts, people are forced to save in ways that are not diversified, making them vulnerable to risks such as theft. These households have no opportunity to establish a credit history or to borrow in order to fund their education, smooth their consumption if their income changes, invest in a small business, improve their house, or pay for any large or unexpected expenses that arise. Households also have limited access to important but often ignored aspects of financial systems, such as property, life, and health insurance. This inability to borrow and save means that many lives in emerging countries are likely to be not only more unpredictable but also more stressful, less productive, and shorter.

For the poor in emerging economies, meaning those that are living on less than $2.50 a day, the lack of access to finance is particularly devastating. Roughly 2.7 billion people across the globe live at incomes less than this level, almost all of them living in emerging countries. But one of the largest problems with living on $2.50 a day is that you do not get $2.50 each and every day. Some days you get more, many days you get much less or nothing at all. Without access to reliable and reasonable financing, it is difficult to borrow in order to eat every day, to smooth consumption, cover unexpected expenses, or invest in education or a business. It is also difficult to save, making it impossible to build an emergency fund in order to reduce risk or accumulate enough funds to make large purchases. The lack of access to finance is one of the principle reasons why the poor stay poor.

Of course, emerging market economies differ greatly from each other and vary across a wide spectrum, from countries with financial systems that closely resemble those in rich countries (such as South Korea) to those that have almost no financial system to speak of (such as North Korea). But to a greater or lesser extent, many of the problems described above are dealt with every day within emerging economies. Yet given this, it is surprisingly difficult to find most of these important differences examined in any detail within economics textbooks that study the workings of financial systems. Despite paying lip service to the notion that finance differs across countries, most economics textbooks, particularly the workhorse "Money and Banking" textbooks, analyze finance through the perspective of modern, advanced-economy financial systems. There are many examples of how this perspective impacts their analysis. To take one example, heterogeneity of all sorts among borrowers and lenders in financial systems is covered only in a superficial manner. As a result, borrowers receive credit whenever the marginal benefits that flow from the loan are greater than the marginal cost of the loan (the real interest rate). Important factors in finance such as limited credit histories, discrimination, financial repression, and a lack of legal systems to enforce loan contracts play little to no role in their analysis.

This lack of attention to emerging markets often extends to macroeconomic policy analysis as well. In most textbooks, governments are politically stable, solvent, and can borrow large amounts at "risk-free" interest rates. Financial markets are integrated with the rest of the economy and with the rest of the world so that there is free flow of goods and capital. As a result, purchasing power parity and interest rate parity are assumed to hold. Exchange rates are assumed to float. Financial crises (asset bubbles, banking crises, currency crises) are rare, with the focus instead being on moderate and periodic business cycles driven by shocks from outside the model.

Taking a look at the bigger picture, economic theory tells us that financial systems are different in emerging market economies in four primary ways. First, finance is first and foremost about information. Without information that can inform risk expectations, finance does not occur. While information abounds in developed countries and reporting requirements are generally enforced, information is often severely restricted and/or unreliable in emerging market economies. This lack of reliable information explains the success of microfinance programs in the emerging world that have solved some of the problems caused by a lack of information through lending to groups as opposed to individuals.

Second, finance also depends crucially upon institutional structures. Legal systems—which protect things such as creditor and shareholder rights, contract enforcement, and property rights—are absolutely vital to well-functioning financial systems. The same holds true for social stability, political stability, and macroeconomic stability. Finally, all financial systems require reliable mechanisms for monitoring and regulating financial transactions to prevent corruption and excessive risk taking that can threaten the stability of the entire system. These institutional structures are crucially lacking in underdeveloped economies. This explains the fact that in most poor countries, the financial sector in general is more underdeveloped than the rest of the economy.

Sometimes these institutional structures differ across countries for cultural and/or sociological reasons. Although financial systems in developed countries all tend to follow structures developed in Western countries and that reflect Western values, financial systems in emerging markets are often considerably different because they reflect a fundamentally different set of values. An example of this is the importance of Islamic finance, which is based upon the notion that usury (the charging of a fee in return for a loan) is immoral and should not be permitted. In a play on Tolstoy's famous quotation about families, developed financial systems are all alike; every emerging market financial system is emerging in its own way.

Third, because of their smaller capitalization, smaller number of transactions, and weaker institutions, financial systems in emerging market economies tend to be less liquid and more volatile. Banking crises, currency crises, sovereign debt crises, asset bubbles and crashes, as well as recessions and depressions are a more regular part of emerging market economies than they are in the developed world, and also with far more drastic economic consequences. Understanding why these financial crises occur and the economic and social impact they have is crucial to understanding economic development in the emerging world.

Finally, the range of options open to policymakers when it comes to monetary and fiscal policy is much different for emerging governments, almost always much more limited. Emerging market governments may not be able to borrow sufficiently to stabilize aggregate demand during a business cycle or to bailout banks after a crisis. Floating exchange rates may be too costly for small economies that are highly dependent on international trade or foreign capital inflows. On the other hand, central banks in emerging economies may not have the credibility to fix their exchange rates without holding excessive amounts of foreign reserves, and they may not be independent enough to withstand pressures to monetize sovereign debt or to maintain targeted inflation rates in the face of budget pressures. These factors primarily derive from immature political systems and the emergent nature of many economies. Without a history of responsible macroeconomic management, many emerging market economies have little credibility with financial markets.

Despite all of these and other important differences, there is no textbook written for upper-level undergraduate students, lower-level graduate students, and informed readers of economics that explicitly focuses on describing the workings of financial systems in emerging market economies. This book looks to fill this gap by focusing on describing the important characteristics of financial systems in emerging market economies and their differences from those in developed countries. This book surveys both theoretical and empirical research on the workings of financial systems in the emerging world, and it does so in as non-technical a way as possible. It also includes numerous case studies examining financial systems in specific countries and specific events. The final chapters of this book describe and compare financial systems within four different regions that make up the majority of the emerging market world: Sub-Saharan Africa, the Middle East, Asia, and South America.

This book is divided into five parts.

Part I: The importance of finance in emerging market economies

The primary purpose of this part is to provide a broad overview of important facts and the basic workings of financial systems in emerging market economies. It presents many of the theoretical concepts related to financial intermediation that will be the foundation of the analysis used throughout the rest of the book. Chapter 1 covers basic information that might typically be included in a standard Money and Banking course, but with an emphasis on discussing these topics from an emerging market perspective. Included is an examination of the theoretical and empirical support for the claim that financial systems are crucial to economic growth, and vice versa. This chapter also looks at the mechanics of how banks and financial markets operate, including a discussion of the advantages and disadvantages of each of the primary forms of financial intermediation: bonds, stocks, financial intermediaries (banks), and foreign exchange. This is followed by a general description of the structure of emerging market financial systems, including a look at (1) one measure of aggregate financial development (the World Economic Forum Financial Development Index), (2) the relative importance of various forms of financial intermediation in emerging economies, and (3) how the relative importance of different financial instruments varies between developed and emerging economies and how various regions of the emerging world differ from each other. This chapter concludes with an introduction to financial remittances from migrants working in rich countries and the important role these remittances play in formal (and informal) finance in emerging economies.

One of the important themes of this book is that information is the most important input into finance. Because finance involves trading money across time, there is inherent uncertainty in finance that discourages financial intermediation unless lenders can be given some assurance that the risk they are assuming is acceptable given the amount of return they are expecting to receive. Borrowers and lenders can only provide these assurances and effectively balance costs and benefits when sufficient information is available. Without adequate information, borrowing and lending will not take place. The most important difference between emerging and developed financial systems is that the information that is available to lenders is much more limited and considerably less reliable in emerging economies, posing a significant barrier to finance. Chapter 2 develops the economic theory behind these arguments by discussing the important concepts of asymmetric information, heterogeneity, adverse selection, moral hazard, credit rationing, and the external finance premium. These concepts not only explain the lack of financial development in emerging economies, but also help explain why emerging market economies are so volatile. This chapter also includes a discussion of the factors that limit information and curb the ability of lenders to overcome this lack of information within emerging economies. Governments and legal systems (or the lack thereof) play predominant roles in these information failures. This chapter concludes with a look at two new developments in emerging financial systems that allow potential borrowers and lenders to overcome some of these information deficiencies. The first is micro-finance, or the act of providing small loans and other financial services to the very poor who have not previously had access to formal finance. Microfinance loans typically are given to groups of people rather than individuals. The second is the development of information technology, particularly cellphones, which have greatly increased both information and access for many who have never had the ability to use formal finance before.

Part II: Domestic finance and policies in emerging markets

Part II examines financial systems in emerging markets and focuses on the domestic factors, such as government policy and cultural and social norms, that shape a country's financial system. While most emerging markets are increasingly part of the global economy, it is important to first understand the things that make each emerging country unique. Chapter 3 examines institutions and their role in shaping financial systems. The term "institutions" is often vaguely used, but in this book institutions will be defined as the incentives created by governments and societies to engage in mutually beneficial transactions. In other words, it is the factors that encourage people to engage in productive behavior, such as financial intermediation, and not destructive behavior, such as theft. Institutions are not created within markets. Instead, they are the policies, laws, and social norms that encourage things such as the sharing of information, adherence to the rule of law, and the ability to manage and reduce the costs of conflict. This chapter evaluates exactly which institutions are most important in creating efficient financial systems and also reviews the empirical data that attempts to quantify exactly how important these institutions are to financial development. The debate over the role in culture in shaping productive institutions is also surveyed. Sometimes institutions are structured specifically to increase government control and limit financial transactions. The rationale and costs of such governmental policies, known as financial repression, are also examined here. In order to get a deeper understanding of exactly how institutions can differ across emerging economies and their impact on the efficiency of financial intermediation, a case study comparing China's largely state-owned financial system to the privately owned but highly regulated financial system in India concludes the chapter.

Chapter 4 examines fiscal policy and sovereign debt in emerging market economies. The chapter begins by analyzing the government budget constraint, particularly the important role of sovereign debt in keeping emerging government budgets in balance. Unfortunately, the long history of sovereign debt lending to countries is also a long history of countries defaulting on this debt. Periodic default is true whether we are talking about the emerging world or the developed world (as Greece knows all too well). This chapter looks briefly at this history and examines the causes and consequences of sovereign debt crises. Likewise, the determinants of sovereign risk premiums and their role in increasing the costs of debt—as well as providing a justification for debt relief—are examined. One way that many countries have avoided outright default on their sovereign debts is to increase their money supply in order to pay their bills through seigniorage. In extreme cases, sovereign debt crises have led to hyperinflations and economic and financial collapse. This chapter explores the conditions under which hyperinflations occur, their economic consequences, and the impact of monetary strategies to end them, such as currency boards and dollarization. It concludes with a brief case study of the most significant outbreak of sovereign debt and inflation crises among emerging economies, the Latin American debt crises of the 1980s.

Chapter 5 examines two other types of financial crises that emerging markets are historically vulnerable to: asset bubbles and banking crises. Asset bubbles have long played a large role in generating financial and macroeconomic instability throughout the emerging world. This chapter begins with a discussion of the possible causes and consequences of asset bubbles, both from a theoretical and an empirical perspective. This is followed by a brief introduction to the debate surrounding how monetary policy should respond, both before and after an asset bubble "pops," and a case study of one potential asset bubble currently in the making within China's housing market. Asset bubbles are often associated with banking crises. In the next section, a brief history of banking crises is presented along with an examination of various theories as to their causes and empirical studies of their potential costs. The role that government policies such as bank bailouts, lending regulations (or lack thereof), and deposit insurance play in preventing (or exacerbating) banking crises is also discussed. Finally, a case study of the bank and asset market crashes in Mexico in 1994, commonly referred to as the "Tequila crisis," is discussed.

Part III: International finance in emerging markets

Finance has become increasingly internationalized; this is particularly true when it comes to finance in emerging markets because of their smaller size and their reliance on international trade and foreign capital. Much of the historic globalization that has taken place throughout the world over the last three decades has been driven primarily by trade in financial assets, not just trade in goods and services. This part examines how international finance shapes financial systems and economic development in emerging economies.

Chapter 6 begins with a look at cross-border capital flows and financial liberalization, or the elimination of rules, regulations, and taxes that are placed on the movement of financial assets into and out of a country. The long history of international capital flows to emerging economies is summarized briefly. This is followed by a discussion of the potential benefits and costs of liberalizing capital accounts, both in theory and in practice, based on empirical studies of capital account liberalization across countries. While liberalization is traditionally associated with eliminating rules and regulation, there is a strong rationale for implementing stronger, but targeted, prudential regulation of foreign capital to limit certain risky behaviors, which will also be examined in this chapter. Also, the importance of sequencing reform in terms of what financial reforms should come first and how quickly liberalization should proceed is also discussed. This chapter concludes with a case study comparing the process and impact of financial liberalization in Asia and Sub-Saharan Africa.

Chapter 7 examines monetary policy and exchange rate management in emerging economies. The potential list of objectives that central banks in emerging market economies should aim to achieve are more numerous—and more difficult to obtain—than those in developed countries for many reasons, not the least of which is the lack of credibility that many central banks suffer from because of past policy mistakes. One of the most important objectives for central banks in emerging markets is to minimize exchange rate volatility in order to facilitate financial and trade linkages with the rest of the world. In this chapter, the exchange rate policy trilemma, or the impossibility of achieving fixed exchange rates, liberalized capital accounts, and independent inflation and interest rates, is explained. Because of this trilemma, countries that liberalize capital flows face a tradeoff between the costs and benefits of fixing their exchange rate or allowing it to float. The implications of this choice, as well as alternative exchange rate strategies aimed at obtaining different balances in costs and benefits along this tradeoff, are evaluated here as well. Today one of the most important intermediate strategies between fixing and floating exchange rates is for central banks to set an explicit inflation target. This approach is rapidly gaining in popularity among emerging market economies, and the rationale for this approach, as well as its recent empirical success, is evaluated. Finally, in order to illustrate the benefits and pitfalls of alternative exchange rate policies in practice, a case study of the currency board strategy employed by Argentina in the 1990s, and the resulting financial crisis that occurred there in 2001, is examined.

Chapter 8 focuses on one specific danger of fixed exchange rate regimes—currency crises—both in isolation and in initiating systemic banking crises. This chapter begins with a basic review of the balance of payments account and the causes of exchange rate misalignment that can create imbalances which set the stage for currency crises to occur. This is followed by an assessment of the two broad categories of theories that attempt to explain the causes of currency crises and contagion (or the correlation of capital flight across countries). The first is fundamentals-based theories, in which overvalued exchange rates and large current account deficits lead to capital flight and large devaluations. The second is belief-based theories of currency crises, in which self-fulfilling changes in beliefs lead to capital flight within and across countries. The discussion then moves to an examination of the twin crisis phenomenon, in which currency crises and banking crises occur simultaneously, as well as triplet crises, in which currency, banking, and asset market crashes occur at the same time. The various linkages and interactions between these crises are investigated. Many recent twin and triplet crises have occurred, the largest of which was the East Asian financial crisis of 1997–1999, which is reviewed here. This chapter concludes with an examination of two additional questions regarding emerging market financial systems that are currently being hotly debated. First, what are the reasons for and the implications of the recent trend among emerging market economies (particularly in Asia) to maintain undervalued exchange rates and accumulate exceptionally high levels of foreign exchange reserves? Second, what has been, and what should be, the role of the IMF when financial crises strike emerging economies?

Part IV: Describing financial systems in emerging regions of the world

Having examined the crucial theoretical issues at stake for financial systems in emerging markets, and having often painted emerging market economies in broad brush-strokes, it is important to take a closer look at financial systems in different regions of the emerging world and at a few specific countries within these regions. In this part, four broad regions are examined that include over 90 percent of emerging economies: Sub-Saharan Africa, the Middle East and North Africa, Latin America, and Asia. While there is considerable heterogeneity within these regions, there are also remarkable similarities between countries in each region from which important insights can be drawn. Specific focus is given to the major economies in each region, countries that can be characterized as financial successes and countries that can be classified as financial disasters.

Chapter 9 begins by examining Sub-Saharan Africa, not only the poorest of the emerging regions of the world but also the region that has shown the least financial and economic progress over the last 40 years. After a description of some of the shared characteristics of Sub-Saharan financial systems, particularly the importance of informal finance in Sub-Saharan Africa, this chapter takes a closer look at the steady progress of financial liberalization and financial innovation across the region. Next, a look at the challenging environment for monetary policy in Africa and the significant hurdles faced by central banks to promote financial development and macroeconomic stability. Nigeria is the largest economy in Africa, and a closer look at the country provides an excellent example of how rampant corruption and other institutional failures can significantly limit financial and economic development. In contrast to large Nigeria, small Botswana is examined as an example of how even the most seemingly "backward" of countries can create institutions that facilitate financial development and improve standards of living. The fact that the Democratic Republic of Congo, which is also discussed here, is a historic failure despite its wealth of resources once again illustrates the importance of institutional structures when it comes to encouraging financial development that helps create economic development. Finally, this chapter discusses how the lack of developed financial systems creates additional risk for poor countries, as illustrated by the 2007 global financial crisis in the developed world and its impact on Sub-Saharan economies.

Chapter 10 looks at financial systems in the Middle East, including North Africa. After a description of some of the shared characteristics of Middle

Eastern financial systems, this chapter takes a closer look at the region's largest country in terms of population: Egypt. Egypt's economic performance over the last 40 years has been disappointing, in large part because of their inefficient, government-run financial system that is similar to those of many of the economies in the region. This chapter also presents a case study of the biggest financial failure in the region—Iran—which illustrates the devastating impact that unchecked financial repression can have on economic growth. In contrast to Egypt and Iran, the United Arab Emirates has fostered one of the most highly developed financial systems in the world, and become one of the richest countries in the world on a per-capita basis, despite its small size. In part, this success has been fueled by its adoption of liberalized, outward-looking financial policies. Success has also been fostered in the United Arab Emirates and many other emerging market economies by the use of sovereign wealth funds, which are also described and evaluated in this chapter. One additional topic covered in this chapter is the increasing impact of Islamic finance on Middle Eastern financial systems. Under Islamic finance, financial transactions are governed by the *Qur'an* as dictated by *Shari'a* law which prohibits the charging of interest on loans, among other things. As a result, alternative financial arrangements have to be made in order to be strictly consistent with *Shari'a* law. The nature of some of these arrangements and their impact on financial development in the Islamic world are summarized here.

Chapter 11 examines financial systems in Asia. This region incorporates the most dynamic emerging market financial systems, it has been the largest recipient of foreign capital inflows, and it has seen the largest declines in poverty over the last three decades. Despite the large number of widely varying countries in the region, there has been an "Asian model" of financial development that has been generally followed across the region and which is described here. This Asian model incorporates export promotion, undervalued exchange rates, financial systems dominated by large banks, directed lending by the government, and connected lending between corporate conglomerates. This chapter examines the financial structures of the two largest and fastest-growing countries in the world, China and India, and compares their different approaches to financial development. In China, the financial system has played a leading role in driving economic development through government-directed investment by state-owned banks to state-owned firms. Private firms primarily find credit through a large and unregulated underground lending market. While this system has pumped unprecedented levels of investment into the economy, there are real questions about the efficiency of these investments, the overall stability of the banking system, and the sustainability of this approach. In India, financial development has largely been the result of overall economic growth and has not been driven by financial liberalization or improved institutions. As a result, India's financial system is relatively underdeveloped outside of its dynamic stock markets and is a hindrance to overall growth. The important differences between state-led financial development and market-driven development is particularly evident in many of the economies of South East Asia, which were particularly hard hit by the

East Asian crisis in 1997. This chapter ends with a case study comparing the different approaches of Indonesia and Malaysia to financial liberalization after the East Asian crisis.

Chapter 12 discusses the financial systems of Latin America. The characteristics that generally define finance in Latin America are summarized, followed by a look at one aspect of the region's financial system that exemplifies Latin America for many: offshore financial centers in the Caribbean. Next, the region's largest economies are examined: Brazil and Mexico. Both economies are similar in that after years of disastrous financial and economic policies, including significant financial crises in the mid-1990s, both financial systems have liberalized and significantly improved their macroeconomic environment. At the same time, there are significant differences between the countries in terms of their openness to foreign capital and the role of government ownership in their banking systems. Migrant remittances are a particularly important aspect of Latin American finance and have become the second-largest source of capital flows to the region (larger than financial aid). These remittances present unique challenges and opportunities and their regional impact is described here. This chapter then turns to look at the disaster that is the Argentinean financial system, which is an excellent case study in how instability—social, political, and macroeconomic—kills financial intermediation and undermines economic growth. The chapter concludes with a look at dollarization in Latin America, the significant costs it imposes on many aspects of finance in the region, and potential strategies for de-dollarizing economies.

Part V: Conclusions

Chapter 13 concludes the book and summarizes the ten most important lessons learned from recent successes and failures in financial development among emerging market economies. One of the most important themes of this book is that while trial and error have been important factors in advances in our understanding of how financial systems work, the development of better economic theories of how financial systems work has played just as important a role in this improved knowledge. This final chapter reviews many of these advances in our understanding while also highlighting the important challenges for financial development still to be faced by emerging market economies in the future.

Acknowledgments

There is no such thing as a solo act when it comes to the long and treacherous act of writing a book. There are many people who deserve to be thanked. This includes my many colleagues at Cornell College who were generous with their time and their schedules, allowing me to take the time I needed to write this book. I am particularly appreciative of my good friend Professor Rhawn Denniston for his sage professional advice and not-always-so-sage sense of humor. I also want to express my gratitude to Richard and Norma Small, who were the benefactors of the distinguished professorship in their names that financed a great deal of the research that went into this book. But most of all, it would be difficult to undertake such a project without the support and joy my family constantly gives me. To my wife, Debra DeLaet, and my girls, Edie and Daphne, thank you is not enough, but it will have to do for here.

Part I

The importance of finance in emerging market economies

1 Finance and development

Introduction

What is the role of financial development in economic development? Surprisingly, this is a question that did not pique the interest of many economists until relatively recently. For over 100 years, the conventional wisdom on this question was that financial development would happen automatically and by itself, but only after macroeconomic development had already occurred. The economist Joan Robinson (1952) summarized this "laissez-faire" view of finance as: "Where enterprise leads, finance follows." This thinking is still implicit in the way that many historians have told the story of economic development in the United States and Europe, including the Industrial Revolution, where the role of financial development is typically down-played and the role of technological development (that somehow takes place magically with little investment in research and capital accumulation) takes center stage.

This view of finance as passively responding to overall progress is one that is not consistent with the larger scope of history. In the words of historian Niall Ferguson (2008): "The evolution of credit and debt was as important as any technological innovation in the rise of civilization, from ancient Babylon to present-day Hong Kong." Empires—from Rome to Britain—rose and fell based on their ability to marshal financial resources when they needed them to prosecute wars or to keep their populations pacified.

A few prominent economists did argue that finance plays an important role in initiating, not just following behind, economic growth. Joseph Schumpeter's (1912) model of creative destruction and technology cycles emphasized the important role of finance in allocating resources to entrepreneurs. Through financial intermediation, entrepreneurs are able to gain access to the resources needed to create the new technologies that are the engines of growth. According to him, entrepreneurship is impossible without the "bankers and other financial middlemen who mobilize savings, evaluate projects, manage risk, monitor managers, acquire facilities and otherwise redirect resources from old to new channels."[1] Schumpeter identified Britain's strong and efficient financial system as a primary reason why the Industrial Revolution began there and not elsewhere.

Interestingly enough, the root meaning of the word finance is consistent with Schumpeter's view of why it is so important. As noted by Robert Shiller (2012), the word *finance* derives from the Latin *finis*, which is often translated as "end" but was also used as a synonym for "goal." In this context, finance can be thought of as part of the process of facilitating the economic goal of development and growth.

But despite the arguments of a few economists such as Schumpeter, the Nobel Prize winning economist Robert Lucas (1988) essentially summarized the consensus opinion of economists in the early 1990s when he said that the role of finance in economic development was "over-stressed." Given how little it was actually stressed in the literature, this in essence meant that it should not be stressed at all.

Over the last 20 years, however, economists' thinking about the interaction between financial development and economic development has changed quite dramatically, because of both theoretical advances and improved empirical research. On the theory side, many new models have been developed by economists such as Ben Bernanke and Mark Gertler (1989, 1990) and Joseph Stiglitz and Andrew Weiss (1981), who show how market failure in financial markets can limit financial development and create instability that can limit economic growth. These models will be the focus of subsequent chapters. On the empirical side, both econometric research and the experiences of emerging market economies, including many in Asia such as Hong Kong and Singapore, have clearly illustrated exactly how financial development can stimulate economic development. This empirical research is summarized by Patrick Honohan (2004), World Bank economist and Governor of the Central Bank of Ireland, as follows: "The causal link between finance and growth is one of the most striking macroeconomic relationships uncovered in the last decade."

Setting aside the research of economists, anyone who has spent time in much of the emerging world understands the trap that many of the poor find themselves in when they lack the financial resources today that will eventually help to feed them tomorrow. The development economists Abhijit Banerjee and Esther Duflo (2011) tell the story of a street vendor in Chennai, India that paid her supplier an effective interest rate of slightly less than 5 percent a day. While this may not sound like much, borrowing $1 today at these rates would lead to a debt of nearly $20 million if left unpaid for a year. Many of these poor not only cannot affordably borrow through formal channels, they also cannot save their money safely with reasonable returns and have no access to insurance to smooth consumption and offset unexpected expenses. The lack of affordable finance is a large part of the poverty trap that plagues much of the developing world.

This chapter examines the nature of finance and discusses why, intuitively, financial development is crucial to economic growth. This is followed by a brief review of the empirical literature examining the relationship between financial development and economic growth. Next, the chapter provides an introduction to the primary methods of finance—financial intermediaries (principally banks), bonds, and stocks—and a discussion of the merits and disadvantages of each.

The relative importance of these alternative methods of finance differs across countries. To understand how, a brief survey of the financial structure of a selection of emerging economies is examined, including a look at the empirical evidence regarding whether financial structure matters for economic growth. This chapter concludes with a look at one source of finance unique to the emerging market economies: remittances from migrant workers in developed nations back to their families and friends still living in emerging economies.

What is finance and why is it important to economic growth?

Finance is not an easy concept to define. For most, they know finance "when they see it." The simplest definition is that *financial intermediation* is the trading of money across time. By *money*, economists mean any asset that is generally accepted in trade. Money is a tool for eliminating the need for barter and provides three significant benefits to its holders. First, money is a medium of exchange, making trade easier as compared to bartering. Barter requires a double coincidence of wants, meaning that you have to have what your trading partner wants and your partner has to have what you want. Money allows individuals to break this link by allowing them to separate the selling of the things that they have from the purchase of the things that they want. Second, money is a store of value, meaning it is a way to save and, as a result, conduct your purchases at a time that is different from when you sell your wares. Third, money conveys important information by being a unit of account, or a common standard by which to measure value and denote prices. This reduces confusion and increases efficiency.

In modern economies, the most commonly used methods of measuring money are *M1* (currency in circulation and checking account deposits at banks payable on demand) and *M2* (*M1* plus savings deposits, money market deposits, and small certificates of deposits issued by banks). *M1* includes assets that are clearly money, while *M2* includes additional assets that, while not generally used in payments for goods and services, are clearly very liquid, meaning that they can be easily converted into money. Of course, historically many different assets have served as money, from gold to sea shells to cigarettes. The disadvantage of these commodity monies is that their supply is inflexible and highly variable, leading to constraints on trade and unpredictable changes in the prices denoted in these monies. With paper, or *fiat money*, governments can control the aggregate supply of money and, with proper management that maintains the public faith in its value, regulate the supply of money in a way that enhances price and economic stability.

Given the importance of money, it is obvious why individuals who have productive uses for it now but do not currently have sufficient amounts of it would be willing to trade money in the future for money today. This is exactly what financial intermediation facilitates. What makes finance unique from other economic transactions is this element of time. Anyone who trades money today for money tomorrow is accepting significant risk from many different sources. For example, there is risk regarding future changes in how much money is worth, or its purchasing power, based on changes in the prices of goods and services in the future (i.e. inflation or deflation). There is also the risk that the borrower will not meet their obligations and fail to pay the lender on the terms agreed upon (i.e. default).

Time is also a crucially important element in the economic development of emerging market economies. Because of the power of compounding, small increases in growth rates which are sustained over time lead to large increases in the level of output. A country growing at 2 percent a year will double in size every 36 years, while a country growing at 4 percent would quadruple in that same amount of time.[2] Thus, financial intermediation that enables poorer countries to obtain money sooner also allows these countries to invest in productive inputs sooner, grow faster sooner, and advance along their development paths more quickly.

Financial systems are the markets and organizations that facilitate financial intermediation at an aggregate level. Financial systems take advantage of economies of scale to increase the amount of financial intermediation and reduce its costs. Development of financial systems can directly increase economic growth (and welfare) within economies in many different ways. Here are five of the most important.

Financial development allocates resources to those with the most productive uses for these resources. Finance allows individuals without wealth to invest in education, in physical capital, or to start a business. As mentioned earlier, Schumpeter (1912) argued that finance was the fuel for all types of investment activities, entrepreneurial behavior, and risk taking. Without finance, only those with the wealth to fund these activities themselves will undertake them. There is absolutely no guarantee that those with wealth will also be those with the most productive uses for it. According to Frederic Mishkin (2006b), "the financial system [is] the brain of the economy.... It acts as a coordinating mechanism that allocates capital, the lifeblood of economic activity, to its most productive uses by businesses and households."

Contrary to the assumptions of many, the poor do save. The problem is that they generally do not save through formal methods, such as in bank accounts, which are likely to funnel this money to productive investment (and also generate a return for the saver). Banerjee and Duflo (2011) report that in 18 less developed countries, only 7 percent of the rural poor and 8 percent of the urban poor have formal savings accounts and in many of these countries the number is less than 1 percent. Instead, saving largely takes place through the purchase of real, non-productive, assets: livestock, larger houses, and paying in advance for shop credit.

Another important way financial development increases allocative efficiency is by improving the quality of information that is available by expanding the number of people engaged in the financial system. More participants create greater demand for information services such as real-time asset prices, accounting systems, credit rating agencies, financial rating firms, and financial reporting firms. Reliable information is crucial to accurately evaluating risk, and the more information that is available, the better the decisions made by borrowers and lenders. More information also allows for better monitoring of lenders after they receive financing, reducing the chances of default and further increasing efficiency.

Financial development provides incentives to save and invest within an economy. By allowing resources to be used in the most productive ways, financial systems increase the potential return and reduce the risk of savings. This increases the aggregate amount of savings, which, in turn, increases aggregate investment in human capital, physical capital, and entrepreneurial activities. Walter Bagehot (1873) argued that financial development, and the resulting increase in the scale of financial intermediation that accompanied it, was what initiated the Industrial Revolution. Finance provided sufficient resources to entrepreneurs to fund the enormous amounts of investment that were needed to take advantage of existing manufacturing technologies. Many of these technologies had existed well before the mid-1700s but could not be implemented without finance.

Financial development allows both savers and borrowers to reduce risk, encouraging productive activities. Finance takes place across time, making it risky, which in turn reduces the amount of finance that takes place and increases its costs. If risk can be reduced, financial intermediation will increase, allowing greater and more efficient investment. Well-developed financial systems mediate risk in a number of ways. First, they *hedge* risk, meaning they allow people who want to reduce risk to transfer it to others who are willing to accept more risk (for a greater return). An example of this is a company issuing a share of stock. The company receives a source of funds they are never obligated to pay back, reducing their risk. The buyer of this stock accepts the risk of an uncertain return for an uncapped share of the company's profits. Lending for longer periods is also a way to hedge risk away from borrowers and to lenders. Second, financial systems *pool* risk by aggregating the savings of many different individuals. This allows an individual borrower to effectively rely on many different sources for any single loan, reducing the chances of an interruption in finance. Third, financial systems *diversify* risk by allowing savers to hold many different types of assets from many different borrowers, spreading risk more thinly over a larger group. Finally, financial development reduces *liquidity* risk, meaning that it becomes easier to buy or sell a financial asset when a financial system is larger because there are more buyers and sellers and there are more transactions taking place.

Financial development increases the number of trades, reducing transaction costs and increasing efficiency. The concept of *economies of scale*, where the average cost declines as the quantity produced increases, is fundamental to understanding why financial systems, as opposed to informal financial transactions, are so important to economic growth. More financial trades (often referred to as *financial deepening*) allow for greater specialization within the financial industry and also allows for financial institutions to invest in technologies and processes that reduce transaction costs. Financial deepening also facilitates specialization outside of the financial industry by allowing firms to outsource certain activities using trade credit to buy and sell goods they might have been forced to produce, often inefficiently, by themselves. These sorts of specialization gains are at the heart of the increases in productivity that drive long-run economic growth.

Financial development serves as a source of insurance for firms and households, reducing aggregate risk and encouraging productive behavior. The availability of life, property, and health insurance are all contingent upon the availability of financial assets for insurance companies to safely save premiums in until they are dispersed. More than this, the ability to borrow at reasonable interest rates to help cover unexpected costs—such as natural disasters, health emergencies, a loss of income, or other unexpected losses—is itself a form of insurance for households and firms. Without the insurance that having access to finance provides, many households and firms are forced to act in ways that minimize their exposure to risk, such as keeping the scale of their investments low, but that also minimizes their productivity.

The empirical evidence on the relationship between financial and economic development

Does financial development cause economic development, or is it just a symptom of economic development? Econometric studies conducted over the last two decades have reached a consensus answer to this question: financial development directly increases economic growth through better allocation of resources and reducing transaction costs (efficiency) and also by increasing the aggregate quantity of savings and investment through reducing risk (scale).

A few individual studies deserve discussion. The seminal study on this question was conducted by King and Levine (1993), who find that historical measures of bank development across 77 countries are significant predictors of investment, productivity, and growth 10 to 30 years into the future. This result has since been affirmed in many other studies using variants of King and Levine's approach.[3] This research cumulatively suggests that doubling the supply of credit within the average emerging market economy would increase growth by about 2 percent a year, meaning that doubling credit would double a country's income level over 36 years.[4]

Taking a somewhat different approach, Buera *et al.* (2011) examine the relationship between financial inefficiency and differences in productivity and income across countries. Using a quantitative model, they find that financial distortions impact the allocation of capital and entrepreneurship away from sectors of the economy that have larger financing needs (e.g. manufacturing), reducing total factor productivity, investment, and economic growth. The authors estimate that differences in financial development can explain up to 80 percent of the differences in income between a rich and an emerging market economy such as the United States and Mexico.

Other studies have taken a more microeconomic perspective and have focused specifically on the impact of financial development on the poor. Beck, Demirgüç-Kunt, and Levine (2007) find that between 1980 and 2005, financial development disproportionally increased the incomes of the bottom 20 percent of the income distribution as well as reduced the proportion of people living in extreme poverty (defined as living on less than $1 a day). Of these improvements in the incomes of the poor, roughly two-thirds come from increases in aggregate growth and one-third come from growth specific to the poorest households. Demirgüç-Kunt and Levine (2008) attempt to identify the sources of this income growth among the poor. They survey the empirical literature and find that financial development increases economic opportunity as measured by increases in entrepreneurial activity, physical capital, schooling, and health as well as by decreasing transaction costs and even reducing discrimination.

Instead of measuring financial development as increases in the size and number of financial transactions, Beck *et al.* (2007) focus on participation and access to financial services. They find incredible variation in financial access across countries. For example, Ethiopia has roughly one branch bank per 200,000 residents, as compared to Indonesia which has 17 branches per 200,000 residents (in the United States, this number is over 60). In Bangladesh, there is one ATM for every 1.7 million residents. In Bolivia, the average loan is 28 times the level of per-capita GDP in the country, while in Iran the average loan is only 4 percent of per-capita GDP. Overall, 40 to 80 percent of all individuals in emerging economies lack access to formal banking services. Across different measures of access, the authors find that increased financial access leads to increased economic growth.

Other studies have focused on the microeconomic impact of informal finance and the day-to-day financing activities of the poor in order to implicitly examine the welfare and growth impacts of financial underdevelopment. Collins *et al.* (2009) interviewed 250 households living on less than $2 a day over the course of a year. In the author's words, "One of the least remarked-on problems of living on $2 a day is that you don't literally get that amount each day." As a result, even the poorest households rely heavily on finance in one form or another. Their research illustrates how poor households, lacking access to formal financial systems, make do in other informal ways. In order to provide insurance against unexpected expenses, the poor are forced to save in non-productive ways such as burying currency, giving money to a neighbor, or paying in advance for shop credit. Also, savings clubs (known as "merry-go-rounds" in Africa) are popular, where individuals contribute to savings "pots," each member receiving the pot on a rotating basis. When borrowing, the poor are forced to rely on wage advances, not pay their bills, borrow from neighbors, and pawn their goods. The authors find that none of the households they followed used fewer than four different methods of informal finance, and many used over ten different techniques, often changing their mix daily. Likewise, in a survey of households in Udaipur, India, Banerjee and Duflo (2011) found that two-thirds of poor households had loans. For these low-income borrowers, 37 percent of the borrowing came from shopkeepers, 23 percent from relatives, 18 percent from moneylenders, and only 6.4 percent from formal lenders. Across 18 less developed countries, they find that less than 5 percent of the rural poor and less than 10 percent of the urban poor have formal loans.

Often, these informal lending relationships can serve as a form of insurance that can reduce risk. In a survey of poor in rural Nigeria, Udry (1994) finds that the average family was a borrower or lender to 2.5 other families. Interestingly, when a borrowing family suffered a loss they would still regularly pay back their loans, but when the lending family suffered a loss they would actually be repaid more than they originally lent as a means of reciprocity. The problem with such complicated informal lending and insurance relationships is that they are quite expensive and often not reliable, leaving households vulnerable to shocks such as unexpected health problems, robbery, and declines in income. This vulnerability prevents them from being able to maintain consistent levels of consumption, physical investment, and schooling. As evidence of this, Udry found that the informal lending relationships in Nigeria did not eliminate consumption volatility for poor households, even when total income in the village was unchanged. Likewise Beegle *et al.* (2005) find cross-country evidence that income volatility is linked to higher levels of child labor and lower levels of schooling despite the existence of informal finance.

This lack of insurance to protect against income volatility also keeps the entrepreneurial activities of the poor very small in scale, reducing not only the risk they expose themselves to but also their potential returns. For example, studies have found that households with lower wealth and less access to finance are more likely to engage in lower risk and lower return activities as well as less likely to start their own businesses.[5]

The other problem with informal lending is that it is very expensive. Banerjee and Duflo (2011) find in Udaipur, India that those living in extreme poverty (less than $1 US a day) pay an average interest rate of 57 percent a year. Across less developed countries, interest rates for the poor are consistently between 40 and 200 percent a year, significantly higher than formal interest rates. While not dispositive, these studies surveying the impact on the financial behavior of poor households suggest that emerging economies have a great deal to gain from financial development that brings with it increased access to formal finance.

In reviewing this research, it is important to recognize that it is quite likely that the causation between finance and economic growth also works in reverse and that economic development can facilitate financial development. This can occur because higher incomes increase net worths, making it less risky to borrow and lend. A larger economy also increases the number of transactions that take place, including bond and stock market transactions, which makes these markets more liquid and reduces risk as well as transaction costs. Finally, many of the prerequisites for economic growth, such as stable legal and political systems, are also prerequisites for financial development (more on the role of institutions in Chapter 3). Consistent with these theoretical arguments, Levine (1997) finds that across 80 developed and emerging economies, measures of financial development increased as aggregate income increased.

Forms of financial intermediation in financial systems

The different needs, risk preferences, and required returns of different borrowers and lenders have created both the demand for and supply of many different types of financial assets. Here is a brief summary of the four principle forms of financial intermediation within financial systems.

Bond markets. *Bonds* are financial instruments in which (1) the amount borrowed (the *principle*) is repaid at a fixed point in time (its *maturity date*); (2) interest payments are made regularly at fixed points in time, and (3) the interest rate is fixed throughout the life of the bond.

From a borrower's (or the bond issuer's) perspective, bonds are attractive because they offer flexibility. Bonds can be short-term or long-term (often as long as 30 years), allowing borrowers to obtain financing for long-term investments in which profits are not realized for many years. Bonds also offer borrowers the advantage of predictability; bondholders cannot place additional conditions on issuers as long as their interest rate payments are met. The disadvantage of bonds for borrowers is that they require fixed payments which, if not met, lead to default. This, in turn, can lead to significant restrictions on the issuer's future activities or even bankruptcy.

For lenders (or the purchasers of bonds), bonds typically offer a degree of predictability by allowing them to lock in for a fixed period higher returns than typically offered by savings accounts issued by banks. The disadvantage to lenders is that holding bonds exposes their savings to two distinct forms of risk. First, there is *default risk*, or the risk the borrower will not meet their financial obligations. Default risk can vary considerably across bonds depending upon the characteristics of the issuer, the details of an individual bond instrument, and the legal systems that allow for (or fail to allow for) enforcement of bond contracts. Many bonds have clauses in which they legally receive higher priority in the case of default, while other bonds are *subordinated*, meaning they receive lower priority in the case of default. Second, rising market interest rates reduce the attractiveness of existing bonds with fixed interest rates, leading to a fall in the prices of these bonds in secondary markets. When this happens, bondholders can be exposed to significant losses if they attempt to sell their bond before its maturity date (this is referred to as *interest rate risk*).

Stock markets. A common *stock* (or *equity*) is a financial instrument that grants its buyer a share of limited ownership of a corporation. Stockholders' power is limited by the fact that they are only allowed to vote for the board of directors of the corporation and do not have the right to play a direct role in managing the firm's day-to-day operations. Stockholders' liability is limited in that they cannot lose more than the price of the stock they purchased. Stockholders have a right to share in the net income of the corporation, either through *dividends*, or payments made by the firm to stockholders, or through increases in the price of the stock as the net worth of the firm increases.

The advantage to borrowers (the corporation issuing the stock) is that stock does not lock them into fixed payments. This lowers the default risk that the corporation faces and provides it with additional financial flexibility. The disadvantage to stock issuers is that they lose a share of any future profits, some degree of privacy as publicly traded corporations are required to make more financial data public, and some degree of control over the corporation's operations.

For lenders (stockholders), equity offers the potential of uncapped returns subject to the future profitability of the corporation. With higher potential returns, however, also comes higher default risk. When a corporation goes bankrupt, stockholders only receive what is left after all creditors and bond-holders have been compensated. Stocks are also risky because future profit-ability is highly unpredictable, making the prices of stocks quite volatile. Uncertainty regarding the "correct" price of stocks often fuels speculative behavior that magnifies price movements and risk. John Maynard Keynes (1936) compared stock markets to a beauty contest in which the best strategy for picking the winner is not to use your own opinion of who is most beauti-ful, but to predict which contestant the other judges will think is most beauti-ful. Such subjectivity means that fundamental attributes of stocks may play a relatively minor role in price movements over short periods, leading to extreme price volatility and risk.

Financial intermediaries. Financial intermediaries are organizations that facilitate the transfer of money from small savers to borrowers. Financial inter-mediaries take many forms. *Insurance companies* collect premiums from con-tract holders and use these premiums to purchase large asset portfolios, making payouts to contract holders when specific events occur. *Mutual funds* issue shares and use the proceeds to purchase large portfolios of assets, changes in the value of which are reflected in the price of the mutual fund's shares. *Finance companies* are often tied to consumer product corporations and provide financ-ing to the purchasers of these products by raising funds, primarily through bond issues. Finally, *banks (depository institutions)* primarily raise funds by issuing deposit accounts and certificates of deposit, and primarily use these funds to make commercial and consumer loans and to purchase bonds.

Commercial banks (banks that emphasize lending to firms and households) are the most important financial intermediaries, and the most important source of finance in general, in emerging market economies. They provide a wide array of borrowing and lending services that are crucial to well-functioning financial systems. They also specialize in providing these services to households and small firms that are the most dependent on finance and that also constitute a large segment of emerging market economies.

Banks offer many advantages to savers. Banks accumulate the savings of a large number of individuals and invest these funds across a wide variety of bor-rowers and financial assets, pooling and diversifying both savings and invest-ment, which reduces risk. Banks also specialize in dealing with small borrowers, allowing them to take advantage of economies of scale and develop expertise in information gathering. By doing this, banks are able to obtain better information on potential borrowers so that they can make better decisions and keep transaction costs low, increasing returns and lowering risk. Finally, by reducing transaction costs banks are also able to offer savers a wide variety of services, such as checking accounts, that would otherwise be prohibitively expensive.

While banks minimize risk, they are still risky institutions because they are illiquid. Banks borrow short term (usually there are few restrictions on deposit withdrawals) but lend for longer, fixed terms. This exposes them to both liquidity risk and interest rate risk. In addition, their customer base and assets tend to have higher levels of default risk because they specialize in dealing with small borrowers. As a result, there is significant risk in holding bank deposits. So much, in fact, that changing perceptions of this risk are often acute enough to scare depositors and trigger a *bank run* in which each depositor tries to withdraw their savings before the bank runs short of liquidity. Bank runs can lead to the immediate failure of any bank, even one fundamentally profitable. To reduce the risk of bank runs in order to stabilize banking systems, most governments offer some form of deposit insurance that promises to repay depositors in the case of a default by their bank.

From the perspective of borrowers, banks provide significant advantages. The biggest is that banks are typically the only option for small, medium, and even large borrowers. Raising money by issuing bonds or stocks is not an option for most firms in most emerging economies because these markets are not well developed. Even when financial markets are an option, there are large transaction costs associated with obtaining funds directly through financial markets, such as the fees charged by *investment banks*, or financial institutions that specialize in issuing stocks and bonds.

Bank lending does have disadvantages for borrowers. Bank lending is typically more expensive; interest rates on bank loans usually exceed the interest rates on most bonds. Bank lending involves fixed interest payments, leading to the possibility of default. Because of the higher default risk of the clients that banks typically serve, bank loans are usually accompanied by much more intrusive monitoring conditions than bond debt. The time and effort spent accumulating information as well as the conditions imposed in order to receive a loan are costly to borrowers. Most importantly, commercial loans from banks tend to be short term, but firms typically invest money in long-term projects. This creates risk and costs for firms that they cannot eliminate unless they are able to issue long-term bonds or stocks.

It is important to highlight the significance of another type of financial institution easily ignored: insurance companies. As mentioned, one of the main facts that characterize the life of the poor in emerging economies is its volatility. With little wealth and limited social safety nets provided by the government, poor households have little margin for error when faced with a negative shock to their income or wealth. These shocks cannot be hedged, as they are in developed countries, through the purchase of health, life, and property insurance. As a result, the poor find that their economic lives are much more vulnerable, making investing and planning for the future difficult. This in turn negatively impacts their productivity and their ability to sustain economic improvement in their lives.

Having broader access to insurance services would be an excellent way for households in emerging economies to protect their well-being and encourage economic growth. But insurance providers cannot exist in a vacuum. Insurers need a stable legal, political, and economic environment in order to assume the risks associated with providing insurance. In addition, insurance firms need high-return/low-risk financial assets in which to invest their premiums, particularly long-term assets such as bonds and stocks. Thus, the impact of financial development on access to insurance is another way that finance can increase economic development.

The foreign exchange market. Foreign exchange is the trading of one currency for another currency, either at current (spot) prices or at fixed future prices. The foreign exchange (FX) market, like bond markets and some stock markets, has no physical location but is simply a network of currency traders working for major financial institutions, primarily international banks. The FX market is by far the largest financial market in the world. FX trades average over $4 trillion (roughly one-third of the US economy) a day. The total volume of FX trades is nearly 100 times the actual amount of trade in goods and services made worldwide. The vast majority of FX trades are made to facilitate international capital movements, such as the buying and selling of international financial instruments, or made by traders speculating on the prices of exchange rates and foreign assets.

A brief look at financial development and financial structure in emerging economies

To set the stage for future discussions, it is valuable to make a first attempt at broadly characterizing the level of development in emerging market financial systems and examine how they are structured in terms of the relative importance of bank, stock, and bond financing.

It is not easy at all to come up with a single, simple measurement of financial development. In measuring financial development, both the size of banks, bond markets, and stock markets as well as how broad financial access is spread and the efficiency of intermediation are all important. In addition, there should also include some measure of the overall stability of the financial system, which includes the legal, political, policy, and economic environment of the economy. Finally, some measure of the openness of the financial system to international finance should be incorporated. As one measure of financial development, the World Economic Forum has created the Financial Development Index (FinDI), which comprises multiple sources of data measuring these factors for 57 of the largest economies in the world.[6] This index ranges from 1 to 7, with 7 being the highest level of financial development.

Table 1.1 presents the FinDI rankings for 2011 and 2010, as well as each country's ranking in terms of level of GDP (measured at purchasing power parity (PPP)). Not surprisingly, developed economies dominate the top of the FinDI rankings. Malaysia is the highest-ranked emerging market economy,

Table 1.1 Financial Development Index rankings

Country	2011 rank	2010 rank	2011 score	2011 GDP rank
Hong Kong SAR	1	4	5.16	36
United States	2	1	5.15	1
United Kingdom	3	2	5.00	8
Singapore	4	3	4.97	38
Australia	5	5	4.93	18
Canada	6	6	4.86	14
Netherlands	7	7	4.71	22
Japan	8	9	4.71	4
Switzerland	9	8	4.63	37
Norway	10	15	4.52	46
Sweden	11	12	4.51	33
France	12	11	4.44	46
Belgium	13	10	4.38	31
Germany	14	13	4.33	5
Denmark	15	16	4.30	52
Malaysia	16	17	4.24	29
Spain	17	14	4.24	13
South Korea	18	24	4.13	12
China	19	22	4.12	2
Austria	20	19	4.11	35
Finland	21	20	4.11	53
Ireland	22	18	4.10	56
Saudi Arabia	23	26	3.90	23
Bahrain	24	23	3.90	103
United Arab Emirates	25	21	3.89	48
Israel	26	27	3.86	50
Italy	27	25	3.85	10
Kuwait	28	28	3.73	58
South Africa	29	32	3.64	25
Brazil	30	31	3.61	7
Chile	31	30	3.61	41
Jordan	32	29	3.48	96
Poland	33	35	3.45	20
Czech Republic	34	33	3.40	43
Thailand	35	34	3.32	24
India	36	37	3.29	3
Panama	37	39	3.23	88
Slovak Republic	38	36	3.22	62
Russia	39	40	3.18	6
Peru	40	48	3.16	39
Mexico	41	43	3.16	11
Morocco	42	41	3.15	57
Turkey	43	42	3.14	16
Philippines	44	50	3.13	32
Columbia	45	47	3.09	28
Kazakhstan	46	49	3.06	51
Hungary	47	45	3.03	54
Tunisia	48	N/A	3.00	67

continued

Table 1.1 Continued

Country	2011 rank	2010 rank	2011 score	2011 GDP rank
Egypt	49	38	2.99	26
Vietnam	50	46	2.98	40
Indonesia	51	51	2.92	15
Romania	52	44	2.85	45
Argentina	53	52	2.69	21
Ukraine	54	53	2.62	37
Pakistan	55	54	2.58	27
Bangladesh	56	56	2.58	44
Tanzania	57	N/A	2.55	80
Ghana	58	N/A	2.55	77
Venezuela	59	55	2.44	34
Nigeria	60	57	2.44	30

Source: World Economic Forum, IMF.

coming in 16th place, which is higher than its relative ranking according to GDP of 29th place. This makes Malaysia unusual; note that most emerging economies are typically ranked lower in the FinDI than when ranked according to GDP. The most significant examples of this are China (2nd in GDP, 19th in FinDI), India (3rd in GDP, 36th in FinDI), Brazil (7th in GDP, 30th in FinDI), Turkey (16th in GDP, 43rd in FinDI), Argentina (21st in GDP, 53rd in FinDI), and Nigeria (30th in GDP, 60th in FinDI). Of course, the flip-side of this observation is that many developed countries score quite highly on the FinDI relative to the size of their economy, for example Hong Kong (36th in GDP, 1st in FinDI), Singapore (38th in GDP, 4th in FinDI), Australia (18th in GDP, 5th in FinDI), and Switzerland (37th in GDP, 9th in FinDI).[7]

Emerging market economies scored highly in the FinDI in 2011 among the components of the index that measure financial stability. This is the result of the fact that emerging economies were relatively unscathed by the 2007 global financial crisis. The high economic growth rates in much of the emerging world coupled with generally sound macroeconomic management and manageable levels of debt meant that countries such as South Korea, Malaysia, China, Saudi Arabia, and Poland improved significantly in recent FinDI rankings. However, emerging economies continued to score relatively low with regard to measures of the overall development of their bond and stock markets, the quantity of long-term lending, financial access for households and small and medium-sized firms, and the quality of their legal systems. This is consistent with the econometric findings of Beck, Demirgüç-Kunt, and Levine (2010), who find no significant financial deepening among middle- and low-income countries in general over the last two decades.

Figure 1.1 presents data on the size of bank assets (BSA), non-bank assets (NBA) (including insurance companies, mutual and pension funds, etc.), stock market capitalization (SMC), and domestic bond issues (DBO) for a selected group of emerging economies. In general, banks play a disproportionately large

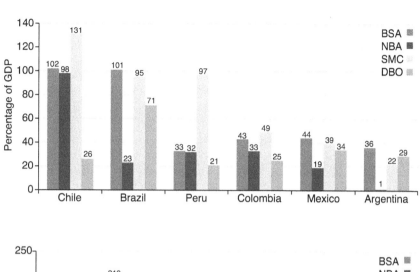

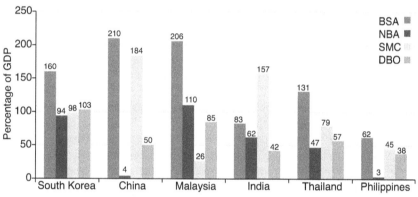

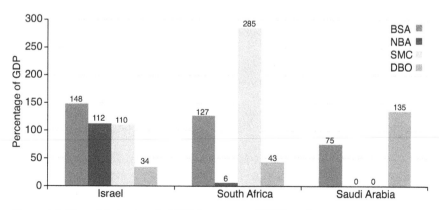

Figure 1.1 Financial structure in 2007 (in percent of GDP).

role in finance in emerging economies. However, there are a few examples of countries in which stock markets are slightly larger than their banking systems (Chile, Columbia, Peru, India, and South Africa). In these countries, however, this growth in their stock markets appears to have come at the expense of their bond markets. Other than Saudi Arabia, there are no financial systems that are dominated by bond market capitalization. Other than South Korea, there are no examples in this figure of emerging market financial systems that have high levels of financial development (ratios close to 100 percent of GDP) across all four types of financial assets.

Overall, stock market capitalization has grown greatly in emerging economies, from only $83 billion in 1983 to $45 trillion in 2009, while volume in these markets (meaning the total value of transactions) has risen from $1.2 billion in 1983 to $80 trillion. China alone has seen its stock market capitalization rise from only $369 million in 2003 to an incredible $3.4 trillion in 2011, making it the second-largest stock market in the world.[8] One factor that has contributed greatly to the levels of stock market capitalization in emerging market economies is the privatization of state-owned enterprises (SOEs). *Privatization* refers to the sale of state-owned assets to the private sector, often in the form of issuing stock. In 2009, 132 of the *Fortune* Global 500 companies were previously SOEs and had been privatized, representing half of the market capitalization of non-US companies.[9]

Does financial structure—meaning the mix between bank, bond, and stock financing—matter when it comes to economic growth? The circumstantial and empirical evidence suggests that it does not. When looking across developed countries, we see countries that are heavily weighted toward banks, such as Germany and Japan where bank finance accounts for 80–90 percent of total finance. However, in countries such as the United States and the United Kingdom, banks account for only 40–50 percent of total finance. France, Germany, and Italy have bond markets that are roughly twice the size of their stock markets. The opposite is true in Japan, the United Kingdom, and Greece, where stock markets are two to three times the size of the bond markets. Only in the United States is there a rough balance between banks, stocks, and bond financing. Demirgüç-Kunt and Levine (2001) find no consistent empirical evidence across 48 countries between 1980 and 1997 that financial structure has any quantifiable impact on access to finance, the number of new firms, or economic growth.

This said, clearly it is in a country's best interests for borrowers and lenders to have a diverse range of financial assets at their disposal, given that each type of asset has specific advantages and disadvantages for borrowers and lenders. A country with no bond market is a country in which long-term borrowing is going to be difficult, and this can impact investment and growth in the long run. In those emerging market economies in which one type of financial asset is clearly missing—which is most emerging market economies—clearly there are efficiency gains to be had by improving this type of financial intermediation.

Remittances to emerging market economies

In 2010 there were roughly 200 million migrants across the globe. A large majority of these migrants are individuals moving from emerging countries to developed countries in search of higher incomes (wages are on average five times higher in developed countries, measured at purchasing power parity). Many of these migrants send payments back to their family and friends. These remittances are the second most important source of external finance for emerging economies, behind only foreign direct investment but ahead of foreign portfolio investment (i.e. bonds and stocks) and foreign assistance. The World Bank reports that in the decade preceding the global financial crisis remittances grew at a real rate of nearly 13 percent a year and total remittances were more than $480 billion in 2012 (although as much of 50 percent of remittances are missed through direct transfers of unrecorded cash).[10] Table 1.2 presents the 15 largest remittance recipients in 2009 and 2010 both in terms of total volume and as a share of GDP. For larger countries, remittances are bigger in absolute levels but small relative to the size of their economy. For the 15 countries with the largest remittance flows relative to GDP, remittances are greater than 13 percent of GDP.

For recipient countries, remittances have become a crucial avenue for financial development by serving as a source of funds and by increasing financial access through increasing the interaction between the poor and the financial sector. While the size of remittances varies greatly, they are large in terms of total transfers, but only because there are a large number of small transfers. For example, El Salvadorian migrants working in the United States send back an average of more than $5,300 a year (38 percent of their income). However, the average remittance transaction is only approximately $300.[11]

Table 1.2 Largest emerging market remittance recipients in 2009 and 2010

Remittances received in 2010 ($ billions)		Ranked by share of GDP in 2009 (%)	
India	55.0	Tajikistan	35
China	51.0	Tonga	28
Mexico	22.6	Lesotho	25
Philippines	21.3	Moldova	23
Bangladesh	11.1	Nepal	23
Nigeria	10.0	Lebanon	22
Pakistan	9.4	Samoa	22
Poland	9.1	Honduras	19
Lebanon	8.2	Guyana	17
Egypt	7.7	El Salvador	16
Vietnam	7.2	Jordan	16
Indonesia	7.1	Kyrgyz Republic	15
Morocco	6.4	Haiti	15
Russia	5.6	Jamaica	14
Serbia	5.6	Bosnia	13

Source: Yang (2011).

Empirical evidence suggests that emerging economies benefit in a number of ways from these remittances. Aggarwal *et al.* (2006) find across 99 developing countries that higher levels of remittances are associated with a variety of measures of increased financial development. Adelman and Taylor (1990) find that $1 of remittances sent to Mexico increased GNP by $2.69 in urban areas and $3.17 in rural areas.[12] Adams and Page (2005) find that remittances are associated with reductions in poverty. Mishra (2005) finds that remittances act as a form of insurance for those in the home country and increase in response to declines in aggregate income in the home country. Other studies have shown that higher levels of remittances are associated with increased schooling, health, and entrepreneurial activity.[13]

Of course, remittances are no panacea for emerging economies. Remittances represent the loss of productive workers, which can negatively impact growth, particularly when these migrants have unique skills that are in short supply (otherwise known as "brain drain"). In addition, remittance services often involve large transaction costs. While many remittances are sent by established money-transfer firms such as Money Gram or Western Union, many migrants from smaller countries or more remote areas rely on informal brokers and small operators that charge exorbitant prices. The World Bank (2010) estimates that sending $200 between developed and emerging economies costs an average of 9 percent in transaction and exchange rate fees. The cost of remittances between emerging economies can be even more expensive. For example, it costs nearly 25 percent of the remittance to send $200 from Kenya to Tanzania. These high costs are in part because most remittance payments are relatively small (roughly $200 at the median) and the fixed costs of these transactions are relatively large, on average $10. But these large costs are also a function of the low levels of financial development and financial access that exist in many emerging financial markets.

The World Bank reports that remittance fees fall within a receiving country as financial development increases, when the number of service providers increases, and when the number of migrants rise. The incredible expansion of mobile phones throughout the developing world also promises to reduce these transaction costs (more on mobile-phone-based banking in the next chapter).[14] Best of all for those receiving remittances, there is also evidence that as fees fall, the size of remittances increases disproportionally.[15]

Remittances also have benefits for the migrant, outside of simply helping family and friends. Remittances are also a means for migrants to save within their home country. With the growth of mobile-phone-based remittance services and reduced regulations on foreign capital flows, migrants are better able to save in emerging market economies than ever before. In fact, the governments of Israel and India have successfully sold diaspora bonds directly marketed to migrants in developed countries to help pay for public investment projects. Nigeria, Kenya, and the Philippines have pilot projects being developed to do the same.

Conclusions

Financial development is an important driver of economic development. Many of today's rich countries have used specialization in financial services as a leading sector for propelling economic growth, and many emerging economies today in Asia and in countries such as Chile, Brazil, and South Africa are attempting to do the same. Financial development not only benefits poorer countries, but it directly benefits the poorest populations within these countries. Many empirical studies have been conducted over the last 20 years showing that not only does financial development directly increase aggregate income, but it also disproportionally benefits those at the bottom of the income distribution living in poverty. It does this in five ways: by increasing the total amount of finance available, by increasing access to finance for those with the most productive uses for it, by reducing the risk of financial transactions, by providing these services at lower transactions costs, and by providing insurance to help protect against the volatility of economic life.

As a result, it is imperative that emerging economies find ways to facilitate financial development. History and the empirical record suggest that the method through which formal finance takes place—whether through banks or financial markets—is not nearly as important as the fact that it takes place. To understand how countries can encourage financial development, we must first understand the factors that influence financial intermediation and the inputs that go into creating it. The next chapter begins this process of building a deeper understanding of the production process behind financial intermediation.

2   Information and finance

Introduction

What goes into the making of financial intermediation? What is its production process? Based on our discussion in the previous chapter, the fundamental defining characteristic of finance is risk. Because finance takes place across time, and because no one has perfect information about a borrower's ability or willingness to repay in the future, engaging in a financial transaction is always an act of faith guided by judgment. According to Walter Bagehot (1873), credit is "the disposition of one man to trust another." No lender will extend credit without some reasonable expectation that the borrower can meet the conditions of the financial transaction they are engaging in. There is only one way to create this reasonable expectation: the borrower has to provide specific, quality, and persuasive information about their ability and commitment to meeting their financial obligations. The most important theme of this chapter is that information is the most important input into financial intermediation. If lenders do not have the proper information and cannot be given adequate assurances of repayment, credit will not be granted regardless of other factors, including the interest rate the borrower might be willing to pay.

Information, particularly the lack of it, has many important implications for finance in emerging economy financial systems. This chapter discusses these implications and examines how information failures—particularly asymmetric information—restrict the quantity and increase the price of financial intermediation. We will also look at the empirical literature on how information impacts financial and economic development, as well as its impact on financial volatility. Finally, this chapter examines two modern innovations in financial information. The first is the growth of microfinance, or providing small loans and other financial services to the very poor, typically through lending to groups and not to individuals. The second is information technology, particularly mobile phones, and their growing impact on emerging market financial systems.

Asymmetric information, adverse selection, and moral hazard

It is fairly easy to understand how imperfect information makes it difficult for lenders to evaluate a borrower's *ability* to pay back their obligations. If a lender cannot adequately judge a borrower's financial position, their lending history, or the risk and return of the activities they are going to engage in, then a lender will not extend them a loan.

Evaluating a borrower's ability to pay is often relatively easy because many of the factors involved are observable, such as a borrower's assets. What is more difficult to evaluate is a borrower's *willingness* to pay, which is often not directly observable by a lender. This lack of information possessed by lenders creates a problem of *asymmetric information*, meaning that borrowers always know more about the true risk associated with any loan than the lender does. Asymmetric information exists in part because a borrower knows more about how profitable the uses for borrowed funds are likely to be or what their true net worth and income is. However, the largest source of asymmetric information is the fact that the borrower has better information than the lender regarding their commitment to making future payments and about whether they intend to engage in activities that might reduce their likelihood of making these payments.

The existence of asymmetric information means that financial markets are not perfectly competitive. Asymmetric information creates information externalities that increase the risk of lending, creating market failures that discourage financial intermediation. There are two important implications of these information externalities: adverse selection and moral hazard.

Adverse selection. Asymmetric information creates a perverse lending incentive before a loan even takes place. This comes from the fact that individual borrowers who have the highest default risks are the ones who are most likely to seek loans. The obvious reason for this is that risk-loving individuals who are most likely to engage in risky behavior are likely to do so with their own money as well as a lender's money. At the same time, conservative borrowers are less likely to assume risk and suffer losses that would require them to request a loan to cover it. Likewise, it is the poorest borrowers that have the most need, but also the smallest margin for error, which are most likely to ask for a loan. Taken together, these observations imply that the pool of borrowers that are applying for loans is riskier than the population in general. This phenomenon is referred to as *adverse selection*. Lenders know about this problem but they cannot eliminate it because they do not have perfect information to adequately separate the riskiest borrowers from the safest borrowers. As a result, financial intermediation is discouraged by the higher risk of lending created by asymmetric information.

Moral hazard. A second perverse incentive is created by asymmetric information after a loan is given. When a loan is granted it encourages riskier behavior from the borrower because the lender assumes some of the downside risk of a project the borrower undertakes; if a project fails and the borrower defaults, then the lender is going to be out a portion if not all of their money. However, the lender usually does not have a claim upon the upside benefits of these projects; if the borrower realizes large profits, they do not have to share any of it with the lender (this is less true when it comes to stocks than it is for bank lending and bonds). When borrowers are able to allocate some of the downside risk of a project to others while keeping all of the upside benefits for themselves, it creates incentives for borrowers to engage in riskier behavior than they would if they were using their own money. This incentive problem is referred to as *moral hazard*. Moral hazard is endemic in financial systems and comes from many sources. When you consider the fact that most financial institutions and individuals are both borrowers and lenders (for instance, banks make loans but also take in deposits) it is possible for an agent in an economy to be both a victim of moral hazard at the same time that they are guilty of engaging in moral hazard behavior. By increasing the risk of finance, moral hazard discourages all kinds of financial intermediation.

Dealing with information problems and risk

If a lack of quality information is the most important obstacle to conducting financial intermediation, then the obvious solution is for lenders and borrowers to develop processes that help generate better information and reduce the incentives to engage in adverse selection and moral hazard behavior. Developed countries have developed these systems, but most emerging countries have not. It is this fact that is the most important difference between finance in developed and emerging economies.

Consider applying for a loan. In a developed country, a name, an address, and a social security or tax identification number instantly allows a lender to gain access to a wide variety of residency, income, and credit histories from both publicly available sources—such as tax records—or from private credit reporting agencies. In most emerging economies, no such social security or tax identification numbers are available. In fact, because of unreliable birth records, there may not be any record of an applicant's name (coupled with the fact that in many cultures names are much more fluid and/or complicated). Addresses are often not available because of non-existent property registries and surveying. And even if you have a name, an address, or a tax number, no organization exists to assemble the attached information into a reliable economic history.

Verifying income is difficult for many of the same reasons. In addition, because so many more people work in informal markets, they often get paid in cash that does not create a paper trail. This is particularly true for many small businesses, which often have few detailed records to demonstrate profitability or cash flows.

These problems can be overcome, but they involve creating information and legal systems that can mitigate the problems of asymmetric information and moral hazard. Here are some of the things that can be done to create these information and legal systems.

Develop credit information registries. Private companies can be used to collect and produce information and sell this information for a profit. This could include journalist and news service organizations (such as the *Wall Street Journal* and the *Financial Times*), credit rating agencies (such as Moody's or Standard and Poor's), or investment advising firms. While private information services can provide valuable information, they are plagued by a free-rider problem: it is easy for people who have not paid for the information produced by these organizations to use the information. The easiest way to do this is for a free-rider to watch and follow the behavior of other investors who have purchased information. As a result of free-riding, private companies alone will produce an inefficiently low amount of information because of their inability to fully capture the revenue from the information they produce.

One potential solution to the free-rider problem is to treat credit information as a public good and for the government to create public rating registries that collect and distribute the information that it collects. This includes information generated by legal systems (i.e. titles, criminal records, etc.) and also information created by tax records and through the provision of social welfare programs (health care, pensions, and education). Many emerging market economies have developed such public registries, or are in the process of doing so, because markets commonly fail to provide such information services in poorer countries.

A good example of a country that is currently investing in this idea is India with its "Unique Identity" program (UID), where biometric information (fingerprints and retinal scans) will have been collected on more than 600 million people (half of India's population) by 2014. The idea is to reduce fraud and identity theft by keeping better information records on all Indian citizens. It will also allow Indians to receive cash transfers from the government directly into their own bank accounts, thereby creating a credit information registry that can increase financial access for all Indians.

Use government regulations to increase transparency. Realizing that asymmetric information leads to market failure in financial systems and that the free-rider problem means that the market will provide an inefficiently low amount of information, governments have a role in setting regulations that increase financial transparency. This can be done in many ways: imposing reporting requirements on publicly held firms, requiring tax returns to be submitted, setting accounting and financial standards on firms, and creating and enforcing laws aimed at reducing financial fraud. Most importantly, all of this information must be made public and be accessible through a formalized system of name registration or by providing identification numbers.

Use financial intermediaries, not financial markets. Banks (and other financial intermediaries) have two important information advantages over bond and stock markets. First, banks specialize in lending to and generating information about small, information-limited borrowers. They do this in a number of ways. One way is by establishing long-term relationships with small borrowers, allowing these borrowers to build a credit history. Another is by establishing ties to the local communities in which they operate, generating information through personal contacts.

The second information advantage that banks have is that all of the information they generate is private, meaning that it is not subject to being used (and its value diluted) by free-riders. The value of private information is another important factor in encouraging banks to develop long-term relationships with their customers.

The information advantages that banks possess, particularly on smaller borrowers, are important in explaining a fact highlighted in the previous chapter: banks are responsible for a very large proportion of finance in most emerging market economies. Financial underdevelopment is associated with a lack of information, which banks are best able to deal with. Because information availability is likely to increase as financial systems develop, it is reasonable to expect that the importance of banks should diminish over time in favor of bond and stock markets within growing emerging economies. This is exactly what happened in many developed economies during the twentieth century.

However, the informational advantages of banks have their limits. It is still the case that the very poor in many countries do not have access to bank lending because banks find it extremely difficult and very costly to get information about the very poor, particularly those who live in rural areas, those who live in informal urban housing, or those who only work in informal jobs.

After the loan: monitor and impose restrictive covenants. Having information before a loan is given only helps deal with the adverse selection problem. Obtaining information on behavior after a loan is given, through things such as financial reporting requirements, helps discourage moral hazard behavior. Successful lenders are constantly monitoring their borrowers. In addition, many debt contracts have *restrictive covenants*, meaning requirements or prohibitions on certain behaviors by a borrower that are aimed at reducing default risk. These could be requirements that forbid a borrower from using loans for anything other than a designated purpose, they could require borrowers to hold insurance or maintain certain levels of net worth, or they could be covenants that necessitate the regular provision of financial information.

Monitoring and enforcing restrictive covenants are expensive for both borrowers and lenders. This is one advantage that informal moneylenders have over formal banks. Because moneylenders often use physical threats or social pressures to enforce contracts, they do not have to incur the costs of monitoring that formal lenders do. As a result, under some circumstances they may be able to lend at lower rates than formal lenders.

Lend money short term and not long term. When loans are extended for only short periods of time, the renewal of a loan can become a "carrot" to be dangled in front of a borrower to encourage them to engage in appropriate behaviors and reduce moral hazard. Of course, the inability to obtain long-term credit is extremely costly for small businesses that would like to engage in long-term investments.

Require collateral and high net worths. Collateral is the assets of a borrower that are transferred to the lender in the event of default.[1] Requiring collateral in order to obtain a loan is the most widely used, and most effective, method of overcoming the problems of asymmetric information. Losing the rights to collateral imposes a known loss on borrowers if they default, increasing the stake that a borrower has in meeting their loan commitments. This limits adverse selection before a loan is made and moral hazard behavior after a loan is made. The net worth of a borrower can be a substitute for collateral, but only if the borrower is rich enough.

Higher net worth not only limits the probability of default on a loan (reducing adverse selection), but increases the chance that the borrower will be fully responsible for any losses (reducing moral hazard incentives). The importance of net worth and collateral in overcoming asymmetric information is at the heart of the old adage in finance that "only the people with money can borrow it."

Unfortunately, each of these methods of dealing with asymmetric information problems—credit information registries, government transparency regulation, financial intermediaries, monitoring and restrictive covenants, short-term lending, and collateral—is likely to be less effective in emerging market economies than in developed countries. Here are some reasons why.

A lack of privately produced information. There is a negative feedback loop between the lack of financial development in emerging economies and a lack of information. Financial underdevelopment means fewer financial transactions, less financial access, less participation, and less financial information produced. Of course, less financial information then hampers financial development in a vicious cycle.

A lack of effective contract enforcement mechanisms. One of the reasons that emerging economies are not rich economies is that they often do not have the proper legal systems in place that allow them to enforce financial contracts in an efficient, cost-effective, and timely manner. Borrowers often ignore restrictive covenants or collateral requirements because they know that it will take years to enforce these contracts, if ever. Borrowers in some countries might also be able to use political connections, or make bribes, to stop this process altogether. Finally, some borrowers who default know that credit records are so poor that they can easily disappear, only to borrow again later. Under these circumstances, there will be no mitigation of adverse selection and moral hazard.

Even when formal contract enforcement mechanisms are in place, a great deal of finance in poorer countries takes place informally, often involving oral contracts that are difficult to enforce in the legal system.

A lack of effective government regulation. The same reasons why some governments cannot enforce contracts are why they cannot effectively enforce regulations on providing financial information. Weak legal systems, corruption, and politics make it impossible for some governments to ensure reliable financial information and accounting transparency. In addition, a lack of established accounting principles and professional expertise in many countries limits the quality and usefulness of financial reports.

High and variable interest rates. In many economies, fragile macroeconomies, repressed financial systems, and a lack of financial development lead to high and variable interest rates. Higher and more variable interest rates increase the problems of adverse selection by making loans attractive only to those that can earn the highest returns (and engage in the highest risk). It also necessitates earning higher returns once a loan is given, encouraging borrowers to engage in more risky behavior and increasing the incentives for moral hazard.

A lack of collateral and net worths. In emerging economies, those living in poverty (less than $2.50 a day) make up 40 to 60 percent of the population. At these income levels, it is difficult to accumulate sufficient collateral and net worths to make the poor attractive customers for formal finance. Emerging market economies are also filled with start-up businesses and small and medium-sized firms. These are the firms that are most likely to have limited access to formal sources of finance because of the lack of credit histories and limited assets to use as collateral. There are many stories that could be told of successful entrepreneurs who had difficulty in finding their first loan, including Narayan Murthy and Nandan Nilekani, the founders of the hugely successful Indian software firm Infosys, who had difficulty getting their first loan because banks could see no inventory in their firm to use as collateral.

Hernando de Soto, in his popular book *The Mystery of Capital* (2000), identifies one of the important reasons why the poor do not have access to collateral. Because of underdeveloped legal systems, many emerging market economies make it extremely expensive and time-consuming for the poor to obtain legal title to the assets that they informally own. De Soto documents just how extreme some of these difficulties in many countries can be. For example, in the Philippines obtaining legal title to untitled urban land involved 168 steps that took between 13 and 25 years.[2] In Haiti, purchasing government land involved 176 steps that would take 19 years to navigate. De Soto estimates that the total value of real estate without proper legal title in the emerging world was more than $9 trillion in the year 2000. To put this number in some perspective, it is 93 times the amount of foreign aid given to the developing world over the last three decades. Without legal title and formal ownership, this land and capital cannot be used as collateral or to supplement a borrower's calculated net worth. Coupled with the difficulty of enforcing collateral requirements in many emerging economies, these trillions of dollars of "dead capital" cannot be used to overcome asymmetric information problems and facilitate financial development, placing severe constraints on economic development.

The external finance premium and credit rationing

Asymmetric information increases the risk associated with financial transactions. It also plays an important role in reducing the quantity and increasing the price of financial intermediation. Two widely influential models explain how and why this occurs. Together, they form the basis of the modern economic theory of financial intermediation.

The external finance premium. In a series of papers, Ben Bernanke and Mark Gertler (1987, 1989, 1990) examine the determinants of what they refer to as the *cost of credit intermediation*, otherwise known as the *external finance premium*. From the perspective of borrowers, the external finance premium is the costs borrowers pay to obtain finance when they cannot obtain it internally through their own net worths or retained profits. The external finance premium is determined by a multitude of factors, only one of which is the interest rate. The costs of producing reliable accounting information needed to overcome the problems associated with asymmetric information are also a large portion of the external finance premium. Accountants, information systems, and bookkeeping can be quite expensive, particularly for small borrowers. Borrowers are also likely to have to incur monitoring costs, to adhere to restrictive covenants, and to provide collateral; these activities have a significant opportunity cost associated with them. When borrowing is done through bond or stock markets, there are significant underwriting costs that are incurred when investment banks market and sell these assets to the public. Finally, it is important to note that lenders also incur significant costs as they monitor their borrowers. The costs incurred by lenders are likely to be passed on to borrowers either directly through fees or indirectly through higher interest rates.

Bernanke and Gertler's principal insight is that the size of the external finance premium is directly related to the size of the asymmetric problem, meaning the levels of adverse selection and moral hazard associated with each individual financial transaction. When the financial fundamentals (net worths, assets, and cash flows) of lenders and borrowers are high and borrowers have the ability to produce quality information about these fundamentals, then the external finance premium will be low. This will encourage financial intermediation and financial development. But when financial fundamentals are weak, information is poor, and adverse selection and moral hazard are rampant, then the external finance premium will be large and many borrowers will be priced out of formal financial markets, limiting financial access and development.

It is important to note that the financial fundamentals of lenders and not just borrowers impact financial intermediation. A lender's willingness to extend credit is not only a function of the borrower's financial position but of their own financial position as well. When lenders have lower net worths, they are forced to reduce their risk exposure and move toward holding more liquid, less risky assets. If they are to engage in any new lending, lenders will be forced to charge higher interest rates and require more information, more collateral, and more monitoring. This increases the external finance premium and reduces the efficiency and the quantity of lending, just as it does when borrowers have weak financial fundamentals.

Credit rationing. Like the external finance premium model, models of credit rationing agree that weaker financial fundamentals and a lack of financial information limit financial intermediation. However, the mechanism by which this occurs is different. Models of credit rationing focus on the fact that lenders often use a number of non-price commitments to reduce risk, such as requiring collateral and asking for co-signers on loans. These terms are not a direct factor in the costs incurred by a borrower (for example, a firm can still use their collateral in production during the life of a loan), but they are still conditions that are often difficult to meet. As a result, many borrowers find that their credit is limited regardless of the price they are willing to pay for it; in other words, they are quantity rationed, not price rationed.

Joseph Stiglitz and Andrew Weiss (1981), in one of the most influential papers in modern macroeconomics, develop a model of credit rationing in which the effective return a lender receives on a loan is more complicated than just the nominal interest rate alone. In this model, changes in interest rates impact the default rates of borrowers. When interest rates rise, it creates incentives for a riskier group of lenders to apply for loans (adverse selection) and encourages riskier behavior from those that are given loans (moral hazard). Realizing this, lenders keep interest rates at levels lower than what would clear the market in an attempt to reduce these risk externalities. This means that persistent disequilibrium and an excess demand for credit exists in financial markets, where many borrowers are willing to pay higher interest rates to receive more credit but lenders will not provide it because of its impact on risk. Credit rationing also implies that interest rates are inflexible, or "sticky," particularly under high-risk conditions.

In Stiglitz and Weiss' model, the risk externalities created by adverse selection and moral hazard make it too risky to price ration finance through charging higher interest rates. Instead, lenders impose credit limits on their borrowers. The level of this credit limit depends upon the expected default risk of an individual borrower. This, in turn, depends upon the borrower's financial fundamentals, which includes a borrower's net worth, the amount of collateral they possess, and the quality of the information that a borrower can provide. Borrowers that have weaker financial fundamentals are the most likely to have lower lending ceilings imposed on them. This credit rationing reduces financial intermediation and can constrain consumption, investment, and economic growth.

Using a similar model, Stiglitz and Greenwald (2003) show that changes in the financial fundamentals of lenders can also affect the credit constraints imposed on borrowers. As the financial fundamentals of lenders decline, they are forced to reduce the riskiness of their portfolios. To avoid additional risk from moral hazard and adverse selection, they do this by tightening credit limits as opposed to raising interest rates. Credit rationing is particularly severe on those borrowers that have the weakest financial fundamentals.

Credit rationing takes place in many different forms in financial systems and not only impacts the level of finance provided within an economy but can also impact financial structure, or the mix between bank, stock, and bond financing. For example, consider *equity rationing*, or the lending constraints on firms in stock markets. Equity rationing is imposed on firms both internally and externally. Internal equity rationing takes place when quantity limits are self-imposed by the managers of firms despite the fact that equity has a significant advantage over debt in that there is no bankruptcy risk associated with it. Managers impose internal equity limits because new stock issues dilute the return on existing equity, the maximization of which is management's primary responsibility. Also, issuing new equity may send unwanted signals to markets and shareholders that the managers of the firm think the stock price is overvalued.

Equity rationing is also imposed externally on firms through stock markets. Hellmann and Stiglitz (2000) present a model in which equity rationing takes place among investors when firms have private and asymmetric information about their investment projects. When investors reduce the price they bid on a stock (which increases the cost of equity to firms), it causes a riskier pool of firms to issue equity (adverse selection) and also encourages firms that already have equity financing to engage in riskier investment projects in order to increase their returns (moral hazard). To counteract this, investors equity ration individual firms by placing limits on the amount of equity they are willing to hold.

Bond market rationing is also likely to occur in financial systems. When bond investors do not have sufficient information to discriminate between the risks of various firms, then savers will credit ration all bond issuers. As a result, the safest firms will likely go elsewhere for their financing, either to stock markets or, most likely, to banks, which may have superior private information and be able to offer more credit on better terms. This means that the pool of borrowers left in bond markets is riskier and are credit rationed to an even greater extent; just one more reason why credit rationing reduces the overall level of financial intermediation in an economy. It also helps explain why bank financing tends to dominate bond market financing, particularly in poorer emerging economies with less quality information.

Empirical evidence on credit rationing and the external finance premium. A strong prediction of the two models just discussed is that borrowers that have the weakest financial fundamentals and with less information about these fundamentals are the most likely to face higher financing costs and tighter credit limits. These borrowers are likely to be poorer, smaller, and younger than the average borrower. A great deal of empirical evidence exists in developed countries, primarily the United States, that indicates that, in fact, poorer, smaller, and younger borrowers do pay larger external finance premiums and are more likely to be credit rationed.[3] A great deal of work has also been conducted recently focusing on emerging market economies. A number of these studies were reviewed in Chapter 1 during the discussion of how financial development disproportionally benefits the poor, who are most likely to be credit constrained.[4]

At the microeconomic level, Beck, Demirgüç-Kunt, Laeven, and Levine (2008) and Beck, Demirgüç-Kunt, and Maksimovic (2008) find empirical evidence across emerging economies that smaller firms and poorer households are most likely to be credit constrained and also most likely to benefit from financial development. A number of other authors have investigated the behavior of households and firms in specific countries. These studies find that the investment levels of small firms closely track their income, suggesting external finance is too difficult or too expensive for them to obtain.[5] They also find that the poorest households have the highest default risks, are least likely to own their own businesses, behave in more risk-averse ways, and are more likely to use informal finance.[6]

One potentially powerful method of investigating the impact of credit rationing is using randomized experiments. Studies in Sri Lanka and Mexico investigated how small businesses reacted to receiving a grant of either $250 or $500. The return from the first $250 of the grant was over 60 percent a year in Sri Lanka and over 120 percent in Mexico, suggesting significant untapped economic opportunities because of a lack of finance.[7]

At the macroeconomic level, de Wet (2004) finds that emerging market governments are regularly credit rationed by international investors, as evidenced by the fact that the quantity supplied of sovereign government bonds is persistently greater than the quantity demanded of these bonds for many countries. This would be consistent with the credit rationing model in which interest rates are lower than what is needed to clear the government bond market because of the externalities generated by asymmetric information. Likewise, Zoli (2004) finds evidence that emerging governments face credit limits and that when sovereign debt levels grow past these limits countries are likely to face discreet cut-offs in credit from foreign investors.

Finally, other studies have looked across countries to identify a relation between information provision and levels of financial intermediation.[8] Djankov *et al.* (2007) find that levels of credit are higher in countries with more information sharing through better public credit registries and private information firms. In fact, they find that information sharing systems are more important to financial deepening in low-income countries than improvements in the legal enforcement of contracts.[9]

Macroeconomic volatility and credit rationing in emerging economies

Why is macroeconomic performance in emerging market economies more volatile? Table 2.1 presents data between 1960 and 1997 on average output growth and the standard deviation of output growth and employment in OECD (developed) and non-OECD (emerging) countries. While average growth in non-OECD countries was only one-fourth of that in OECD countries over this period, output growth and employment were more than twice as volatile. While OECD countries spent 9 percent of this time in recession, non-OECD countries spent 20 percent of the time in recession.

A good deal of theoretical and empirical evidence suggests that financial systems have played an important role in the growth volatility of emerging market economies. As examined in more detail later in this book, many economic crises in the emerging world were sparked by financial crises. During

Table 2.1 Average growth and volatility of growth and employment, 1960–1997

Variable	Non-OECD		OECD	
	Mean	Number of countries	Mean	Number of countries
Growth	0.7%	163	2.7%	23
Std.dev. of growth	6.1%	163	2.6%	23
Median std.dev. of growth	5.2%	163	2.2%	23
Std.dev. of employment	0.098	83	0.035	21

Source: Easterly *et al.* (2001).

these financial crises, such as the East Asian crisis of 1997–1999, countries that had experienced remarkable levels of economic development slipped into depression within a matter of weeks as capital flight and financial panic ran rampant.

Easterly *et al.* (2001) investigate the sources of financial and economic volatility in emerging market economies. Macroeconomic data provides some clues to the factors that affect the net worths of lenders and borrowers, which in turn affect default risk, the external finance premium, and the amount of credit rationing within an economy. The authors find three key results. First, the emerging economies that grew the fastest were countries that were more open to international trade, had higher levels of financial development as measured by their ratio of private credit to GDP, and had higher levels of capital inflows. One interpretation of these facts is that these factors are correlated with improved financial fundamentals in the economy, reducing the external finance premium and the amount of credit rationing that takes place at the microeconomic level. Also, financial development at the macroeconomic level loosens the credit limits imposed by foreign investors.

Second, the authors find that measures of financial volatility, such as capital flow volatility, are closely correlated with output volatility across emerging economies. This is not surprising given what we have observed regarding the importance of finance booms and busts in instigating business cycles. In addition, the authors find that measures of openness are also strongly correlated with growth volatility, which suggests that economic openness increases efficiency and growth, but also exposes economies to potential capital outflows that can destabilize financial fundamentals and economic activity.

Finally, the authors find that financial development, as measured by a country's credit-to-GDP ratio, has a non-linear impact on growth volatility. In its initial stages, financial development reduces economic volatility because it increases economic efficiency, improves financial fundamentals, improves information, provides insurance to stabilize production and consumption, and reduces risk. As the financial system becomes larger relative to the rest of the economy, however, the risk and inherent volatility associated with financial fundamentals and scarce information in many emerging economies begins to dominate, increasing growth volatility. Figure 2.1 presents Easterly *et al.*'s estimated relationship between output volatility and the credit-to-GDP ratio. The turning point is roughly when the credit-to-GDP ratio reaches 100 percent, which is a benchmark commonly used to separate developed from underdeveloped financial systems.

Thus, increasing openness and the size of the financial system relative to the economy is good for growth, but it increases the importance of credit intermediation and financial fundamentals in determining economic performance. These financial fundamentals can be unstable, particularly in emerging market economies because of the financial fragility of many poorer households and firms as well as the difficultly of obtaining quality financial information. This can lead to financial development also becoming a source of macroeconomic volatility for emerging economies during the earlier stages of growth. Later chapters will return to this question of financial volatility—particularly financial crises—in order to gain a deeper understanding of the role that financial development may—but does not have to—play in creating economic instability in emerging market economies.

The microfinance revolution

Microfinance is a term used to refer to the act of providing small loans and other financial services to the very poor that do not have access to formal financial services. These poor have little collateral, little information on which their credit worthiness can be judged, often live in rural areas that are subject to high transaction costs, and regularly suffer from financial discrimination for class or racial reasons. Microfinance seeks to design lending schemes in which small entrepreneurs and households can gain access to the modest amounts of finance they need to expand the scale of their businesses or stabilize their spending. The fundamental idea here is that small amounts of finance can be used to break out of the poverty traps the poor find themselves caught in, where being poor forces them to produce at a small scale and creates volatility in their household spending, but producing at a small scale and having volatile household spending causes them to be poor.

The most popular model of microfinance was first developed by the Grameen (derived from the word "rural" in Bengali) Bank in Bangladesh. Grameen Bank was founded in 1976 by Muhammad Yunus, the 2006 winner of the Nobel Peace Prize for his work there. Yunus' impetus for starting the bank was his belief that, in his words, "all human beings are born entrepreneurs."[10] Yunus made his first

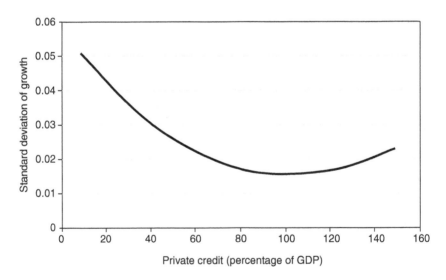

Figure 2.1 Growth volatility and private sector credit (source: Easterly *et al.* (2001).

loan of $27 to a group of more than 40 women who crafted bamboo. Today the bank has more than eight million Bengali customers in 76,000 villages. All this in a country in which less than 5 percent of the adult population has access to formal loans from the banking system.[11]

The key component of the Grameen model as it was originally formulated is group lending. Small loans are made not to individuals but to small groups of people, usually of around five. The idea is that group lending allows for greater repayment of loans by creating incentives for individuals in these groups to monitor and screen each other as well as to use peer pressure to increase the social penalties for default.[12] In other words, group lending is a way to limit the problems of adverse selection and moral hazard by increasing information and the costs of default. The informational advantages offsets the fact that group lending also creates a problem of moral hazard by encouraging individual members of the group to borrow excessively because they can pass the risk along to other members of the group.

Overall, the emphasis on group lending has been very successful for Grameen in terms of increasing rates of repayment.[13] Grameen reports that 98 percent of its loans are repaid, although this number is likely somewhat overstated as it is relatively easy to reschedule most loans in the Grameen system.[14]

The Grameen model also incorporates a number of other innovations in lending. Loans are progressive, meaning that they start small at high interest rates (typically 20 percent) and for very short terms. However, once a group establishes a record of repayment, the loans get larger for longer terms and at lower interest rates. Collateral is sometimes required, but what qualifies as collateral is very broadly defined and can be something that has value only to the borrower (e.g. family relics). The payment schedules on microloans are inflexible and usually require weekly fixed payments. Customers are required to participate in training sessions that offer business, health, and life skills development. Grameen, under a program referred to as "Grameen II," has also begun to focus on developing savings accounts, insurance accounts, and even pension savings accounts for their customers.

Grameen business loans are typically used to increase inventory (23 percent of total loans), invest in capital to expand production (25 percent), and invest in livestock and poultry (46 percent).[15] Other microfinance organizations focus much more on providing consumer credit that grants households the ability to stabilize their spending on food and schooling. The average Grameen loan in 2010 to a group of five was $384, with loans ranging between $100 and $5,000. While this does not sound like a great amount of money, most of the customers for these loans are living at or below $2.50 a day, meaning that these loans are quite significant as a fraction of income. In 2010, the four largest microfinance banks in Bangladesh provided almost 90 percent of all loans in the country, distributing more than $2.6 billion in loans to more than 22 million borrowers.[16]

One final defining characteristic of microfinance is that it primarily goes to women. Grameen makes 98 percent of its loans to women. There are many reasons for this. First, Grameen did not start off targeting loans to women, but evolved that way as women had higher repayment rates than men. Women are also much more likely to be credit rationed because of their lack of economic standing in many countries and because of outright discrimination. This is despite the fact that many women are entrepreneurs, often working as shopkeepers and street vendors where their lack of capital and inventory is less of a barrier. Finally, there is also quite a bit of evidence that finance that is directed at women more directly benefits the welfare of the entire household. Khandker (2005) reports empirical evidence that borrowing by a woman has a greater impact on per-capita household spending for food, schooling, and health care than borrowing by a man.

Many microfinance organizations have embraced this women-centric viewpoint. Microfinance organizations such as Thusang Basadi ("Women's Finance House") in Botswana have made women's empowerment, as measured by increasing their female customers' range of choices over the daily conditions of their lives, the primary goal of their work. Thusang Basadi uses the group lending approach to not only administer loans but also provide women support networks and financial training for every aspect of their lives, both working and in the home.

Today microfinance across the globe serves somewhere between 150 and 200 million customers worldwide, translating into more than half-a-billion people that benefit on a daily basis from microfinance.[17] This number sounds large, but pales in comparison with the more than three billion people that live in moderate poverty (less than \$2.50 a day). Not only does microfinance fail to help most poor households, but the benefits and the costs of microfinance for those who do receive it are still a topic of some debate in the economic development profession.

Studies that focus on the microeconomic impact of microfinance generally show that it does have benefits for the poor that receive microloans. For example, Morduch (1999) estimates that \$1 in finance for the very poor has five times the impact on income compared to the marginally poor. Karlan and Zinman (2010) conducted a randomized trial in South Africa comparing the outcomes of those receiving and those not receiving microfinance over the course of two years. They find that those households that were granted loans had lower instances of poverty and hunger as well as higher rates of schooling and employment. In another paper, Karlan and Zinman (2009) find evidence in Manila that the welfare impact of microfinance on households through consumer credit is significant and greater than its impact on small businesses. Banerjee *et al.* (2009) conducted a similar randomized experiment in Hyderabad, India in which some households were given access to a standard microfinance program and others were not. They find that those neighborhoods that received microfinance were more likely to start new businesses and purchased more durable goods. However, there was no evidence of increased empowerment of women or higher spending on education and health.

Taken as a whole, these microeconomic results, and others like them, suggest marginal, but not dramatic, improvements in quality of life of the poor as the result of microfinance programs. The reasons that microfinance is not more beneficial may stem from what makes it work in the first place: its emphasis on group lending and regular fixed payments. These characteristics keep administrative and default costs low, but also make it a less attractive alternative for many poor borrowers to moneylenders (or to not borrowing at all).[18] As a result of such observations, many microfinance organizations, including Grameen, have begun to provide more flexibility in loan terms and payment schedules in order to accommodate the fact that the poor have irregular cash flows. In addition, while clients are still required to interact in groups, under Grameen II all loans are individual liability loans so that members of the group are not required to cover the losses of other group members. Giné and Karlan (2009) conducted a randomized trial of microborrowers and find that moving to individual liability loans (while still requiring borrowers to participate in lending group meetings) increases the number of loan customers and reduces drop-out rates without significantly impacting repayment rates.

When microfinance programs have been evaluated at a macroeconomic level based on their overall impact on poverty, the empirical evidence on its benefits are more mixed. A number of studies have failed to find clear support for the argument that microfinance reduces aggregate poverty, although the evidence in specific countries such as Bangladesh is stronger.[19] This could suggest that not all microfinance programs are equally effective. It may also be the result of failing to empirically separate the impact of microfinance from other factors affecting poverty.

Probably the most important issue shaping the future of microfinance is the debate between economic sustainability and expanding services to the poorest of the poor. Many economists argue that microfinance organizations need to focus on attracting more depositors and outside investors, increasing the scale of their lending operations, and generating sufficient profits to be independently viable and not simply reliant on donors. In other words, microfinance organizations need to act more like for-profit banks. As evidence of this, 50 percent of microfinance organizations say that they are liquidity constrained, but only 27 percent offer savings accounts.[20] This lack of capital inhibits these institutions' abilities to expand lending. On the other hand, many others argue that microfinance organizations should not focus on profitability but on increasing access to the extremely poor, even if it means taking losses. Microfinance organizations should continue to accept subsidies, primarily from foreign donors, in order to continue to emphasize social goals such as expanded lending to those living in extreme poverty.

Cull *et al.* (2009) report that less than half of microfinance organizations show a profit, with not-for-profit organizations subsidized by donations at levels equal to 40 percent of their capital. Despite these subsidies, microfinance continues to be expensive: the median interest rate is 25 percent, but interest rates are often greater than 40 percent for many lenders. This is twice the interest rates charged at traditional banks, indicating that microfinance borrowers are being credit rationed by banks.

Compartamos Bank in Mexico epitomizes the tradeoffs faced. Compartamos is a microfinance bank that has focused on economic sustainability, regularly earning a return on equity of greater than 50 percent a year.[21] It has been so profitable that Compartamos raised $1.6 billion in an initial stock offering in 2007. This capital allowed Compartamos to expand access and the size of their loans to many Mexicans. But critics charge that it comes at the price of an increase in the costs of finance, limiting financial access to those who are the neediest. The average effective interest rate (including value-added tax) on a Compartamos loan in 2007 was 94 percent!

The key driving factor behind these high interest rates are the high transaction costs associated with microfinance. The screening and monitoring activities associated with microfinance are largely fixed and do not vary much with the size of the average loan. As a result, the administrative costs are very large as a percentage of microloans, despite adopting methods to keep these costs low such as group lending and requiring regular fixed payments. Given this, some argue that these financing costs are best thought of as fees; converting these costs into annual interest rates exaggerates their size and is not consistent with how the poor think about these loans.[22] For example, someone who pays $1 to borrow $20 for one day in order to meet their children's school fees might consider this a worthwhile investment, but pays an effective annualized rate of over 1,400 percent. However, it is still clear that while expressing these fees as an annual percentage might unreasonably exaggerate the costs of microfinance, it is also true that some of the poor are priced out of the microfinance market without subsidies, even despite the fact that microloans are on average less than half as expensive as borrowing from moneylenders.[23]

Unfortunately, the entire debate over the costs of microfinance misses one of its most important benefits. The economic lives of the poor are highly uncertain and irregular. For many of these poor, having a reliable and flexible source of funds during periods of need as well as a reliable and flexible way to save money when they are flush is very valuable, despite its high costs. Moneylenders and family may not have money to lend when the poor need it most, while saving by holding money, buying livestock, or lending to a neighbor exposes one's wealth to a wide range of risks.[24] Microfinance can significantly reduce the riskiness of the lives of the poor at costs that are reasonable given the lack of options available.

These tensions between profits and social goals have recently come to a head in many emerging economies, including India where microfinance makes up over half of total finance in the country. A state government in India has charged that microfinance organizations indirectly played a role in the suicides of 85 farmers after crop failures left them, or members of their loan group, unable to repay their loans.[25] In response, the government has passed new laws lowering interest rates and rescheduling payments on many microloans. In addition, a few microloan officers were arrested. While politically popular, these kinds of actions will increase both the risk and the costs of microfinance, leading to more credit rationing of the poor than existed before.[26]

Information technology and microfinance in emerging economies

The continued development of mobile phone technology throughout the world has the power to greatly magnify the benefits of microfinance and increase the financial access of the poor. Figure 2.2 presents data on mobile phone subscriptions in the developed and emerging worlds. On average, two-thirds of those living in the emerging world have access to mobile phones, although this number is only about one-fourth among the poorest emerging economies. This is a far greater number than those who have access to ATM machines, branch banks, computers, landlines, or traditional deposit accounts.

Mobile phones can amplify the power of microfinance in two ways. First, mobile phone microfinance can indirectly increase formal financial intermediation by increasing information and the profitability of small firms. Entrepreneurs can use their phone to find out market information about where to best sell their goods and where to obtain their inputs most cheaply. Mobile phones offer firms the ability to sell their goods through texting, which not only reduces transactions costs (such as eliminating the need for middlemen) but also provides access to larger markets that allow small firms to better take advantage of economies of scale. Mobile phones also allow small entrepreneurs and households the ability to establish a transaction record that is the first step toward establishing the credit history needed to get a loan. More profitability and information will reduce the external finance premium and credit rationing that many small firms and households face.

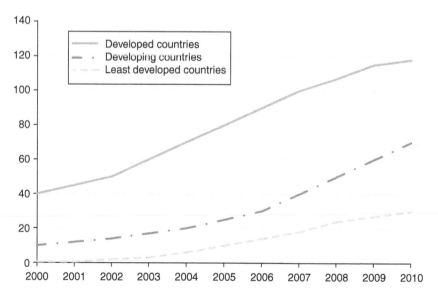

Figure 2.2 Mobile-phone subscriptions (per 100 people) (source: *The Economist*, December 11, 2010).

Second, mobile phone microfinance can directly increase formal finance by providing financial services to those in rural or poor areas where it is very costly to provide these services. Mobile phones allow for branchless microbanking, meaning it gives people the ability to make cash transfers, deposits, and withdrawals through their cellphones and not through personal transactions at branch banks.

According to a recent survey, there are more than 20 countries in the world today in which more than 10 percent of adults report they have used mobile money; 15 of these countries are African.[27] The best example of how branchless microbanking can work is Kenya's M-Pesa program (M for mobile, *Pesa* meaning "money" in Swahili), developed by Kenya's largest mobile operator Safaricom. This program allows for transfers of money via text messages. In 2012, 68 percent of the Kenyan population used M-Pesa and conducted transfers amounting to roughly 20 percent of Kenyan GDP.[28] The M-Pesa program is a network of 20,000 small retailers, many of whom also sell mobile phone minutes or food as street vendors, which have agreed to become mobile money managers as well. Any subscriber to the M-Pesa program (which is available to anyone with a mobile phone) can go to one of these money managers and make a deposit or withdrawal of currency. These transactions are recorded in each customer's e-account electronically via texting, and a return text serves as a receipt to verify the transaction. Mobile money managers have to manage both the balances in their electronic accounts ("e-float") as well as the amount of physical currency in their possession. The average agent conducts more than 100 transactions a day. To facilitate the management of these transactions, intermediary agents have entered the market to help groups of money managers transfer currency and e-float among themselves in order to eliminate shortages or surpluses.

The M-Pesa program allows millions of Kenyans to transfer money, particularly between urban areas where many people have migrated for work and their home villages. It has also saved significant amounts in transaction costs and untold hours of waiting in line to pay bills or to make a financial transaction at the small number of branch banks in the country. Kenya only has 1.38 branch banks and 0.56 ATMs per 100,000 residents.[29] Mobile banking also offers users ways to reduce the fees associated with international remittances. M-Pesa has recently partnered with Western Union to let people in 45 countries transfer money directly to M-Pesa users in Kenya.

The next step for M-Pesa, and programs like it that have spread throughout Africa and even into places such as Afghanistan, is for these money managers to begin making small loans to their regular customers from which they can get sufficient information or collateral. These forms of "semi-formal" lending have already begun. But a whole range of financial options might eventually be available from mobile banking. One is the availability of mobile foreign investment. With more than 200 million migrants working abroad, mobile phone technology is not only changing the nature of remittances (see the previous chapter), but it is also changing the nature of diaspora lending. Because migrants have better information and closer contacts about their home country than other foreigners do, they can often serve as middlemen, or as direct sources, for finance. This is particularly true for countries with large diaspora, such as India and China, which have played a large role in connecting these countries to global financial systems. For example, two-thirds of Chinese foreign direct investment comes from areas in which a majority of their population is ethnically Chinese (Hong Kong and Taiwan). With mobile phone technology, the ability of migrants to overcome information deficiencies and expand financial access for both large and small borrowers is becoming easier for a wider range of countries.

One final and interesting mobile finance program in Kenya is referred to as "Kilmo Salama" (safe farming). Here, farmers are charged small fees, subsidized by large agribusinesses, to insure their investments (seeds, fertilizer, etc.) against crop failure.[30] Farmers register for the program by choosing the closest automated weather station in their area. If there is a crop failure, as measured by the weather conditions reported electronically by this weather station, then farmers can be compensated directly into their mobile e-accounts. By significantly reducing transaction costs and increasing information, these kinds of information technology have the potential to significantly reduce risk, facilitate financial intermediation, and reduce the volatility of the lives of the poor.

Conclusions

Financial intermediation is about much more than matching someone who has money with someone who does not and is prepared to pay for it. It is about the willingness to assume the risk of lending money today for money tomorrow and the ways that this risk can be mitigated. The only way to facilitate this willingness in a world of imperfect and asymmetric information is by providing enough information to assure lenders that their risk of default is being adequately compensated.

As emphasized in this chapter, asymmetric information is the primary reason for market failure in financial markets and the fundamental reason behind the credit rationing and high external finance premiums that plague underdeveloped financial systems. This is why information is the primary input in generating financial intermediation. But information is not created in a vacuum. It is dependent upon a whole range of incentives that exist within and outside emerging economies. Some of these incentives can be created by new developments such as microfinance, with its focus on group lending, as well as by mobile phone banking, which reduces the transaction costs of financial services. However, from a larger perspective, governments and societies also play an important role in shaping the incentives that govern financial and economic development. It is this discussion that is covered in more detail in the next chapter.

Part II

Domestic finance and policies in emerging markets

3 Institutions and financial systems

Introduction

Most things need to be surrounded by the proper environment in order to grow. The development of financial systems in this respect is no different from the development of animal or plant life. There exists a range of conditions under which finance will take place and even thrive. But outside of this range, financial intermediation will wither. The purpose of this chapter is to broadly describe the general environment needed for financial systems to thrive.

An important insight of this chapter is that there is no single blueprint for building a successful financial system. Instead, building a financial system is more like composing music: there are some broad rules, but *inspiration* and *context* are just as important. Inspiration is a result of having the proper incentives in place to encourage efficient financial intermediation. Instead of the word inspiration, economists typically use the term *institutions* to denote the incentives created by governments and societies to engage in mutually beneficial transactions (such as financial intermediation). Institutions are not created within markets. Instead, they are the policies, laws, and social norms that encourage things such as the sharing of information, adherence to the rule of law, and the ability to manage and reduce the costs of conflict. As a result, institutions are key to reducing the uncertainty and risk associated with finance. Very importantly, institutions are also context-specific, meaning that a certain set of institutions might have very different implications for financial development in one country than it would have in another country and context.

In order to understand the importance of institutions more clearly, this chapter begins with a list of factors most likely to be associated with institutions that foster financial development. It also looks at the empirical research on institutions and examines the role that culture may or may not play in shaping institutions. Next, this chapter discusses financial repression, or government policies aimed specifically at increasing governmental control of the financial system at the cost of limiting financial intermediation. The rationale for financial repression, policies associated with it, and its costs in terms of limiting financial development are all discussed. This leads to an introductory discussion of what constitutes prudential government regulation of financial systems (to be continued throughout the rest of the book). This chapter concludes with a case study comparing and contrasting the institutions that impact financial development in the two largest, and fastest-growing, emerging market economies: China and India.

The determinants of institutions

The definition of institutions just provided is extremely broad and non-specific. There is a good reason for this: institutions themselves are shaped by a wide variety of factors that are not easy to delineate. In theory, anything that impacts incentives—even things as intangible as widely shared attitudes—can impact institutions. In examining institutions here, however, the focus will be primarily on the role of government policies, laws, and social norms and how these factors influence incentives and impact behavior within financial systems.

One of the most important things to keep in mind regarding institutions is that they are the air that financial systems breathe; institutions are essential, but often invisible. Institutions are not created by markets, but they form the background environment in which the more obvious market activities of borrowing and lending take place. While many things go into determining institutions, economic research suggests that the following factors are most important in shaping the effectiveness of a country's institutions.

The protection of property rights. Having strong property rights means that an individual's property is adequately protected from expropriation by the government or by other individuals. This expropriation could take many forms. In many emerging economies without strong property rights it often comes in the form of not having adequate legal systems to enforce contracts. As discussed in the previous chapter, overcoming asymmetric information is at the heart of every financial transaction. Debt contracts typically include many clauses that define the collateral that will be forfeited in the case of default as well as many monitoring and screening requirements that are intended to increase the flow of information between borrowers and lenders. If these contract provisions cannot be enforced, or if there is a concern that they cannot be enforced, these important methods of overcoming the problems of asymmetric information become moot and financial intermediation will suffer.

Many times, property is expropriated passively because property rights have never been well defined in the first place. This was the insight of Hernando de Soto's work (discussed in the previous chapter) on dead capital and the costs of failing to develop legal processes that can adequately grant title to many people living on informal property. These processes include developing public asset registries as well as the laws to support them.

In order to have an adequate legal system, not only do the proper laws have to be in place but there also has to be an adequate number of properly trained law enforcement officers, lawyers, and judges. In many emerging market economies, the problem is not with the law but with its enforcement. In Nigeria, the cost of recovering collateral in the case of default can be more than 30 percent of the total amount of debt. Contract disputes in Bangladesh can cost more than 60 percent of outstanding debt and take an average of 1,442 days to reach a conclusion. India has more than 300,000 open legal cases that are ten years or older.[1] This lack of enforcement increases uncertainty and creates significant disincentives to borrow and lend.

Limiting corruption and theft. High amounts of corruption and theft reduce property rights. In practice, corruption can take two different forms. Decentralized corruption refers to corruption that takes place at an individual level and is independent from other acts of corruption. For example, the loan officer that demands a payment before a loan application is considered, or a bureaucrat who asks for a payment to "speed the process" of obtaining a legal title to a piece of property to be used as collateral in a loan; these are examples of decentralized corruption. Centralized corruption is top-down corruption that is organized. This often includes organized crime and political corruption: for example, when a political party demands a kickback in order to pass a preferential law that benefits a particular firm. In its extreme, centralized corruption can lead to kleptocracy, where the primary objective of government becomes the maximization of grift. While both forms of corruption are costly, it is decentralized corruption that is the most costly.[2] When corruption is centralized, there are incentives to act like a "corruption monopolist" and limit the overall amount of corruption in order to increase its price or the size of the bribe. With decentralized corruption, there are no limiting factors on the amount of corruption, meaning it can often devolve into an endless series of bribes that can put a halt to formal financial transactions.

One can think of corruption as a tax, but in fact corruption is more costly than a tax because of the uncertainty associated with it. The size of a tax is typically known before a transaction takes place. Because bribes cannot take place in public, they are variable and magnify the risk already associated with financial transactions.

Facilitating conflict management. Having legal systems that allow for the fair enforcement of contracts is one important mechanism for facilitating conflict. But at a broader level, having strong institutions that are conducive to financial development requires there to be the proper political and social structures in place that encourage stability and cohesion among the population. This means having the political structures, legal systems, and social norms that can manage conflict between those of different ethnic groups, income levels, ideologies, or special interests.

One conflict in particular needs to be dealt with in any economy, and that is the conflict between elites and the poor. On one hand, political institutions have to protect the poor against elites amassing excessive power and manipulating institutions in their favor, such as by limiting competition in order to gain monopoly profits. On the other hand, the poor make up a large majority of the population in many emerging market economies. If policies are left to majority rule, the institutions put into place may not be favorable to financial development. For example, given that there are more poor people than rich and more borrowers than lenders, a simple majority rule political system might vote for the invalidation of debt contracts. This would benefit borrowers in the short run but put a halt to financial intermediation, helping no one over time. This phenomenon is often referred to as the *tyranny of the majority*. For these reasons, well-functioning representative democracies that attempt to balance majority and minority rights as well as those of the elites with those of the disadvantaged should be more conducive to financial development.

Providing macroeconomic stability. Financial stability is a function of macroeconomic stability. Lenders are less likely to accept the risk of financial intermediation when overall macroeconomic risk is high. This risk can come from business cycles, high and volatile inflation rates, high levels of debt (bringing with it the danger of sovereign debt crises and dramatic shifts in fiscal policy), periodic banking crises, and exchange rate instability. Each of these can change the financial fundamentals of borrowers and lenders and have dramatic impacts on the level of credit within an economy. The role of monetary and fiscal policy within emerging economies will be discussed in more detail in later chapters, as will the causes of sovereign debt crises, banking crises, asset bubbles, and currency crises. At that time we will examine the exact role that macroeconomic policy plays in creating and mitigating financial volatility.

Proper regulation of the financial system. As discussed before, there are many good reasons to think that financial markets are imperfectly competitive and that laissez-faire policies will not lead to socially optimal outcomes, particularly because of the existence of asymmetric information. Stiglitz *et al.* (1993) delineate seven major failures in financial markets that justify government regulation and supervision in emerging market economies.

1   The monitoring of borrowers is a public good because information is a public good. As a result, many people are free-riders of information and it is undersupplied in free markets. Government policies that increase information sharing and facilitate the monitoring of borrowers—such as setting accounting standards, establishing credit information registries, requiring public information disclosure—increase the aggregate levels of financial development and create positive externalities for everyone in an economy.

2   The managers of banks need to be monitored as well. Because they are lending the money of their depositors, they are subject to the same moral hazard and adverse selection incentives as those who borrow from banks. Governments can help minimize the risky behavior of bank managers by setting accounting standards, requiring public disclosure of institutional performance, requiring diversification of assets, setting loan safety standards, limiting exposure to exchange rate risk, and preventing corruption and fraud. Most importantly, governments can reduce moral hazard by requiring banks to maintain adequate capital from their investors. This is the equivalent of requiring collateral from borrowers; when banks have their own capital at stake through capital adequacy requirements, shareholders have more incentive to monitor managers and managers have less incentive to take excessive risks.

3 Financial crises create negative externalities. Bank runs, sovereign debt crises, currency crises (all to be discussed in more detail in later chapters) negatively impact everyone in an economy, even those not directly engaged in the formal financial sector. By creating bank deposit insurance and empowering central banks to serve as lenders of last resort, governments can play a role in reducing the risk of financial crisis and preventing extremely costly recessions and depressions.

4 Because banking is subject to significant economies of scale, financial systems tend to be highly concentrated; this is particularly true in emerging market economies. This lack of competition can lead to monopoly behavior that restricts credit. Governments can encourage financial competition by removing domestic barriers to entry as well as by encouraging competition, particularly from foreign banks, which can help overcome these market failures. More foreign banks can also solve other market failures created by asymmetric information by improving information technology, by transferring knowledge ("best practices"), and by increasing bank capital.

5 Adverse selection and moral hazard lead to credit rationing, particularly among the most vulnerable: those with lower net worths, newer borrowers, and borrowers with less-established credit histories. The allocative efficiency of the financial system can be increased if governments can develop institutions that help facilitate financial access and the flow of credit to these rationed groups. This could include policies that subsidize lending to the poor, either directly (government education loans, for example) or through microfinance institutions. It can also include anti-discrimination policies in lending.

6 A lack of education among the populace, particularly among the poor and disadvantaged, creates additional forms of asymmetric information that can lead to market failure and inefficient decision making. Governments can help solve these problems through public education, particularly in regard to educating the population about how finance works.

7 Many emerging financial systems suffer from missing insurance markets. This makes it difficult to transfer and pool risk within these financial systems, reducing the overall efficiency of finance. Governments can help replace these financial markets through the provision of social safety net programs such as public retirement insurance, public health insurance, unemployment insurance, and disability insurance.

The term *prudential regulation* is used in this book to refer to government policies and regulations that are aimed at reducing risk and increasing the efficiency of financial intermediation. Prudential regulation includes the following: capital adequacy requirements, accounting standards, information transparency requirements, asset diversification requirements, loan safety standards, limits on exchange rate risk exposure, deposit insurance, lender of last resort, limited barriers to entry, corruption prevention, and other limits on risky financial behavior. One of the most important objectives of this book is to develop a deeper appreciation of what constitutes appropriate and beneficial prudential regulation that reduces financial volatility and facilitates financial development, and distinguish these policies from other government practices that only limit financial intermediation.

Empirical evidence on institutions

A vast literature has developed over the last two decades examining the empirical evidence on institutions in an attempt both to determine which institutions are most important to financial and economic development and to identify how quality institutions are created in the first place. While this literature is too large to entirely review here, a few studies are worth highlighting.

Regarding the question of how strong institutions are created, many studies have focused on the historical foundations of institutions. One of the most widely cited studies along these lines was done by Acemoglu *et al.* (2001a). In this study, the authors argue that different colonization strategies led to different institutions being adopted in different countries. In those countries in which the climate and health environment, as measured by settler mortality rates, was conducive for permanent settlement of immigrants, colonization strategies focused on establishing policies and institutions that were consistent with long-run economic growth and financial development. This includes establishing representative political systems and equitable legal systems. This was most likely to be the case in colonies within temperate climate zones (North America, Australia, New Zealand). But in other countries, settler mortality was incredibly high. In Nigeria in the mid-1800s, roughly 2,000 deaths occurred each year to maintain a constant level of 1,000 settlers in the country! In these countries where mortality was high, primarily in Latin America and Sub-Saharan Africa, the economic incentives faced by immigrants encouraged extractive colonization policies, such as mineral exploitation and slavery, which were not consistent with the creation of quality institutions and sustained economic growth.[3] The authors show that settler mortality rates in the mid-1800s are positively correlated with various measures of poor institutions today, including the risk of government expropriation and less democratic political systems. The authors argue that this is evidence of the importance, and persistence, of the historical origins of institutions.

Other economists have focused more specifically on the historical origins of legal systems across countries. Levine (2005) looks at differences in the performance of legal systems between countries that were colonized by Britain and adopted the English common law system as opposed to former French, Spanish, and Portuguese colonies that adopted the civil law system. Under common law, the law is built from individual case laws in a bottom-up fashion where judges play the predominant role. In a civil law system, the state is the sole interpreter of the law and the law is created in a top-down fashion. Under the argument of the *legal origins theory*, common law is better able to evolve over time in order to effectively protect property rights and enforce contacts as the economy evolves because it is more flexible and less procedural. In fact, Levine finds empirical evidence that common law systems have more shareholder protections, lower costs of capital, greater economic and political freedom, and higher levels of financial development.

A good example of how these two legal systems have historically protected property rights in different ways can be seen in how differently land squatters were treated in North versus Latin America. The civil law system used in Latin America placed a premium on protecting the property rights of the large *hacienda* landowners, who were then able to protect their property rights using their political powers at the state level. Squatters' rights were limited. In fact, indigenous populations were completely tied to specific *haciendas* without any individual property rights under what was known as the *encomiendas* system. Squatters were often not eligible to be compensated by landowners for improvements they made to the land they lived on (which reduced incentives for squatters to invest in improving land). This plays a large role in explaining why so many people today in Latin America live on the unimproved land their families have lived on for decades, yet their property rights are not recognized by the government through the provision of legal title. In the United States and Canada, on the other hand, squatters were given significant rights. Many colonies adopted systems in which squatters were allowed to buy title to land at a price set by a jury if the legal owner would not pay for improvements made by squatters. In addition, government-owned land was widely distributed among the population in North America through a long series of laws, such as the Homestead Act of 1862 in the United States. A similar bias against the property rights of non-elites has been found in India, where states in which landlords were awarded strong property rights over cultivators still have lower levels of investments in capital, health, and education today.[4]

Quite a bit of empirical work has been conducted examining the impact of legal origins on the quality of legal systems and on economic development, much of it indicating that there is a close positive relationship between common law systems, better protection of property rights, and faster growth.[5] On the other hand, empirical studies such as that conducted by Armour *et al.* (2009) find that if the behavior of civil and common law legal systems are evaluated over time and not just at one point in time, there has been significant convergence between the two systems, particularly in regard to shareholders' protections, over the last 15 years. Regardless of the origins of legal systems, many studies have found that more effective legal enforcement, particularly contract enforcement and protection of shareholders' rights, increase efficiency and financial development.[6]

Other studies have focused on political instability and how it can weaken institutions. For example, Detragiache *et al.* (2005) find that political instability in a country directly increases corruption and reduces financial development.[7] Political systems that are more open—meaning they allow broader participation and limit the power of elites—have been found to be correlated with more competition in the financial sector and greater financial development.[8]

Specifically focusing on financial regulation, many empirical students have found that regulations that promote monitoring and the disclosure of information enhance financial development. Likewise, studies have found that increasing the openness of a banking industry to foreign competition and improving the overall quality of financial regulation are correlated with higher levels of financial development.[9] These findings are consistent with the arguments presented earlier by Stiglitz *et al.* that prudent but limited financial regulation is needed to maximize financial development. However, the existence of endemic corruption in many emerging market economies limits the possibility of such effective regulation taking place, making financial systems more unstable because of it. Barth *et al.* (2006) find empirical evidence that some prudential regulatory policies borrowed from developed countries actually reduced financial development in emerging economies. This is because policies that increase the regulatory power of bureaucrats might also increase the opportunities for corruption in countries without the proper institutions already in place.

Do culture and beliefs play a role in creating strong institutions?

One of the most controversial and sensitive subjects in economics is the role that culture may or may not play in economic and financial development. *Culture* can be defined as the customary beliefs and values that ethnic, religious, and social groups transmit fairly unchanged from generation to generation. In any society, social groups monitor and screen individuals in an effort to ensure conformity to cultural standards. Some of these cultural standards may promote strong institutions that foster financial development, others may not. Because culture changes very slowly, cultural attributes that discourage financial development have long-lasting impacts on economic growth. To highlight one example, the cultural beliefs that led to the caste system of India, under which certain elite social groups exclude other groups from participating in the benefits of trade, is an illustration of how culture can reduce overall economic and financial development.

The idea that culture plays a role in economic development is an old one. The modern discussion was initiated by Max Weber (1905), who argued that the Protestant belief system—which encourages thrift, industry, and self-reliance—is most conducive to the creation of wealth and is the major reason behind the rapid economic advance of Protestant-majority countries during the Industrial Revolution.

This idea of the "work ethic" has been most recently promoted by the historian David Landes (1999), who also argues that beliefs and attitudes toward growth are driven by culture, although he accepts the fact that multiple cultures can create individuals that are "rational, ordered, diligent, and productive" (1999: 177) In Landes' opinion, cultures that emphasize education (particularly for females), emphasize precision, do not attach a social stigma to wealth creation, and promote rational dissent are those cultures that will develop economically and financially. For example, Landes argues that South America's lack of relative development stems in part from the cultural attitude of the Spanish and

Portuguese toward financial transactions. The Iberian countries adopted a "squeeze" approach to growth that focused on exploiting existing resources in Latin America, not on manufacturing and finance. As opposed to North America, few European families permanently migrated to Latin America. The institutions established in Latin America, such as limits on squatters' property rights and the exclusion of peasants from legal and financial systems, reflect the centralized power of the Catholic Church as well as a tradition of entrenching power in the hands of a small number of elites who often lived in Europe.

Culture and beliefs can also directly impact economic and financial development through its impact on policy. For example, Islamic prohibitions on usury, or the charging of interest, play a very important role in financial intermediation in countries with large Muslim populations. Islamic finance will be discussed in greater detail in Chapter 10.

While culture is not something that can be easily quantified, some economists have attempted to measure various aspects of culture in an attempt to identify its empirical impact on economic and financial development. Guiso *et al.* (2004) attempt to measure the benefits of *social capital*, defined as the benefits accruing to the members of a community from their participation in social networks, using data on voter participation and blood donation rates in various regions of Italy. They find that higher measured social capital is positively associated with many different measures of financial development: higher credit, more checking accounts, more informal loans, greater stock holdings, greater stock market capitalization, and greater diffusion of firm ownership.

Social capital is closely related to the idea of trust. Trust plays an important role in any economic transaction, but particularly in financial transactions because they take place over time, are difficult to monitor, and are subject to the problems of asymmetric information and risk. Each of these problems is particularly acute in emerging economies. In the words of Nobel Laureate Kenneth Arrow (1972: 357): "It can be plausibly argued that much of the economic backwardness in the world can be explained by the lack of mutual confidence." When information is lacking, mutual trust between borrowers and lenders can be one way to overcome the problems of adverse selection and moral hazard.

Zak and Knack (2001) use cross-country surveys that attempt to measure levels of trust across countries. They find that having more measured trust within a country is associated with higher levels of investment and growth. The impact is quite large: a 17 percent increase in measured trust leads to a 1 percent increase in investment. They find that income inequality, more ethnic heterogeneity, and higher levels of discrimination reduce trust. Algan and Cahuc (2010) collect data that looks at the trust levels of children of US immigrants over time in order to gauge how "trusting" the society their parents have immigrated from is. They find that trust levels inherited from their home countries are a significant predictor of the level of economic development in the home country. Religion is also an important determinant of beliefs and trusts. Guiso *et al.* (2006) find that increased religiosity is associated with higher levels of trust, lower transaction costs, higher savings, more efficient allocation of resources, and greater entrepreneurial behavior.[10] Finally, trust appears to be a function of the number of social and economic interactions between individuals. Feigenberg *et al.* (2010) find that more frequent group meetings among those in microfinance programs reduced defaults by facilitating reciprocity among members.

One final factor impacting culture is ethnic diversity within a country. For many reasons, ethnic diversity can lead to conflict, discrimination, inequality, an inability to resolve conflicts, and low levels of trust. Multiple studies have found that increased ethnic diversity is correlated with many measures of poor institutions, including increased government expropriation, lower competition, more corruption, fewer public services, weaker contract enforcement, and lower financial development.[11] The negative impact of ethnic diversity on finance can be observed in microcredit group lending. Karlan (2005) finds that within microcredit groups in Peru, group members with closer ethnic and geographic ties were less likely to miss payments or drop out of their group when they did miss a payment. Interestingly, closer ties also meant that group members were more likely to forgive delinquent payments because they better understood the circumstances surrounding the member that defaulted. This suggests that better monitoring is taking place when clients are more closely culturally connected.

Financial repression

Some emerging market economies have adopted policies aimed specifically at limiting financial intermediation and increasing government control over the financial system. Policies associated with financial repression include the following:

1　*Foreign capital controls.* Restrictions on the flow of international capital are imposed that limit borrowing and lending across borders and place limits on the foreign ownership of domestic banks and other financial assets.
2　*Barriers to entry.* Limits on competition exist in some countries that restrict the number of private banks. These restrictions are aimed at increasing the market share of a small number of private banks or of state-owned banks.
3　*Interest rate controls.* These controls are often ostensibly aimed at reducing the costs of lending for the poor. However, below market interest rates also reduce incentives to save and can lead to additional credit rationing as credit demand will be persistently larger than credit supply.
4　*High reserve and bond holding requirements.* By requiring banks to hold a greater amount of required reserves on deposits or mandatory levels of sovereign bond holdings, governments essentially force banks to lend money to them at reduced interest rates by coercing them to hold more government assets.
5　*High inflation.* Inflation, particularly if it is unexpected, reduces the real value of debt and reduces real interest rates. This can create large losses for lenders. Any increase in inflation or uncertainty about future inflation will significantly curtail financial intermediation.

6 *Directed lending and other restrictions.* Directed lending occurs when governments require banks to make a certain amount of loans to industries/firms deemed an economic priority. Governments also place credit restrictions on certain types of loans, such as consumer lending, in order to favor other sorts of lending, such as commercial lending.

7 *Exchange rate controls.* Governments impose exchange rate controls that require the trading of foreign currency to take place at official exchange rates, typically at higher than market rates that favor the government and make foreign imports more expensive.

Why do governments adopt financial repression policies? One reason is that financial repression can be an important source of revenue for governments. Monopoly banks make large profits that can be taxed, either directly or indirectly by imposing higher required reserves or bond holding requirements. Financial repression that favors state-owned banks can increase the revenues they generate. Interest rate ceilings allow the government to borrow at reduced interest rates. The higher the levels of required reserves that banks have to hold, the greater the revenues that can be made through *seigniorage*, or from creating more money and increasing inflation. Directed or restricted lending may be aimed at industries that provide the government revenues through taxes, because they are state-owned businesses or because they are a source of foreign currency. Exchange rate controls essentially serve as a tax on foreign trade. In sum, these sources of revenue are very important for many emerging economies that have a narrow tax base and an inefficient tax-collection system.

Second, financial repression can be used to give governments control over domestic savings and, as a result, a cheap form of financing. To the extent that repression limits domestic bond and stock markets, domestic residents only have the option of saving in banks (often state-owned) or in domestic bonds issued by the government. These savings can then be used to cheaply fund government spending priorities.

Third, financial repression policies are often adopted on behalf of political special interests. These can be to protect the interests of the elites by restricting competition and increasing monopoly power, limiting information and transparency, or reducing prudential regulation. The poor can also be a special interest, and many financial repression policies such as interest rate ceilings, exchange rate controls, higher inflation (because it reduces the real value of debt), and directed lending by state-owned banks have all been advocated as means of helping the poor.

A final special interest often advocating for financial repression is corrupt bureaucrats and politicians. Interest rate controls, exchange rate controls, capital controls, lending restrictions, and entry barriers all transfer power to bureaucrats and politicians that can then use this power to gain bribes. An insightful way to think about the problem of special interests is to recognize that there is an asymmetric information problem created when the public elects representatives to do the government's work. Because bureaucrats and politicians know more about their preferences for corruption and about the economic impact of any policy of financial repression that they enact, both adverse selection and moral hazard are created that increases the amount of financial repression and corruption. Corruption and financial repression are likely to be particularly acute in countries where information is lacking due to a lack of a free press, transparency, education, or fair elections.

Financial repression is costly for the same reasons that financial development is beneficial. Financial repression prevents financial markets and institutions from allocating resources most efficiently, reduces the incentives to screen and monitor, reduces incentives to save, limits incentives to keep transaction costs low, and can lead to more credit rationing by artificially keeping interest rates low. Many studies have found the costs of financial repression to be significant. Roubini and Sala-i-Martin (1992) use interest rate controls, required reserve ratios, and inflation as measures of financial repression. They find that each of these is correlated with reduced financial development and economic growth.[12] A significant literature has also been developed finding significant evidence that international capital controls are costly and that the liberalization of capital flows can be significantly beneficial. For example, Galindo *et al.* (2002) find that financial liberalization increases growth by 1.3 percent on average, with larger growth impacts in industries that are more reliant on external finance. Their results indicate that liberalization increases both the size and efficiency of financial systems. Tornell *et al.* (2003) find that in countries with repressed financial systems, financial liberalization increased growth by a remarkable 2.4 percent a year between 1980 and 1999. Figure 3.1 presents growth rates before and after liberalization for a group of emerging market economies in their study. The authors find that most of these large increases in growth are directly attributable to large increases in credit and investment rates.

Beck, Demirgüç-Kunt, and Peria (2008) examine financial repression as it pertains to barriers to entry and bank access. They find that barriers to entry are associated with other indicators of poor institutions, such as limited competition and weak legal systems. These policies reduce financial development and income by increasing the transaction costs associated with finance. Table 3.1 presents their data on the costs of maintaining a checking and savings account across a selection of countries. For example, in Uganda and Sierra Leone it can cost upwards of one-fourth of average family income to maintain a checking account. Assuming that households are able to pay no more than 2 percent of their income in banking fees, the authors calculate that a large percentage of the population is barred from access to financial services in many countries (see the last two columns of Table 3.1). In Uganda and Sierra Leone, checking account fees are more than 2 percent of household income for 90 percent of the population. Even the fees in the first two columns that are closer to 1 percent of average income are still prohibitively large fees for basic banking services. Other costs not included in Table 3.1 are just as extreme. For example, just to open a checking account in Cameroon costs $700, which is greater than Cameroon's annual per-capita GDP. In Kenya, as in other countries, the fees to withdraw from a savings account are between 5 and 10 percent of the withdrawal amount.[13] These financial services are expensive in non-monetary ways as well. For example, the authors report that in Pakistan it takes more than a month just to process a loan application. All of these costs are the direct result of financial repression policies.

Many other studies have shown that the existence of state-owned banks limit financial development. In a comprehensive review of the empirical literature on state-owned banks, Megginson (2005) finds that an increase in the relative size of the state-owned banking sector reduces financial efficiency, development, and growth within a country.[14] This is because state-owned banks are more likely to lend to governments and to make decisions based on political patronage. Because they are not driven by profits to keep risks low, state-owned banks also have less incentive to monitor and screen borrowers in order to reduce adverse selection and moral hazard, making their lending portfolios less efficient and more risky.

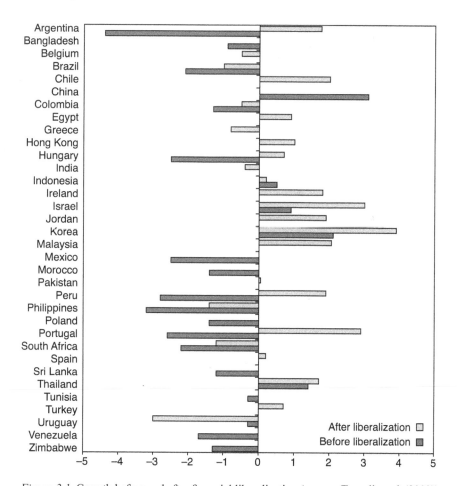

Figure 3.1 Growth before and after financial liberalization (source: Tornell *et al.* (2003)).

Table 3.1 Banking fees in some emerging market economies

Country	As % of per-capita GDP		Lowest percentage of population for which fee is more than 2% of household income	
	Checking acct. annual fee	Savings acct. annual fee	Checking acct. annual fee	Savings acct. annual fee
Bolivia	0.80	1.80	5	17
Brazil	0.8	0.03	12	1
Cameroon	7.9	1.2	54	3
Egypt	0.4	0.1	1	1
Ghana	5.9	0.6	37	1
India	0	0.2	0	1
Indonesia	2.8	0.7	10	1
Israel	0.04	0	1	0
Kenya	12.8	2.1	81	10
Madagascar	5.2	0	40	0
Malawi	22	3.6	94	33
Mexico	0.4	0.2	2	1
Sierra Leone	26.6	0	89	0
South Africa	2.1	0.9	31	12
Turkey	0.3	0.1	1	1
Uganda	24.9	3.4	93	33

Source: Beck, Demirgüç-Kunt, and Peria (2008).

There is no consensus among economists, however, that financial repression necessarily has to be harmful, nor that all countries with repressive financial policies should immediately act to liberalize. There are many potential reasons why financial repression does not have to be a drag on growth. Reasonable interest rate ceilings can actually limit credit rationing by allowing banks to be choosier, reducing overall risk. A lack of net worth among financial institutions is a significant drag on credit growth in many countries and policies that limit competition or reduce the cost of acquiring capital can increase the profitability of existing banks, allowing them to lend more. Directed lending can focus banks on generating higher social returns, as opposed to only corporate profits. For example, directed lending can be used to increase investment in industries crucial to macroeconomic development, such as export industries that are highly productive. Finally, directed lending is more stable and less sensitive to market swings, potentially helping to protect the economy from financial crises.

In essence, what the defenders of financial repression are arguing is that moderate amounts of financial repression are just a form of prudential regulation. There is empirical support for some of these assertions. Demirgüç-Kunt and Detragiache (1999) find that deregulation of interest rates and reductions in barriers to entry increase financial volatility in countries that lacked the institutional and legal frameworks to limit financial risk. Klein (2003) finds that opening foreign access to stock markets increases the size and returns in stock markets, but only for countries beyond a certain level of economic development (per-capita income greater than $2,000).[15]

Others point to the success of many East Asian financial systems—particularly those of Japan, South Korea, and Taiwan—as evidence of the benefits of limited financial repression. While there were important policy differences between these countries, governments in these countries were heavily engaged in directed lending of long-term credit to export-intensive industries. They also subsidized targeted lending, imposed interest rate controls, and restricted entry of foreign and domestic banks to promote the growth of a small number of large banks. Bond and stock market development was not emphasized. Each country also favored large state-owned banks that helped finance their governments and their directed lending initiatives. Finally, each country encouraged the creation of corporate conglomerates that merged banking and industrial firms in an effort to overcome problems of asymmetric information and increase credit. (The argument against this kind of connected lending is that it can degenerate into "crony capitalism" where lending decisions are based on relationships, not economic fundamentals.)

Japan, South Korea, and Taiwan have been three of the greatest economic development success stories of the twentieth century, so it is hard to argue with the overall results. However, the question is: did these countries grow because of or in spite of these financial repression policies? Critics of these policies have argued that financial repression was harmful, but not very. Repression was moderate and became less invasive as these economies developed. Many of the repressive policies enacted were primarily directed at ensuring financial stability and avoiding risky and inefficient lending.[16]

Proponents of the East Asian model of growth point to the high levels of savings and investment rates these countries were able to achieve. Directed lending was particularly pushed into highly productive export-oriented sectors that set the foundation for sustained economic growth. They also emphasize that repression helped foster remarkably stable financial systems, at least until the deregulation of the 1980s led to the financial crises of the 1990s. Finally, other proponents have argued that policies such as barriers to competition were needed to create large banks that could maximize domestic savings, credit expansion, and investment given the significant capital needs that existed in many industries after the devastation of war. Given these large banks, interest rate ceilings were then needed to reduce rates from monopolistic levels to more competitive levels.[17]

One final argument offered by proponents of moderate financial repression is that many similar policies were followed by developed countries, such as the United States and Western European countries, during the gold standard and Bretton Woods eras before the global financial integration of the 1970s and domestic deregulation of the 1980s. In taking a broader perspective on history, financial repression appears to be a fairly common step in early to middle stages of economic development.

Regardless of where one comes down on this issue, the policies adopted in East Asia were uniquely adapted to their situation. Many countries in South America and Africa have tried similar policies but have been unable to obtain similar results, as will be discussed in the last section of this book when we look at the financial systems in these regions in more detail.

Finally, there is also strong evidence that while financial repression is costly, quickly reforming in a "cold-shower" approach may not be the best way to enact reform. For example, the complete removal of interest rate ceilings may lead to spikes in interest rates that could increase moral hazard and adverse selection problems, leading to increases in credit rationing. In addition, instantaneously liberalizing foreign capital flows, particularly before effective systems for prudential regulation of these inflows are built, may lead to unsustainable credit growth and speculation that can set the stage for a future financial crisis, as we will see has happened many times in the past when we examine financial crisis episodes in more detail. General rules for sequencing financial liberalization will also be examined in later chapters, particularly Chapter 6.

Comparing the institutions of China and India

China and India together comprise 2.5 billion people, or more than a third of the world's population. They have also been the two fastest-growing countries in the world over the last decade. After growing more slowly than China for years, India, as reported by the IMF, grew faster in 2011, at 10.4 percent compared to China's 10.3 percent. An important question related to these incredible growth performances continues to spark interest: are these huge countries growing because of their financial systems or in spite of them? Chapter 11 presents a more detailed examination of this question, but a brief characterization of some of each country's most important institutions is presented here.

At the beginning of the Chinese growth boom in the early 1980s, China had no formal legal or property rights system because of the Marxist policies it followed throughout the 1960s and 1970s. The Chinese property rights system in place today, often referred to as the "household responsibility system," looks nothing like a Western property rights system argued for by Hernando de Soto. Local officials of the Chinese government assign land to households via long-term leases (50–70 years for commercial property and 70 years for residential) that are created by the government and, of course, can be broken by the government. Holders of these leases then have the rights to any profits or capital improvements they make to the land. While the government promises to renew expired leases at market rates, the lack of certainty regarding the permanent ownership of land makes it impossible for the private sector to use their capital as collateral in order to obtain credit.

Because of this lack of protection for individual property rights, formal finance is not an option for most firms in China's private sector (where almost all of the growth in China is occurring). Instead, China's private sector deals with this lack of formal institutions and formal finance by relying on informal financial networks that work within informal institutions. Much of the informal finance that takes place in China flows through underground lending markets, which are technically illegal but still ubiquitous in some regions of the country.[18] These underground lending markets include financial transactions through middlemen, pawnshops, trade credit, credit cooperatives, and rotating savings and credit associations.[19] Within these underground lending markets, private entrepreneurs have developed alternative institutions (typically with local governments turning a blind eye) that avoid formal systems and instead are locally self-governing and based upon social norms. Particularly important to these informal institutions is a Confucian belief system in China that emphasizes family, social order, and trust as well as the importance of personal relationships, referred to in China as *guanxi*. These social ties often cross borders as many ethnic Chinese have access to Chinese contacts in Hong Kong, Taiwan, the United States, and across the globe. These underground lending markets not only allow private businesses to gain access to credit that is unavailable to them through the formal financial system, but also allows them to get this credit quickly and to subvert Communist Party interference in their operations.

When private firms do gain access to formal finance, they are typically forced to borrow in small amounts from multiple banks with help from third-party guarantees, who serve as co-signers for these loans. Local governments, with loans from state-owned banks, also make loans to over 40 percent of private firms, often through the same underground lending markets that are technically illegal.

Chinese formal institutions discourage formal finance in many other ways. The World Bank's *Doing Business 2011* collects quantitative and qualitative data on business regulations and the protection of property rights for 183 countries. Table 3.2 presents data from this report for 17 of the largest emerging

Table 3.2 Comparing legal systems and institutions in emerging economies

	World Bank, Doing Business 2011 (rank out of 183 countries)							2010 corruption perceptions index rank (out of 178 countries)
	Overall ease of doing business	Starting a business	Registering property	Getting credit	Protecting investors	Enforcing contracts	Closing a business	
China	79	151	38	65	93	15	68	79
India	134	165	94	32	44	182	134	87
Argentina	115	142	118	65	109	45	77	105
Brazil	127	128	122	89	74	98	132	69
Egypt	94	18	93	72	74	143	131	98
Indonesia	121	155	98	116	44	154	142	110
Korea (South)	16	60	74	15	74	5	13	39
Malaysia	21	113	60	1	4	59	55	56
Mexico	35	67	105	46	44	81	23	98
Pakistan	83	85	126	65	28	155	67	143
Peru	36	54	24	15	20	110	96	78
Philippines	148	156	102	128	132	118	153	134
South Africa	34	75	91	2	10	85	74	56
Sri Lanka	102	34	155	72	74	137	43	91
Taiwan	33	24	32	72	74	90	10	33
Thailand	19	95	19	72	12	25	46	78
Turkey	65	63	38	72	59	26	115	56

Source: World Bank (2011); Transparency International (2011).

market economies. China ranks 79 out of 183 countries in the overall index of the ease of doing business. Looking at the individual components in this index, China scores particularly poorly on the ease of starting a business and on protecting investor's property rights. China looks relatively better in the enforcement of contracts and registering property, despite the fact that there are only 150,000 lawyers in all of China (the same number that is in California), or only one lawyer per 8,082 people (compared to the United States where there is one lawyer per 273 people).[20] To make things even worse, only one-fifth of Chinese lawyers have an actual legal degree.[21] This lack of professionalism impacts not only China's legal system but also its accounting systems and its ability to meet international information disclosure standards.

Legal systems are also weak in China because of the cultural belief that it is more important to maintain *guanxi* than it is to maintain adherence to the formal law. In the words of businessman James McGregor, "Your network of family and personal relationships are more important than the rules of the road."[22] As a result of its weak legal system, there is a persistent willingness in China to ignore established laws or work around them. As a local saying goes, "Green means go, yellow means go, and red means find another way around." This entrepreneurial spirit when it comes to dealing with the "rules of the road" is a large part of the reason why the Chinese have been so good at developing informal institutions (such as underground lending markets) and other work-arounds that have allowed economic growth to occur in China at a breathtaking pace despite its weak formal institutions. But it makes it difficult for China to build quality formal institutions in the future if they are being built only to be ignored.

China also scores poorly in regard to perceptions of corruption, which is measured by Transparency International (2010). In the last column of Table 3.2, one can see that China ranks 79 out of 178 countries and ranks 7 out of the 17 emerging countries in this table. The influence of the Chinese government in the economy plays an important part in this low ranking. China's financial system is dominated by four large, state-owned banks that are not profitable and typically make decisions heavily influenced by Communist Party members and based largely on relationships (and personal payoffs), not profits.

Finally, the Chinese financial system is closed to wholly owned foreign ownership of banks and it is difficult for foreigners to purchase Chinese financial assets, save publicly traded equity, in general. While there has been some gradual movement toward allowing some foreign banks to operate in China through partnerships with Chinese banks (for example, JP Morgan and Morgan Stanley were allowed to invest in one Chinese bank in January 2011), foreign banks can only participate as bit players and are restricted from conducting many different types of financial transactions.

The result is that the financial development of the Chinese economy is weak relative to the strength of its entire economy (see the Financial Development Index in Table 1.1). But despite the weakness of its institutions, China continues to grow. This is, in part, because of the high Chinese savings rate (nearly 50 percent of GDP in 2011) that generates so many funds for investment that growth can continue even if these funds are not efficiently allocated. This is also because of the underdeveloped nature of the Chinese economy, making most forms of investment more productive because of diminishing marginal returns (but sure to decline as the economy becomes more developed). China can also continue to grow despite its widespread corruption because China is a classic example of a country characterized by centralized, not decentralized, corruption which, as discussed earlier, is much less damaging to overall economic growth.

Many worry that China's remarkable record of growth will soon be imperiled by the underlying weakness of the Chinese financial system, which in turn is imperiled by the weakness of its formal institutions. Despite having reasonable levels of government debt, multiple credit agencies warned in early 2011 that Chinese debt could be downgraded because of worries about hidden defaults in the Chinese banking system. Despite reporting 20 percent increases in profits in 2010 and less than 1 percent of loans as non-performing, many experts believe the true number of non-performing loans is greater than 12 percent, a rate that is not sustainable. The majority of these bad loans are the responsibility of local governments that regularly speculate in property, small businesses, and the stock market based on personal gains and *guanxi*. These bad loans coupled with rising inflation and a relatively low amount of bank capital in the financial system puts China at risk of a costly financial crisis.[23]

As opposed to China, India has a long-established legal system as well as the oldest banks and financial markets in Asia, dating back to the early years of British colonization. India also has strong laws protecting creditor rights and a common law legal system that has proven to be effective and flexible in protecting property rights in many other countries. But despite having *de jure* ("according to the law") financial institutions that look good on paper, India's de facto ("in practice") institutions are even worse than those in China. India scores much lower in the World Bank's Doing Business Index than China, ranking 134 out of 183 countries (refer back to Table 3.2). In the more detailed rankings, the only areas where India scores higher than China are in credit availability and creditor protection.

The principal problems in India are corruption and an incompetent legal system. In regard to corruption perceptions, India ranks 87th among 183 countries and 10th among the 17 emerging countries in Table 3.2. Worse yet, corruption in India is generally of the growth-killing decentralized type, conducted by countless government workers and bureaucrats throughout every level of India's public sector. Stories of bribery and thievery among India's bureaucrats are common. For example, Banerjee and Duflo (2011) tell the story of a small Indian business owner who spent 4.5 million rupiah in bribes to police officers to recover the money lost from a 20 million rupiah bad check. They ultimately recovered only four million of the debt. Over 80 percent of business owners report that it is difficult to get necessary licenses because of bribes.[24] Much of this corruption is centered in the police and judiciary, making the enforcement of property rights and contracts very difficult.[25] India ranks second-to-last in the world in the enforcement of contracts (China ranks fifteenth). Currently, there is reported to be a 30 million case backlog in the Indian legal system, with roughly one-third of these cases being over three years old. There are 25,000 cases pending to the Supreme Court (taking between eight and 20 years to complete).[26] The costs of enforcing a contract are estimated to be four times what they are in China.

India also suffers from excessive regulation and red tape. The time and number of procedures associated with obtaining licenses and permits are twice that of the developed world. India ranks in the bottom 20 in the world in the ease of starting a business. For example, to obtain permission to build a warehouse in Mumbai takes an average of 200 days and costs 2,718 percent of per-capita income.[27] Of course, the reason for much of this red tape is to increase the number of opportunities for bureaucrats to charge bribes. India also ranks low in information disclosure. Once again, the disclosure laws on the books are strong, but accountancy standards and enforcement are weak in practice.

The implication of these weak financial institutions in India is that family businesses and informal finance dominate the Indian economy. Family businesses reduce external financing needs and minimize the exposure to corruption. But it also increases risk and limits the size, efficiency, and management expertise of Indian businesses. It also keeps the size of Indian banks and bond markets small relative to the size of the economy.[28]

All of this said, the Indian stock market has been growing rapidly since it was deregulated in 2003. Also, the efficiency and profitability of the Indian banking industry has been increasing recently. Indian banks have been growing at 18 percent a year, pushed forward by deregulated interest rates, a growing influence of foreign banks, and, most importantly, a microfinance boom that has increased competition in the industry and broadly increased financial access for poorer households and smaller entrepreneurs. Microfinance now accounts for half of all credit in the Indian economy. This is an important area in which India, where the government has significantly subsidized microfinance, differs from China, where microfinance has been actively discouraged by the government in favor of government lending (and implicitly informal finance). Microfinance has allowed many smaller borrowers to bypass some of the corruption and inefficiency in the Indian system. Microfinance is an important area where India's future financial development holds promise and where it must thrive if India is to permanently eclipse China as the world's fastest-growing economy.

Conclusions

Institutions reduce risk and shape the incentives that are crucial to well-functioning financial systems. We know what factors are important to having institutions that promote financial development and economic growth: protecting property rights, enforcing contracts, keeping corruption low, managing conflict, maintaining macroeconomic stability, and instituting prudential financial regulation aimed at reducing financial risk and increasing information. But these things are only broad principles; there are many sets of *microinstitutions* that can be fundamentally consistent with achieving these principles. China is a good example of this. China's institutions do not match Western microinstitutions in most ways. But they generally work within the context of China's culture, society, government policies, and history (or at least they are not so a large an impediment at this stage of China's development to prevent it from growing).

India illustrates another important point about institutions, which is that it is not what is on paper (*de jure*) that counts, but how things are actually done in practice (de facto). Institutions rely on people, not principles. To the extent that institutions do not create incentives that discourage individuals from engaging in corruption or in other non-productive activities, no set of appropriate laws will guarantee financial development. India has advanced by gradually improving their financial institutions, but also through the development of informal finance and microfinance that has allowed many Indians to operate within a second financial system with its own set of incentives.

One final point that must be made about institutions is that it is hard to rank which individual factor is most important or needs to come before others. This is because each of the factors that determine quality institutions are interrelated. It is difficult to say whether protection of property rights is more important than limiting corruption because in practice they can only be achieved at the same time through a similar set of policies.

Once good institutions are in place, the bulk of the economic evidence suggests that gradual financial liberalization through eliminating excessive financial repression policies—interest rate controls, capital and exchange rate controls, barriers to entry, lending restrictions, high inflation—can be beneficial. But eliminating financial repression will only generate stable and sustainable growth once the proper financial institutions and prudential regulatory policies are in place. Also, it is important that the transition to these liberalized policies take place gradually over time, giving the financial system a chance to learn, plan, and adjust to the new environment.

There is one additional financial institution that plays an important role in financial systems in emerging market economies: the public finance policies of governments. Public finance was only briefly touched upon in this chapter but demands much closer examination. This is the purpose of the next chapter.

4 Fiscal policy and sovereign debt

Introduction

Fiscal policy and monetary policy play a crucial role in shaping financial development in emerging market economies for two reasons. The first is that fiscal and monetary policies shape incentives and institutions, which, as we discussed in the previous chapter, are absolutely fundamental to creating the foundations for efficient financial systems. Fiscal policy determines tax levels and the structure of a taxation system, it determines both the level and the priorities of government spending, and it determines a country's debt level and how it finances this debt. In setting monetary policy, a central bank determines the rate of money growth within an economy as well as serves as a lender of last resort and a regulator of the financial system. Together, fiscal and monetary policy directly impact many of the macroeconomic variables that play crucial roles in the functioning of financial systems, including interest rates, inflation rates, levels of credit, and exchange rates.

But fiscal and monetary policies also influence financial systems through another channel. Governments are the creators of many different types of financial assets. The two most important are the *money base* (currency plus bank reserves within the banking system) and *sovereign bonds* (bonds issued by the government). These assets serve as "foundation" assets for every financial transaction that takes place within an economy. The monetary base is the core of the money supply, which in turn determines the price level and is the financial asset that is traded in any financial transaction. Sovereign bonds are a core asset for banks and savers, and also provide valuable financial information by serving as an important benchmark interest rate in any economy.

This chapter focuses on the importance of fiscal policy to the functioning of financial systems within emerging market economies. It begins with a discussion of the government's budget constraint and the challenges emerging economies face in managing this constraint. One attractive option for governments is to issue sovereign debt to cover their budget deficits. Of course, the danger of issuing sovereign debt is that it requires fixed payments that create the possibility of a sovereign debt crisis, when the government's ability to borrow comes to a sudden stop and it is forced to default on its debt payments. We examine the long history of sovereign debt crises across the globe and discuss why they occur, the costs they entail, and the policies governments can adopt to try to avoid them.

One cost of sovereign debt crises is that they have often been associated with high inflation or even *hyperinflation* (inflation of greater than 1,000 percent a year) episodes. This chapter examines why inflation is correlated with sovereign debt and what can be done to break this link. Another cost of sovereign debt and inflation is *dollarization*, or the abandonment of the local currency for a foreign, or "hard," currency. We examine the implications of dollarization and how it often works in practice. This chapter concludes with a case study of the Latin American debt crisis, which was an acute occurrence of fiscal deficits, debt crises, hyperinflations, and dollarization across a large number of Latin American countries in the 1980s and 1990s.

The government budget constraint

Like any other actor in an economy, governments face a budget constraint. However, unlike other actors, governments have a unique ability to create financial assets, namely money and sovereign debt (bonds), in order to finance any discrepancy between its spending and its revenue. The government's budget constraint can be summarized as follows:

$$G - T = \Delta MB + \Delta B \tag{4.1}$$

This equation says, quite simply, that any difference between a country's government spending (G) and tax revenue (T)—or the budget deficit ($G-T$)—must be paid for by issuing new financial assets. These assets can be changes in the monetary base (ΔMB) created by issuing new currency, creating new bank reserves, or requiring banks to hold more reserves. The other option is to borrow by issuing sovereign bonds (ΔB).

The simple fact is that for many emerging economies it is extremely difficult to keep government spending in balance with tax revenue. On the revenue side, many emerging governments do not have the fiscal institutions in place to collect sufficient tax revenues. An IMF study found that emerging market economies only collect 18.2 percent of their GDP in taxes compared to the developed country (OECD) average of 37.9 percent.[1] This is in part because the informal sector is much larger in poorer countries, which is more difficult to tax. But inefficient tax bureaucracies are also to blame. While developed countries rely more heavily on income and business taxes, allowing tax revenue to be more efficiently generated from higher-income individuals, less developed countries do not have the accounting and information systems in place to collect sufficient information on incomes. Coupled with weak legal systems, this leads to rampant tax evasion. As a result, many countries are forced to rely more heavily on tariffs and consumption taxes—in other words, taxing goods instead of incomes— because these taxes are harder to evade. However, these forms of taxation are more regressive, disproportionally taxing the poor and limiting tax revenue. Finally, special interest politics also play a role in taxation. In countries with unequal incomes, rich individuals with a great deal of political power can shape the tax system in their interests. For example, property taxes were extremely low, below 4.2 percent, in 21 of 22 emerging economies examined in one study.[2]

While tax revenues are often limited, the needs for government spending are significant in emerging economies. Because of the large numbers of people living at or near poverty, demands for social safety net spending (health, food) are great, as are the needs for public infrastructure (roads, bridges, information technology, sanitation) and education.

One large magnet for government spending in many emerging economies are state-owned enterprises (SOEs), which typically constitute 7 to 15 percent of GDP in emerging economies but absorb nearly 20 percent of investment. The rationale for having SOEs is twofold. The first is to provide for the creation of natural monopolies in the utilities, communications, and transportation sectors. The second is *import substitution*, or the belief that domestic industry cannot survive unless protected from international trade and subsidized by the government. This argument has been particularly influential in the financial, manufacturing, and agricultural sectors. Unfortunately, SOEs have typically been inefficient, isolated from competition, and have operated in domestic markets too small for them to take advantage of economies of scale. As a result, they have ultimately become large drains on the government's resources. Losses in SOEs are often as great as 3 percent of GDP in many emerging economies.[3]

Since the 1980s, however, *privatization*, or the sale of state-owned assets and enterprises to the private sector, has taken place at a rapid pace in emerging market economies. More than $2 trillion of SOE assets have been sold since 1997. This has provided resources to governments from the sale of assets (when these resources have not been wasted because of corruption), reduced the drain of SOEs on public resources, and generally (but not always) increased economic efficiency in these firms.[4] It has also greatly increased the capitalization of many emerging stock markets, as privatization has often taken place through public stock sales.

Given the disconnect between their spending needs and their tax revenues, most emerging market economies have persistent fiscal deficits that must be financed with either increases in the monetary base or borrowing by issuing bonds. The advantage of increasing the monetary base is that these are assets that pay zero rates of interest and do not have to be repaid. The disadvantage of increasing the monetary base is that this also increases the money supply, increasing the price level and changing interest rates, exchange rates, and other macroeconomic variables in ways that may destabilize financial intermediation and economic activity (more on this later).

The other option is to issue sovereign bonds. These bonds can come in two forms. *Domestic debt* is in bonds that are issued under national financial laws. As a result, they are primarily attractive to domestic residents and typically, although not always, denominated in the domestic currency. These bonds are often attractive to domestic residents who, because of financial underdevelopment and/or financial repression, have few other alternatives for saving, particularly in their domestic currency. They are attractive to governments because they allow the government to borrow in the domestic currency, reducing the exchange rate risk of borrowing in hard currencies. Domestic debt is also important for governments that offer social welfare programs that make payments in the domestic currency. Of course, the problem with domestic debt is that for many emerging market economies, sufficient levels of domestic debt cannot be raised to meet their fiscal needs. However, economic growth in the emerging world has increased the ability of many emerging governments to borrow domestically. While 40 percent of debt in emerging countries was domestic in 1900, today over 80 percent of total debt is domestic, much of this debt long term.[5]

The other form of sovereign borrowing is *external debt*, or borrowing subject to international financial law and typically denominated in a foreign currency. External debt can take the form of bonds designed to be sold to private foreign investors or as bilateral or multilateral lending from other governments or from international organizations such as the World Bank or IMF. With the increasing globalization of financial markets, external debt is an option for more emerging market economies than ever before, but its danger is that it must be paid back, typically in a foreign currency. As a result, external debt exposes a government to substantial exchange rate risk that magnifies the risk of default. This is because a government's revenue and assets are typically in its domestic currency but its external debt liabilities have to be paid in a hard currency. In the event of a depreciation of their exchange rate, this currency mismatch significantly increases the probability of default on any external debt.

The determinants of sovereign borrowing and debt crises

It should be obvious why issuing sovereign debt is an attractive option for many emerging market governments in deficit. But it is less obvious why savers, both foreign and domestic, would choose to hold their savings in sovereign debt, particularly when the ability to force any government to meet their financial obligations on these bonds is more limited than the ability to force a private bond issuer to make good on their commitments. In the case of domestic debt, it is the government that makes the laws under which bond agreement is adjudicated, giving the government an easy way to repudiate its debt. In the case of external debt, international bankruptcy laws are notoriously difficult to enforce, particularly when you consider that there can be several thousand different bondholders spread across many different countries. The days when one country could openly invade another country in an effort to enforce debt contracts, as Britain did in Egypt and Istanbul in 1882 or the United States did in Haiti in 1915, are hopefully past.

There are important reasons, however, why governments have incentives to repay their sovereign debt, which in turn creates incentives for savers to purchase this debt. Default can limit the government's future access to borrowing, imposing significant costs on the defaulting government. In the case of domestic debt, default means failing to repay the country's own citizens, creating important political consequences. Default on external sovereign bonds can discourage other forms of foreign lending to an emerging country, such as foreign direct investment, because foreigners may perceive this default as an increase in the risk of doing business within the country. Any increase in perceived risk can also increase exchange rate volatility and reduce bank credit to firms, significantly limiting investment and trade. Finally, there is the possibility that the foreign assets held abroad by a defaulting country could be seized by foreign creditors, although in practice this is a long and difficult process.[6]

Despite these significant incentives to repay, Reinhart and Rogoff (2009) compile a comprehensive list of historical external debt crises and show that most countries, typically in their early stages of development, have experienced at least one sovereign debt crisis. Many countries are "serial defaulters" with multiple and periodic debt crises. For example, France had eight external defaults between 1500 and 1800, but zero since. Spain had seven crises in the 1800s and 13 crises before 1900, but zero since. More recently, to take two examples from emerging economies, Nigeria has defaulted five times since its independence in 1960, while Argentina has defaulted three times on its external debt since 1982, including the largest ever default in 2001 of $95 billion. Defaulting on domestic debt is also quite common; the authors identify over 70 domestic debt defaults since 1800.

The easiest way to understand why defaults are so common across countries is to understand how the accumulation of debt impacts the government's flows of funds, often referred to as the net transfer equation:

$$NT = (g - r)D \tag{4.2}$$

where NT is the net transfer (net inflow) of funds to the government, D is the level of debt, g is the rate of increase in the debt, and r is the average interest rate paid on the debt. From this equation, we can see that as long as the growth rate of debt accumulation is larger than the interest rate paid on this debt, then a country is creating a positive inflow of funds from issuing debt to cover its budget deficits. However, if the growth rate of the debt falls below the level of the interest rate paid on the debt, sovereign debt is creating a net outflow of funds that will add to the deficit and create the possibility of a debt crisis.

Based on historical analysis, Reinhart and Rogoff argue that there are two phases to any debt crisis. The first is the boom phase, when the levels of domestic and external debt increase relative to the size of the economy.[7] This boom phase can be fueled by many factors, possibly market psychology coupled with a lack of transparency ("hidden deficits"). In the next chapter, we will examine the economic explanations of asset and credit booms in more detail.

The second, or critical, phase of the debt crisis occurs when there is a significant decline in the confidence of lenders that the country is both willing and able to make the payments on its debt. When this happens, a "sudden stop" in sovereign lending can occur, significantly reducing g. In addition, increases in perceived risk associated with this sudden stop can increase interest rates, or r, on any sovereign debt that is not fixed rate but short term in nature. As a result, it is possible for g to fall significantly below r, creating an outflow of funds that the government may find itself unable or unwilling to pay. The fact that perceptions and expectations play such an important role in determining debt crises raises the possibility that debt crises can be self-fulfilling; in other words, if markets come to believe that a debt crisis will occur, new lending will come to a sudden stop, interest rates will spike, and a debt crisis will, in fact, occur.

In predicting when a sudden stop in lending or a spike in interest rates will occur, note that perceptions regarding both the government's *ability* as well as its *willingness* to pay play a role in determining a country's capacity to borrow and the price it pays to borrow. While fundamental indicators such as debt-to-GDP ratios clearly play a role in determining g and r, other, less quantifiable factors also play a role, such as the quality of a country's financial institutions, its financial transparency, its future growth prospects, and the government's reputation regarding its commitment to meeting its obligations. As a result, it has often been observed that for two countries with the same levels of debt relative to the size of their economy, one country may suffer from a sudden-stop in lending and a debt crisis, but the other may not. The country that defaults would be said to suffer from *debt intolerance*, which is largely a function of market expectations based on reputation.

Levels of debt intolerance can differ widely across countries. For example, Reinhart and Rogoff find that only 16 percent of all debt defaults occurred at debt-to-GDP levels greater than 100 percent, but 20 percent of defaults occurred at debt-to-GDP levels of 40 percent or below. They also find that the default and inflation history of a country matters when trying to identify when debt intolerance exists and the exact debt-to-GDP level that is likely to trigger a crisis within a specific country. In general, debt-to-GDP levels above 35 percent appear to significantly increase the probability of default for those countries with poor default histories, but this level can be as low as 20 percent for "serial defaulters."

One additional factor may play a role in a country's level of debt intolerance, and that is whether markets perceive a country's fundamental problem to be one of illiquidity or insolvency. A country that is *insolvent* has a long-run and fundamental imbalance in its budget, often the result of limited economic growth prospects that will not change with additional lending. If judged to be insolvent, a country will be more debt intolerant and much more likely to suffer from a debt crisis. A country that is *illiquid*, on the other hand, has a short-term imbalance in its budget, possibly caused by a sudden increase in interest rates or a difficulty in rolling over its short-term debt. A country whose fundamental problem is one of illiquidity is much less likely to suffer from a sudden-stop in new lending and a debt crisis.

How should governments respond when a sovereign debt crisis occurs? Countries on the verge of default have multiple potential options to avoid default, none of them good. One option is to repudiate, or refuse to repay, their debt and suffer the full consequences of a default. Short of this, a country can attempt to reschedule their debt, meaning they can negotiate with the holders of their debt to postpone and/or reduce their debt payments. Debt holders may agree to this because they feel that by accepting something less than full repayment they can maximize their total expected payback in a process known as eliminating *debt overhang*. The primary difficulty with debt rescheduling is that there are significant coordination problems in negotiating with thousands of different bondholders, each of which have different investment objectives and each of which have incentives to free-ride off those bondholders who do agree to debt rescheduling.[8] The final option that a country in danger of default has is to change the other variables in their budget constraint by cutting spending, raising tax revenue, or increasing the monetary base. (The options of cutting government spending or raising tax revenues are often referred to as *austerity*.) In reality, countries on the verge of default typically adopt a mixture of these options.

Regardless of the policies adopted to deal with debt crises, the economic impact is often severe. Sovereign debt crises are typically associated with capital flight, dramatic depreciations of the exchange rate, spikes in interest rates, declines in credit, reductions in asset prices, higher unemployment, and significantly reduced economic growth.[9] Reinhart and Rogoff find that, on average, external debt crises lead to 1 percent reductions in GDP. Domestic debt crises reduce GDP by 7 percent on average. However, there is a great deal of variability across countries depending upon the severity of the crisis and the extent of the default.

Sovereign risk premiums and debt relief

Even those countries that do not default on their debt pay a penalty when investors judge that there is increased risk of default. That penalty is a higher interest rate on their sovereign debt, known as the *sovereign risk premium*. Figure 4.1 presents average sovereign risk premium data for selected countries from 1997 to 2009 as measured by the Emerging Market Bond Spread Index (EMI), an index that calculates the average difference in interest rates between sovereign bonds from an emerging economy and US treasury bonds of similar maturities. This index is measured in *basis points*, or 0.01 percent. Obviously, there are significant differences between the interest rates various emerging market economies pay on their debt, indicating that quite a bit of variation exists in expected rates of default across these countries as well.

Bellas *et al.* (2010) find that over the long run, macroeconomic fundamentals are the primary determinants of a country's risk premium. These macro fundamentals include the debt-to-GDP ratio, the level of its foreign reserves, the proportion of debt that is short term, the trade balance, the budget deficit, measures of political risk, and the inflation rate. In other words, the ability to repay debt significantly impacts the price that a country pays for incurring debt. The positive correlation between sovereign risk premiums and debt-to-GDP ratios is roughly 0.8. This strong correlation can be seen for selected countries in Figure 4.1. Note, however, that this correlation is not perfect, both because other fundamentals matter but also because fundamentals only measure the *ability* to repay debt, they do not measure market perceptions about a country's *willingness* to repay its debt. In addition, the authors find that non-country-specific factors such as measures of financial volatility and liquidity in global financial markets can also impact sovereign debt premiums over short periods.

Because debt levels impact both sovereign risk premiums and the likelihood of experiencing a costly debt crisis, many have pushed for broad debt relief for emerging market economies on the basis of both economic and moral reasons. The primary economic reason is that debt relief may eliminate debt overhang and actually increase the amount of debt many developing countries are able to repay, while at the same time reducing sovereign risk premiums and freeing resources to spend on economic development. Others have made moral arguments that much of the debt accumulated over the years in many emerging countries was squandered by bad governments, since replaced, or accumulated as part of a country's colonial heritage. As a result, these countries should not be held morally responsible to repay for the past sins of others, referring to these past obligations as *odious debt*.

Organized debt relief programs have existed for emerging market economies since the 1980s. Since 1996, a program has been adopted by G8 countries, the IMF, the World Bank, and other multinational organizations to provide

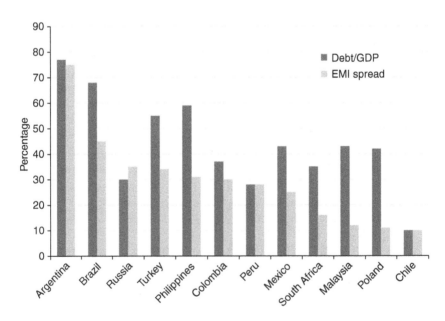

Figure 4.1 Public debt and sovereign risk spreads (source: *Bloomberg*; IMF, *World Economic Outlook*).

systematic debt relief to what are referred to as Highly Indebted Poor Countries (HIPCs). Under the HIPC program, poor countries that are significantly indebted can qualify for relief of up to two-thirds of their debt in exchange for the adoption of "sound economic policies," typically meaning macroeconomic reforms of their fiscal and monetary policies. Currently 40 countries (29 in Sub-Saharan Africa) qualify for the program and 35 of these have received some level of debt relief, totaling $71 billion in relief.

Such debt relief programs have been widely criticized for doing either too little or too much. Some critics argue that too few countries qualify for debt relief and even when they do, complete forgiveness of their debt is impossible. Other critics, such as the economist William Easterly (2007), argue that debt relief encourages poor policy by encouraging adverse selection and moral hazard. He notes that those countries that are the most indebted are also the countries most likely to have adopted poor economic policies. Granting debt relief to these countries effectively rewards bad economic policy (adverse selection). And once a country qualifies for debt relief, it is now able to borrow more, further encouraging the continuance of policies that got them in debt in the first place (moral hazard). Easterly points out that between 1989 and 1997, the 41 most highly indebted countries were forgiven $33 billion in debt, but borrowed $41 billion over the same period. Easterly also shows that HIPCs have more overvalued exchange rates, are more likely to be at war, and receive less foreign direct investment than other emerging market economies, indicating the persistent failure of their economic policies in spite of debt relief programs.

Inflation and central bank independence

Countries with significant levels of debt have options other than austerity. They can pay their bills by increasing the monetary base, otherwise known as *seigniorage*. Seigniorage is an attractive option for many emerging country governments because it can be done stealthily by a central bank. A central bank can purchase the bonds issued by the government with increases in the monetary base and essentially "monetize" any new debt issuances. At the same time, increases in the money supply create inflation, reducing the real value of any outstanding domestic debt denominated in the local currency. As a result, increasing the monetary base is a particularly effective method of reducing existing debt levels.

Of course, the long-term consequences of the inflation created by monetizing debt are very costly. If the inflation is anticipated it can create significant transaction costs as the public tries to hold less money to avoid the inflation tax. To pick an extreme example of transaction costs, inflation reached nearly 7,000 percent in Brazil in 1990. As a result, it became common for Brazilian workers to get paid twice a day—each time a little more—and to take a wheelbarrow to work to haul their money around in so that they could more quickly run to the market to spend it before it lost more value. Inflation also creates *menu costs*, or costs associated with changing prices. Finally, even when inflation is expected, it makes it difficult to determine exactly what the appropriate price is when prices are changing often. As a result, it creates confusion and risk, which can discourage economic and financial transactions.

If unanticipated, inflation creates even greater costs. In regard to financial intermediation, unexpected inflation reduces the real value of debt and reduces real interest rates, lowering the net worths of savers and lenders. Over time this can significantly discourage financial intermediation and encourages capital flight. Consider the example of Argentina. Between 1960 and 1994, its average inflation rate was 127 percent a year. A depositor with $1 billion in the bank in 1960 and who kept all of this in Argentinean pesos would have been left with the real equivalent of $0.0007 (one-thirteenth of one cent) by 1994!

Because of the danger it poses to savers, unexpected inflation also worsens debt intolerance and makes it harder in the future for a country to issue additional domestic debt in the local currency. Unexpected inflation also increases macroeconomic uncertainty and reduces efficiency by interfering with the information conveyed by prices. Finally, inflation is also often associated with other policies of financial repression, such as controls on exchange rates, interest rates, and capital flows.[10]

The cross-country empirical evidence indicates that the correlation between budget deficits, sovereign debt, and high inflation is strong. Bruno and Easterly (1998) find a strong correlation between budget deficits and inflation rates, while Reinhart and Rogoff (2009) find a correlation of 0.75 between inflation and default on external debt between 1940 and 2007. High debt levels are the reason why most emerging market countries in Africa, Asia, and Latin America have experienced at least one high inflation episode (inflation greater than 40 percent) in their history since their independence.

However, not all countries during every debt crisis have resorted to monetizing their debt. Why? Sargent and Wallace (1981) argue that it has to do with the institutional structures that exist within the central banks of different countries. Some countries have central banks that operate under a *fiscal dominance* model, where the central bank is directly tied to the government's treasury and is under the direct control of the executive branch of the government. In these cases, fiscal policy needs dominate monetary policy decisions, leading to inflation when budget deficits and debt get out of control. An alternative model is one of *monetary dominance*, where the monetary authorities in the central bank have independence from the executive branch and have the freedom to choose the targets of their policies (known as *political independence*), choose the policies to meet these targets (known as *policy independence*), or both. In this case, the monetary authorities are more likely to restrict money growth and inflation to rates that maximize long-run growth and not just short-term fiscal needs.

Reinhart and Rogoff (2009) find empirical evidence of another determinant of fiscal dominance policies: the balance between domestic and external debt. They find that fiscal dominance and high inflation policies are most likely when countries have issued large amounts of domestic debt in their domestic currency because inflation allows the government the possibility of directly reducing the real value of this debt. They estimate that inflation rises on average by 3 percent during defaults on external debt, but by 170 percent during defaults on domestic debt, remaining above 100 percent for years following the default.[11]

In looking at the empirical evidence regarding the impact of central bank independence on monetary policy, Cukierman *et al.* (1992) find no evidence that legal independence of the central bank reduced inflation in emerging market economies, but did find that a lower turnover of central bank governors (likely the result of more monetary independence in practice) did reduce inflation. A 2009 IMF study reports a significant trend since the mid-1990s among both emerging market and developed countries toward granting more political and policy independence to their central banks.[12] This increased independence has occurred both formally, meaning via changes in the law, and informally, meaning in practice. Empirical evidence suggests that greater central bank independence has been associated with significant reductions in both the level and volatility of inflation across emerging market economies.

Dollarization

High inflation episodes have eroded the confidence that many emerging market residents have in their local currencies and in their central bank's ability to protect its value, even years after high inflation episodes have passed. As a result, many residents resort to *dollarization*, or the use of hard currencies such as US dollars, for making purchases and when saving and lending. In practice, dollarization can take many forms. Informal dollarization takes place when private individuals choose to hold their assets and issue liabilities in foreign currencies. This impacts bank balance sheets as banks prefer to lend in hard currencies and the public prefers to save in hard currencies. Informal dollarization is common in many countries with high inflation histories.

Uruguay provides one example of how informal dollarization works. As an aftereffect of the periodic spikes in inflation and large devaluations that have occurred in the Uruguayan peso approximately every 20 years, today roughly 70 percent of savings and credit in Uruguay is conducted in dollars. Most high-priced goods are sold in dollars and smaller items are sold in pesos. In the words of a Uruguayan, "I can't tell you the price of bread in dollars or the price of a car in pesos." The government has tried to reduce the extent of dollarization in the economy gradually, principally by restraining inflation and focusing on macro-economic stability but also through measures such as issuing more domestic debt. In 2000, all of Uruguay's sovereign debt was denominated in dollars, but in 2011 only about half of it was. This provides Uruguayans, and foreigners, opportunities to save in pesos. It also gives the Uruguayan government an opportunity to borrow in the local currency in which most of their costs are also denominated. However, the fact remains that the power of Uruguayan monetary policy and its ability to protect the stability of its financial system is significantly limited by dollarization. To protect against exchange rate fluctuations that would severely destabilize their dual-currency economy, the central bank is forced to hold extremely large amounts of dollars (roughly $8 billion in 2011, or 15 percent of GDP).

Other countries have moved to more formal systems of dollarization, such as currency boards or currency unions. Under a *currency board*, a central bank holds hard currency to fully back any domestic currency they issue, usually on a one-to-one basis, in order to maintain a fixed exchange rate. In a *currency union*, many countries join together to run a currency board, with an international central bank created to manage a common currency and monetary policy for the group. Under either system, independent monetary policy, as well as influence over domestic interest rates, credit, bank lending, etc., is given up in an effort to stabilize the local currency to a hard currency. The largest currency unions among emerging markets are the West African Economic and Monetary Union, the Central African Economic and Monetary Community currency union (both of which peg their currencies to the euro), and the East Caribbean Monetary Union (which pegs to the US dollar).[13]

The principal ideas behind the adoption of currency boards and currency unions are ones of stability and credibility. Given the often disastrous monetary and inflation histories of many of these countries, tying their own hands by adopting a currency board or union is an attempt by these governments to establish credibility for their commitment to lower inflation and create exchange rate stability. Of course, any currency board or union is only as strong as the policymakers' commitment to following its rules. For example, Argentina's currency board, which fixed the Argentinean peso to the dollar between 1991 and 2002, worked well until large fiscal deficits and a failure to fully back pesos with dollars led to an abandonment of the currency board and a large devaluation of the peso (more on the Argentinean financial crisis in Chapter 7).

The process of dollarization is a difficult one to end once it has begun. Countries that have had repeated high inflation episodes have higher rates of dollarization that persist well beyond the time when inflation has abated. Even with the implementation of financial repression policies—such as banning hard currencies, limiting hard currency deposits in banks, or forcibly converting foreign currency deposits into the local currency (all of which can lead to capital flight out of the country in other forms)—dollarization often remains a persistent challenge for many emerging market economies to deal with. A more detailed discussion of de-dollarization in Uruguay and other Latin American countries is included in Chapter 12.

The Latin American debt crisis of the 1980s

One of the most significant series of sovereign debt crises occurred in Latin America during the 1980s. The genesis of the Latin American debt crisis stemmed from two concurrent phenomena that began in the 1970s. The first was the petrodollar boom. *Petrodollars* refer to the explosion in dollar holdings that originated from the increase in oil prices and revenues to oil-producing countries, such as OPEC countries. Many of these petrodollars eventually were saved in international banks, leading to a boom in dollar-denominated lending (much of it short term) throughout the world, but particularly to emerging market economies. Table 4.1 presents data on the explosion in debt-to-GDP ratios for a selection of emerging market economies. In just five years between 1975 and 1979, total emerging market external debt more than doubled from $180 billion to $406 billion, while debt service payments tripled to roughly $75 billion a year. In terms of our net transfer equation (4.2), there was a large increase in the growth rate of debt accumulation, *g*, throughout the emerging world. This was particularly true in Latin America, where the growth prospects looked to be strong and many countries, such as Mexico and Venezuela, had significant petroleum reserves available to service their debt.

The second important factor in the buildup to the Latin American crisis was the low real interest rates in global financial markets during the 1970s. As illustrated in Table 4.2, these low (even negative) real rates were driven by the fact that nominal interest rates lagged behind the buildup of inflation in the United States during this period. These low real rates triggered an intense scramble by many investors to find investments with higher rates of return, often in the sovereign debt of emerging economies, particularly in Latin America. In terms of our net transfer equation, this reduction in real interest rates, *r*, coupled with the increase in *g*, spurred large transfers of resources into emerging market economies. Sometimes these capital inflows were used to increase investment and productivity. Unfortunately, often these inflows into Latin America were squandered on inefficient SOEs, import substitution policies, populist social policies, overvalued exchange rates, and corruption.

The boom times for foreign capital inflows to Latin America ended abruptly in 1981. First, oil prices declined. Then, the US Federal Reserve moved to reduce inflation by steeply increasing real interest rates. Latin American countries quickly found that their opportunities to issue new debt had dried up, the real cost of rolling over their existing debt had increased (by nearly 12 percent between 1975 and 1981), and that the net transfer equation had moved decidedly against them. A recession in developed countries and a decline in the region's terms of trade contributed to a miserable macroeconomic picture in Latin America that triggered a sovereign debt crisis, capital flight, massive credit rationing, and precipitous declines in investment and consumption.

Table 4.1 Ratios of public debt to GDP, 1976–1981 (%)

Country	1976	1977	1978	1979	1980	1981
Argentina	15.0	18.0	18.7	20.1	21.3	29.6
Brazil	19.8	20.9	21.3	22.2	28.5	30.1
Venezuela	11.7	17.2	28.6	35.2	36.3	40.0
Mexico	22.0	31.4	32.2	30.8	29.1	34.3
Nigeria	3.9	5.8	9.4	12.2	13.9	16.9
Philippines	31.0	33.8	36.8	35.5	34.6	36.3

Source: World Bank (2012).

Table 4.2 Real international interest rates in Latin America, 1974–1984 (%)

Year	US nominal prime rate	US inflation rate	US real prime rate
1974	10.8	13.1	−2.2
1975	7.9	11.1	−2.9
1976	6.8	8.3	−1.3
1977	6.8	8.5	−1.4
1978	9.1	7.2	1.7
1979	12.7	9.2	3.2
1980	15.3	11.9	3
1981	18.9	10.1	8.1
1982	14.8	7.5	6.8
1983	10.8	5.1	5.5
1984	12.0	4.8	6.9

Source: IMF (2009).

Given the lack of credible, independent monetary institutions in most Latin American countries at this time, one of the first ways that many governments responded to these debt crises was to monetize their debt through inflation. Table 4.3 presents data for the average inflation rate in the seven largest Latin American economies in the 1980s and 1990s. Inflation was above 20 percent in all of these countries in the 1980s, but averaged over 220 percent when weighted according to the GDP of each country. These figures miss some of the extremely high inflation rates that existed in the smaller countries of Latin America like Bolivia (where inflation peaked at greater than 10,000 percent).

Mexico was the first to move toward default on their sovereign debt in 1982. By the mid-1980s, 28 of the 32 countries in Latin America had appealed to the IMF for a bailout to prevent a sovereign debt crisis, receiving a total of more than $145 billion in loans. As conditions to these loans, the IMF required two groups of policy reforms. The first was *austerity policies*, meaning reductions in budget deficits, devaluation of currencies, and reductions in inflation rates. The

Table 4.3 Inflation rates in Latin America (%)

Country	1980s	1990s
Argentina	437.6	14.9
Brazil	336.3	199.9
Chile	20.3	9.4
Colombia	23.7	20.1
Mexico	65.1	18.3
Peru	332.1	38.1
Venezuela	23.2	43.3
Average	176.9	49.1
Weighted average by GDP	223.3	92.3

Source: IMF (2009).

second was *structural reform policies*, meaning market-oriented reforms of labor and financial and goods markets. These policies were implemented with the primary goal of increasing long-term productivity and re-attracting foreign investment in what Paul Krugman (2008) has referred to as "the confidence game." However, in the short run these reforms reduced aggregate demand and magnified the precipitous falls in growth throughout the region. Latin American GDP growth in the 1980s was close to zero on average during what is often referred to in the region as "the lost decade."

The US Treasury spearheaded two programs to provide some debt relief to Latin American countries, in part to help stabilize regional economies, but also to prevent a full default that could jeopardize the solvency of nine large US banks with significant exposure to Latin America debt. The first was the Baker plan in 1986, which focused on debt rescheduling but provided little real debt relief to Latin American countries and was largely ineffective. The second was the Brady plan in 1989, which demanded market reforms in exchange for outright debt forgiveness and the provision of additional IMF and World Bank loans. While more successful, the Brady plan suffered from significant coordination failures associated with getting all of the various bondholders to agree to debt forgiveness.

By the 1990s, capital flows to the region had begun to return and growth had resumed, although only moderately. Proponents of the IMF's and the Brady plan's austerity and structural reform policies argue that placing the emphasis on growth set the stage for faster development in Latin America in the 1990s and 2000s. They also argue that these policies, particularly those that reduced inflation rates across the region in the 1990s (see Table 4.3), encouraged domestic financial development that has allowed these countries to borrow more in their domestic currencies, reducing exchange rate risk and the threat of external debt default. Critics charge that these austerity and structural reform policies were the economic equivalent of kicking someone when they are down and that the lack of significant debt relief remained a significant drag on growth in the region for another decade or more. Despite two decades of solid growth in the region since the Latin American debt crisis, countries such as Bolivia, Guyana, Nicaragua, and Honduras remain on the IMF's HIPC list. In addition, extensive dollarization remains today as a lasting remnant of these debt crises in many countries across Latin America.

Conclusions

By serving as an important determinant of institutions and as the creator of crucial financial assets such as the monetary base and sovereign bonds, emerging market governments can use fiscal and monetary policy as a tool to spur financial development and generate stability in the chaotic process of economic development. Those countries that have developed rapidly, particularly many of those in Asia, have shown how prudent fiscal policy that limits debt growth and maintains inflation stability can become a means of financing important public programs while also helping create a strong foundation for sustained financial development.

Unfortunately, we do not have to look too widely today or too far back in history to find many examples of the alternative, where irresponsible debt accumulation has led to debt intolerance and destabilizing debt crises. There is an extensive history of debt crisis throughout the history of economic development, including many in countries that today are developed countries. These debt crises have often led to the monetizing of debt by central banks controlled by governments willing to trade the short-term advantages of stealthily paying their bills with seigniorage for the long-terms costs of high inflation, devastated financial systems, dollarization, and stunted economic development.

This said, one of the most remarkable macroeconomic developments in the last 20 years has been the dramatic improvement in fiscal and monetary restraint that emerging market economies have shown. Unlike the 1980s and early 1990s, today emerging market economies account for only 17 percent of all government debt issued globally and have an average debt-to-GDP ratio of 37 percent of GDP. Compare this to developed countries where this ratio averages over 100 percent. Recent sovereign debt crises have taken place in Europe, not Latin America or Africa. Coupled with more independent central banks, this greater fiscal restraint has also led to lower and more stable inflation rates in emerging economies. However, given the regular occurrence of sovereign debt crises and high inflation episodes throughout history, it is naively optimistic to think that debt crises and hyperinflations are strictly a thing of the past in emerging economies.

The next chapter turns to two other important and often catastrophic sources of financial instability often tied to sovereign debt crises: banking crises and asset bubbles. Once again, these crises have an extensive history in emerging markets and present significant challenges to financial and economic development.

5 Asset bubbles and banking crises

Introduction

The purpose of this chapter is to investigate the causes and consequences of asset bubbles and banking crises in emerging market economies. Unfortunately, these two types of financial crisis occur regularly across countries, both rich and poor, and have managed to significantly impede the pace of financial and economic development in the vast majority of emerging economies at some point in their history.

It is important to start by clearly defining what we are talking about. The term *asset bubble* refers to a rise in the price of an asset above what can be justified by the asset's financial fundamental value. In the words of Nobel Laureate Joseph Stiglitz (1990: 13), "If the reason that the price is high today is only because investors believe that the selling price is high tomorrow—when 'fundamental' factors do not seem to justify such a price—then a bubble exists." As Stiglitz's definition suggests, an asset bubble is likely to exist when swings in the psychology of the market dominate the real characteristics of an asset. The problem with bubbles, of course, is that they burst, and the resulting collapse in prices can lead to large losses of wealth, increases in perceived risk, and declines in confidence that can depress financial intermediation and economic growth.

A *banking crisis* refers to a situation in which numerous banks simultaneously find it impossible to roll over their short-term borrowing and/or experience a sudden withdrawal of deposits that leads to widespread illiquidity or insolvency throughout the banking system. Banking crises are common because banks are structured in ways that make them vulnerable to liquidity crises. Banks are inherently illiquid because they hold long-term assets (primarily loans) but borrow using short-term liabilities (savings accounts, short-term bonds, etc.) Any interruption in a bank's ability to roll over its short-term debt or a sudden large withdrawal of deposits (a *bank run*) can lead to the failure of even the most stable and profitable of banks.

Asset bubbles and banking crises are best studied together because they often occur at the same time, in large part because there are important feedback effects between the two that are examined in this chapter. Also, similar factors are at the root of both asset bubbles and banking crises: namely, fragile fundamentals caused by insufficient prudential regulation, risky lending driven by moral hazard, and speculative behavior. One final reason to study asset bubbles and banking crises together is that their impact on financial instability and economic growth are similar. In addition to examining these issues, this chapter presents a case study of one of the more well-known, illustrative, and costly examples of asset bubbles and banking crises in emerging economies: the 1994 Mexican "Tequila" crisis.

The causes and consequences of asset bubbles

Why would the prices of some assets rise above levels that can be justified by their fundamental economic characteristics? One of the first observations to be made about asset bubbles is that they do not generally occur in many types of assets, such as bonds or agricultural products, but are most likely to occur among long-lived assets with no specific maturity: stocks, real estate, mineral commodities. When considering why this is the case, the answer points to the importance of speculation. Assets with no maturities have longer horizons over which their returns must be evaluated, leading to more uncertainty and a reliance on speculative assumptions. Unlike assets with a fixed life, such as bonds, assets with no maturity never have any principle that must be repaid, meaning there is no anchor to their prices. The importance of uncertainty and speculation is at the heart of *belief-based theories* of asset bubbles.

The most influential proponent of the role of beliefs in driving asset bubbles is Charles Kindleberger (1989). Examining case studies from developed countries, Kindleberger identifies four factors that drive asset bubbles. First, speculative manias and panics are a fundamental aspect of human psychology and market behavior. While speculation is necessary for markets to behave efficiently, it often leads to excessive volatility because it is human nature to become overly exuberant or pessimistic when faced with uncertainty.[1] This is largely because of the second of Kindleberger's four factors, the irrationality of market participants. In his opinion, which is not significantly different from that of other economists such as John Maynard Keynes (1936) or Hyman Minsky (1982), rationality is more of "a long-run hypothesis" as opposed to an accurate portrayal of how market participants make decisions in the short run. In the short run, people make highly subjective decisions based on limited information that is often only tenuously linked to real changes in the economy. The actions of individuals are then magnified by *herding behavior*, or the tendency of investors to try to follow market leaders because they think that they are smarter or better informed. This herding behavior can make the booms and busts associated with asset bubbles self-fulfilling in the sense that when everyone thinks that prices will rise, they rise, and vice versa.

All booms need fuel, which leads us to the third and fourth factors in Kindleberger's theory. Kindleberger argues that all asset bubbles start with some new form of financial innovation or technology (i.e. new types of financial assets, changed institutions, new markets, etc.) that encourages investors to think that old paradigms, and the prices associated with them, no longer matter. There is a well-known adage that "the most expensive words in finance are 'this time it's different'." New financial developments are often used by many investors as the justification for falling into this trap. In Kindleberger's words, new financial technology provides a "narrative" for the bubble.

However, heavily investing in booming assets is not possible without the money to do so, and the fourth and final factor in asset bubbles according to Kindleberger is easy credit. Much of the speculation in asset bubbles is debt-financed, meaning that leverage and risk rise along with asset prices. As profits rise, more and more credit flows into these markets, but only up to a point. At some point, a negative shock, either real or psychological, occurs that triggers a decline in asset prices. Losses begin to build, risk perceptions rise, and the excessive leverage that existed at the end of the boom leads to panic selling and increased credit rationing that magnifies the size of the collapse in asset prices.

While irrationality is at the heart of Kindleberger's theory, it is possible to envision how asset bubbles could be the result of rational investment strategies when herding behavior in financial markets is strong. When one investor's return is closely linked to other investor's behavior, then it might be optimal to buy an asset when everyone else is buying the asset and count on the existence of a "greater fool" to sell this asset to in the future, even if its current price is beyond anything that can be justified by economic fundamentals. When everyone follows such a strategy, an asset bubble can result.[2]

Other models of asset bubbles can be characterized as *fundamentals-based theories* because they focus on real shocks that initiate booms and busts in asset prices. Kaminsky and Reinhart (1999) and Higgins and Osler (1997) emphasize the role that financial liberalization plays in freeing banks to engage in riskier behavior. This can encourage moral hazard lending and a rapid expansion in credit and leverage. Much of this credit gets funneled into asset markets, creating debt-fueled price booms. Kaminsky and Reinhart estimate that real estate and stock prices rise on average by 40 percent following financial deregulation. At some point, however, this buildup in leverage and asset prices reverses itself in reaction to a negative real shock that eventually will occur, such as an increase in interest rates or a depreciation of the exchange rate. As asset prices begin to decline and defaults rise as a result of excessive leverage, credit tightens and the collapse of asset prices accelerates.

It is important to note that both belief-based and fundamentals-based theories of asset bubbles agree on a number of points. First, they both emphasize the role of credit growth in financing speculative behavior. Second, moral hazard plays an important role in creating incentives to assume risk in these models because the downside risk of speculation is shared with lenders when this speculation is debt-financed.

The third thing that all of these theories have in common is their policy prescriptions for preventing asset bubbles from occurring. There is agreement that indiscriminate financial deregulation is dangerous and that prudential regulation that aims to limit leverage, excessive credit growth, and moral hazard lending is essential to dampening bubble behavior. Note that this is different from saying that financial repression is justified. What these theories argue for is a measured approach to liberalization that focuses on minimizing its short-term impact on financial instability. However, Kindleberger and his followers are skeptical that prudential regulation can ever completely overcome human nature or that asset bubbles can ever be completely prevented.

The final point of agreement among these models is that asset bubbles are likely to be more common in emerging market economies than in developed economies. There are at least three reasons for this. First, as discussed before, there is a decided lack of financial information in many emerging financial markets. As a result, decisions are made under more uncertainty, leading to more speculative behavior and possibly increasing the likelihood of herding behavior, either rational or irrational. Less information also means more moral hazard and adverse selection, increasing risk and financial volatility. Second, emerging markets generally have poorer institutions, meaning prudential regulation is weaker. Many emerging markets have long been characterized by financial repression policies, and when liberalization occurs it is often enacted by regulators with little experience or knowledge about how to keep an appropriate eye on much more dynamic and complicated financial markets. Third, most financial markets in emerging economies are not as developed, have fewer participants, and are not as liquid. As a result, these markets are less efficient and are more prone to excessive price swings and volatility.

One point where there is significant disagreement among economists is how aggressive central banks should be in preemptively "pricking" asset bubbles before they get too large. On one hand, many economists (particularly proponents of belief-based models) argue that central banks can diminish the volatility of asset markets and stabilize financial intermediation by tightening the money supply and credit during asset booms in order to limit the amount of debt-financed speculation. The less asset prices rise during a bubble, the less they will have to fall during the "pop." Such a strategy represents a switch from traditional monetary policy where the focus is on aggregate inflation in goods and services, not narrow inflation in asset prices.

Other economists, such as the chairman of the US Federal Reserve Ben Bernanke (2002), argue that monetary policy is a blunt instrument most effective at controlling macroeconomic variables, such as inflation and output, and is not able to specifically target asset markets alone. Tightening monetary policy and raising interest rates to slow asset prices will not only slow the growth of these prices, but also slow economic growth in general. In the words of Bernanke, using monetary policy to prevent a bubble is like trying "to perform brain surgery with a sledgehammer."

A second problem with using monetary policy to preemptively burst asset bubbles is that it is extremely difficult to contemporaneously determine whether increases in prices are driven by bubbles or fundamentals. If bubbles were easy to identify, then investors would never be caught holding these assets when a bubble collapses. There is little reason to think that central banks are better at identifying asset bubbles *ex ante* than investors. In the words of Nobel Laureate Robert Lucas, "If these people exist, we can't afford them."[3] As a result, unless a central bank has better information than the market in general, which is unlikely to be true for long periods, the central bank is as likely to attempt to pop a bubble when one exists as it is to make a mistake and attempt to do so when one does not exist. Bernanke's preferred approach to dealing with asset bubbles is to slow the growth of credit by tightening prudential regulation during periods of rapid asset price growth.

Is there a housing bubble in China?

Recent developments in China illustrate exactly how difficult it is to identify asset bubbles and deal with them when they may exist. Since 2009 there has been a great deal of talk in the financial media about a housing bubble growing in China fueled by speculative mania, easy credit, and low interest rates. The first challenge to identifying whether such a bubble exists or not is to examine the economic data, but housing price data is unreliable in most emerging economies, particularly in a country like China where statistics may have been manipulated and many trades do not take place through formal channels. The most reliable housing data comes from private firms. The economic consultancy firm Dragonomics reports that housing prices in major Chinese urban areas rose by more than 10 percent in 2009 and 21 percent in 2010.[4] By another estimate, housing prices in China tripled between 2005 and 2009.[5] At the same time, residential housing has grown from 2 percent of Chinese GDP in 2000 to 6 percent in 2011, while total construction stands at 13 percent of GDP, twice what it was in the early 1990s.

But do these high growth rates in the housing sector necessarily constitute a bubble in a country that grew at nearly 10 percent in 2010 and is doubling in size every decade? Many analysts say it does not and argue that the observed increases in housing prices can be justified by fundamentals.[6] The incredible growth in urbanization in China has increased real demand for houses, pushing prices higher, particularly in the largest cities where housing price data is collected. In addition, unlike in a true bubble, this price growth has not been primarily driven by growth in credit. Mortgage credit in China stands at 40 percent of GDP, roughly half of what it was in the United States in 2007 before its housing bubble popped. However, much of the credit that has been issued has been through underground lending markets (see Chapter 11), in which the transparency and quality of the decision making that goes into making these loans is questionable.

Others argue that the evidence for a bubble is too convincing to ignore. Commerzbank calculates that the housing price-to-income ratio in Beijing is 36, as compared to a ratio of 12 in New York and five in Frankfurt.[7] This means that it takes an average family over 50 years of disposable income to purchase an apartment in Beijing. Housing price-to-rental price ratios in China are twice the global average.[8] Real estate prices in Shanghai in 2012 are approaching those in

Tokyo, but within a country considerably poorer than Japan. These statistics are not consistent with housing prices that are sustainable in the long run. The investment motive to make a profit on "flipping" housing also seems to be rampant in China. In Shanghai, as well as in all of the first-tier cities in China, "ghost neighborhoods" exist in which investors, in an effort to find higher returns for their savings, have purchased apartment complexes that then sit empty, often for years, waiting for a profitable opportunity to sell.

Economist Nouriel Roubini, a consistent pessimist, argues that the bubble is not just in Chinese housing but in fixed investment in general, which has risen to 50 percent of GDP in 2011. He argues that investment at these levels is not sustainable in the long run.[9] Eventually the returns on investment will fall, triggering defaults and a bust in investment spending across the entire Chinese economy.

In the midst of the debate regarding whether a bubble exists in China or not, it now appears that the central bank of China thinks that a bubble does exist. In June 2011, the People's Bank of China (PBOC), China's central bank, imposed a new regulation that all mortgages on second homes must require 40 percent down payments in an effort to reduce debt-financed housing purchases. The PBOC also raised interest rates to deflate housing prices, contrary to the admonitions of Bernanke and others regarding the dangers of using monetary policy to fight bubbles. These actions came at a time when the first indicators of what could be a significant deflation of housing prices were first being observed.[10] In 2011 housing prices were estimated to have declined in more than half of all Chinese cities and Standard and Poor's estimates that housing prices declined by 10 percent for the year.[11] These declines in housing prices not only threaten the housing sector of the economy, but also threaten weak Chinese banks and economic growth in general if the declines pick up pace.[12] On the other hand, optimists, including the Chinese government, argue that these falling prices are only a modest correction and the market is headed for a "soft landing."[13] Although it is very uncertain at the time of this writing how this will all play out, what is more clear is that definitive guidelines for identifying and preemptively dealing with bubbles remain elusive.

The causes and consequences of banking crises

Banking crises are, unfortunately, quite common phenomena. Honohan and Klingebiel (2003) count 112 banking crises in 93 countries between 1970 and 2000 (not including the numerous banking crises that have occurred during the global financial crisis that began in 2007). These banking crises have typically been extremely costly for governments, who have had to help recapitalize crisis banks as the result of guaranteed (either explicit or implicit) deposit insurance. Table 5.1 presents one estimate of the 15 costliest banking crises between 1980 and 2001 in terms of the size of the government bailout as a percentage of GDP.[14] Honohan and Klingebiel estimate that the cost of the average banking system bailout is roughly 13 percent of GDP. These costs do not include the opportunity costs of lost wealth and income, which can also be significant.

Table 5.1 Worst banking crises since 1980

Country	Crisis dates	Estimated cost of bailout (as % of GDP)
Argentina*	1980–1982	55
Indonesia*	1997–1998	55
China	1990s	47
Jamaica*	1994	44
Chile*	1981–1983	42
Thailand*	1997	35
Macedonia	1993–1994	32
Israel	1977–1983	30
Turkey*	2000	30
Uruguay	1981–1984	29
Korea	1998	28
Côte d'Ivoire	1988–1991	25
Japan	1990s	24
Uruguay	1981–1984	24
Malaysia*	1997–1998	20

Source: Caprio and Klingebiel (2003).

Note
* Indicates a country with multiple banking crises since 1980. The reported crisis is the largest.

Once again, there are two broad categories of theories explaining the origins of banking crises: belief-based theories and fundamentals-based theories. In belief-based theories, banking crises are the result of bank runs in which depositors (or bondholders) withdraw their funds from banks based on sudden changes in expectations and losses of confidence. In the words of Walter Bagehot (1873: 86), the father of modern central banking, "Credit—the disposition of one man to trust another—is singularly varying." Charles Kindleberger presents a theory of banking crises similar to his theory of asset bubbles, where periodic manias and panics driven by irrationality lead people to erratically change their behavior based on how they believe others will behave. This herding behavior leads depositors to suddenly withdraw their deposits based on the fear that others may withdraw their deposits first and leave the bank without enough reserves to meet outflows. Likewise, the holders of a bank's short-term debt might become reluctant to roll this debt over if they lose confidence that other debt holders will roll over their debt, because failure to do so would put the bank at risk of failure. These fears of bank runs and banking crises are endemic because of the inherent illiquidity of banks. In such belief-based models, banking crises are self-fulfilling because once it becomes widely believed that a banking crisis might occur, then a banking crisis will occur regardless of the real financial fundamentals of the banking system.

Belief-based banking crises do not necessarily have to be driven by irrationality. Diamond and Dybvig (1983) show how rational depositors can initiate bank runs when the best response of one depositor depends upon the actions of other depositors. Once a depositor believes there is a sufficient probability that others will withdraw their deposits from the bank, a self-fulfilling bank run can take place without any real change in the financial position of the bank prior to the bank run. In these models, multiple equilibriums are possible with outcomes ranging from bank stability to a bank run. Depositors' beliefs about the probability of which equilibrium will occur determines which equilibrium actually does occur.

Fundamentals-based theories of banking crises focus on the factors that weaken the financial positions of banks. One type of banking crisis that has often occurred in emerging markets are banking crises driven by financial repression. As discussed previously, many emerging market governments have used their banking systems as a means to monopolize savings and generate cheap sources of finance for their government spending. Governments have often done this by forcing banks to hold large amounts of sovereign debt and currency reserves. When the government itself becomes unable to meet its financial obligations, it is forced to default on its debt or rely on seigniorage, increasing inflation. In either case, banks will suffer losses that can ultimately lead to insolvency and a banking crisis. This type of banking crisis is really just another form of domestic default on sovereign debt, which was discussed in the previous chapter.

A second type of fundamentals-based banking crisis originates from large and negative shocks to the capital and profitability of banks that puts the entire system at risk of insolvency.[15] Such negative shocks could come from many potential sources:

Recessions. Declines in economic growth reduce incomes and profits, leading to increases in credit risk and bankruptcies that can reduce bank capital below threshold levels, triggering a banking crisis.

Terms of trade shocks. Banks in many emerging markets are often not sufficiently diversified and lend extensively to a small number of industries. Any terms of trade shock that negatively impacts certain sectors of an economy, particularly commodities, can lead to declining profits and increased defaults in these industries that, in turn, can lead to large losses for banks that can cause a banking crisis.

Increasing interest rates. Banks generally lend long and borrow short, meaning that the costs of their liabilities are more sensitive to increases in interest rates than the return on their assets. This exposes banks to a great deal of interest rate risk, where spikes in interest rates can reduce bank capital and profits. Higher interest rates can also increase credit risk and default by increasing moral hazard and adverse selection within the banking system.

Exchange rate depreciation. Banks often have currency mismatches in their balance sheets when they have more foreign-denominated debt than foreign-denominated assets. Whenever this occurs, a depreciation of the local currency can raise the value of a bank's debt more than it raises the value of its assets (as measured in the foreign currency), leading to a decline in net worth and bank capital. Even when banks carefully protect against currency mismatches and try to balance foreign-denominated assets and liabilities, banks commonly find themselves making foreign-denominated loans to local firms that generate all of their profits in the local currency. As a result, any depreciation in the local currency makes it less likely that firms can meet their debt payments in the foreign currency, increasing the number of bankruptcies and non-performing loans a bank experiences and reducing bank capital.

Unexpected inflation. Inflation that is not anticipated reduces real interest rates on bank loans and significantly reduces the real value of the long-term loans a bank has made, reducing profits and bank capital.

Unexpected deflation. Deflation that is not anticipated increases real interest rates and significantly increases the real value of the long-term loans a bank has made. However, this will only increase bank capital and the profits of banks if borrowers are able to maintain their payments on these loans. In fact, there are many instances, for example during the Great Depression, when sustained deflation led to huge increases in bankruptcy rates by dramatically increasing levels of real debt and real interest rates. These bankruptcies served to decrease, not increase, bank capital and triggered banking crises.

Irving Fisher (1933) was one of the first to identify the role that credit-fueled asset bubbles coupled with deflation played in contributing to the banking crises experienced worldwide during the Great Depression. In his debt-deflation theory, the buildup of debt and increases in leverage that occur during booms make financial systems particularly vulnerable to losses incurred by deflation-fueled bankruptcies.

Sovereign debt crises. A debt crisis increases the probability that banks will suffer a default on their holdings of government bonds. For reasons we discussed in the last chapter, debt crises also increase expected inflation and interest rates as well as decrease the exchange rate, all of which reduce the profitability and capital of banks. Maybe most importantly, debt crises can shake public confidence in the economy and the financial sector, leading to a self-fulfilling banking crisis.[16]

Asset bubble collapses. As discussed in the previous section, asset bubbles are usually fueled with debt, much of this provided by banks. This debt increases moral hazard in asset markets, further ballooning the bubble until it collapses, reducing net worths, increasing bankruptcies and defaults, and leading to large losses in bank capital that can trigger a banking crisis. As a result, throughout history there has been a close link between asset bubbles and banking crises, where a collapse in an asset bubble can start a banking crisis, but a banking crisis can lead to the disappearance of credit that further exacerbates the collapse of the asset bubble.

If so many shocks can potentially cause a banking crisis, how do banks ever stay afloat in the first place? The answer, of course, is that well-run banks are aware of these potential risks and take actions to mitigate and insure against them. Just as importantly, countries with quality financial institutions make sure that appropriate prudential regulations are in place to force banks to limit the risks they expose themselves to. These prudential regulations would include, but are not limited to, restrictions on risky asset holdings (particularly in assets prone to bubbles such as housing and stocks), restrictions on deposit and credit growth, limits on loans to single borrowers or industries, limits on short-term foreign-denominated debt, and possibly even interest rate ceilings (to limit moral hazard lending). Bank capital requirements are also an important part of prudential regulation. The Basel Accords, which are international agreements setting capital adequacy standards on banks based on the risk of their assets, are one attempt to limit risk in banking systems by ensuring that banks hold sufficient capital based on the risk of their assets. However, the Basel agreements only apply to the largest international banks and are voluntarily administered by domestic governments. As a result, the vast majority of banks in emerging economies are not subject to Basel, and even when they are, there are large variances in how strictly they are enforced.

Since the 1980s, many emerging market governments have liberalized their banking systems in an effort to reduce financial repression, but have not at the same time been able to create the appropriate level of prudential regulation to prevent the excesses that can lead to banking crises. As reported by Honohan and Klingebiel (2003) earlier in this section, 112 banking crises have occurred in 93 countries between 1970 and 2000. However, before 1970, Eichengreen and Arteta (2002) report that only one banking crisis occurred between 1945 and 1971 for the 21 countries in which there is reliable data. This increase in the frequency of banking crises has come at the same time that financial systems across the globe have significantly liberalized. Because restrictions on bank behavior have often been indiscriminately removed, banks have engaged in riskier behavior that has led to moral hazard fueled lending booms. This has left them more vulnerable to banking crises. Emerging market economies are particularly vulnerable to indiscriminate deregulation because they typically have weaker bureaucratic structures that are more easily co-opted by political interests, lack strong legal institutions, have less quality information, have fewer resources for the enforcement of prudential regulation, have thinner markets, have fewer shareholders to impose market discipline on banks, and possess less experienced regulators.

Fundamentals-based models of banking crises have much different policy prescriptions for preventing and mitigating banking crises than belief-based models. Belief-based theories argue that because bank runs trigger banking crises and are largely self-fulfilling, crises of confidence can be prevented through the government provision of deposit insurance and/or the existence of a strong central bank that can serve as a lender of last resort. According to Bagehot (1873: 86),

> after a great calamity, everybody is suspicious of everybody; as soon as that calamity is forgotten, everybody again confides in everybody. ... The Bank of England is bound, according to our system, not only to keep a good reserve against a time of panic, but to use that reserve effectually when that time of panic comes.

However, in fundamentals-based models, deposit insurance and crisis lending only encourages moral hazard. When banks can use insured money to finance their lending and are then bailed out when they make bad loans, banks are much more likely to engage in the kinds of risky behaviors that make banking crises much more common. Instead, fundamentals-based models argue that appropriate prudential regulation of lending aimed at reducing the riskiness of bank behavior and limiting the growth of credit during booms is the most reliable method of preventing banking crises.

Once a banking crisis is imminent or has already begun, all theories agree that the only way to limit the damage to the financial system and to the entire economy is for prompt and aggressive bailouts of any bank that the authorities believe can be and should be saved. These decisions as to which banks are "savable" and which are not is extremely complicated in practice and should hinge on whether the bank is well run and fundamentally profitable but is suffering from short-term illiquidity problems. However, too often bailout decisions are made only on the basis of political connections or are indiscriminately granted to every bank, regardless of the level of corruption or competence.

Government-financed bank bailouts should involve both lending to banks in order to increase bank liquidity, but also purchasing bank capital in order to reduce leverage ratios. Such bailouts are the best way to stabilize the financial system and restore credit so that economic growth can resume. However, there are two significant problems with generous and extensive bailouts. The first is that bailouts can be expensive—in some cases, egregiously so (once again, refer to Table 5.1). In fact, the bailout costs from banking crises can be so large as to trigger a sovereign debt crisis. The second problem is that bailouts encourage moral hazard and increase both risk in the banking system and the probability that more banking crises will occur in the future. In most emerging market economies, not a single bank has ever been allowed to fail. This can only mean that moral hazard is a large and dangerous problem in most emerging market financial systems.

Empirical evidence on banking crises

It is difficult to directly test belief-based theories of banking crises because beliefs are difficult to measure and because these theories do not impose any empirically testable hypotheses on measurable fundamentals. In addition, explicit or implicit deposit insurance and crisis lending has become commonplace in almost every country, which limits the occurrence of bank runs and self-fulfilling banking crises.

There is substantial evidence that a lack of prudential regulation and poor economic fundamentals play crucial roles in most modern banking crises. Demirgüç-Kunt and Detragiache (1998) examine 31 banking crises in developed and emerging economies between 1980 and 1994. They find that an index measuring institutional quality, which is a proxy for the quality of prudential regulation, is a significant predictor of banking crises. Many measures of deteriorating fundamentals such as slow economic growth, high inflation, high real interest rates, high credit growth, and current account deficits are also correlated with banking crises. Finally, the authors find that explicit deposit insurance is associated with an increased frequency of banking crises, suggesting that moral hazard lending plays a role in their buildup. Joyce (2011) finds that many of these same fundamentals are correlated with banking crises, but also finds that higher levels of external debt and less foreign direct investment are positively correlated with banking crises.

Seemingly contradicting these studies, Barth *et al.* (2006) look at a larger number of countries and fail to find that prudential bank regulations and higher bank capital requirements reduce the incidence of banking crises. They argue that this result may be due to the fact that prudential regulations often increase the opportunities for corruption when, as is often the case in many emerging economies, the proper legal and law enforcement institutions are not in place to regulate the regulators. Their work reemphasizes the important point that it is not regulation per se, but the kinds and quality of regulation that matter in reducing risk in the banking system.

Focusing specifically on countries that have conducted financial liberalization, Kaminsky and Reinhart (1999) find that in 26 banking crisis episodes, 18 of them occurred within five years of significant financial liberalization. Eichengreen and Arteta (2002) examine 78 banking crises and find that in countries where financial liberalization has recently taken place and where there existed high pre-crisis levels of credit growth and low levels of bank capital, banking crises were significantly more likely to occur.[17] This is consistent with the argument that indiscriminate deregulation leads to lending booms that increase leverage and risk in the banking system, making banking crises more likely. Mishkin (1999) finds that credit grows at an unsustainably high rate following deregulation, averaging between 15 and 30 percent a year in emerging economies.

Other studies have examined the relationships between asset bubbles, sovereign debt crises, and banking crises. Reinhart and Rogoff (2009) find that stock and housing bubbles consistently precede banking crises in both developed and emerging economies. They identify 40 examples of stock price collapses (with an average decline of 25 percent) tied to banking crises since 1920 and seven examples of housing bubbles tied to banking crises since 1997 alone. In another study examining the relationship between debt crises and banking crises, Reinhart and Rogoff (2011) once again examine a large historical database of financial crises and find that booms in external debt levels consistently precede banking crises as part of the overall boom in credit. However, their econometric results indicate that banking crises cause sovereign debt crises, but not vice versa. These results suggest that the bailout costs incurred by the government can trigger debt crises, but that debt crises themselves do not have predictive power in explaining banking crises.

The costs of banking crises, both in terms of the size of the bailout and in terms of lost GDP, are very difficult to measure. There is a variety of timing, accounting, and definitional issues related to determining exactly what constitutes the true costs of a banking crisis.[18] Reinhart and Rogoff (2009) estimate that the average banking crisis results in an increase in government debt of 86 percent, or a near doubling of the public debt. This is both because of spending on the bailout and because of increased government spending and declines in tax revenue associated with the economic slowdown that occurs. They estimate that banking crises are associated with recessions that last on average for two years and lead to a 5 percent decline in output from trend.[19] However, there is quite a bit of variability across different crises. Boyd *et al*. (2005) find that 30 percent of countries experiencing a banking crisis suffered no declines in output growth. These crises primarily took place in developed countries. However, for those countries that did experience an economic slowdown the authors find that the present value of lost output from trend was between 60 and 300 percent of pre-crisis GDP, while output remained below trend for an average of five years.

Regarding estimates of the costs of the bailout alone, Honohan and Klingebiel (2003) estimate that the average bailout costs roughly around 13 percent of GDP, while Boyd *et al*. (2005) find these costs average between 8 and 10 percent of GDP. However, once again, there is quite a bit of variability across crises (as can be seen in Table 5.1).

The Mexican "Tequila" crisis of 1994

The Mexican financial crisis of 1994 was one of the most severe and costly banking crises of the modern era. As is often the case, the crisis was largely unforeseen at the time, but in hindsight it is easy to see that the factors that led to the crisis had been building for a long time. Mexico's 1994 banking crisis actually began back in 1982 during the Latin American debt crisis (discussed in the last chapter). At that time, Mexican banks suffered from a high degree of financial repression. Half of all bank loans went to the government, which meant that Mexico's sovereign debt crisis also led to a banking crisis in Mexico. In response, the Mexican government nationalized all banks in an effort to prevent their failure. These newly state-owned Mexican banks did relatively little lending and remained inefficient, but they were able to recapitalize with the help of an infusion of capital from the government.

In the early 1990s, the Mexican government began to re-privatize these banks. Given the inefficiency of these state-owned banks, privatization was a good idea in theory. Unfortunately, as has commonly been the case in many other emerging market economies, privatization took place rapidly and without sufficient transparency to prevent corruption. Given that during the era of financial repression Mexican banks engaged in only the most basic transactions and lent little to the private sector, little expertise existed among bank officers to help guide these banks now that they were operating in liberalized and much more competitive globalized financial markets. Significant barriers to entry were not removed and the Mexican banking system remained highly concentrated, so that state-owned banking monopolies were replaced with privately owned banking monopolies. Four Mexican banks held over 70 percent of all bank assets.[20] Most importantly, little prudential regulation was put in place to moderate banks' behavior once they were deregulated. Bank capital requirements were lower than international standards and connected lending and corruption were rampant. In fact, 20 percent of large bank loans were made to the banks' own directors. These loans had lower interest rates and higher default rates than average.[21]

When a recession struck the United States in 1991 and worldwide interest rates fell, foreign capital quickly found a home with higher returns in the newly deregulated Mexican financial system. The lack of prudential regulation enabled a domestic lending boom driven by moral hazard. As can be seen in Figure 5.1, bank credit increased by 25 percent a year between 1988 and 1994 as total bank credit rose from 10 percent of GDP to over 40 percent.[22] At the same time, capitalization in the Mexican stock market rose from only $4 billion in 1985 to $200 billion in 1993, while foreign investment in all financial assets rose from $5 billion a year in the late 1980s to $20 billion a year in the early 1990s. In fact, Mexico became the largest emerging market borrower in the world; much of this debt was short term and in dollars. All of these capital market inflows gradually appreciated the Mexican peso above levels that, as was to become obvious in 1995, were not sustainable.

As the lending boom progressed, loan quality fell and default risk increased. Figure 5.2 presents the level of non-performing loans as a share of total loans in the Mexican banking system. Even before the crisis, non-performing loans were at 8 percent, much higher than sustainable levels, and bank capital in Mexico had fallen below international standards.[23] Many Mexican banks had so many bad loans that they essentially became "zombie banks," financially dead because of their lack of capital, but not closed by the government because of a lack of oversight and the costs that would be incurred if depositors were bailed out. These insolvent zombie banks had even greater incentive to engage in moral hazard lending, essentially willing to go "double or nothing" now that they had little more to lose.

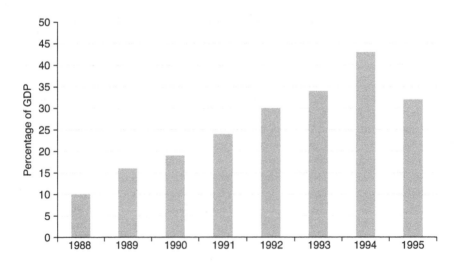

Figure 5.1 Bank credit to private enterprises in Mexico (source: Mishkin (2006a)).

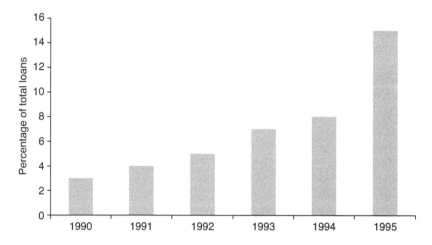

Figure 5.2 Non-performing loans as share of total loans in Mexico (source: Mishkin (2006a)).

In 1994, two shocks shook this house of cards. First, the United States raised interest rates as its economy began to grow faster. Second, a revolt in the Chiapas region and the assassination of a presidential candidate increased the perceived political risk of operating in Mexico. Foreign capital began to flee Mexico and interest rates spiked dramatically to over 90 percent. Stock prices declined by 40 percent and the economy began to contract.

Before the crisis, the Mexican government had significantly reduced its government debt and deficits, in large part through the Brady plan for debt relief that was discussed in the previous chapter. As the crisis began, however, the Mexican government tried to keep its head above water by borrowing more, largely because of a need for dollars to defend its fixed exchange rate. The government borrowed in dollars using *tesobonos*, or short-term dollar-denominated bonds. In January 1994, only about $1 billion of *tesobonos* were issued (5 percent of the public debt), but this number rose to $18 billion by December (55 percent of the public debt). However, eventually capital flight reached a level where the central bank was left without sufficient amounts of dollar reserves despite this new borrowing and a 50 percent devaluation of the peso took place in December.[24] This devaluation was the trigger for both a sovereign debt crisis and a banking crisis. The 50 percent devaluation of the peso essentially doubled the real value of dollar-denominated sovereign debt (at a cost of 10 percent of Mexican GDP) and also the value of dollar-denominated bank liabilities. At the same time, defaults skyrocketed and bank capital fell because many firms' profits were made in pesos but they borrowed from banks in dollars; devaluation left them unable to meet their payments on these dollar loans.

All of these events—the banking crisis, the asset price collapse, the sovereign debt crisis, the political crisis, and the exchange rate devaluation—increased defaults and reduced bank capital, forcing banks to dramatically reduce credit. This collapse in financial intermediation lowered consumption, investment, and economic growth. As growth fell, defaults, asset prices, and the sovereign debt crisis worsened, further reducing growth in a vicious cycle. Eventually, GDP in Mexico fell by roughly 10 percent in a year, while poverty rose above 35 percent of the population and even crime rose by 50 percent.

A partial reprieve was granted in 1995 by the US government and the IMF, who provided a $50 billion loan to Mexico to prevent default on its debt and recapitalize its banks. The bank bailout itself ended up costing roughly 20 percent of GDP, higher than average although less than in many other banking crises.[25] After the crisis, Mexico adopted a series of financial reforms to reduce moral hazard and risk, including increasing bank capital requirements, tightening limits on connected lending, and creating credit information bureaus. Barriers to foreign ownership of banks were also lifted and today more than 80 percent of Mexican banks are foreign-owned.[26] Economic growth and bank profitability did resume in 1996. However, today the Mexican banking system remains weak, in large part because of insufficient legal systems and property rights protection. Bank lending as a percentage of GDP stood at less than 20 percent in 2011, lower than where it stood before the crisis at 40 percent and also less than the emerging market average of 75 percent. In addition, only 25 percent of the Mexican population has access to formal finance. A more detailed look at the Mexican financial system today is included in Chapter 12.

The Mexican Tequila crisis followed a script that has become disturbingly familiar across emerging market economies. Baliño and Sundararajan (1991) examined seven banking crises in emerging economies in the 1980s and 1990s and found that before the crisis they all had (1) high levels of non-performing loans, (2) recently deregulated their financial industry, (3) booms in economic growth and credit, (4) inflation in asset prices, and (5) international trade imbalances that signaled overvalued exchange rates.

Turkey in 2000–2001 and Argentina in 2001 also experienced banking crises that were preceded by indiscriminate liberalization of their financial systems that initiated credit booms, increasing non-performing loans, and currency mismatches. In each of these countries, spikes in interest rates, political instability, and a depreciation of the exchange rate triggered asset price collapses, sovereign debt crises, and banking crises in scripts very similar to Mexico's.[27] Tiny Iceland, after a remarkably reckless privatization of its banking system in 2001, experienced credit and asset price booms followed by a sovereign debt crisis and banking crisis in 2007 that may be among the largest in history. The bank bailout in Iceland is estimated to eventually cost the government more than 75 percent of its pre-crisis GDP.[28]

Conclusions

Asset bubbles and banking crises can be costly enough to set back economic and financial development in emerging market economies for years, sometimes even decades. The direct costs of banking crises and asset bubbles are significant: government bailouts of banking systems that can cost half a year's worth of GDP or more and that can even be large enough to initiate sovereign debt crises. The indirect costs can be even more devastating: reductions in wealth and losses in confidence that reduce financial intermediation, limit investment and consumption, and stunt economic growth.

There are good reasons to think that both beliefs and fundamentals play a role in creating asset bubbles and banking crises. The importance of beliefs means that both can be self-fulfilling; if enough people believe that an asset collapse or banking crisis is about to happen, it will. But it is also clear that weak financial fundamentals play an important role in both phenomena. Recent asset bubbles and banking crises have followed similar scripts. They begin with a lack of prudential regulation (often the result of recent financial liberalization) that is followed by a spike in moral hazard lending, credit booms, and currency mismatches. Emerging markets are particularly vulnerable to these things occurring. They end when leverage and risk reach a point that defaults begin to occur, net worths and prices begin to fall, and panic selling sets in. Together, all of these factors explain why asset bubbles and banking crises are, in the words of Charles Kindleberger, a "hardy perennial."

A brief review of the Mexican financial crisis in 1994, among others, illustrates that one of the other defining characteristics of asset bubbles and banking crises is that they interact with each other and with other forms of financial crisis such as sovereign debt crises and currency crises (which will be discussed in more detail in Chapter 8). The interactions between asset price collapses, banking crises, sovereign debt crises, and currency crises create the kinds of massive losses and international panic that are the driving force behind catastrophic economic depressions and global financial crises. It is to the international aspects of finance in emerging market economies that we turn in the next part of this book.

Part III

International finance in emerging markets

6 Financial liberalization and capital flows

Introduction

One of the most remarked upon trends in modern economics is *globalization*, or the increasing interconnectedness of economies across the globe. Globalization in the trade of goods and services, however, has been around since the late 1800s, although it was significantly interrupted by the Great Depression and two world wars. What is new today is *financial globalization*, or the free movement of financial assets across borders, and the extent to which it involves not just finance between developed countries but now also finance in emerging market economies. There has been a pronounced trend among emerging market economies toward freeing capital to move more easily between countries through the process of *capital account liberalization.*[1] Capital account liberalization involves the removal of constraints on the flow of *foreign portfolio investment* (the purchase by foreigners of financial assets such as stocks and bonds), *foreign direct investment* (investment by foreigners in structures, equipment, and organizations usually involving some operational control), and bank borrowing/lending across countries. Figure 6.1 presents data on net private capital inflows (inflows minus outflows) to the 30 largest emerging economies since the 1980s. Net private capital inflows to the largest emerging market economies were over $1 trillion in 2011 and 2012. This is below pre-global financial crisis levels in 2007 but up over 50 percent since 2009. However, despite this sustained (but volatile) growth, emerging market economies continue to attract only about one-fifth of all international private capital flows.

Capital account liberalization in emerging economies has involved many of the following policy changes: (1) eliminating domestic controls on foreign lending and borrowing, (2) removing limits on bank deposit expansion and debt holdings in foreign currencies, (3) abolishing interest rate controls, (4) allowing foreign ownership of domestic banks, (5) eliminating multiple (or black market) exchange rates, and (6) allowing the free movement of financial assets between citizens of different countries. Figure 6.2 presents one measure of *de jure* capital account liberalization in developed and emerging market economies, the Chinn–Ito (2008) Index.[2] This index indicates that both developed and emerging economies have liberalized their laws significantly since 1970. While developed countries remain more open, emerging market economies have significantly narrowed the gap since 1990.

However, the freeing of capital flows to emerging markets has been surprisingly controversial among economists. While there is agreement among economists that free trade in goods and services promotes economic development, there is no similar consensus that free trade in financial assets necessarily provides the same benefits. Recent experience, particularly across Asia, shows us that international capital flows have the potential to fuel increases in investment and productivity that can speed the pace of development in emerging economies. However, international finance is different from domestic finance in many important ways: there are larger asymmetric information problems, different (and weaker) institutions and legal systems involved, more government influence through tariffs and exchange rate policies, and real disparities in power between major international financial firms and local banks. All of these differences mean that international capital flows have the potential to create costly instability in ways that domestic financial development does not.

The purpose of this chapter is to summarize the history of international capital flows to emerging economies and understand the potential benefits and costs of liberalizing capital accounts, both in theory and in practice. We will also talk about the process of capital account liberalization, including what economic theory and the empirical evidence tell us about how liberalization should be sequenced, what capital controls are important to eliminate, and what prudential regulations need to be maintained and even strengthened in conjunction with liberalization. This chapter concludes with brief case studies of the very different impacts of capital account liberalization in two regions of the emerging world: Asia and Sub-Saharan Africa.

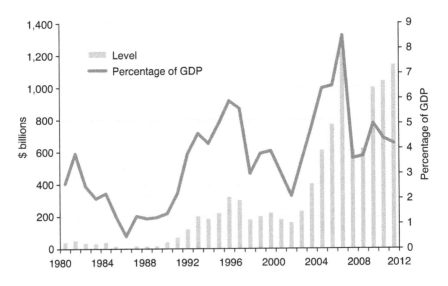

Figure 6.1 Emerging market net private capital inflows (source: *Institute of International Finance Research Note*, September 25, 2011).

The determinants of capital inflows and outflows

Why would foreign investors look to emerging market economies, and vice versa? International capital flows to any emerging market economy are driven by a mixture of internal (or pull) factors and external (or push) factors. The internal factors are those that impact the domestic return on an emerging market financial asset: domestic interest rates, economic growth rates, savings rates, return on equity, and expected inflation rates. It also includes any controls or taxes on the movement of capital. Finally, internal factors include the liquidity of financial markets and the perceived macroeconomic and financial risk within an economy.

External factors are those outside the control of an emerging economy: world liquidity, world interest rates, world economic growth, exchange rate movements, and the demand for international diversification. Because most emerging economies are a relatively small part of the world economy, these factors are exogenous from their perspective. In other words, it is external factors that determine the *relative* return on emerging economy assets.

Capital outflows from emerging market economies are determined by the same factors, with two important differences. The first is that capital outflows from emerging countries are often driven by the desire of domestic citizens of emerging countries to diversify their savings and reduce the risk they are exposed to when they save domestically. Most investors generally view their emerging market investments, even those within their own country, as riskier

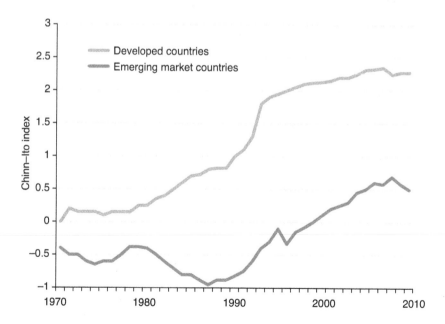

Figure 6.2 A measure of capital account openness (source: Ito and Chinn (2012)).

than their investments in the developed world. This is partially because these investments are actually riskier (for both economic and political reasons), but also because the quality of the information in emerging economies is often poorer, even when you live there. As a result, many emerging economies have permanent capital outflows that are as great, or greater, than their capital inflows. Some of the poorest countries in the world are net lenders, despite the fact that they are attracting high levels of capital inflows. This is also a big part of the reason why many developed economies, particularly the United States, are net borrowers with positive net capital inflows.

The second difference between the factors driving inflows and outflows is that the central banks of emerging economies have a large demand for accumulating international reserves in order to protect their economies from sudden capital outflows and to manage their exchange rates (see the next chapter for a discussion of exchange rate policy management and sterilization). In East Asia, 59 percent of all capital inflows are held by the central bank as international reserves. In Latin America, this number is 35 percent—remarkably large given the significant investment needs of many of these countries.[3]

Barry Eichengreen (2003a) identifies four international lending booms since the Industrial Revolution. His case studies, as well as empirical work on this question, point to a relatively wide range of both internal and external factors that drive international capital flows.[4] The first capital flow boom began in 1880 and lasted until the beginning of World War I in 1914. This boom was driven by expansion in world GDP, financial innovation (such as improvements in communication and transportation), and liberalization of capital markets in Europe and the United States. Capital flows reached 3.5 percent of world GDP, a level that has not been seen since. However, almost all of these flows were between rich countries, with very little going to emerging market economies.

The second boom era occurred between the end of World War I and the Great Depression. However, the Great Depression marked the beginning of an extended period of restricted capital flows that lasted until the 1970s. Controls limiting the flow of international capital were a key part of the Bretton Woods system created in 1945. This inflexible fixed exchange rate system required countries to adopt financial repression and capital controls in an effort to discourage speculation and reduce capital flow volatility that could undermine these fixed exchange rates. Skepticism regarding international capital movements during this era was best expressed by one of the principle architects of the Bretton Woods system, John Maynard Keynes (1933: 760), who stated: "Ideas, knowledge, science, hospitality, travel—these are the things which should of their nature be international. But let goods be homespun whenever it is reasonable and conveniently possible, and above all else let finance be primarily national."

During the 1960s and 1970s, international capital flows began to gradually expand as the Bretton Woods system collapsed and a boom in petrodollars led to a significant surge in world savings. A large proportion of this new capital began flowing for the first time to emerging market economies, particularly in Latin

America, that offered strong growth prospects, higher interest rates, and a willingness to issue debt denominated in dollars. Unfortunately, the debt boom of the 1970s led to the debt crisis of the 1980s, which was primarily centered in Latin America.[5]

The 1990s has spawned a fourth international capital flow boom. For the first time, emerging market economies in Asia and Latin America are at the forefront of this boom. The majority of capital inflows to emerging markets are in the form of foreign direct investment and equity, not debt. Net inflows remain large despite the fact that many emerging economies experience large capital outflows to rich countries as well. As mentioned above, for some countries these outflows are driven by the desire to reduce risk and gain diversification. For other countries, most notably China, these outflows are the result of a huge demand for international reserves. In 2011, China held more than $3 trillion in international reserves at the same time that it received roughly 30 percent of all net private capital inflows to the emerging world.[6]

The growth in capital inflows to emerging countries has been driven by internal factors such as increased capital account liberalization, improved domestic financial development, improved macroeconomic policies (including lower inflation and debt), greater political stability, and strong growth in emerging market economies. It has also been driven by external factors, such as lower global interest rates and slower growth in developed economies. Financial innovation has also played a large role, particularly innovation driven by improved communication and information technology. Information technology has significantly increased efficiency by reducing the need for middlemen, by increasing the number of transactions and liquidity, and by creating new financial assets that allow investors to better hedge and diversify risk. Information technology has also fostered the growth of institutional investors, such as mutual fund companies. Most importantly, however, information technology has reduced the costs of information, making it easier for foreign investors to monitor and screen their investments and to overcome the disincentives created by asymmetric information.

Despite this growth in capital inflows to emerging countries, a question remains as to why even more capital does not flow to emerging market economies. Emerging economies still only receive about one-fifth of all capital flows during the latest capital flow boom. The fundamental economic concept of diminishing marginal returns would suggest that most capital should flow to the emerging world because returns on capital should be higher where capital is most scarce. But diminishing marginal returns alone ignores the equally important concept of risk and asymmetric information. Those countries that do not have the proper financial institutions in place—including legal protections for foreign investors, accounting and transparency requirements, and proper macroeconomic management—are not able to establish the credibility with markets necessary to attract enough foreign capital to significantly spur development. Emerging countries that have weak institutions, or that continue to follow policies of financial repression, or that have a history of economic mismanagement (and as a result suffer from debt intolerance) will fail to attract much foreign capital regardless of the potential returns it might offer. Until very recently, this would be true of most emerging market economies.

The benefits of capital account liberalization, the arguments for capital controls

Liberalizing foreign capital flows has the potential to generate many of the same benefits that general financial development creates. As discussed in Chapter 1, financial development increases allocative efficiency, encourages financial deepening which reduces transaction costs, encourages savings and investment, reduces risk through better hedging and diversification, and increases the quantity and quality of information so that credit rationing is minimized. All of these things contribute to faster economic growth and higher standards of living for both the rich and poor.

But capital account liberalization also offers additional potential advantages over and above those of domestic financial development alone. Foreign capital flows provide countries with the ability to smooth their consumption while sustaining high investment rates through foreign borrowing. In this way, capital flows offer emerging market economies a way to stabilize consumption against fluctuations in their domestic growth rates. The entry of foreign banks encourages competition and fosters the transfer of best practices and human capital that can increase the efficiency of the domestic banking system. Increases in foreign competition can also weaken domestic political special interests and encourage the elimination of financial repression policies. Because capital account liberalization forces countries to compete for capital flows, it forces countries to adopt international institutions, such as capital requirements (through things such as abiding by the Basel treaties), improved accounting standards, improved legal systems, and generally accepted standards of prudential regulation for banks and financial markets. Finally, opening financial systems to foreign capital flows creates additional incentives for countries to follow better macroeconomic policy and even allow more political freedom, because failure to do so can lead to destabilizing capital flight. Many proponents of capital account liberalization point to the decline in global inflation—which averaged 16 percent a year in the 1980s, over 20 percent a year in the 1990s, but has declined to only 5 percent a year in the 2000s—as an example of how liberalization imposes external discipline on policymakers that they would not otherwise face.

If capital account liberalization creates so many benefits, why is its adoption so controversial? The reason is that foreign capital flows have the potential to undermine economic stability. As can be seen in Figure 6.1, large swings in net private capital inflows can occur, primarily because of changes in net portfolio investment. Foreign direct investment is typically less volatile because it is usually long term and often in physical assets. Foreign portfolio investment, on the other hand, is more volatile for many reasons. First, because emerging market economies are subject to frequent recessions, sovereign debt crises, asset bubbles, and banking crises. Second, foreign investors often have poorer information than domestic investors, leading them to have higher perceived risk that leads to more volatile saving and investment decisions. Third, enforcing financial contracts is often much more difficult for foreign investors, leading to them to be more likely to sell in a panic if they perceive an increase in default risk. Finally, governments, which themselves can be a source of volatility, are heavily involved in foreign capital flows through their tax policies and through their management of exchange rates.

The most unstable forms of foreign portfolio investment are short-term debt that needs to be regularly rolled over and debt that is denominated in a foreign currency. Overreliance on these forms of foreign capital increases the likelihood of sudden episodes of capital flight that can, in turn, lead to the collapse of asset prices, currency crises, sovereign debt crisis, and banking crises.[7] The details of how capital flight interacts with other types of financial crises will be discussed in more detail in Chapter 8, where we will see that sudden capital flight episodes can be extremely costly not only in terms of banking and financial system bailouts, but also in terms of lost output during the resulting economic recessions and even depressions.

Instead of broad liberalization of all forms of foreign capital flows, many economists and policymakers argue that some forms of foreign capital should be restricted. Restrictions on the holdings of risky assets by banks and the imposition of capital adequacy requirements are widely recognized as appropriate forms of prudential regulation that are justified by the need to minimize the impact of moral hazard and adverse selection on systemic risk. By the same logic, restrictions on the most volatile forms of foreign capital are also an appropriate form of prudential regulation. Proponents of capital controls particularly focus on restrictions of "hot money," or short-term foreign-denominated debt that can quickly leave a country and is subject to the risk of currency mismatch in the event of depreciation in the domestic currency. Joseph Stiglitz (2000) argues that indiscriminant capital account liberalization encourages hot money inflows that make emerging economies vulnerable to self-fulfilling speculative attacks, particularly because of the informational failures and moral hazard that exists in most emerging financial systems. Stiglitz notes that these hot money inflows are significantly procyclical, meaning that they amplify booms and busts. As a result, hot money inflows do not provide emerging countries with insurance that stabilizes consumption and investment but instead serves to destabilize short-term growth. At the same time, because this hot money is short term and foreign denominated, it is unlikely to be used to finance the long-term investments that many poorer countries are desperate for.

Stiglitz argues that inflows of short-term foreign capital inflows should be regulated. In practice, this could be done in many different ways. In the early 1990s, Chile imposed a holding period on all short-term foreign investments as well as required that 20 percent of all foreign inflows had to be held at the central bank on reserve. These restrictions essentially served as a tax on short-term foreign capital inflows. In 1998, Malaysia imposed restrictions on capital outflows requiring a minimum period that any foreign capital inflow had to remain within the country before it could leave. Other countries have placed regulations on banks to limit the amount of foreign-denominated liabilities or assets that they can hold.

While capital controls sound reasonable in theory, there are two reasons to question their effectiveness in practice. First, there is significant empirical evidence that capital outflows do not cause, but are a symptom of, financial crises.[8] In other words, they are not at the root of the volatility problem in emerging economies. Second, capital controls are often ineffective because they are easy to subvert. The problem is that many investors have significant profit incentives to find loopholes in these controls when large differences in returns exist between countries. It is relatively easy to hide who is purchasing assets by using holding corporations and other financial chicanery. Many emerging market countries do not have the institutions or the bureaucracies in place to properly monitor these transactions. In addition, many bureaucrats are corruptible and imposing capital controls only provides these bureaucrats the power to discriminate among investors in return for bribes.

Empirical evidence on this question suggests that capital controls are not generally effective in limiting overall capital inflows to emerging economies. In addition, there is little evidence that capital controls make financial crises less likely, although they may make them less costly when they occur.[9] However, Montiel and Reinhart (1999) find that these controls do have an impact on the composition of inflows, encouraging more long-term foreign direct investment and less portfolio investment.[10] To the extent that foreign direct investment is preferable because of its stability, this improves overall welfare. But this only occurs if quality bureaucratic institutions are in place that can limit discrimination and corruption. Also, these benefits have to be weighed against the microeconomic costs of capital controls, which Desormeaux *et al.* (2008) find to be large, particularly for small and medium investors and the firms that they lend to. All of this said, in 2011 the IMF changed its policy recommendations to emerging economies and endorsed the use of capital controls in the face of "unsustainable" surges in short-term inflows.[11]

Sequencing financial liberalization

As we learned in Chapter 5, indiscriminant and rushed financial liberalization has repeatedly led to asset bubbles and banking crises throughout the world over the last 30 years. Time and time again, countries have rushed liberalization without the proper prudential regulations first put into place. Based on this experience, we can now ask what we have learned about how financial deregulation can take place in a way that will maximize its benefits while minimizing the potential volatility it brings. Should certain economic and financial reforms take place before others?

Once again, there is a wide variety of opinions on these issues, but the approach that comes closest to summarizing the consensus of most economists in this area is expressed by McKinnon (1992).[12] His suggestions are based upon the fundamental principle that financial liberalization can only increase growth when the microeconomic fundamentals for solid growth are already in place. So the first step of capital account liberalization should be the deregulation of domestic goods markets at the microeconomic level, which includes opening these markets to international trade. Greater international trade will increase the efficiency of domestic markets, improving both the productivity of future foreign capital inflows and also reducing default risk.

The second step should be macroeconomic stabilization. Because financial repression policies are often adopted in order to raise government revenues, a system of revenue collection and sustainable spending budgets has to be in place so that liberalization will not immediately lead to budget deficits, sovereign debt crises, and inflation. Having sensible macroeconomic policies in place will also help establish credibility with markets that will make the country attractive for long-term foreign investment.

Third, domestic financial systems should be liberalized after a system of prudential regulation is put into place. Domestic stock and bond markets should be deregulated before banks in order to encourage long-term lending before short-term lending. As discussed repeatedly, banks should be subject to regulations aimed at limiting moral hazard and adverse selection in order to reduce risk and ensure financial stability. The most important of these prudential regulations are bank capital adequacy requirements (see Chapter 3 for a full discussion of exactly what prudential regulation entails). This may mean that the government has to privatize state-owned banks in order to generate funds for the recapitalization of banks, while at the same time being realistic about which non-performing loans need to be written off. In addition to prudential regulation, countries should establish a deposit insurance program and ensure that their central bank can serve as a strong lender of last resort.

Fourth, only when domestic financial markets have been sufficiently liberalized should foreign capital flows be liberalized. Efficient, stable, and flexible domestic systems are crucial to ensuring that foreign capital inflows are used productively and do not fuel financial booms and busts. Fischer and Reisen (1993) argue that capital account liberalization itself should also be staged. The first to be allowed should be foreign direct investment because it is stable, long term, and directly contributes to productivity and human capital accumulation. Banking systems should be opened to foreign inflows next, but only after sufficient bank capital and prudential regulations are in place. Third, interest rates should be deregulated gradually with an eye toward monitoring the moral hazard behavior that may result from higher interest rates. Next, foreign capital outflows should be deregulated, followed by eliminating barriers to foreign banks operating within the country. Foreign bank entry comes late in the process in order to give domestic banks a chance to prepare to compete with what are likely to be larger and more efficient international banks. Finally, controls on foreign portfolio investments in stock markets, followed by short-term debt markets, should be eliminated. In this way, the riskiest inflows are allowed only when the entire economy has had a chance to develop enough to be prepared for them.

Two points are important to emphasize regarding the staged-liberalization approach presented above. First, Dani Rodrik (2007) convincingly argues that capital account liberalization should not be a one-size-fits-all process, but that reform has to account for the unique institutions and environments in each country. For example, capital account liberalization should look very different in India, which has a Western-style legal system and individual property rights, than it does in China, where property rights are largely reserved for the state. In India, the primary concern should be for the destabilizing effects of hot money inflows. In China, the primary concern should be over foreign direct investment and how it can be conducted in a way that is consistent with communal property rights.

Second, and probably most importantly, this staged approach requires that liberalization take place gradually over a very long period (possibly decades) so that markets, firms, expectations, and institutions have a chance to adjust. The length of this process will depend upon the institutions that are initially in place, the efficiency of the political system needed to implement these changes, and the overall pace of economic and financial development.

Having said all of this, there is an alternative point of view that says that liberalization sometimes must proceed before institutions can change. According to this counterargument, liberalization increases competition and creates an environment in which market discipline is imposed upon firms, special interests, and institutions that are not competitive. Kaminsky and Schmukler (2003) present empirical evidence that the rule of law improved before liberalization in only 18 percent of countries they surveyed, but it improved in 64 percent of these countries after they liberalized. For countries that liberalized first, liberalization led to more volatility in the short run but less volatility in the long run. While a minority viewpoint, the argument that liberalization should drive institutional reform, and not vice versa, might be a viable, if high-risk, strategy for some countries and in some environments.

Empirical evidence on the impact of capital account liberalization on growth

Investigating the impact of capital account liberalization on economic growth has become one of the most popular research questions among macroeconomists. This is in part because its theoretical benefits are controversial, but also because empirical studies have often obtained contradicting results. A brief introduction to this expansive literature review is presented here.

Literature reviews of the studies investigating the impact of financial liberalization on economic growth have found that there is only mixed evidence that capital account liberalization leads to increases in long-term growth.[13] To cite one specific study, Edison *et al.* (2004) find that capital account liberalization unambiguously increased growth in only three of ten countries they examined. However, there are many caveats to this result. The first deals with the importance of institutions. Without institutions such as prudential regulations in place, there is no reason to think that liberalization will increase economic growth, and it might actually harm growth. Many studies have looked at exactly this question and have found that capital account liberalization is beneficial to growth only when good institutions and quality governance are first in place.[14] Rajan and Zingales (2003) find that having institutions that encourage competition in the domestic financial system is crucial to generating growth from capital account liberalization. This is because competitive financial systems reduce the power of special interest groups, which improves other institutions and makes it more likely that foreign capital will flow to where it is most productive.

The second caveat is that the results of these studies often turn on the question of how you empirically measure liberalization. Which policies should be included, and which should not? Even more importantly, is it how the law changes that counts (*de jure*) or is it how these laws are implemented in practice (de facto) that should count in any measure of capital account liberalization? The Chinn–Ito Index of openness included in Figure 6.2 is actually a measure of *de jure* liberalization. Kose, Prasad, Rogoff, and Wei (2009) find that de facto measures of liberalization, such as capital inflow and outflow data, are correlated with higher growth in emerging market economies, but there is no significant relationship with *de jure* measures of liberalization. This is likely part of the reason why many previous studies that use *de jure* measures failed to find evidence of a significant growth impact from liberalization.

A third caveat is that the impact of liberalization, as discussed above, depends crucially upon how it is sequenced. There is solid empirical evidence that countries that liberalize too quickly do not experience growth benefits from it. Edwards (2001) finds that capital account openness increases productivity, but only for countries that have reached a certain income level. Given that income is correlated with stronger institutions, this result once again indicates the importance of having strong institutions in place before liberalization. It also points to the fact that capital account liberalization should not be a priority policy item for the poorest countries. Similarly, Eichengreen *et al.* (2009) find that opening capital accounts only increases growth within countries that already have developed financial systems, strong accounting systems, and legal rights for creditors.[15]

One final caveat is that capital account liberalization is most likely to increase economic growth in the short run, not the long run, because of diminishing marginal returns to investment. However, it will have a long-run impact on the level of income. Studies that focus on the correlation between liberalization and long-run average growth may not find a relationship between the two because of this effect. In looking at growth over the short run, however, Henry (2007) finds a strong relationship across multiple studies that capital liberalization does increase growth over a five-year period. Similarly, Bekaert *et al.* (2005) estimate that the impact of capital account liberalization is a 1 percent increase in growth over five years.

While the results from macroeconomic cross-country empirical studies on the impact of liberalization have often varied, the studies that have focused on the more microeconomic impacts of capital account liberalization on financial development have consistently found that it is beneficial. Henry (2003) finds that stock market liberalization in emerging economies reduces the cost of capital by 2.4 percent, increases investment by 1.1 percent, and growth in output per worker by 2.3 percent a year.[16] Demirgüç-Kunt *et al.* (1998) find that reducing barriers to foreign bank entry in emerging economies increases efficiency in the banking system while stimulating overall financial development and macroeconomic growth.[17] Given that there is a strong relationship between overall financial development and economic growth, these are important but indirect channels through which capital account liberalization improves economic growth.

Capital flows in Asia and Africa

No two regions of the world have had more different development experiences over the last century than Asia and Africa. In 1900 Asia was 25 percent poorer than Africa. By 2000, Asia had become 250 percent richer and the disparity continues to grow rapidly. There are many reasons for this divergence, but one of them is the different experiences that each region has had with capital account liberalization.

In Asia, financial systems were generally closed, highly regulated, and moderately repressed until the early 1980s.[18] At that point, financial systems, including foreign capital controls, were broadly reformed and gradually liberalized over an extended period. This liberalization generally followed the conventional wisdom expressed in this chapter regarding the importance of gradual sequencing of reform. An emphasis was placed on opening product markets to international trade and having developed domestic financial markets in place before controls on foreign capital flows were loosened. Interest rates were deregulated over a number of years, but only after barriers to foreign entry of banks and deposit insurance programs were put in place. Prudential regulation was also strengthened and supervisory power centralized.

The result of this staged liberalization began with growth in investment, followed by output growth, and finally by growth in foreign capital inflows. Foreign capital has flowed to a wide and diverse range of industries in Asia. In 2011, net private capital inflows to the seven largest Asian economies, including India, were over $500 billion, roughly 50 percent of the total flows to all emerging markets.[19] Of this $500 billion, roughly $250 billion was in equity and foreign direct investment. The first graph in Figure 6.3 presents data on net capital flows to Asia as a percentage of GDP between 2008 and 2010. The volatility of capital inflows, even during this short period, is obvious. The steep decline in capital flows in 2008 was primarily the result of external factors, largely the global financial crisis and the recession in the United States. This downturn has been followed by a strong recovery in inflows.

The process of financial liberalization being followed by China today is generally consistent with the Asian model first followed more than 20 years ago.

Like its neighbors in the past, China is a repressed financial system dominated by a weak banking system with many state-owned banks and high levels of non-performing loans. Having achieved some microeconomic deregulation and macroeconomic stabilization, China is deregulating its stock markets and allowing limited access to foreign banks, but only gradually. In terms of prudential regulations, China has increased capital adequacy requirements and has tightened bank lending standards in order to limit the growth of credit. Serious problems remain, such as China's inefficient state-owned banks, high rates of non-performing loans, and a potential asset bubble occurring in its housing market (more on these problems in Chapter 11). Despite these problems, China's financial development policies would have to be considered successful because in many ways they have followed conventional economic wisdom, even if in China's own uniquely unconventional ways.

In 2011 China received about one-third of all capital that flowed to emerging economies, roughly $375 billion.[20] However, Chinese capital controls on hot money are quite restrictive and, as a result, these flows are heavily weighted toward equity and foreign direct investment. The second half of Figure 6.3 presents data on capital inflows to China between 2007 and 2010. Once again, despite strict restrictions on hot money, a heavy reliance on foreign direct investment, and strong economic growth during this period, foreign capital flows to China have still been quite volatile.

Of course, the process of capital account liberalization in Asia has not been without significant bumps in the road. The East Asian financial crisis (see Chapter 8) was one of the largest and most dramatic financial crises in history. Inadequate prudential regulation allowed a boom to occur in foreign capital flows to the region before the crisis (particularly hot money capital flows), creating a great deal of currency mismatch that played an important role in magnifying the size of the crisis. Likewise, similar booms in capital inflows into stock markets today in India and China (see Chapter 11) may again threaten future financial crises in the region.

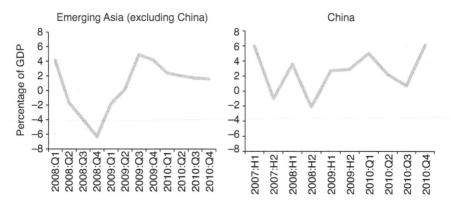

Figure 6.3 Net capital inflows to emerging Asia (source: IMF (2011c)).

The history of capital account liberalization in Africa, begun later than Asia in the mid-1980s, has been much different. In general, capital account liberalization in Africa has occurred while domestic financial liberalization has remained incomplete. Interest rate controls remain common, real interest rates are often negative, black market exchange rates regularly exist, state-owned banks do a majority of the lending, and there is little competition in most banking sectors. Non-performing loans are high while bank capitalization is weak, particularly in state-owned banks. Institutions—particularly legal, accounting, and political systems—are fragile or often non-existent. Macroeconomic stabilization has also not taken place. While inflation rates and budget deficits in the region are generally lower today than they have been in the past, the lack of stable political institutions in many African countries has given these governments little credibility with investors.

The impact of capital liberalization in Africa can be summarized with two observations. First, many African countries have been able to attract foreign investment. While Africa receives only one-tenth of total private net capital flows to emerging economies, which in 2010 amounted to $90 billion, these flows have grown fast and are large relative to the size of their much smaller economies. Figure 6.4 presents data on net capital inflows to Sub-Saharan Africa both in levels and as a percentage of GDP. Not only has the level of net capital inflows grown significantly, but as a percentage of GDP these inflows recently have been higher than in other emerging economies from other regions, even Asia (refer back to Figure 6.3). Half of all net capital inflows to Sub-Saharan Africa go to the two largest economies in the region, Nigeria and South Africa.

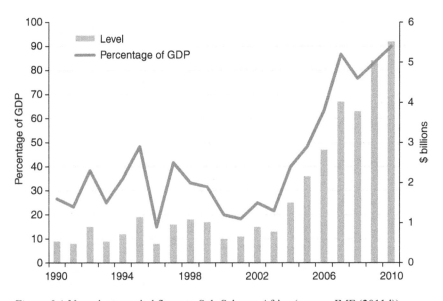

Figure 6.4 Net private capital flows to Sub-Saharan Africa (source: IMF (2011d)).

However, the second impact of capital liberalization in Africa has been instability and frequent crises, with no obvious impact on economic growth. While overall capital flows to Sub-Saharan Africa in Figure 6.4 appear somewhat stable, this aggregate number masks wide swings in flows within specific countries. Capital flow reversals have contributed to frequent financial crises within Africa. Naudé (1996) finds that financial liberalization in Africa actually increased spreads between foreign and domestic interest rates, increased risk and the level of non-performing loans, and increased the probability of banking crises. In regard to economic growth, Serieux (2008) reviews the empirical evidence from 19 sub-Saharan countries that liberalized their capital accounts and concludes that private savings, investment, and credit remained flat afterwards with no significant impact on growth.[21]

These results, and others like them, are the result of two related problems that are prevalent in African financial systems. The first problem is poor management and the lack of strong institutions that can direct foreign capital to where it will be most productive, not just where it will gain the largest speculative return. The second problem is that because of inefficient financial systems, foreign capital in Africa has not been widely distributed but instead has been concentrated in raw materials and natural resource industries. While these industries are often highly productive, they are also very cyclical and contribute greatly to the boom/bust nature of many African economies.

Conclusions

The bulk of the theoretical and empirical evidence reviewed in this chapter suggests that liberalization of foreign capital flows can be very beneficial for emerging market economies. Foreign capital offers all of the benefits of financial development but in a way in which domestic consumption can be protected and the benefits of higher investment can be enjoyed more quickly. Foreign capital also brings with it increased competition, which directly increases efficiency, and also external discipline for building higher-quality institutions and better policy management.

However, the recent experience of emerging economies also suggests that it is possible to have too much of a good thing, particularly if it comes before you are ready for it. There is a story regarding Milton Friedman, legendary Nobel economist and proponent of free markets, who argued to a Chinese official during a visit there that liberalization should take place as quickly as possible. "To cut the tail off the mouse, don't do it inch-by-inch." To which the official replied, "My dear professor, our mouse has so many tails, we do not know which one to cut first."[22]

This same thing could also be said of capital account liberalization; foreign capital can be so volatile and have such a wide impact on the economy that to open these flows before the financial system is ready for them is to potentially invite disaster. Foreign capital is volatile because emerging financial systems often have poorer-quality information and weaker institutions for enforcing their contracts. As a result, panic and capital flight is common. Too often, capital account liberalization has been pursued indiscriminately. Foreign capital has rushed in before proper institutions, prudential financial regulations, and competitive domestic financial institutions are in place. When this happens, such as in Sub-Saharan Africa, any negative shock can lead to massive capital flight and financial instability without obtaining the benefits of higher long-term growth. However, the experience of Asia shows us that when capital accounts are opened only in the final stages of financial liberalization when flexible financial systems and basic prudential risk regulations are already in place, capital inflows can fuel growth with only moderate increases in volatility (although financial crises can still occur, such as during the East Asian financial crisis).

The key appears to be moderation and gradual liberalization. Moderation in foreign capital flows may be enforced through prudential regulations such as restrictions on credit growth and capital adequacy requirements. But explicit controls on capital, particularly hot money inflows, may also be justified. However, any benefits they might bring must be weighed against the costs incurred by investors, the fact that capital controls are easily avoided, and that controls can lead to bureaucratic corruption.

One of the most important factors that influence capital flows was not examined in this chapter: the role of central banks in setting monetary policy and managing the exchange rate. This is the topic to which we turn in the next chapter.

7 Monetary policy and exchange rate management

Introduction

Central banks have numerous responsibilities they must manage. They serve as the primary banker for the government. They also serve as a banker for domestic banks, providing check clearing and other financial transfer services as well as lending to banks in order to stabilize credit growth and serve as a lender of last resort during bank panics. Central banks also play a key role in enforcing and monitoring bank regulation (and repression, as the case may be). Finally, central banks are responsible for helping economies achieve domestic macroeconomic objectives by using monetary policy to maintain levels of interest rates, credit growth, financial stability, and inflation that are consistent with full employment and strong output growth.

Central banking is even more difficult in emerging market economies than in developed economies. Emerging market economies generally are more vulnerable to supply shocks and have more unstable financial systems, more dysfunctional political systems, and also weaker financial institutions. More than that, central banks in developed countries have the luxury of focusing on domestic, or internal, economic balance and can largely ignore external factors, such as trade balances or capital flows. This is because these economies are large and, as a result, can generally force smaller economies to adjust to them, and not vice versa. Emerging economies do not have the same luxury. Emerging market economies, particularly fast-growing economies that are heavily reliant on international trade and foreign capital flows, cannot allow their countries to become too unbalanced relative to external economic conditions. They must closely monitor trade balances and capital flows in an effort to prevent slipping into a situation where the levels of these variables become unsustainable, forcing a costly adjustment that could interrupt much-needed economic growth.

The exchange rate is the primary link between external factors (such as the trade balance and capital flows) and internal factors (such as inflation, financial stability, and output growth). In the effort to achieve both external and internal balance, the primary tool that central banks have at their disposal is their ability to use monetary policy to influence the exchange rate. By selling (purchasing) their domestic currency for foreign currency, central banks can depreciate (appreciate) their exchange rate. Changes in the exchange rate directly impact external factors such as the trade balance and capital flows by changing the price of exports, imports, and the return on financial assets. In turn, changes in these variables impact internal factors such as inflation, financial intermediation, and economic growth.

Unfortunately, there are no simple rules for exchange rate management to guide central banks in emerging economies. Central banks have a wide range of possible strategies to choose from. At one extreme are floating exchange rate strategies that accept short-term exchange rate volatility (and external instability in trade and capital flows) in return for flexibility to respond to domestic internal economic conditions, such as inflation and financial stability. At the other extreme are strategies that involve fixed exchange rates, where the central bank essentially trades short-term exchange rate stability (and external stability) for a loss of flexibility in managing domestic factors such as financial stability or inflation. Between these two extreme strategies are numerous intermediate, or hybrid, strategies that attempt to balance the potential costs and benefits of the two extreme alternatives.

The primary purpose of this chapter is to examine the tradeoffs and implications of various exchange rate strategies that emerging market central banks employ, as well as understand how alternative strategies might impact financial and economic development. The chapter begins with a discussion of nominal and real exchange rates and the importance of making a distinction between the two when deciding what is the "right" exchange rate at any given time for a central bank target. Next, the *exchange rate policy trilemma* is discussed, which refers to the irreconcilable tradeoff central banks face that prohibits them from maintaining open capital accounts, fixed exchange rates, and monetary policy independence at the same time. This trilemma means that countries that want to liberalize their capital accounts must choose between fixed and flexible exchange rates.

Given the difficult choices that must be made, this chapter summarizes the potential advantages and disadvantages of the extreme exchange rate strategies of "hard" fixed exchange rates and "pure" floating exchange rates as well as discusses intermediate strategies such as target zones and crawling pegs. One of the new trends in this area is the adoption of inflation targeting in lieu of exchange rate targeting, which will also be examined. This chapter concludes with the cautionary tale of the Argentinean economic crisis of 2001–2002 that illustrates the potential costs of choosing the wrong exchange rate strategy.

The objectives of monetary policy

Traditional, or "classical," economic theory argues that the primary goal of central banks when managing their exchange rate should be to keep the current level of the exchange rate at the "right" level—meaning its long-run equilibrium level based on economic fundamentals.[1] Of course, there are questions to be asked about this classical view of exchange rate management. The first is:

why would an exchange rate differ from its long-run equilibrium in the first place? There are many possible reasons. Capital inflows and outflows, asset bubbles, temporary aggregate demand or supply shocks, and wage and price inflexibility can all lead to short-run movements in exchange rates. In addition, emerging economies that are financially repressed and have restrictions on the flows of foreign exchange will not see their exchange rate stay at its long-run equilibrium.

Deviations from the long-run equilibrium exchange rate can lead to the misallocation of resources that can limit growth, increase credit risk, and create financial instability. If the exchange rate becomes too high it can price a country's exports out of international markets, increasing trade deficits and reducing economic growth. If the exchange rate is too low it can increase the price of imports and commodities, driving up inflation while at the same time driving down consumption and investment. Low exchange rates can also encourage unsustainable capital inflows that can create costly financial and economic volatility. Under the classical view, these realities provide incentives for central banks to minimize deviations of its exchange rate from its long-run equilibrium.

What then determines a country's long-run equilibrium exchange rate? The Classical answer depends upon making a distinction between the *nominal exchange rate*, which is the price of one country's currency in terms of another country's currency, and the *real exchange rate*, which is the amount of goods in one country that can be traded for a similar amount of goods in another country. Nominal exchange rates are determined by foreign exchange markets and are widely reported; real exchange rates are not directly observable and must be estimated. To understand how a real exchange rate is estimated, let E represent the nominal exchange rate as measured by the price of the domestic currency in terms of a foreign currency. To keep things simple, let's assume the foreign currency is dollars so that E equals the number of dollars obtained per unit of the domestic currency (\$/Dom). The real exchange rate, denoted as ε, equals the price of domestic goods relative to foreign goods (domestic goods/foreign goods), which can be calculated as follows:

$$\varepsilon = E \frac{P^{Dom}}{P^{\$}} \tag{7.1}$$

In this equation, P^{Dom} is the price of a basket of goods in domestic currency prices and $P^{\$}$ is the price of the same basket of goods purchased internationally in dollar prices.[2] Thus, this simple equation calculates the real domestic price of a basket of goods relative to its international costs, adjusted for the nominal exchange rate. A real exchange rate less than 1 would indicate that the real prices of goods are cheaper domestically than internationally.[3]

The classical theory of *purchasing power parity*, or the law of one price, says that in a frictionless world with no trade barriers and where international trade is costless, markets will equilibrate prices across borders until the real exchange rate equals 1 ($\varepsilon = 1$). Under these conditions, the nominal exchange rate simply reflects changes in the relative price level in dollars versus that in the domestic currency such that:

$$E = \frac{P^\$}{P^{Dom}} \tag{7.2}$$

Here, any relative increase in the domestic price level will cause the nominal exchange rate to decline proportionally, and vice versa.

Purchasing power parity has only a tenuous relationship to the real world that most emerging market economies operate within. For emerging market economies, there is no such thing as costless international trade. Tariffs, quotas, taxes, high transportation costs, and numerous other barriers to international trade generally prevent the real price of goods from equilibrating with international prices in emerging market economies.[4] However, the point of discussing purchasing power parity here is that when determining the "right" nominal exchange rate to target, the central bank must consider what the appropriate real exchange rate should be that will keep the costs of domestic goods in line with the price of international goods given the institutions, trade barriers, and policies that exist within the country. To fail to do this threatens to significantly misallocate resources, create unsustainable trade balances and capitals flows, and distort domestic consumption and investment in ways that could negatively impact growth over the long run.

When a central bank is faced with the problem that the current real exchange rate is not equal to what they think its long-run equilibrium rate should be, they have three options. The first two are passive options. The central bank can choose to let domestic prices and wages adjust to get the real exchange rate back in line, but given the inflexibility of many emerging market labor and goods markets there are reasons to think that this process will be extremely slow. Second, the central bank can let the nominal exchange rate adjust on its own in the foreign exchange market. History indicates that this adjustment process can also be quite slow and that exchange rates are often highly variable in the short run, exposing the economy to macroeconomic volatility in the mean time.[5] The third, more active option is for the central bank to discretionarily manage the real exchange rate by using monetary policy to move the nominal exchange rate. Changing the nominal exchange rate through buying or selling its currency for foreign exchange in the appropriate manner can move the real exchange rate back into line with its long-run equilibrium value.

The exchange rate policy trilemma

Central banks have to manage their exchange rates under multiple constraints. In a perfect world, emerging market policymakers would like to achieve three objectives. First, they would like to open capital accounts to attract foreign capital inflows in order to encourage investment. Second, they would like to stabilize exchange rates in order to limit risk and encourage international trade and capital inflows. Third, they would like to maintain monetary independence and reserve the right to use discretionary policy to influence domestic interest rates and credit in ways that will stabilize and stimulate economic growth. The problem is that achieving all three of these goals simultaneously is impossible. Figure 7.1 graphically illustrates what is known as the *exchange rate policy trilemma*. Countries can only occupy one side of this triangle and achieve two of the three goals placed at its corners.

To understand why this trilemma holds, consider a country with an open capital account. If this country makes the decision to fix their exchange rate, the central bank can only do this by standing ready to adjust its monetary policy so that it is always ready to buy or sell its currency at the pegged, or targeted, exchange rate. But if capital can freely flow in and out of the country, the central bank will not be able to control external changes in these capital flows. Instead, it will have to solely react to changes in capital flows at the expense of being free to manage domestic macroeconomic variables such as interest rates, inflation, or output growth. In effect, the central bank must give up monetary independence in order to peg its exchange rate. It must choose either the left or the right side of the triangle.

It is possible for a country to fix their exchange rate while at the same time maintaining flexibility to respond to domestic macroeconomic conditions, but only if changes in capital flows are removed as a factor in creating exchange rate volatility. In other words, only in an environment where there are strict controls on the flow of foreign capital can a central bank achieve both fixed exchange rates and monetary independence (and reside on the bottom side of the triangle).

Another way to understand this trilemma is through the theory of *interest rate parity*. Interest rate parity is essentially the same concept as purchasing power parity but applied to interest bearing financial assets. According to interest rate

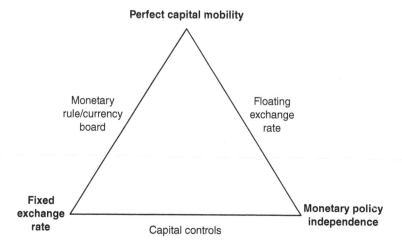

Figure 7.1 Exchange rate policy trilemma (source: Krugman *et al.* (2011)).

parity, if there is perfect capital mobility between an emerging economy financial system and international markets, then arbitrage will ensure that the return on similar assets will be the same across borders. This return must include any gains or losses associated with expected changes in the exchange rate. In other words, the following must be true:

$$i^{\$} = i^{Dom} + \%\Delta E^{e} \tag{7.3}$$

where $i^{\$}$ is the foreign interest rate in dollars (and is exogenous from the point of view of an emerging market economy), i^{Dom} is the domestic interest rate in the domestic currency, and $\%\Delta E^{e}$ is the expected change in the nominal exchange rate over the period that the asset is held. Notice that this is added to the domestic interest rate because an appreciation of the domestic currency relative to the dollar increases the effective return on holding domestic assets.[6]

As already mentioned, interest rate parity holds when capital accounts are completely liberalized. In this environment, we can see from this equation that central banks cannot set both the exchange rate and domestic interest rates at the same time. If the central bank chooses to fixed its exchange rate (setting $\%\Delta E^{e} = 0$), then capital flows will force domestic interest rates to equilibrate with dollar interest rates (for equivalent assets). If the central bank chooses to prioritize control over the level of its domestic interest rates and keep it at a different level than dollar interest rates (i.e. maintain monetary independence), it must give up control of future movements in its nominal exchange rate. If the central bank wants to control both domestic interest rates and the exchange rate, it must regulate capital flows so that the interest rate parity condition does not hold with equality.

The tradeoffs between fixed and floating exchange rate strategies

Capital account liberalization has been beneficial enough to become the dominant trend among emerging economies. Given this fact, according to the exchange rate trilemma, emerging central banks then have to make a difficult choice between fixing their exchange rate (at the cost of monetary independence) or floating their exchange rate (at the expense of exchange rate volatility).

There are different ways to fix and float. At one extreme, a country can adopt a *hard peg*, meaning that it can adopt institutional rules that prevent the exchange rate from changing. One version of a hard peg is full dollarization, or the complete abandonment of the domestic currency, such as has been done in Ecuador, El Salvador, Panama, and Liberia. Full dollarization not only means a complete loss of monetary independence, it also means that the central bank cannot serve as an unlimited lender of last resort (it can only lend up to its amount of dollar holdings) and that the government cannot raise any revenue through seigniorage.[7] A slightly less extreme hard peg is a *currency board* arrangement, where the central bank can only issue domestic currency that is 100 percent (or more) backed by foreign reserves. Many times these currency boards become part of the country's constitutional arrangements, significantly curtailing the monetary independence of a central bank.

However, most fixed exchange rate strategies are less radical *soft pegs*, meaning that the central bank chooses a peg but has some ability to change the peg if needed. Under a soft peg, the central bank stands ready to buy and sell the domestic currency at the fixed peg, holding enough international reserves to make sure they can support this pegged rate in the event of a surge in capital outflows. As a result, the only thing that ensures that the peg is maintained is the central bank's commitment to the peg and its ability to defend it based on the amount of foreign reserves it possesses.

At the other extreme is a pure floating exchange rate strategy where the central bank never intervenes in the foreign exchange market (except to make necessary transactions to fund government operations). Under pure float, the exchange rate is only a function of current supply and demand for the domestic currency in foreign exchange markets. For most emerging market economies, adoption of pure float would mean that their exchange rate would be highly volatile for many of the same reasons that their financial systems are highly volatile: asymmetric information, thin markets because of a lack of financial development, and weak institutions that increase risk.

Often times, emerging market economies refuse to choose between these two extreme options and instead adopt a hybrid approach to managing their exchange rate. But before we discuss these intermediate strategies, it will help to understand the conditions under which one of the polar options of a hard peg or pure float would make sense for an emerging market economy. There are numerous factors that impact the benefits and costs of these two strategies:

Transaction costs and the level of exchange rate risk. Many emerging market economies are small and foreign exchange markets in their currency are underdeveloped, reducing the efficiency of currency trades and leading to large brokerage fees. For the same reasons, smaller underdeveloped economies also tend to have more volatile exchange rates that increase the exchange rate risk associated with holding domestic currency for trade or investment. Higher transaction fees and exchange rate risk discourage international trade and capital flows, negatively impacting economic growth. As a result, the larger the transaction costs, the less developed the financial system, and the more reliant the emerging economy is on international trade, the greater the benefits of fixing over floating. Empirical evidence points to the fact that more stable exchange rates do promote international trade and economic integration for emerging market economies.[8]

It is important to note here that promoting stability in international trade can conflict with promoting stability in capital flows. If a country's primary goal is to promote stability in trade, then that country should choose to peg to its principal trade partner's currency, or a weighted average of its trading partners' currencies when there is no dominant trade partner. Choosing such a peg will stabilize the real exchange rate. However, many times a country's primary goal is to promote capital inflows. Because most international capital transactions take place in dollars, pegging to the dollar is typically the best way to attract these inflows. However, pegging to the dollar may not be consistent with maintaining a real exchange rate that is consistent with its long-run equilibrium level and may increase the chances that a country experiences a currency crisis (more on this in the next chapter).[9]

The source of exogenous shocks. Because of their small size and relative openness, emerging market economies are more vulnerable to economic shocks. Shocks can be categorized into three groups. A nominal shock is one that primarily changes aggregate demand and real variables only in the short run before nominal variables can adjust. An example would be a sudden change in the money supply or a change in expectations. A real shock would be one that primarily changes aggregate supply and results in permanent changes in real variables. An example would be a sudden decline in a country's terms of trade (such as from a fall in commodity prices for a commodity exporting country) or a change in productivity (such as from a change in institutions). Finally, a financial shock would be some exogenous change in financial stability, default risk, or the supply of credit within an economy. Such changes could be driven by asset bubbles, banking crises, or changes in prudential regulation.

Assuming that prices and wages in most emerging markets are relatively inflexible, then different exchange rate strategies provide preferable outcomes for different types of shocks.[10] For real shocks, the real exchange rate should be allowed to change because the long-term equilibrium exchange rate should also change. The best way to do this in the face of an inflexible price level would be for the central bank to allow the nominal exchange rate to adjust. Thus, floating nominal exchange rates (and monetary independence) are preferable when real supply shocks are predominant.

On the other hand, in the face of nominal shocks the central bank does not want to allow the real exchange rate to change. As a result, fixing the nominal exchange rate will keep the real exchange rate stable when the price level is inflexible. Hence, fixed exchange rates are preferable when nominal demand shocks are predominant.

Unfortunately, simple conclusions cannot be drawn for financial shocks. Instead, the advantages of each strategy depend upon the institutions and financial structure that exists within the economy. However, floating exchange rates do give central banks much more flexibility to respond to financial crises, particularly to act as a lender of last resort, than do rigid fixed exchange rate strategies that preclude monetary independence.

The low-inflation credibility of the central bank. A significant advantage of floating exchange rates is that it gives central banks the independence to pursue short-term domestic objectives. But this can also be a significant disadvantage because many central banks have shown themselves unable to maintain a commitment to important long-term goals such as low inflation when they are given too much policy freedom. Instead, because of political pressures, corruption, or just incompetence, central banks have often acted in ways that might aid short-term goals—such as temporarily faster credit growth or the need to fund budget deficits through seigniorage—at the expense of higher inflation over the long run.

Barro and Gordon (1983) illustrate how the conflict between short-term and long-term goals can lead to unnecessarily high inflation. In their simple model, the central bank publicly announces its monetary policy but the public cannot directly observe what the actual monetary policy is that the central bank follows. As a result, the public must set their expected inflation rate based on their expectations of what they think will be true about the actual monetary policy the central bank chooses. The public knows that the central bank has incentives to increase inflation above what it announces because this would stimulate growth and raise more seigniorage. So if the central bank publicly announces a policy of low inflation, should the public believe them or not? Barro and Gordon show that the answer to this question depends upon how credible the central bank's announcement is. If the bank is viewed as credible, then the public will set their expected inflation rate low. But if the announcement is not credible, then the public will set their expected inflation rate much higher. When this happens, the central bank is forced to inflate in order to prevent a "negative surprise" from occurring that could threaten economic growth. In the end, when the central bank is not credible, higher inflation occurs without any higher output growth.[11]

This idea—that optimal long-run policy is incompatible with the incentives that shape policy in the short run—is referred to as *time inconsistency*. Time inconsistency stands at the heart of all modern theories of how monetary policy should be conducted (as well as modern public policy analysis of any sort). Because of this time inconsistency problem, a central bank that is not viewed as having a credible commitment to low inflation will find it very difficult to achieve low inflation. On the other hand, credible central banks will be able to achieve lower inflation without any drag on output growth (and obtain a proverbial "free lunch").

How do central banks achieve low-inflation credibility with the public? The most obvious way is to earn a reputation as an inflation fighter: keep inflation low for an extended period. However, there are many problems with this approach. First, gaining a reputation could be costly in the short run as it would require the central bank to keep inflation much lower than what is expected, slowing economic activity and potentially creating financial instability. Second, reputation is fleeting: reputation is not necessarily transferable when there is turnover among the bureaucrats at the central bank. Likewise, a sudden exogenous shock that spikes inflation, such as a change in commodity prices, could ruin years of reputation building. Finally, good reputations are very difficult to build in many emerging market economies because of bad neighbors. When markets lack information, and possibly interest, about specific emerging market economies, markets often lump groups of emerging market economies together, making it difficult for a single, well-managed country to garner a reputation independent of its neighbors.[12]

Barro and Gordon argue that a less costly and more permanent solution to the time inconsistency problem is for the central bank to be irrevocably committed to a *monetary rule*, or a single, observable monetary objective consistent with low inflation. For example, a law or constitutional amendment that strictly required the central bank to maintain a fixed rate of money growth could be seen as a credible commitment to maintaining low inflation by many observers. This would even be true for countries with the worst reputations, assuming that the rule cannot be easily changed and that there are sufficient institutional arrangements in place to make sure that it is enforced and that outcomes are transparent. (For emerging market economies with weak political institutions, these last conditions make it unlikely that any rule would be viewed as credible enough to work.)

An alternative monetary policy rule that is attractive to many emerging central banks is a fixed exchange rate policy. A commitment to maintaining a fixed exchange rate is essentially a commitment to adopting the monetary policy, and inflation rate, of the country that the currency is being pegged to. How effective a fixed exchange rate policy is in generating low-inflation credibility depends upon the existing credibility of the central bank and the extent to which the policy is seen as being binding and enforceable. Strict and binding institutional arrangements such as a currency board have been adopted as a means of gaining credibility where little has previously existed (see the discussion of Argentina later in this chapter). For other central banks with better reputations, less binding soft exchange rate pegs may be viewed as credible enough to get the public to lower their expected inflation rates.[13]

The stability of fiscal policy. The stronger the fiscal position of a country, the more likely that a fixed exchange rate policy will be beneficial. This is true for three reasons. First, history has shown us many times that unsustainable fiscal policy eventually leads to unsustainable monetary policy because of the temptation to rely upon seigniorage. This will eventually lead to higher inflation and a depreciating exchange rate. Fixed exchange rates and large budget deficits are incompatible in the long run, a point we will return to in the next chapter.

Second, fixed exchange rates have fiscal costs for governments that they must be able to cover. If monetary policy is dedicated to the maintenance of its pegged exchange rate, the central bank will be less able to serve as a lender of last resort in the event of a banking crisis, forcing fiscal policy to pick up the slack. The government may also need to fund large holdings of foreign reserves to support the exchange rate peg, particularly under a currency board system.[14]

Finally, if independent monetary policy must be sacrificed when following a fixed exchange rate policy, countercyclical fiscal policy can serve as a substitute to stabilize output growth and unemployment in the event of any downturn. But this can only happen if the fiscal resources are there to be used.

The dangers of moral hazard and currency mismatch. One way of viewing a fixed exchange rate regime is that it is a policy in which exchange rate risk is purposely transferred from the public to the government. When considered in this way, it becomes obvious how fixed exchange rates encourage moral hazard behavior in international finance. International borrowers and lenders are more likely to engage in riskier transactions if they believe that the risk of any change in the exchange rate is being assumed by the government. For emerging market economies, moral hazard is likely to result in excessive "hot money" foreign capital inflows that are short term, speculative, and expose a country to the dangers of capital flight.

Moral hazard can also lead to currency mismatches and liability dollarization. Borrowing in a foreign currency is attractive to banks and businesses because such credit is cheaper and more easily available. When exchange rates are fixed by central banks, banks and business may be lured into thinking that foreign-denominated debt no longer carries any exchange rate risk. This is only true as long as the central bank is able to maintain its peg. But when the central bank cannot, as we saw during the Mexican Tequila crisis in 1994, the Argentinean crisis of 2001 (examined later in this chapter), and as we will see in our discussion of the 1997 East Asian crisis, the result is absolutely devastating for financial systems and economic development.

The quality of financial institutions and the level of financial development. Because fixed exchange rates encourage moral hazard and increase the risk of currency mismatches, adopting a rigid peg without the proper prudential regulation policies and monitoring in place to limit this risk is like giving a child a hand grenade to play with. When these institutions do not exist, floating exchange rates force those in financial markets to incorporate exchange rate risk into their decision making, leading to better allocations of resources.

However, there is an irreconcilable conflict here. While weak financial institutions make floating exchange rates more attractive because of the risk of currency mismatch, a general lack of financial development makes floating exchange rates less attractive because underdeveloped financial systems do not have strong markets in place to handle the excessive exchange rate volatility that comes with a floating exchange rate. As a result, many emerging markets adopt fixed exchange rates as a method of encouraging financial development, even when it is clearly a risky thing to do given that most underdeveloped financial systems also have underdeveloped financial institutions and lack the proper system of prudential regulation.[15] This contradiction is one of the primary reasons why, at this time, there is no consensus among economists regarding the best exchange rate management regime for emerging market economies at various stages of development to follow.[16]

Intermediate exchange rate regimes and inflation targeting

In reality, few countries choose either of the extreme options of a hard fixed exchange rate peg, such as a currency board, or pure float. This is in part because neither regime grants any discretion to policymakers. Under either of the options of fixing or pure float, the central bank essentially gives up the ability to make day-to-day decisions on how to manage the exchange rate. When choosing to float the central bank pays no attention to movements in the exchange rate. When choosing to fix, the central bank simply responds to supply and demand conditions for their currency and acts according to the rule of the pegged exchange rate that is in place.

Many central banks prefer to retain some day-to-day flexibility in their approach to managing their exchange rate in order to obtain some balance between exchange rate stability and other macroeconomic objectives. As a result, a large number of central banks adopt intermediate, or hybrid, approaches between rigid pegs and pure floating exchange rates. One option is a *target zone* in which the central bank announces a central peg for the exchange rate but allows the exchange rate to float within a band around this peg. Only when the exchange rate reaches either the upper or lower limit of this band will the central bank intervene. By making the band wider, the central bank is obviously retaining more independence, while a narrower band creates more exchange rate stability. Announcing the size of the band publicly helps stabilize expectations and may help generate some credibility for the central bank. However, it also creates the possibility of destabilizing speculation during times when the exchange rate is approaching one of the band limits in anticipation of the central bank's intervention. Target zones are most attractive to those countries that would benefit from fixed exchange rates but are subject to many external shocks, particularly real shocks, which demand more exchange rate flexibility than a rigid peg.

A second option is a *crawling peg* in which the central bank targets a real exchange rate in a manner that allows the nominal exchange rate to change at a pre-specified rate. Crawling pegs make the most sense for countries that want to peg their exchange rate but that also maintain monetary policies that are inconsistent with a rigid peg. An example would be a country that would like to peg to the US dollar but that maintains an inflation rate higher than that of the United States. Over the long run, maintaining a fixed nominal peg will eventually lead to an increase in the real exchange rate, meaning that domestic goods will become more expensive than goods priced in dollars and create trade deficits and a loss of international reserves. But under a crawling peg, this country could gradually let the value of their currency fall so that the real exchange rate remains steady. For example, if inflation in the country is 8 percent and dollar inflation is 3 percent, the central bank should allow the domestic currency to steadily depreciate by 5 percent a year in order to stabilize the real exchange rate. Crawling pegs can also be adopted in the face of market conditions that necessitate an appreciating exchange rate but when the central bank does not want to interrupt export promotion by allowing the real exchange rate to rise too quickly.

Another option is managed (or "dirty") float, meaning a policy of allowing the exchange rate to float while maintaining the discretion to occasionally intervene in the foreign exchange rate market if the real exchange rate deviates too far from its long-run equilibrium. Managed float does nothing to stabilize expectations or help create credibility for the central bank's policies. However, it does maintain the most policy independence for the central bank. It also gives central banks more options for maintaining some exchange rate stability than pure float, particularly in the face of large external shocks. Given the dependence of most emerging markets upon exports and capital inflows, while many emerging countries may profess to float, in reality they exhibit a "fear of floating" that causes them to manage their exchange rate actively at certain times.[17] As a result, pure float is not common among emerging market economies; managed float is the most common.

Figure 7.2 attempts to categorize countries—both developed and emerging—according to the exchange rate strategy they followed, de facto, in 2008.[18] A strong majority of emerging market economies have adopted a soft fixed exchange rate peg. Managed float is less common, as are other hard peg strategies. However, according to Eichengreen and Razo-Garcia (2006), the current trend among emerging market economies is toward intermediate regimes such as managed float and crawling pegs. They argue that increased capital mobility in many emerging market economies has made it more difficult (and dangerous) for these countries to adopt either rigid pegs or pure float.

In regard to which currencies are being pegged to, 66 emerging countries either have adopted the dollar as its currency, peg to the dollar, or manage their exchange rate against the dollar. Only 27 countries do the same with the euro (outside the euro area itself), while a smaller number peg to another currency or a basket of currencies.[19]

A final exchange rate management strategy that is currently becoming more popular is *inflation targeting*. Under an inflation targeting regime the central bank is mandated (through a law or a change in the constitution) to follow the primary goal of achieving a publicly announced numerical target for the inflation rate. If this target is not achieved, there must be some consequences for the policymakers in the central bank so that the inflation target is credible. (In democratic countries, publicly announcing the inflation goal will create some market

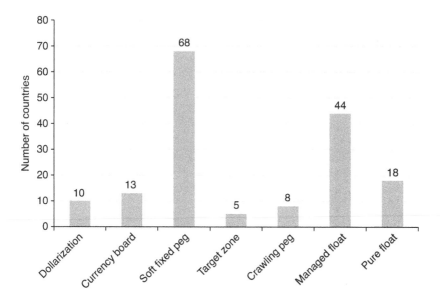

Figure 7.2 Emerging market exchange rate regimes in 2008 (source: IMF (2009)).

and political pressures that can serve to punish central bankers.) However, within this broader goal of achieving their inflation target, the central bank does have the flexibility to respond to secondary objectives, such as exchange rate stability.

According to its proponents, inflation targeting regimes allow emerging market economies to achieve the best of all possible worlds. If the inflation target is viewed as credible by markets, it will stabilize inflation expectations which will, in turn, lead to more stable real exchange rates. A credible inflation target will also reduce inflation by mitigating the problem of time inconsistency in monetary policy. Finally, it gives the central bank some flexibility to respond to short-run shocks, particularly if the central bank is judged not just on short-term inflation but on inflation measured over longer periods (one to two years).

However, in macroeconomics there are rarely perfect policy solutions, and inflation targeting is no exception. One problem critics of inflation targeting raise is that it is often difficult to sufficiently punish policymakers; without this, policymakers may fail to achieve their targets and the targets will not be seen as credible. This is particularly true within countries that lack quality financial and political institutions. An even bigger problem with inflation targeting is that while inflation rates are primarily determined by monetary policy in the long run, the central bank does not perfectly control the inflation rate in the short run. Many types of shocks, both real and nominal, can influence short-run inflation. As a result, how can a central bank ever be held responsible for something that it does not perfectly control? And how can any inflation target then ever be viewed as credible?

One final problem with inflation targets is that they can force central banks to enact procyclical monetary policies in the face of real supply shocks. For example, in the face of a negative shock to a country's terms of trade that increases the price of imported goods, a rigid inflation target would force the central bank to cut the money supply and reduce inflation when the standard stabilization policy would be to increase the money supply in order to avoid a slowdown in economic activity.[20]

All of this said, the early returns for countries that have adopted inflation targets are quite positive. Empirical studies have found that emerging market countries generally have higher inflation and output volatility than developed countries because of poorer institutions, less credible monetary policies, and more frequent shocks. However, the 13 emerging market economies that adopted inflation targets before 2002 have been able to reduce both the level of inflation and the volatility of output relative to their peers, suggesting that inflation targeting improves both the quality of institutions and the credibility of policy.[21] Referring back to Figure 7.2, 15 of the 18 countries that are classified as having a pure floating exchange rate have also adopted an inflation target, indicating once again how reluctant emerging economies are to let their currency float without an anchor. Of the 44 emerging economies that are classified as having followed managed float exchange rate regimes, ten of them have also adopted an inflation target.

An excellent example of the potential benefits of inflation targeting is Chile. In the 1970s, Chile had an average inflation rate of 90 percent and also experienced the excessive exchange rate and financial volatility that goes along with such high rates of inflation. Chile was able to reduce inflation to 25 percent by 1990, at which point it committed to an inflation targeting strategy in order to reduce it even further. Chile began with an inflation target band between 15 and 20 percent in 1991, but gradually lowered and narrowed this band over the decade. By 1999, inflation had fallen to 2.3 percent and has averaged 3 percent a year since, which is its current inflation target. At the same time, Chile was able to grow its economy at a very impressive rate of 8 percent a year. Of course, it is also important to recognize that in many ways Chile possessed the perfect environment for inflation targeting to work. The central bank was independent and was able to make a strong commitment to its inflation target. The country also had a sound financial system with strong prudential regulation. Chile also has low budget deficits and strong capital inflows. All of these factors significantly enhanced the credibility of the inflation targeting regime in Chile, but also means that Chile may not be an applicable role model for other emerging market economies without these same factors in place.

Argentina's currency board and the crisis of 2001

Argentina has a long history of doing relatively little with a lot. In the early 1900s, Argentina was as rich as the United States in per-capita terms. But despite a wealth of natural and human resources, a century of economic mismanagement and political instability has left Argentina today with income of only about one-third of per-capita US GDP. Argentina's most recent crisis in 2001 actually began in the 1980s. During the Latin American debt crisis, Argentina monetized its debt like many of its neighbors, leading to a hyperinflation of more than 2,000 percent a year. Argentineans today still refer to the building that houses the Central Bank of Argentina as "the scene of the crime"; a building where bullet holes remain in its walls from riots that broke out as a result of the economic and financial turmoil associated with this hyperinflation.

In an effort to reduce inflation and restore credibility to its monetary policy after decades of incompetence, Argentina was one of the first, and by far the largest, emerging country to adopt a currency board system. Under this regime, the Argentinean peso would be convertible with the US dollar on a one-to-one basis. Pesos in circulation would be backed more than 100 percent by foreign reserve holdings of dollars in order to protect against a loss of confidence in the peso. The idea behind this currency board was to credibly reduce money growth and inflation while at the same time fixing the exchange rate of the peso to the dollar. In addition, the currency board promised to protect the independence of a central bank that had shown itself to be part and parcel of the volatile Argentinean political system. In other words, the currency board would be a way to force the Central Bank of Argentina to make the tough decisions it had never been able to make in the past.

For a while, the currency board system appeared to work quite well. Inflation fell from 2,300 percent in 1990 to 5 percent in 1994 while the economy grew at

7.6 percent a year. For the first 11 years of the currency board, the economy grew at 3.4 percent a year, much better than the negative 1 percent growth rate during the preceding 11 years.

In the middle of this decade of relative prosperity associated with the currency board, Argentina also significantly strengthened the prudential regulation of its financial system by improving accounting standards, strengthening the rights of creditors, increasing capital requirements, and restricting the levels of hot money that could be held by banks. In fact, the World Bank lauded Argentina as the second-best emerging market country in terms of the quality of their system of prudential regulation. The Argentinean banking system was also restructured as many state-owned banks (which were half of all banks in the country) were privatized and insolvent banks were either closed or recapitalized. Foreign banks were also allowed to enter the country and their presence rose from 15 percent of total bank deposits in 1994 to 70 percent by 2000. Overall, Argentina's credit-to-GDP ratio doubled from 15 percent in 1991 to 30 percent in 1999.[22]

Unfortunately, there were three significant problems with this "Argentinean miracle" of the 1990s. The first is that within this strong system of prudential regulation there were few restrictions on dollar-denominated debt, leading to a significant dollarization of liabilities in the banking system. In fact, the currency board system encouraged dollarization of debt by propagating the belief that pesos and dollars are, and always would be, perfectly convertible with each other. The proportion of debt denominated in dollars doubled between 1993 and 1998 to nearly 40 percent of total debt. In fact, for Argentinean firms that operated in the non-tradable sector (meaning they earned their revenues in pesos), 75 percent of their debt was in dollars![23] This extreme currency mismatch meant that a collapse of the currency board would lead to financial devastation across the economy.

The second problem was Argentina's lack of fiscal discipline. Part of this economic boom was fueled by external debt-financed spending by the government. Argentina's sovereign debt-to-GDP ratio rose from 27 percent in 1992 to 38 percent by 1998. Making this debt increase worse, almost half of it was denominated in dollars. This incredible growth in sovereign debt occurred despite the fact that Argentina had suffered through a sovereign debt crisis less than ten years earlier. Argentina has long been the classic example of a debt intolerant country. Its political structure—where the federal government collects most of the taxes but the provinces primarily determine expenditures—coupled with the strength of its labor unions and the crassness of its special interests politics make Argentina chronically undisciplined when it comes to fiscal matters.

The third problem was the general microeconomic inefficiency of Argentinean labor and product markets. As just mentioned, labor unions and labor regulations are very strong in Argentina. Because of this, labor and goods markets are inefficient and wages and prices are very inflexible. This is a large problem when a fixed exchange rate system such as a currency board is adopted because the currency board prohibits exchange rate movements from serving as a factor of adjustment to economic shocks. As a result, any negative shock experienced by Argentina could not be offset by nominal movements in the exchange rate, wages, or prices. Instead, these shocks would directly impact real variables such as unemployment and output.

In 1999, Argentina began to experience such shocks in many different forms, the most important of which was an appreciation of the dollar (and, as a result, the peso) by 25 percent between 1999 and 2001. This appreciation was magnified by a devaluation of the Brazilian real after it experienced a financial crisis. In addition, a fall in commodity and food prices, which are Argentina's primary exports, significantly worsened Argentina's terms of trade and trade deficit. A sharp recession immediately struck, reducing output by 2 percent a year in 2000 and 2001.

As the economic situation worsened, capital began to flee Argentina and the central bank's reserve of dollars began to disappear. Fewer dollars mean fewer pesos under the currency board system, which increased interest rates and further worsened the economic situation. In December 2000, the IMF granted Argentina a $40 billion loan to help it defend its currency board in the face of capital flight, but by March 2001 these dollars were largely gone and Argentina announced it was no longer backing its peso to the dollar alone but to a basket of currencies. The public understood this for what it was—a devaluation in violation of the currency board agreement—and immediately panicked. Confidence in the entire financial system disappeared, leading to extreme capital flight and bank disintermediation.

Argentina's government and central bank only worsened the situation by, as is consistent with its history, refusing to abide by its own laws and generally accepted standards of conduct. The government required banks to hold more of its sovereign debt, weakened prudential regulation, and sacked the chief regulator. The central bank began printing up small-denomination bonds (which were essentially currency but were not subject to the currency board rules) in order to raise seigniorage.

Despite these actions, Argentina was able to receive an additional $6 billion loan from the IMF in August 2001, but by this point it was too little, too late to avoid a full-fledged bank run. More than 80 percent of all deposits left the Argentinean banking system during the first half of 2001. The government's attempt to stem the banking crisis by limiting withdrawals from banks to $250 a week per person only led to riots and the fall of the government. The new government immediately defaulted on its public debt, including that owed to the IMF and World Bank, and formally abandoned the currency board in January 2002, at which point the peso immediately depreciated by two-thirds of its value. Given the extreme currency mismatch in the Argentinean economy, most firms and all banks became instantly insolvent. A two-thirds depreciation of the peso meant that the real value of dollar-denominated debt tripled in terms of pesos!

In order to restore some semblance of financial stability, the Argentinean government explicitly violated established property rights and adopted a policy of "pesofication." Under this policy, dollar debt was forcibly converted into peso debt by the government. The conversion rate was not determined by market exchange rates but by the government. The general public was able to convert their debt at a rate of $1 for 1.4 pesos (a relatively good deal for the public given that the current exchange rate was $1 = 1.5 pesos). However, the government converted its own debt at $1 = 1 peso, the same rate as under the currency board. Banks, and any other holders of debt, were robbed by these transactions. All lenders lost because they received significantly less than they should have received if their dollar debt had been converted to pesos at market rates. Banks particularly suffered because the government had forced banks to hold more dollar-denominated Argentinean debt early in the crisis, but then these banks were repaid in a considerably devalued peso after the currency board was abandoned. One of the reasons it was so politically easy for the Argentinean government to rob banks is that after the liberalization of the mid-1990s, 70 percent of the banking industry was operated by foreign banks.[24]

In 2002, the Argentinean economy was in free-fall. The economy contracted at an annual rate of 15 percent in the first quarter, unemployment stood at 20 percent, inflation rose to 30 percent, and the percentage of the population living in poverty rose to over 50 percent. The economic situation did gradually improve in 2003, aided by a spike in food prices. However, economic confidence in Argentina did not improve after the government's egregious violation of property rights and its endless squabbling with the IMF, World Bank, and private creditors over how to end its sovereign debt crisis.[25]

There are many important lessons to be learned from the 2001 Argentinean crisis, but one stands out as particularly important. This lesson is that the choice of exchange rate regime is no substitute for sound economic fundamentals. It is impossible for any monetary or exchange rate rule, such as a currency board, to overcome weak financial institutions. In the end, exchange rate policies are less important than managing systemic risk and having quality prudential regulation and monitoring in place. This is particularly true for the risk associated with currency mismatch, which can never be completely eliminated through the choice of an exchange rate regime. In hindsight, it is clear that a currency board could never work in Argentina given their dysfunctional institutions and their inability to play by the rules. Outright dollarization would have been a better option if Argentina was truly committed to stabilizing inflation and promoting economic integration with the rest of the world, as it would have taken monetary policy entirely out of the hands of the Argentinean government.

Conclusions

When emerging market economies choose an exchange rate strategy, the most important principle to recognize is that there are no simple rules, only tradeoffs. One size simply cannot fit all emerging economies. Instead, the choice of strategy should depend upon the characteristics of the country and the environment in which it operates. Our analysis here suggests that a fixed exchange rate system is most beneficial when the following factors are in place:

- The country is small.
- It is open to both international trade and foreign capital flows.
- It lacks policy credibility and suffers from the problem of time inconsistency that leads to high inflation.
- It is primarily subject to nominal, or aggregate demand, shocks and not real, or aggregate supply, shocks.
- The country has sound fiscal policies.
- It has less developed financial markets.
- The country has strong financial institutions.

What becomes evident from looking at this list is that no emerging market economy is completely characterized by all, or none, of these factors. As a result, the choice of an exchange rate management strategy is always fraught with uncertainty and danger; hence, the attractiveness of many intermediate strategies between pure float and rigid fixing. These strategies—such as target zones, crawling pegs, and inflation targets—are ways of mitigating the risk of making the wrong choice while at the same time attempting to capture some of the benefits of credibility and exchange rate stability.

As we learned in the Argentinean crisis of 2001, no exchange rate strategy by itself can ever grant governments credibility and the power that comes with it. Credibility—and financial stability—can only be earned through the hard-won development of financial institutions and the exhibition of a real commitment to adhering to the rules that are in place even when it is not easy to do so. Failing to credibly commit to these rules can lead to currency crises, financial crises, and economic collapse. These are the topics we turn to in the next chapter.

8 International financial crises

Currency and twin crises

Introduction

In this final chapter on international finance in emerging market economies we return to the topic of financial crises. As emerging economies have liberalized and globalized, they have gained significant benefits in terms of financial development and economic growth. But these gains from financial openness have come at the cost of increased financial and macroeconomic volatility, not only in the form of sovereign debt crises, asset bubbles, and banking crises, which we have already discussed. There also appears to be some increase in the frequency of *currency crises*, or a large and rapid depreciation in the exchange rate typically associated with sudden foreign capital flight. Many of these currency crises have occurred in conjunction with banking crises in what is referred to as a *twin crisis*. Figure 8.1 presents data on the number of banking crises, currency crises,

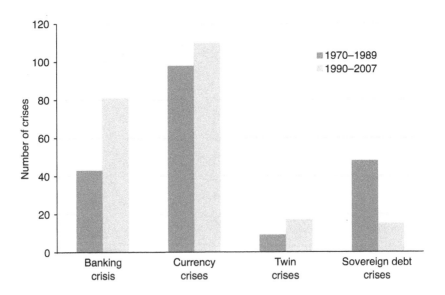

Figure 8.1 Frequency of financial crises.

sovereign debt crises, and twin crises for all countries between 1970 and 2007 broken into two periods. We can see that while there has been a decline in sovereign debt crises in the latter period, banking, currency, and twin crises each appear to have become more common. This increase in the number of crises would be even more dramatic if this figure included crises that occurred during the global financial crisis in 2008 and 2009.

The purpose of this chapter is to examine the causes of international financial crises in emerging market economies. The primary focus is on the causes of currency crises, foreign capital flight, twin crises, and *contagion*, or the spillover of financial crises across countries not related to common shocks. A close examination of the East Asian crisis of 1997–1999 provides the definitive case study of twin crises and of the dramatic costs that are borne by emerging economies when they occur.

In an attempt to avoid currency crises and to promote exports, many emerging market countries have increasingly attempted to keep their exchange rates undervalued, resulting in an unprecedented accumulation of foreign reserves. While there are advantages to such a strategy, this policy also has the potential to fuel financial crises and, in fact, contributed greatly to the 2007 global financial crisis. We discuss why this is the case and the potential long-term consequences of foreign reserve hoarding. This chapter concludes with a discussion of the International Monetary Fund (IMF) and its potential role in preempting international financial crises by serving as a lender of last resort for emerging countries. We discuss the debate over the IMF's role in past crises and the controversies about its role in preventing—or even causing, as many critics charge—financial crises.

Balance of payments and the causes of exchange rate misalignment

Before we examine the causes of currency crises, it is important to understand the role that the balance of payments plays in measuring an emerging country's external balance with the rest of the world. The balance of payments is an accounting system that records the monetary transactions between countries. The balance of payments is based upon the fact that the sources of funds for an economy must equal its uses of funds. The balance of payments is most easily expressed by the following equation:

$$\text{Current Account (CA)} + \text{Capital Account (KA)}$$
$$= \text{Change in Government Intl' Reserves } (\Delta IR) \tag{8.1}$$

The *current account* records the net monetary receipts from trade in goods and services across countries and is closely related to a country's trade balance (exports minus imports). The *capital account* records the net monetary receipts from capital and financial transactions across countries. Finally, the *change in government international reserves* records the net increase or decrease in the amount of foreign assets held by the government (including the central bank).

The balance of payments is really just a simple budget constraint for an economy as a whole. According to the balance of payments equation, it must be true that the aggregate international receipts of funds are equal to the uses of these funds. For example, consider China, a country that runs a large trade surplus and maintains a current account surplus (CA>0) that also generates a surplus of foreign funds. China must find a use for the foreign funds created by this current account surplus. There are two non-mutually exclusive options. Either private citizens must be net purchasers of foreign assets (KA<0) by buying more foreign assets than the amount of domestic assets they sell to foreigners (resulting in a net capital outflow), or the government must be a net purchaser of assets by buying more foreign reserves than it sells (ΔIR>0).

Likewise, any country that experiences a large current account deficit must pay for this deficit by being a net borrower and/or by receiving foreign capital inflows through the government selling international reserves (i.e. CA<0 implies either KA>0 and/or ΔIR<0).

Figure 8.2 presents the average current account balance for emerging market economies as a whole (142 countries). Emerging market economies have gone from running persistent current account deficits in the 1980s and 1990s to running large surpluses in the 2000s. According to the balance of payments, one of two things must then also be happening in emerging market economies. The first is that these countries are running capital account deficits, meaning they are experiencing capital outflows. But from our earlier discussion in Chapter 6 we know that this is not the case and that most emerging economies receive net inflows of foreign capital. This leaves only the second option as possible: the governments and central banks of these countries are accumulating large amounts of foreign reserves.

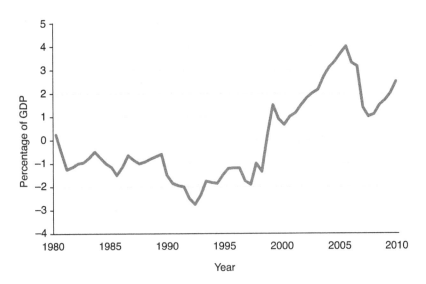

Figure 8.2 Current account balance in emerging market economies (source: IMF (2011g)).

To understand why this is occurring, we first need to examine how changes in a central bank's management of their exchange rate and holdings of international reserves can impact its balance of payments. In the previous chapter, the argument was made that countries that manage their exchange rate should attempt to keep their real exchange rate equal to its long-run equilibrium rate so that the country avoids costly imbalances in its current account that can lead to an inefficient allocation of resources. But now consider alternative strategies. What if a central bank purposefully attempts to keep its real exchange rate *undervalued*, meaning that it keeps its peg at a level such that the real exchange rate is below its long-run equilibrium rate? In this case, the lower real exchange rate will reduce the relative price of exports and increase the price of imports, increasing the balance of the country's current account at the expense of making domestic consumption more expensive. This policy of undervaluing exchange rates has been an important component of the export promotion strategies increasingly adopted in the emerging world. The only way to maintain these current account deficits and to continue to attract foreign capital inflows at the same time, according to the balance of payments accounts, is for the central bank to continue to accumulate large levels of international reserves (otherwise known as *sterilizing* capital flows). We will return to this topic in a later section and discuss the costs and benefits of this strategy of pursuing undervalued exchange rates and international reserve accumulation.

Another policy option is for the central bank to keep the real exchange rate *overvalued*, or above its long-run equilibrium level. This strategy was widely followed by many emerging economies in the 1960s and 1970s and is still widely adopted in Sub-Saharan Africa today. The benefits of this approach is that it reduces the price of imports, which keeps the price of imported commodities and equipment low as well as keeps consumer goods cheap, leading to higher standards of living. However, there are two problems with this strategy. The first is that it reduces domestic competitiveness by discouraging exports in a manner consistent with import substitution policies. The second is that an overvalued exchange rate is inconsistent over the long term with the free movement of capital. This is because such a policy would require a central bank to have an unlimited supply of foreign reserves to support the overvalued exchange rate by selling these reserves to buy its own currency. As a result, for an overvalued exchange rate policy to be viable over any lengthy period, the country must impose strict capital controls, such as currency licenses, import quotas, dual exchange rate systems, or other forms of financial repression. To have an overvalued exchange rate without such controls on capital will eventually lead to shortfalls in foreign reserves and invites inevitable capital flight and a currency crisis.

Currency crises and contagion

Currency crises occur when central banks are no longer able or willing to defend an overvalued exchange rate they are pegging. These overvalued exchange rates can be the result of purposeful policy, as just described, or they can occur inadvertently, meaning the central bank finds itself in a position where the market believes the exchange rate is overvalued but the central bank does not. In either case, a point comes when markets begin to anticipate a devaluation of the currency and withdraw their resources from the country, leading to capital flight. This then forces the central bank to defend its peg by selling its international reserves for its currency until either the capital flight abates or they reach the point where they no longer have the international reserves. When a central bank reaches this point where they can no longer defend their peg by selling international reserves, it is forced to allow its currency to float, resulting in a sudden and large depreciation in the exchange rate that is the defining characteristic of currency crises.

Most overvalued exchange rates that lead to currency crises are of the inadvertent variety, which raises the question: how do central banks find themselves unwittingly in the middle of a currency crisis? There are many potential theories as to why currency crises occur. Like other forms of financial crisis, these theories can be lumped into *fundamentals-based theories* and *belief-based theories* of crises.

The seminal fundamentals-based model of currency crises was developed by Paul Krugman (1979), in which currency crises occur as the result of a pegged exchange rate that is out of line with current macroeconomic conditions. Currency crises are most likely when governments attempt to maintain hard pegs when their fiscal solvency is in doubt (because high budget deficits can lead to high inflation), when they have unstable financial markets and banking systems (that can lead to capital flight), or have low economic growth (that reduces the attractiveness of domestic investment). Under any of these circumstances, downward market pressure will exist on the exchange rate. When this pressure becomes large enough, foreign investors will flee the country, taking international reserves with them until the central bank reaches its breaking point and a currency crisis occurs.

In fundamentals-based models, the best indicator of whether an exchange rate is overvalued is a country's balance of payments. Large current account deficits that cannot be financed with net capital inflows but instead must be financed with negative changes in international reserves will eventually lead to the point where the government runs out of reserves and must devalue. One commonly used rule of thumb is that once a country's current account deficit reaches 5 percent of GDP, its exchange rate is overvalued enough to put it in immediate danger of capital flight and a currency crisis.

Fundamentals-based theories of currency crises fit the facts of many of the currency crises that we have previously talked about, such as the Latin American debt crisis in the 1980s (Chapter 4), the Mexican Tequila crisis in 1994 (Chapter 5), and the Argentinean financial crisis of 2001 (Chapter 7). There is also a great deal of empirical evidence that weak macroeconomic fundamentals such as current account deficits, low growth, high budget deficits, high inflation, capital outflows, and declines in international reserves are all significant leading indicators of future currency crises.[1]

However, other empirical studies find that while fundamentals are important in explaining currency crises, they do not tell the whole story. Eichengreen, Rose, and Wyplosz (2003a) find that for most currency crises it is difficult to identify a specific event that initiated the crisis or to time exactly when the crisis would begin. In addition, they find that countries that have experienced a currency crisis in the past are more likely to experience a crisis again, indicating that credibility plays a role in shaping market beliefs. Finally, these authors find that some currency crisis episodes are difficult to explain based on fundamentals alone. Berg and Pattillo (1999) find that between one-third and one-half of all currency crises are predictable based on fundamentals alone, but that these same fundamentals falsely predict a crisis roughly half of the time.

All of this evidence points to the existence of belief-based currency crises, similar to the belief-based theories of banking crises discussed in Chapter 5. Obstfeld (1996) develops a model of rational expectations in which the return to currency speculators depends upon what each individual speculator believes about the behavior of other speculators. Because speculators realize that each government has a point at which the costs of maintaining a peg begin to outweigh its benefits, there is the possibility of multiple equilibriums and self-fulfilling currency crises depending upon the beliefs that are currently prevalent in the market. If speculators believe that other speculators believe that a currency crisis is going to take place, capital flight occurs and a currency crisis does take place, regardless of the state of existing economic fundamentals.

Proponents of belief-based theories also point to the fact that it is often difficult to identify specific changes in fundamentals that trigger currency crises. Currency crises in the 1990s in Russia, Brazil, and East Asia and even the Argentinean crisis in 2001 each started without a single defining event that served as a trigger, but instead were the result of pressures that had been building for a long time without a crisis occurring. For example, in Argentina budget deficits and worries about sovereign debt default had been building for years but did not lead to a crisis, until they did.

Belief-based theories emphasize the role of credibility as being important in preventing currency crises. As long as the central bank is viewed as being able and willing to defend their peg, a currency crisis will not happen. The ability of a central bank to defend its peg depends upon it having a sufficient amount of international reserves available so that it is able to buy back huge volumes of its currency in order to support its value.

The willingness of a central bank to defend its peg is harder to evaluate. In large part willingness depends upon the institutions that are in place that allow policymakers in the central bank to commit to long-term objectives. It was for this reason that some emerging market economies viewed currency boards as a perfect strategy for fixing their exchange rate because it was assumed (mistakenly) that such boards would change institutions in a way that would make their pegs look more credible. But credibility also depends upon the willingness of policymakers to make difficult decisions, both in terms of their political ramifications and also in terms of their economic implications. For example, many central banks have been forced to make a "Sophie's choice" and raise interest rates in order to stem capital flight and prevent a currency crisis, but this often triggers financial instability and causes a slowdown in economic growth. Those central banks that are not viewed as likely to make such difficult choices, such as the Central Bank of Argentina, will likely find themselves subject to more frequent self-fulfilling speculative attacks.

One of the striking features of currency crises and capital flight is that they have often been linked across countries. During the 1980s, currency crises took place across Latin America, while the currency crisis that began in Thailand in 1997 eventually spread throughout Asia and then to Russia, Brazil, Argentina, and then Uruguay. When a currency crisis in one country increases the probability of a currency crisis in another country, economists refer to this as *contagion*.

Once again, there are *fundamentals-based* and *belief-based theories of contagion*. Fundamentals-based theories focus on the real economic linkages that exist between countries. Fundamentals-based contagion can spread through trade linkages in which an economic slowdown in one country reduces its demand for imports, which in turn reduces exports and output among its trading partners. Contagion can also spread through financial linkages when countries share the same large institutional lenders such as international portfolio funds or international banks. When a crisis occurs in one country and these international lenders incur losses, they are forced to tighten credit and to sell assets from their entire portfolio. In this way, financial crisis in one country can trigger capital flight in others.

However, there are also good reasons to think that beliefs play an important role in spreading contagion through at least three channels. First, as with currency crises, *self-fulfilling contagion* can occur when a crisis in one country leads investors to believe that investors are going to flee other countries, regardless of the economic fundamentals that exist in these countries. When this happens, widespread contagion can occur. Second, contagion can also take place through *herding*. When information is costly to investors, small investors have an incentive to "follow-the-leaders" and mimic the actions of the largest investors with established reputations. As a result, a currency crisis in one country that leads to withdrawals of capital in another country by even one large investor can spook enough other investors to trigger broader capital flight. Finally, a *wake-up call* phenomenon may exist in which a crisis in one country may prompt investors to look for similar weaknesses or policies in other countries. For example, a currency crisis in one country may cause investors to reassess their risk exposure in other countries with similar inflation rates or current account deficits, causing contagion among many countries at once.

The empirical evidence that contagion exists is strong. Eichengreen, Rose, and Wyplosz (2003b) find that a currency crisis in one country increases the probability of a currency crisis in another country by 8 percent on average. The authors find that trade linkages are the best predictors of the spread of contagion, but also find that countries that possess similar macroeconomic policies as the country in crisis are also more vulnerable to contagion, consistent with the wake-up call hypothesis. On the other hand, Kaminsky *et al.* (2003) examine five episodes of contagion since 1980 and find that financial linkages, particularly the existence of leveraged common lenders, played the biggest role in the spread of capital flight. In these cases, when a crisis began in one country, highly leveraged institutional investors were forced to sell off assets broadly across all of the countries in their asset portfolio, spreading price declines and speculative volatility. Not surprisingly, these authors also find that contagion typically follows a boom in foreign capital inflows, particularly hot money inflows fueled by speculative behavior.[2]

An excellent example of contagion driven by financial linkages occurred in Uruguay in 2002. Before its crisis, Uruguay had highly rated sovereign debt and was generally viewed as having one of the strongest financial systems in South America. Uruguay is highly dollarized with nearly 80 percent of its bank deposits in dollars, often held by Argentineans looking for a place to protect their savings from the Argentinean government. When Argentina began its descent into crisis in 2001, Argentineans worried that the crisis would spread to Uruguay because of these close financial ties and withdrew their dollar deposits from Uruguay. This sudden capital flight from Uruguay eventually consumed most of the central bank's international reserves and forced a large devaluation of the Uruguayan peso, a financial collapse, and a severe economic contraction— despite the fact that Uruguay itself was well governed with sound financial fundamentals before the crisis.

Twin crises

Twin crises, or simultaneous currency and banking crises, have become increasingly common over the last two decades. Referring back to Figure 8.1, there has been roughly twice the number of twin crises in the recent period compared to the 1970s and 1980s. This is largely because banking crises have been twice as frequent. As discussed in Chapter 5, financial deregulation in the 1980s and 1990s in emerging economies often took place without regard to creating systems of prudential regulation and supervision necessary to limit moral hazard, asset bubbles, and systemic risk. But twin crises have also been driven by an increased number of currency crises. Emerging market economies today are more vulnerable to capital flight because, as discussed in Chapter 6, capital accounts have often been liberalized without appropriate limitations in place on short-term speculative capital flows and currency mismatches.

But twin crises are not simply currency crises and banking crises that occur independently—there are important linkages between the two such that currency crises magnify the size of banking crises and vice versa. Banking crises can increase the size and frequency of currency crises by increasing perceived risk, encouraging liability dollarization, spurring capital flight (particularly of hot money), and increasing budget deficits and inflation. All of these factors place downward pressure on a country's exchange rate, increasing both the likelihood that the government will not be able to defend its pegged exchange rate and the size of the devaluation once a currency crisis does take place.

On the other hand, currency crises increase the size and frequency of banking crises. The devaluation associated with a currency crisis can devastate bank balance sheets because of currency mismatch, or the extent to which bank assets are in the domestic currency but its liabilities are denominated in dollars. If banks themselves are not directly vulnerable to currency mismatch, meaning that their dollar assets and liabilities are matched on their balance sheet, they are often indirectly vulnerable because many emerging market firms earn most of their revenue in the domestic currency but borrow significantly in dollars. As a result, devaluation reduces the net worth of these firms which can lead to bankruptcies that, in turn, also hurt banks. Coupled with the costs of capital flight and the difficulty that many banks have in rolling over their short-term debts during a currency crisis, it is not surprising that the worst banking crises in history have often been triggered by currency crises. The empirical evidence on twin crises from Glick and Hutchison (2001) indicates that about half of all banking crises lead to currency crises in emerging economies, while about one-third of all currency crises eventually trigger a banking crisis.

Kaminsky and Reinhart (1999) investigate recent twin crisis episodes and find that they have become more frequent in the 1990s and 2000s because of increased financial deregulation; in 18 of the 26 twin crisis episodes they look at, financial liberalization had taken place within the previous five years. The authors also find a regular pattern for twin crises similar to the diagram presented in Figure 8.3. Twin crises begin with financial deregulation absent proper prudential regulations, leading to large increases in foreign capital inflows, particularly hot money that dollarizes the liabilities of banks and firms. This currency mismatch is particularly large when the central bank pegs to the dollar because it encourages greater capital inflows, the ignoring of exchange rate risk, and current account deficits. These capital inflows fuel credit booms and asset bubbles in housing and stock markets. Eventually a negative shock or a change in beliefs occurs that bursts these asset bubbles, often triggering the initial stages of a banking crisis. As foreign investors observe this, they begin to pull their short-term capital out of the country. Capital flight starts slowly but picks up pace as speculation becomes self-fulfilling and herding behavior becomes rampant. Eventually these speculative attacks exhaust the international reserves (or the will) of the central bank, forcing it to abandon its peg and leading to a large devaluation. This devaluation magnifies the panic selling of assets, but most importantly it leads to widespread insolvency because of currency mismatch. This worsens the banking crisis, which in turn magnifies the size of the currency crisis in a vicious cycle that leads to very large devaluations. The collapse of the exchange rate depresses credit which disrupts economic activity and often leads to a sharp macroeconomic downturn.

Kaminsky and Reinhart's analysis suggests that twin crises are caused by poor macroeconomic and financial fundamentals and are not primarily the result of beliefs and self-fulfilling behavior. They present empirical evidence that those countries with the worst financial fundamentals had the highest probability of suffering from a twin crisis as opposed to a single crisis alone. Such countries also suffered the largest economic contractions during their twin crisis.[3]

One of the factors that make twin crises particularly damaging is that policy-makers find themselves in a catch-22 in which they cannot act to alleviate the pressure of one crisis without making the other crisis worse. To mitigate capital outflows that occur during a currency crisis, governments can tighten monetary and fiscal policy in order to increase interest rates. This not only increases the attractiveness of domestic assets, but it also enhances credibility by sending a signal to foreign investors that macroeconomic policy will be more responsible

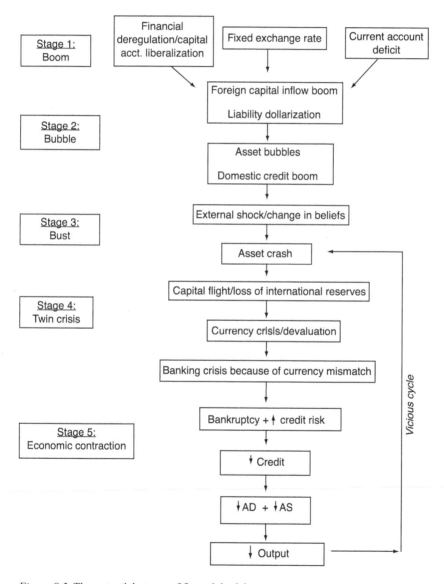

Figure 8.3 The potential stages of financial crisis.

in the future. Unfortunately, in the short run tighter monetary and fiscal policies worsen the banking crisis by reducing aggregate output, which increases default rates. In addition, higher interest rates increase default risk by increasing debt servicing payments and encouraging adverse selection and moral hazard. However, to follow the opposite approach and loosen monetary and fiscal policy would only lead to more capital flight, worsening the currency crisis.

A few studies have attempted to estimate the costs of twin crises. Bordo *et al.* (2001) estimate that the cumulative output cost of a twin crisis is 16 percent of GDP over and above the cost of an average recession, making twin crises very costly. Of this amount, 4.4 percent of the lost GDP is caused by the banking crisis and 8.7 percent is caused by the currency crisis, leaving the incremental lost GDP that is attributable to the interaction between the crises at approximately 3 percent of GDP.[4] Focusing only on emerging market economies, Hutchison and Noy (2005) find similar results that twin crises lead to reductions in output of between 13 and 18 percent of GDP. However, they fail to find any evidence that twin crises have costs that are greater than currency and banking crises separately. Hutchison and Noy also differ from Bordo *et al.* in that they find that banking crises are more costly than currency crises. Their estimates are that currency crises reduce GDP by between 5 and 8 percent over a two-to-four-year period, while banking crises reduce GDP by between 8 and 10 percent of GDP.[5] Thus, questions as to whether currency crises or banking crises are the most costly, and about the costs of interactions between the two, still remain unanswered empirically.

The East Asian twin crises of 1997–1999

The most significant, and shocking, international financial crises in emerging market history occurred between 1997 and 1999 in East Asia. This crisis was centered in the four large economies of Thailand, South Korea, Indonesia, and Malaysia. These countries had experienced historic rates of growth for 35 years preceding this crisis and averaged more than 10 percent a year growth in the five years before the crisis. As a result of the twin crises that struck in 1997, in less than a year these four countries would see incomes fall by more than 10 percent, real wages fall by one-third, unemployment triple, and more than 22 million people slip into poverty.

The origins of the currency crises in East Asia can be traced back to the decisions of these countries to adopt soft pegs and narrow target zones to the dollar. East Asian countries in the region pegged to the dollar despite the fact that their major trading partners were Japan and China. The decision to peg to the dollar was a decision to emphasize attracting foreign capital inflows over stabilizing their real exchange rates and keeping their current account in rough balance. For a long time this helped the region attract large amounts of foreign capital that fueled rapid economic growth. But the dangers of such a strategy revealed themselves in the mid-1990s when the dollar began to appreciate significantly against the major currency in the region, the Japanese yen. Between 1995 and 1997, the dollar rose by 50 percent against the yen as a result of a prolonged recession and banking crisis in Japan coupled with a strong US economy (although an appreciation of this size is difficult to justify based on fundamentals alone).

The fixed exchange rates adhered to by East Asian countries meant that their currencies appreciated right along with the dollar. Most East Asian countries saw their estimated real exchange rates rise by 20 percent between 1995 and 1997. Coupled with other factors, such as strong export growth in China, a decline in exports to Japan, as well as weak world demand for electronics components, these countries began to run sizable current account deficits. Table 8.1 presents data on current account balances in the region. The countries that had the most rigid pegs to the dollar—Thailand, Malaysia, and the Philippines—had the largest current account deficits. If a current account deficit of roughly 5 percent or more is a rule of thumb indicator of when a country is in danger of having an exchange rate that is overvalued enough to put it in danger of a currency crisis, then all four of the largest crisis countries were vulnerable to a speculative attack between 1995 and 1996.

Despite the vulnerability of these countries' currencies to a crisis, the otherwise sound macroeconomic fundamentals of the countries in the region—particularly their low inflation and low budget deficits—seemed to assuage many investors' fears. But a less obvious crisis was lurking in these countries' banking systems.

Asian banking systems (as is discussed in more detail in Chapter 11) dominate financial intermediation in these countries, with banks facilitating over 90 percent of corporate finance. These banking systems are dominated by a small number of very large banks. In the mid-1980s, governments in the region began to deregulate these large and important banks and also liberalize capital accounts. They did this in a relatively short period with little emphasis on creating the prudential regulation that is so important to minimizing moral hazard and systemic risk. Capital adequacy requirements were very low (less than 4 percent, meaning leverage ratios could be as high as 25) and the few limits on risk that did exist were often not enforced by regulators who often were captured by powerful banking and corporate interests.

Table 8.1 Current account balances as percentage of GDP

	1991	*1992*	*1993*	*1994*	*1995*	*1996*	*1997*
Thailand	−8.01	−6.23	−5.68	−6.38	−8.35	−8.51	−2.35
Indonesia	−4.40	−2.46	−0.82	−1.54	−4.27	−3.30	−3.62
Malaysia	−14.01	−3.39	−10.11	−6.60	−8.85	−3.73	−3.50
South Korea	−3.16	−1.70	−0.16	−1.45	−1.91	−4.82	−1.90
Philippines	−2.46	−3.17	−6.69	−3.74	−5.06	−4.67	−6.07
Singapore	12.36	12.38	8.48	18.12	17.93	16.26	13.90
Hong Kong	6.58	5.26	8.14	1.98	−2.97	−2.43	−3.75
Taiwan	6.97	4.03	3.52	3.12	3.05	4.67	3.23
China	3.07	1.09	−2.19	1.16	0.03	0.52	3.61

Source: IMF (2011a).

The eventual results of such an approach should not be surprising to those familiar with the long history of international financial crises (or readers of this book). Foreign capital flowed into these countries, particularly hot money in short-term, dollar-denominated debt. Foreign investment grew between 5 and 15 percent a year, fueling domestic credit booms in which bank lending rose by between 17 and 30 percent a year from 1991 to 1996.[6] This in turn fed real estate and stock price bubbles throughout the region. Behind all of this lending and inflated assets were significant currency mismatch on the balance sheets of firms, which had often borrowed in dollars but earned their revenues in the local currency. When firms are exposed to currency mismatch, the banks that lent them money (money these banks had often borrowed in dollars) are also exposed. For example, in South Korea 56 percent of its total debt was denominated in dollars and 37 percent of this debt was short term.[7] Table 8.2 presents the ratio of foreign-denominated liabilities to foreign-denominated assets in East Asia. The growth of these ratios throughout the region indicates that currency mismatch was prevalent and that any devaluation of the currency could trigger a banking crisis.

Despite these weak fundamentals and dangerous levels of currency mismatch, a banking crisis in East Asia was not inevitable if the banks in the region had been making profitable loans and held fundamentally valuable assets. Unfortunately, this was not the case, as loan quality was extremely weak because of the extensive problem of moral hazard that existed throughout the region's banking systems. Moral hazard was largely unchecked by prudential regulation after the financial deregulation of the 1980s. Low capital adequacy requirements, little monitoring of risk, and few restrictions on speculation led to extremely risky lending behavior by banks.

Moral hazard also resulted from the prevalence of connected lending in the region. Like its banking systems, most industrial production is highly concentrated in a small number of firms throughout East Asia. Conglomerates that merge industrial and manufacturing firms with major banks are common. In South Korea, these conglomerates are referred to as *Chaebols*. The 30 largest

Table 8.2 Ratio of foreign liabilities to foreign assets

	1993	1994	1995	1996	1997
Thailand	6.93	7.73	7.81	11.03	8.12
Indonesia	2.95	4.01	4.26	4.24	5.43
Malaysia	0.83	1.40	1.44	1.48	2.22
Korea	2.98	2.97	3.31	3.75	2.51
Philippines	1.14	0.97	1.10	1.72	1.71
Singapore	1.51	1.62	1.66	1.62	1.38
Hong Kong	1.42	1.43	1.56	1.65	1.59
Taiwan	N/A	N/A	0.61	0.61	0.62
China	0.99	0.94	1.17	1.20	1.36

Source: Corsetti *et al.* (1999).

Chaebols controlled over 75 percent of the South Korean economy in the early 1990s. The idea behind these conglomerates, which were formed in the early stages of these economies' development, is that they would allow strategically important firms to overcome the lending problems associated with asymmetric information by allowing more information to flow between banks and their borrowers. Large conglomerates would also allow these firms to take advantage of economies of scale in finance in order to marshal the credit they would need to fund their huge investment needs. However, there is no bright line between "lending to those that you know best" and "crony capitalism," where credit is offered on the basis of relationships, not economic fundamentals. Unfortunately, there is substantial evidence that this is what the financial systems throughout East Asia had devolved into before the crisis. For example, even before the crisis began it is estimated that as many as 7 of the 30 largest *Chaebols* in South Korea were insolvent, yet were still borrowing at high levels.[8]

One final source of moral hazard in East Asia was the belief among banks that any large losses they incurred would eventually be assumed by the government in a bailout. Even in countries where explicit deposit insurance did not exist, implicit insurance in the form of government assurances (and from the "too big to fail" reality that was true for most large Asian banks) encouraged banks to operate as if the government owned a large share of any of their losses. Not a single bank in any of the four major crisis countries had ever been allowed to fail before the crisis struck. In the event that their governments did not have the resources to cover their losses, these banks could also reasonably expect to be bailed out indirectly by the IMF. As a result, there was little reason to emphasize loan quality before the crisis. Table 8.3 presents the level of non-performing loans for countries within the region. With the exception of China, the countries with the most bad loans before the crisis suffered the largest output losses during the crisis.[9]

These two crises—a currency crisis and a banking crisis—merged and expanded into the largest international twin crises in economic history. The disaster began in Thailand in July 1997 when growing fears about the stability of its financial system and the extent of asset bubbles triggered a speculative attack on

Table 8.3 Non-performing loans as a percentage of total lending

	End of 1996	End of 1997
Thailand	13	36
Indonesia	13	15
Malaysia	10	15
Korea	8	30
Philippines	14	7
Singapore	4	4
Hong Kong	3	1
Taiwan	4	N/A
China	14	N/A

Source: Column 1, Corsetti *et al.* (1999). Column 2, *Bloomberg*, November 11, 1997.

the Thai baht. These fears, and the capital flight of hot money, quickly spread to Indonesia and other smaller countries in the region.[10] However, it became obvious that something very serious was occurring only in October, when both Hong Kong and then South Korea, the largest economy in the region after Japan, began to suffer speculative attacks on their currencies.

The almost complete collapse of the financial systems in the four largest crisis countries took place remarkably quickly. As governments ran short of international reserves, they were one by one forced to devalue. But because of the amount of currency mismatch in the system, these devaluations triggered mass bankruptcies (by the end of 1997, nearly half of all South Korean firms were in default) and losses for banks that spurred further panic selling, capital flight, and devaluation.[11] The devaluations suffered by these countries were massive. Indonesia saw their currency fall by 75 percent in value versus the dollar, meaning that the real value of dollar-denominated debt quadrupled relative to the value of domestic assets. Most banks quickly became insolvent. For example, in Thailand 56 of the 58 largest banks were closed within three months of the beginning of the currency crisis.[12]

The banking crisis fueled declines in capital flows, asset prices, and the exchange rate that further worsened the banking crisis in a vicious cycle, as illustrated in Figure 8.3. The collapse of the financial system depressed credit, consumption, and investment. Output fell sharply while unemployment spiked. Meanwhile, governments in the region had their hands tied by the policy trap described earlier: contractionary policies might restore some confidence in the currency but would also increase interest rates and worsen the banking crisis, while expansionary policies would stimulate output and help banks but worsen the currency crisis.

Contagion is also an important part of the East Asian crisis. Within 18 months, speculative attacks and capital flight had spread not only throughout Asia but as far as Brazil and Russia. While there was a great deal of discussion at the beginning of the crisis about whether it was "manufactured" by large international financial institutions, what is clear is that these speculative attacks followed declining economic fundamentals, and not vice versa.[13] For example, Froot et al. (2001) find that foreign investors did not begin to withdraw significant amounts of their capital from crisis countries before the currency crises in the region had already begun to build.

Regarding the exact source of the contagion, it is clear that trade linkages played an important role within Asia as all of these countries traded heavily with each other and also with Japan, which was also undergoing its own recession. Additionally, financial linkages played a role in spreading contagion as Japan was a major source of capital flows through what is known as the *carry trade*, where investors would borrow in Japan at low interest rates and then invest them in other East Asian countries at much higher interest rates. (One of the reasons this was profitable was because of the fixed exchange rate regimes in the region.) Kaminsky and Reinhart (2000) contend that the losses incurred by Japanese investors because of the recession there caused credit-constrained investors to abandon the carry trade, which then contributed to capital flight and a chain of defaults throughout East Asia in the period leading up to the crisis.

Of course, it is always difficult to completely rule out the role of beliefs in driving the contagion. Many studies have found that fundamentals alone are insufficient in explaining either the timing or the size of the crisis.[14] The fact that the crisis spread outside Asia to countries with much different economic fundamentals suggests that self-fulfilling panic and herding played some role. Others have argued that a wake-up call phenomenon took place where a crisis in a small number of countries raised doubts about the "Asian Miracle" and policies throughout the region.[15]

Recovery from the crisis was relatively quick in coming but not as strong as hoped for. Growth between 2000 and 2006 in the four large crisis countries was 2.5 percent lower than in the pre-crisis period from 1990 to 1996. However, South Korea stands out as an example of how to deal with and recover from a financial crisis. South Korea showed incredible flexibility in responding quickly to its crisis. It quickly renegotiated its sovereign debt with its creditors so that they would eventually be fully repaid. It closed 40 percent of all banks because of insolvency (including one of the largest *Chaebols*) and helped recapitalize the others while forcing them to write off bad loans (the total bailout cost for the banking system totaled 30 percent of GDP). Non-performing loans after this recapitalization fell from over 13 percent to just 3.3 percent.[16] South Korea implemented an ambitious plan of prudential regulation aimed at increasing transparency, capital requirements, and reducing risk. The South Korean central bank was granted more independence and its banking system was opened to foreign competition. All of these actions, and the speed with which they were enacted, helped restore confidence and allowed the South Korean exchange rate to regain some of its value while lowering interest rates, easing both the banking and economic crisis. Problems with crony capitalism, too-big-to-fail banks, and weak accounting standards remain. However, South Korea moved along the road to complete recovery more quickly than most of its East Asian neighbors because of its ability to make hard decisions and implement difficult policies.

International reserve accumulation and undervalued exchange rates

One of the many lessons that emerging market economies seem to have learned during the East Asian crisis is that the dangers of running short of international reserves is simply too costly to contemplate. Table 8.4 presents data on the 20 largest international reserve holdings by country. Emerging market countries are heavily represented on this list, particularly if weighed against their relatively smaller economies. China clearly stands out. In late 2011 it held more than $3.1 trillion in reserves (more than $2,300 per Chinese citizen), up from just $18 billion 20 years ago and $146 billion ten years ago. However, China is not the only foreign reserve hoarder. The top ten countries on this list hold two-thirds of the world's total foreign reserve holdings. Regarding the denomination of these foreign reserves, two-thirds are held in dollars assets, one-quarter in euros, and the rest in pounds, yen, and *special drawing rights* (or SDRs, an international reserve asset created by the IMF).

In the past, a widely used rule of thumb was that a country needed to have enough foreign reserves to cover three months of imports in order to protect its currency against a speculative attack and devaluation. Clearly, many countries on this list are holding international reserves at much higher levels than this rule of thumb suggests. Empirical studies also suggest that it is impossible to reconcile such high levels of foreign reserve holdings with an "insurance motive" to protect against speculative attacks, particularly in Asian countries.[17]

So why are emerging market economies holding so many international reserves? One reason may be that for emerging economies with less developed capital markets, holding international reserves is not just a way to insure against a speculative attack and capital flight but it is also a way to prevent some foreign capital from reaching their private sector during capital inflow booms. These foreign capital inflows, particularly those in foreign currencies, can encourage liability dollarization or even outright dollarization in the economy if they become large enough. In essence, holding international reserves can be a means for central banks to moderate the procyclical flows of capital when financial systems are not strong enough to handle them. Dominguez (2010) finds that, in fact, countries with less developed financial markets do hold more international reserves relative to the size of their economy.

Table 8.4 Largest international reserve holdings, December 2011

Country name	International reserves ($ billions)
China	3,181.10
Japan	1,302.88
Russia	513.98
Taiwan	385.55
Brazil	356.33
South Korea	311.34
India	292.77
Hong Kong	285.41
Germany	263.02
Singapore	245.49
Italy	187.30
Algeria	185.90
Thailand	178.55
France	172.21
United States	149.25
Mexico	149.21
Malaysia	134.08
United Kingdom	123.59
Iran	120.00
Indonesia	111.90

Source: IMF (2011a).

A second reason central banks hold large levels of international reserves is to serve as an emergency fund for the government. By holding high levels of international reserves, central banks have more resources to serve as a lender of last resort, to take aggressive actions with monetary policy, or even help stabilize government spending during a downturn.

However, the most important reason many emerging markets appear to be hoarding international reserves is that many countries have been following a purposeful policy of maintaining undervalued exchange rates. As we saw in Figure 8.2, an integral component of many export promotion strategies has been to run large current account surpluses while maintaining significant levels of capital inflows. According to the balance of payments, the only way to do this is to accumulate large levels of international reserves. Aizenman (2007) summarizes the empirical evidence and concludes that this is the primary factor driving international reserve accumulations in emerging economies, particularly in China.

The potential benefits of undervalued exchange rates are fairly straightforward: export promotion coupled with capital inflows encourages productivity and financial development that increase economic growth. The success of export promotion strategies throughout the world, particularly in Asia, seems to support this tactic.

However, there are also significant dangers and costs associated with a policy of sustained undervalued exchange rates and international reserve accumulation. The first is that it is expensive. One measure of the opportunity cost of holding reserves is the difference between the return on the liquid foreign assets that the central bank holds and the much higher return it could collect from holding less liquid domestic assets. In essence, an undervalued exchange rate policy necessitates poorer emerging economies providing cheap loans to the largest and richest developed countries. Jeanne (2007) estimates that the opportunity cost of holding international reserves for an emerging market economy can vary between 1 and 1.5 percent of GDP a year—quite large for countries that have many pressing fiscal needs.

A second cost to international reserve hoarding is that by facilitating foreign capital inflows, it can also fuel booms in money and credit, leading to inflation and asset bubbles if the central bank is not vigilant in restricting credit growth. Easy credit also means that many of these loans may be driven by moral hazard and adverse selection, not sound economic fundamentals. For example, in 2011, the early signs of higher inflation and a housing bubble were appearing in China, both of which are likely directly linked to the undervalued exchange rate policy followed by the People's Bank of China (its central bank).

Another set of costs associated with an undervalued exchange rate policy is the inevitable consequences, both expected and unexpected, of manipulating the price and market system. Keeping a currency undervalued for a sustained period distorts many economic decisions. From the point of view of the domestic economy, it increases the prices of imports, making consumption more expensive and reducing effective standards of living. It also increases the costs of imported commodities and investment goods, potentially reducing productivity. Finally, it can reduce the efficiency of the financial system. The need to maintain an undervalued exchange rate is often used as an excuse to implement policies of financial repression—such as high required reserve requirements, credit restrictions, etc.—that will decrease financial efficiency and could limit economic growth in the long run.

There are costs to the global economy as well if every emerging market economy tries to maintain undervalued exchange rates, run current account surpluses, and accumulate international reserves—namely, that such a strategy depends crucially on there being developed countries willing to run large trade deficits and accumulate large amounts of debt. During the 2000s, the United States and Europe were willing to play these roles. However, the global financial crisis and sky-rocketing sovereign debt levels among these countries suggest that this situation is not sustainable.

Back in 2005, Ben Bernanke (before he was chairman of the US Federal Reserve) warned of the dangers of this scenario and what he called a "global savings glut."[18] He foresaw the dangers of developed countries being inundated with cheap money, flowing in large part from the hoarding of international reserves and the purposeful policy of maintaining undervalued exchange rates by emerging countries' central banks. While this is primarily true of China, it is by no means alone in following these policies. By encouraging overconsumption, excessive debt, and inflated asset prices in developed countries, Bernanke worried that this "beggar-thy-neighbor" policy would not be sustainable. Eventually debt levels in developed economies would reach levels that would increase the probability of sovereign debt crises and require a sharp reduction in spending. This would not only put economic growth in the developed world at risk, it would also put growth in emerging economies at risk because they need markets for the exports they are producing. This is very much what happened, only much more dramatically than Bernanke could have predicted, during the 2007 global financial crisis and the European debt crisis in Greece, Ireland, and elsewhere in 2010. While these crises have primarily impacted the developed world, they have also slowed growth in emerging markets by roughly 2 percent a year between 2008 and 2010.

More than the costs of the global financial crisis alone, the policy of maintaining undervalued exchange rates followed by China and many other emerging economies directly threatens economic development in these countries in other ways. Despite high levels of economic growth, the citizens in these countries have enjoyed much slower growth in real measures of standards of living and quality of life. Households find themselves faced with high costs for imported goods and commodities, disincentives to consume, and low returns on their domestic savings that distort economic decisions. The fact that many of the benefits of growth are not spread more widely may eventually weaken the commitment of the public to market-based reform. Many emerging market economies recognize the need to wean themselves off export dominance and international reserve hoarding and move to an economy that focuses more on domestic consumption and savings. But this is not an easy transition to make while maintaining the high rates of output growth that many of these countries have become accustomed to and need to ensure political stability.[19]

The role of the IMF in financial crises

With the increased frequency of international financial crises, the role of the IMF in serving as an international lender of last resort has received a great deal of attention in the last few years. The IMF and its role in the international financial system has evolved significantly since its creation. It was founded in 1944 to be the oversight organization of the Bretton Woods system of fixed exchange rates. When Bretton Woods broke down in the early 1970s, the IMF became an organization in search of a mission. It seemingly found this mission in the 1980s during the Latin American debt crisis when the IMF identified a need for an international lender of last resort that could provide low-interest loans to countries with short-term liquidity needs in return for *structural adjustment reforms*—microeconomic market reforms aimed at increasing efficiency and productivity—and *austerity reforms*—macroeconomic reforms aimed at restoring the sustainability of a country's fiscal and monetary policies. In addition to conditional lending, the IMF also provides "surveillance" (better thought of as information gathering in an effort to provide better financial transparency) and technical economic advice to emerging market economies.

The IMF's conditional lending is controversial and has been criticized across the political spectrum. From the left there has been a great deal of criticism regarding the number and type of conditions attached to IMF loans. Some critics see these conditions as infringements on the rights of sovereign nations that force free-market capitalism and globalization on countries when they are most vulnerable. This is the complaint most often voiced by rowdy protestors at the IMF's and World Bank's annual meetings.

A more nuanced version of this complaint is that the IMF too often imposes conditions it cannot enforce nor has any business trying to enforce. In the early years of conditional lending, the IMF attached an average of three structural adjustment conditions to the average IMF loan. By the 1990s, this number had jumped to 12 conditions. This issue came to a head during the East Asian crisis when the IMF imposed an unprecedented number of conditions on its lending. For example, Indonesia accepted 140 structural adjustment conditions with their loan, including things such as requirements to deregulate gasoline and plywood markets. This "grocery list" of reforms alienated many East Asian countries who felt that they were being punished; or worse, that some of these conditions were being imposed by other members of the IMF, particularly the United States and European countries, in order to further their own domestic economic interests. As a result, excessive conditionality weakened the political will to implement the most-needed reforms the IMF requested.

The problem from the point of view of most economists is not that the IMF imposes conditions on their loans. The IMF is not an aid organization; it must be repaid if it is to function, and asking for reforms is a form of collateral that the IMF needs in order to increase the chances that it will be repaid. In addition, the IMF cannot reform countries preemptively; crises are the only time that the IMF has leverage with many recalcitrant countries in order to get them to implement difficult reforms. Finally, and most importantly, there is solid empirical evidence that IMF conditionality does increase growth.[20] The problem here is that many of the things the IMF has asked for in the past are not crucially important and the IMF has no expertise in the area that would justify asking for them (it is unlikely that the IMF has a plywood expert on staff). The biggest danger of excessive conditionality is that the conditions that are important and are in areas where the IMF does have expertise—particularly fiscal policy, monetary policy, and financial system reform—may be ignored along with the less important conditions when too many of them are imposed.

Since the East Asian crisis, the IMF has become increasingly sensitive to these criticisms and has implemented reforms to limit "mission creep." It has issued new directives explicitly limiting its mission to crisis management and short-term lending and away from microeconomic structural adjustment outside of the financial system. In addition, the IMF has announced their intention to more heavily emphasize surveillance over conditionality, meaning that it wants to be more heavily involved in providing technical advice before a crisis strikes than in intervening only after a crisis has begun. In the words of Barry Eichengreen (1999), the IMF needs to become "less of a fireman and more of a policeman." In 2008, the IMF did create a new program that provides three-month loans to countries without the usual conditionality and time-consuming bureaucratic requirements in an attempt to create more nimble and proactive interactions between the IMF and emerging economies.

Others on the right of the political spectrum criticize the IMF for its overly generous lending that they see as encouraging moral hazard which increases, not decreases, the frequency of crises.[21] Because the IMF so readily acts as a lender of last resort for economies in crisis, policymakers within these countries do not incorporate the full risks of the policies that they enact (or fail to enact), counting on a loan from the IMF to prevent a disaster if a crisis strikes. This is likely to be particularly true regarding the adoption of prudential regulation. Credit growth and financial development will be somewhat slower, but more stable, when quality prudential regulations are in place. When easy bailouts from the IMF are available, policymakers are more willing to accept the risk of crises (and less willing to adopt and enforce prudential regulation) in order to gain more economic growth in the short run.[22]

Moral hazard from IMF lending can also trickle down to individuals within countries. Bailouts at the national level from the IMF provide governments with resources for bailouts of individual banks, investors, and corporations, all of which encourages riskier behavior. As a result, IMF bailouts are implicitly providing free crisis insurance to individuals, firms, and banks. For example, IMF lending largely financed the bank bailouts in East Asia, helping governments to assume a large portion of the losses associated with the reckless lending East Asian banks conducted in the early 1990s.

Another example of the way that IMF loans finance moral hazard is through its consistent lending to "repeat offenders": countries that repeatedly rely upon IMF lending over extended periods. Over 70 countries have received "emergency" loans from the IMF for 20 years or more.[23] The reasons behind this are many. First, it is hard for the IMF to say no to poorer countries that are in crisis because these crises represent real human suffering that is hard to ignore. In addition, it is hard for an intergovernmental bureaucracy such as the IMF to get tough on countries given both the geopolitical and internal politics that necessarily go into policymaking. Many countries are too big, and too important, to be allowed to fail. Finally, the financial structure of the IMF necessitates that loans be repaid. The IMF is not an aid agency but instead has a fixed portfolio of resources to lend. As a result, the IMF has often found itself bullied into providing new loans in an effort to avoid default on existing loans. The sordid story of Argentina's long battle with the IMF over the loans it defaulted on during its crisis in 2001 is a case study of how little leverage the IMF really does have over a country once it grants that country a large loan.

The worry is that all of this repeat lending not only increases moral hazard behavior, but it also reduces the incentives for reform and may actually encourage corruption. Knack (2004), among other similar studies, finds a correlation between higher levels of foreign aid and both higher corruption and lower-quality government institutions.

While these criticisms are quite persuasive, ending conditional lending by the IMF is an unacceptably dangerous option. Emerging market economies need an international lender of last resort because they suffer from an inherent lack of resources and credibility at the same time that they are more vulnerable to shocks because of their weaker institutions. Bailouts during financial crises are a necessary evil, and moral hazard is one of the prices that must be paid. All of the historical economic evidence suggests that the dangers of not having a lender of last resort outweigh the dangers of moral hazard. Timely and sizable bailouts coupled with the imposition of appropriate prudential regulations can significantly reduce the costs of a financial crisis, as seen in South Korea following the East Asian crisis. From the IMF's perspective, the primary emphasis must increasingly be on facilitating the adoption of these prudential regulations in exchange for receiving a bailout in order to keep moral hazard to a minimum.

Other actions should also be taken to mitigate moral hazard, such as allowing the IMF more political independence to say no to repeat borrowers or to those countries that do not comply with the conditions attached to past loans. But such reforms would require political will from the member countries of the IMF that may not be realistically possible.

A final group of critics voice a variety of less ideological, more pragmatic criticisms of the IMF related to the policies and policymaking process that the IMF has adopted. Regarding its policies, many critics have complained about the IMF's adherence to what Paul Krugman (2008) refers to as "the confidence game": in response to financial crises, the IMF imposes austerity conditions on emerging economies aimed at reducing inflation, cutting budget deficits, and raising interest rates in an effort to restore the confidence of foreign investors and end capital flight. However, these austerity conditions can make the economic crisis worse by lowering aggregate demand and domestic confidence.

In other words, the confidence game necessitates the following of anti-Keynesian policies to mollify the fears of foreign investors at the expense of domestic citizens. Many critics point to the East Asian crisis as an example of how the IMF's confidence game approach is misguided. The East Asian crisis actually worsened after the IMF made its loans and imposed austerity conditions.

On the other hand, the Keynesian policies adopted in developed countries during recessions are not likely to work in most emerging markets during a financial crisis. Emerging market economies are characterized by weaker institutions, debt intolerance, and debt that is heavily short term and denominated in foreign currency. Because of this, most emerging economies lack credibility, meaning that any loss of confidence is likely to be much more costly and greatly magnify the size of any financial crisis. Expansionary fiscal and monetary policies of a Keynesian nature, such as those typically enacted in rich countries during a crisis (even those that arise from the government serving as a lender of last resort) are likely to trigger inflation and debt fears that will increase capital flight and interest rates. In other words, there is unlikely to be a conflict for emerging economies between restoring foreign investor confidence and stabilizing output. They have to achieve the first or they will not be able to achieve the second.

However, this does not mean that the austerity conditions imposed by the IMF during the East Asian crisis were the right policies to follow. In hindsight, it is clear that fiscal policy had little to do with the crisis; instead, it was rigid exchange rate pegs to an appreciating dollar coupled with weak bank fundamentals that resulted from a lack of prudential regulation. As a result, imposing fiscal austerity did nothing to restore investor confidence but only led to higher interest rates that worsened the banking crisis and also discouraged consumption and investment. In South Korea, austerity imposed by the IMF increased interest rates from 9 percent to over 40 percent. The IMF did quickly reverse itself regarding these austerity conditions after they observed the results, but unfortunately a great deal of economic damage had already been done.

These kinds of policy mistakes by the IMF are related to another set of charges by its critics regarding the process in which policy is created at the IMF. These critics, such as Nobel Laureate and former vice president of the World Bank Joseph Stiglitz (2002), as well as Jeffry Sachs (2005), argue that the IMF is too insular with little outside counsel or creative thinking. Too often decisions are imposed in a top-down manner without any information about details on the ground. The result is "one-size-fits-all" policy decisions that often lead to the IMF trying to solve the last financial crisis, not the current financial crisis. Hence, the conditions imposed on East Asian in 1997 looked quite similar to the conditions that should have been imposed in Latin America in the 1980s.

Part of the reason for this inflexible thinking, according to critics, is the relative lack of influence that emerging market economies have had in IMF decision making. Developed countries, and often the large financial interests that they represent, dominate the IMF. To address with this criticism, in 2010 the IMF's *quota system*, or the contributions each member country makes to the fund's loan portfolio and which also determines their proportion of voting rights, was reformed in order to give large emerging economies more influence. Emerging market countries saw their share of the quota increase to 42 percent of the total. The US controls 17 percent of the quota, while European countries control 32 percent. China has the largest quota of any emerging country with 4 percent of the total.

In addition to reforming its quota system, the IMF has attempted to become more open in other ways. It has changed its bureaucratic structure to incorporate more debate and outside expertise. It has also placed more emphasis on building political capital and opening lines of consistent communication with more emerging market economies. In addition, it has attempted to move away from a "cold shower" approach to reform by encouraging more staged and gradual restructuring. Finally, it has also developed more early warning systems to encourage policy reforms before a crisis takes place. Many of these changes in the IMF's operations have yet to be tested in the heat of a large international financial crisis among emerging economies, however. History tells us that this day will come.

Conclusions

Financial crises have become more frequent within emerging market economies, in large part because many countries have deregulated their financial systems and opened their capital accounts without first having the proper prudential regulations in place. The increasing importance of finance in economic development has magnified the macroeconomic impact of bad policy, fragile financial fundamentals, and volatile beliefs because of a lack of credibility. The danger of over-valued exchange rates and weak banking systems has never been more apparent than during the East Asian twin crises. Countries held as models of development collapsed in short order because they failed to vigilantly manage their exchange rates and mitigate currency mismatch and moral hazard within their banking systems.

Today, emerging markets have under-learned one of the most important lessons from the East Asian crisis, but they also have over-learned another important lesson. Many emerging market economies (as well as many developed countries) still do not appear to have sufficiently taken to heart the dangers of failing to monitor the financial fundamentals of their banking systems through a comprehensive system of prudential regulation and supervision. In this book we have repeatedly returned to emphasizing the dangers of failing to ensure financial transparency, capital adequacy requirements, sustainable credit growth, limits on short-term foreign-denominated debt, and minimizing currency mismatch. While the importance of prudential regulation is obvious, the fact that crises continue to occur suggest that, as the old joke goes, denial is not just a river in Egypt.

The lesson from the East Asian crisis that may have been over-learned is just as important for the world economy. In an effort to protect themselves against currency crises and encourage export growth, many emerging economies have hoarded international reserves in order to keep their exchange rates undervalued. This is a strategy that does not make sense from the point of view of the world economy as a whole, and as a result puts every individual country at risk. This is because it creates an unsustainable imbalance between emerging economies that run large current account surpluses and accumulate international reserves while asking developed countries to run large current account deficits and accumulate debt. The imbalances created by this emerging market savings glut contributed greatly to the 2007 global financial crisis and the 2010 European debt crisis. A real worry is that if emerging countries fail to rebalance their economies toward more appropriate real exchange rates and domestic consumption, the next series of crises will be in emerging market economies. This could occur when the developed world becomes less dependent on debt and a less hospitable market for these countries' exports, which make up a disproportionate share of emerging market growth. Or it could occur because the expansionary pressures of these policies in emerging economies will create inflation, asset bubbles, and banking crises like we have seen many times in the past.

Regardless of when and where the next financial crises take place, the hope is that the IMF has learned lessons from previous financial crises and can serve as a more effective lender of last resort while at the same time limiting the amount of moral hazard and risk it encourages through its bailouts. The IMF's attempts to create more consistent and proactive engagement with emerging market economies are a step in the right direction. The most beneficial change the IMF could make would be to act (and be seen) as more of an independent arbiter, having the power to say no to countries that either fail to comply with important loan conditions or who do not take appropriate steps to limit risk in their own financial system. Of course, good economics of this sort requires large amounts of political will which, unfortunately, is typically observed less frequently than financial crises.

Part IV

Describing financial systems in emerging regions of the world

9 Financial systems in Sub-Saharan Africa

Overview

This final part of the book takes a more detailed look at financial systems in four principal regions of the emerging world. The objective here is to understand different financial systems in different countries and to appreciate their unique paths to financial development. But just as importantly, the objective is to illustrate the important themes developed in previous chapters of the book in order to come to a deeper understanding of the crucial factors involved in financial development across emerging market economies.

Informal finance in Sub-Saharan Africa

Sub-Saharan Africa (SSA) is the poorest region of the world. With a population of 880 million people, per-capita income in the region was only $706 in 2011, which is less than half the per-capita income level in Asia. Over 60 percent of the population lives in moderate poverty (less than $2.50 a day) and more than 40 percent live in extreme poverty (less than $1.25 a day).[1] However, aside from a recent slowdown in growth associated with the global financial crisis, economic growth in SSA has generally been strong for the last two decades and stayed strong in 2011 at 5.5 percent. Eight of the 20 fastest-growing economies in the world between 2005 and 2009 are in SSA.[2]

However, this strong rate of economic development has not been associated with broad-based financial development. According to the World Bank, more than 80 percent of the population in SSA has no access to formal finance through banks, financial markets, and other intermediaries such as insurance firms.[3] Figure 9.1 presents data on deposit and loan accounts per 1,000 adults for commercial banks, which illustrates just how "underbanked" SSA is relative to other emerging market economies and developed countries. Any discussion of finance in SSA has to begin with a discussion of informal finance, which is the only form of finance available to most Africans. This primarily means saving and lending using family and friends, moneylenders, trade and shop credit, and other person-to-person methods of finance.

To understand why informal finance is so common, it is first important to understand why formal finance is not more common in SSA. The primary reason is weak institutions that create a very risky economic environment that discourages financial intermediation. Risk is created by unstable political and social structures in many African countries. It also comes from unstable macroeconomic environments, where high budget deficits, high inflation, current account deficits, excessive regulation, undiversified economies, and a general lack of efficiency have characterized most SSA countries since their independences in the 1960s. Most importantly, risk comes from a lack of information. As we talked about extensively in Chapter 2, information is the most important input into finance because it is the only way to mitigate the risks associated with asymmetric information. In most African countries few formal information systems, such as credit registries, exist for people to accumulate information about themselves in order to qualify for formal loans. As a result, the risks associated with adverse selection and moral hazard are rarely alleviated, leading to pervasive credit rationing and high costs of credit intermediation.

The most important economic fact of life for those living in poverty is that a person living on $2 a day on average does not mean that this person receives $2 each and every day. In fact, the poorer a household is, the more variable its income is likely to be for many reasons. The poor are less likely to work for wages in the formal sector, more likely to have to migrate and/or rely on

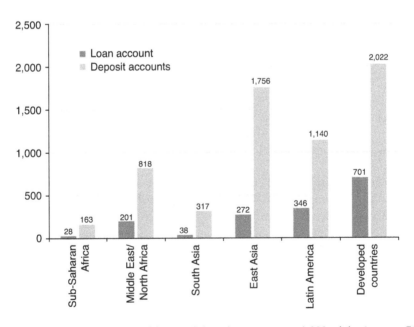

Figure 9.1 Access to formal loan and deposit accounts per 1,000 adults (source: CGAP/ World Bank (2010)).

seasonal work, more likely to rely upon agriculture which is notoriously volatile (particularly in the African climate), less likely to have adequate health care, more exposed to diseases such as HIV/AIDS, and more likely to live in danger-ous areas. These factors, and many more like them, mean that the incomes of the poor are inherently irregular and that economic risk is a central factor in their lives.

Because of their irregular incomes and minimal wealth, managing risk and the timing of money flows becomes the primary objective of finance for poor households. The poor have a regular need to borrow in order to feed themselves, pay for school fees, pay for medical or other emergencies, or to purchase large items such as a house. In SSA, none of these activities can be consistently financed through bank loans. The poor also have a need to save which is also very difficult because their savings options must allow for small, liquid, easy, cheap, and convenient transactions. This rules out bank deposits, which can be prohibitively expensive in many countries. Using bank accounts is also difficult for those with little education or for those living in rural areas without access to branch banks.

As a result, the poor meet their financing needs through informal finance by borrowing and lending to neighbors, moneylenders, pawnbrokers, and shop-keepers. Collins *et al.* (2009) in their book *Portfolios of the Poor* find that the typical South African household they surveyed was using ten different forms of informal finance at any one time on average. Unfortunately, these different forms of informal finance are often expensive, either because of high direct fees or in terms of hidden costs (for example, a shop that provides easy credit is likely to charge higher prices for its goods). Collins *et al.* report that the interest rates on informal loans averaged 30 percent a month in South Africa, although this is somewhat overstated because these loans do not typically incorporate late fees or compounding.[4]

Informal savings also is expensive for the poor; most poor households pay to save, meaning they receive negative interest rates. The reason, once again, is that there are significant transaction costs associated with the small and flexible methods of saving required by the poor. The poor need to have their liquid wealth immediately available whenever they might need it in order to cover any fluctuations in their spending or income. However, they also cannot risk holding their savings themselves where someone might steal it or a family member might spend it. As a result, they are willing to pay a fee to people such as money-lenders to protect it for them, as counterintuitive as that seems to those who are accustomed to operating in developed financial systems where we usually are paid, not pay, to save.

Informal finance has other drawbacks in addition to its high price. It is unreli-able because it is dependent on the goodwill of individuals. And very impor-tantly, it creates very little information record, which is needed so that over time a person can gradually qualify for cheaper and more reliable loans in the formal sector. In the end, this reliance on informal finance creates a financial poverty trap that contributes to keeping the poor poor.

One of the amazing things about the informal financial systems of Africa is how well they work given all of the obstacles they must overcome. Collins *et al.* report that the South African households they surveyed had a median value of assets of only $792 at the end of the year, but these households had financial turnover (meaning inflows plus outflows) of $6,264, which is a much higher rate of activity than you would see in the portfolios of rich households. The poor accomplish this by piecing together numerous informal methods of finance. They save in many straightforward ways, such as by lending to family and neighbors (in exchange for reciprocity when they need to borrow) or paying in advance for shop credit. But they do it in more unusual ways as well. In South Africa, one of the most important ways of saving is through burial societies. Because of the elaborate, long, and expensive funerals that are required in their culture, paying for a burial is one of the biggest financial emergencies that a South African household can face (often costing more than $1,500, or nearly a year's salary for many households). To insure against these expenses, over 80 percent of South Africa's poor belong to a burial society. Members of these societies regularly contribute to a fund that pays them in the event of a death in their family. (Some burial societies rely on contributions only after a member experiences a death in the family, but this form of burial society has higher incidents of reneging, for obvious reasons.) Collins *et al.* find that the burial societies they follow in South Africa provide excellent rates of return to savings. However, these high returns likely reflect the high degree of risk associated with burial societies: 10 percent of them fail to meet their obligations. Thus, even informal financial arrangements designed to reduce risk often end up magnifying the risk the poor face in other ways.

Rotating savings and credit associations (ROSCAs) are also becoming much more popular in SSA, although they have existed in the region in one form or another for over 400 years. ROSCAs are small, informal savings groups (typically 15–30 individuals) where people regularly make payments into a pool and periodically receive the entire pool of funds on either a rotating or sometimes on a lottery basis. There are many different variations of ROSCAs. In some, you can pay more into the pool to increase your chances of winning. Other ROSCAs accumulate funds over time and make loans to its members.

Regardless of the exact form, ROSCAs have many advantages. They provide members with a way to pre-commit to saving. Contributing to a ROSCA is often safer than hoarding cash. The return on ROSCAs tend to be large—often 20 to 30 percent a year. Finally, these groups facilitate social bonding, create financial linkages, and help develop trust among its members. When viewed this way, ROSCAs and other group savings and lending activities can be seen as an evolutionary step in financial development. However, ROSCAs are no replacement for formal finance. They are quite risky because of fraud and thievery, they offer savers little flexibility, they are short term which prohibits their use in saving for a house or an education, and they cannot serve as a buffer in case of emergency because their payouts are unpredictable.[5]

Formal finance is not just discouraged by risk and a lack of information in SSA. It is also discouraged by a lack of quality institutions. Every African country suffers, to a greater or lesser extent, from some of the poor institutional structures discussed in Chapter 3 that inhibit financial development. A few of these factors are particularly harmful in Africa. The first is the lack of legal structures that facilitate trust and credit. Many legal systems in SSA fail to adequately protect creditor rights in a timely manner and do not encourage transparency and the sharing of financial information. In addition, as stressed by Hernando de Soto (2000), many countries in SSA fail to build stable systems to create legal titles for assets such as land, making it difficult to use these assets as collateral in order to reduce risk and encourage credit creation. In part, the lack of individual property rights to land reflects Africa's tribal heritage that emphasizes communal property. The absence of quality legal institutions and title creation processes increases risk, exacerbates credit rationing, and increases the costs of credit intermediation.

The credit rationing caused by weak institutions hurts African households by preventing them from making investments in home improvements, education, and small entrepreneurial ventures. Credit rationing is particularly harmful to small and medium enterprises (SMEs) in Africa.[6] According to the World Bank, over 41 percent of small firms are credit constrained, while 28 percent of medium and 12 percent of large firms are credit constrained. African SMEs are much more likely to report that access to finance is a major constraint on their operations than firms in other regions of the world.[7] These credit constraints are imposed by banks and financial markets, but they are also imposed by international trading partners as evidenced by the relative scarcity of trade credit given to African firms.

The credit rationing of SMEs in SSA reduces growth in the region in many different ways, but principally by reducing investment. For example, one of the primary financing vehicles that many SMEs in other countries use to finance investment is leasing. This is an attractive option for smaller firms because leasing limits the amount of money the firm must pay up-front and instead allows the firm to pay for capital using the cash flows it generates. Unfortunately, because of poor legal systems that fail to protect the property rights of leasers as well as prohibitive tax laws, leasing is not a viable option in most African countries. By reducing investment, credit rationing also limits the ability of African firms to take advantage of economies of scale and is one important reason that African firms tend to be smaller and less efficient than their counterparts in other countries. The credit rationing of SMEs also limits entrepreneurship, technology transfer, and job training, all of which reduce productivity growth and economic development in general.

In the case of small-scale agriculture, the inherent risk associated with farming (or herding) means that farmers are even more credit constrained than other businesses. In addition, farmers are hurt the most by a lack of legal title to land, making it impossible to use their largest asset to collateralize loans. Because they lack finance to support them between growing seasons, farmers are often forced to sell their entire crop immediately at harvest, when prices are at their lowest, and buy seed right before planting, when prices are at their highest.

While farmer co-ops are commonly used in Africa in order to help individual farmers by pooling resources to facilitate borrowing and lending, once again a lack of legal institutions makes this an unreliable form of insurance for most small African farmers.

In terms of improving access to formal finance for African households and firms, two reforms would be most beneficial. First, governments in the region need to do a better job of ensuring the availability of better information. The best method for doing this is to establish credit bureaus and property registries that collect information about financial histories and legal titles for public use. Today, only 60 percent of countries in SSA have credit bureaus and those that do exist only cover a small fraction of the population. One of the biggest hurdles to doing this is the need to first have government information systems that collect basic information, including birth registries, on all of its citizens, something that many SSA countries are currently unable to do. Second, legal systems have to be strengthened in ways that create and protect property rights for asset owners and for creditors. These legal systems not only have to exist, but they have to be able to provide services in a timely manner because protection delayed is protection denied. To cite one example of how slowly some legal systems can work, in Mozambique it takes a creditor an average of 540 days to recover a debt once the borrower declares bankruptcy.[8] While these two reforms seem only common sense, to implement them African governments need to prioritize investing in quality bureaucratic systems, which has been a historical problem in a region of the world where government jobs have often been seen as a means of patronage, not as a source of economic efficiency.

Formal finance in Sub-Saharan Africa

Formal financial systems in SSA are as underdeveloped, if not more so, than their economies in general. As is generally true in poorer countries, SSA financial systems are dominated by banks. Banking systems in SSA typically have a small number of relatively large banks that are usually foreign-owned. Only 19 of the world's 500 largest banks are African.[9] SSA banks have high levels of liquid assets relative to their comparatively low levels of lending, charge high interest rates, and are more profitable (not adjusted for risk) than their counterparts in other regions. Only one-third of SSA countries have stock markets, and those stock markets that do exist (outside of South Africa) are not diversified and have low trading volumes. The same holds for bond markets, which are typically dominated by government issuances. Access to insurance is rare. As a result of all of these factors, long-term finance in Africa is sparse.

What are the driving factors behind this basic lack of financial development? With regard to banks, the primary reason is the high-risk, high-cost environment banks must operate in. Credit risk in SSA is high for the reasons discussed previously: volatile incomes, macroeconomic and political instability, legal uncertainty, and a lack of quality information and collateral. Operating costs for banks are also high for many of the same reasons: a lack of collateral and information increases the costs of loan generation, the relatively small scale of many deposits and loans keep transaction costs large, small and undiversified firms and farms lead to high rates of default, and a lack of efficient legal systems keeps the costs of enforcing loan contracts and collateral forfeiture high.

An additional factor is also at work in discouraging finance in Africa, which is the fact that it is the least densely populated area of the world. Nearly 65 percent of the population in SSA lives in rural areas, as opposed to less than 50 percent in the rest of the world.[10] To make one illustrative comparison, Texas is the median US state in terms of population density; Botswana is roughly the size of Texas but with one-eighth as many people. Because of Africa's incredible geographic size and the fact that transportation and communication infrastructure are limited, the per-person cost of delivering financial services on the continent is very high.[11] High costs lead to high interest rates; between 2000 and 2004 the net interest margin (loan rates minus deposit rates) on bank loans were 6.5 percent in SSA as compared to 4.8 percent for the rest of the world.[12] High costs also drive up the fees for holding deposit accounts at banks. Four African countries—Malawi, Sierra Leone, Uganda, and Zimbabwe—have annual fees on bank accounts that exceed 20 percent of per-capita GDP (refer back to Table 3.1).[13] These higher risks and costs are the main factors limiting the access most Africans have to formal financial markets. Higher risks and limited competition also drive up profit margins for banks; return on bank equity is 20.1 percent in SSA relative to 8.5 percent in the rest of the world.[14]

Limited competition and high risk also drive another important aspect of African banking: relatively low levels of lending relative to their holdings of liquid assets. African banks lend less than their counterparts in other countries with the same amounts of capital. Private credit averages less than 18 percent of GDP across SSA, compared to an average of nearly 60 percent across the world and 100 percent or higher in emerging market economies with relatively developed financial systems, such as China.[15] Credit rationing certainly accounts for a great deal of this scarcity of lending. However, African banks complain about the lack of profitable lending opportunities available to them, either because they have insufficient information on which to judge loan applications or because of a general lack of profitability in many SSA businesses. For example, Ahmed and Islam (2009) report that one-fourth of all investment projects in SSA fail to generate positive returns.

In regard to stock and bond markets, 20 of the 53 countries in SSA have organized stock markets, but only eight have capitalization that is greater than 10 percent of GDP.[16] The average number of listed companies on these markets is 90 corporations. Only one stock market could be thought of as developed, and that is South Africa's, which is the fourth-largest emerging stock market in the world. Outside of South Africa, transaction volume is low (less than 15 percent of GDP a year), the scale of trades is small, returns are generally high (25 percent a year over the last ten years), and there are sizable risk premiums and transaction costs associated with trades.[17] This same shallowness exists in bond markets as well. Only eight countries in SSA have domestic debt markets with a capitalization of greater than 20 percent of GDP. Most of these bonds are held by banks, with only about 30 percent held by the public. Because of the high interest rate risk that exists in Africa because of historically high rates of inflation and macroeconomic instability, most bonds are short term. Roughly 90 percent of bonds have maturities of less than a year.[18]

The relative shallowness of the formal financial sector and the difficulties that the poor face in gaining access to it explain the growth of microfinance across SSA over the last decade. In 2008 there were more than 1,200 microfinance institutions serving nearly four million customers in West Africa alone.[19] As discussed in Chapter 2, by lending to groups as opposed to individuals, microfinance institutions attempt to reduce credit risk by reducing the need for information and using social pressure to ensure repayment when collateral is not available. Microfinance also helps reduce transaction costs by allowing lenders to deal directly with fewer customers, although microfinance remains difficult in the most rural areas of SSA due to prohibitively high transportation and communication costs. From the perspective of borrowers, microfinance often offers finance at lower costs than is available through informal methods. More importantly, however, microfinance provides the poor a more reliable source of finance in an otherwise unreliable world. The importance of maintaining this reliable source of funds is one of the key, and often overlooked, reasons that repayment rates for microloans are so high.

One of the important improvements in microfinance recently has been the movement away from strict and inflexible payment plans and toward providing the poor with more flexibility in the timing of their repayments. This innovation has come as a result of a realization that the cash flows of the poor are irregular and that granting the poor no discretion in the timing of their repayments only forces them to default when it is often avoidable. This new-found flexibility on the part of many SSA microfinance institutions has been aided by another innovation, which is the increasing use of non-traditional collateral, such as family heirlooms, in order to ensure a real commitment to paying back a loan.

Regional differences in Sub-Saharan Africa

While we have discussed SSA as if it is a homogeneous group of countries, in reality there is quite a bit of country and regional variability among financial systems on the continent. West Africa, particularly the francophone countries, is the least financially developed group of countries in Africa. The 14 countries that constitute West Africa have only 90 banks, a large majority of them foreign-owned, with no substantial bond or stock markets outside of Nigeria. There is a regional stock and bond market exchange but only ten firms and 20 bond issues are listed. Financial development has been limited by political instability, high inflation, large deficits, weak currencies, and overall financial repression.

Many have argued that the legal systems in the francophone countries, which are based on the French civil code system and not the common law system typically used in former British colonies, contributes to this lack of financial development. As discussed in Chapter 3, common law systems emphasize bottom-up legal development by granting a great deal of power to judges and to the petitioners of legal cases. As a result, it is argued, common law systems have the flexibility to adjust over time in ways that help to establish and protect property rights. Civil law systems, on the other hand, promote top-down decision making that grants power to state-level politicians that write laws. As a result, its laws tend to favor the elite and special interest groups, often failing to protect the general interest when it comes to protecting property rights. Civil code systems also require that all changes to the law have to go through the political system, making it slow to respond to changes in the economy. Empirical studies suggest that common law countries do have higher levels of financial development than civil code countries, both inside and outside Africa, although there has been convergence between the two over time.[20]

East and Central African economies tend to be resource and agriculture intensive. Largely because of this, financial repression and state-owned banking systems have a long and unfortunate history in the region. Banks have routinely been used as a revenue source for governments by being forced to purchase government debt and hold high levels of required reserves. This reduces the amount of private lending that banks can conduct and exposes them to sovereign debt risk that has repeatedly led to banking crises. Outside of Kenya, banks in East and Central Africa are inefficient and charge high interest rates. Stock and bond markets are rare in the region. Informal finance dominates and even microfinance lags behind other regions of Africa.

Finally, Southern Africa has the most developed financial systems on the continent, particularly in South Africa which, as noted before, has the fourth-largest emerging stock market in the world. South Africa's financial system closely resembles those in developed countries, with a wide array of financial assets and financial intermediaries such as insurance firms. The financial systems in Botswana, Namibia, Zambia, and Zimbabwe all have established, although small, bond and stock markets and banking systems that are dominated by foreign-owned banks (with the exception of Zimbabwe).

Financial liberalization and innovation in Sub-Saharan Africa

Since the mid-1980s, steady financial liberalization has taken place across most of SSA. Financial liberalization began in Africa within an environment of high inflation (typically between 20 and 100 percent a year), state-owned banks that dominated the financial sector, low bank capital, high levels of non-performing loans, little competition among banks, large amounts of directed lending by the government, little prudential regulation, and weak accounting and supervisory standards. In addition, a great deal of lending went directly to the public sector, crowding out private investment. In other words, financial repression and crony finance were the norm across the continent.

Financial liberalization in Africa has largely eliminated interest controls on deposits and loans, reduced quantity controls and the amount of directed lending that takes place, and lessened lending to the public sector. It has also ushered in a wave of privatization of state-owned banks, largely purchased by foreign-owned banks.[21] Today more than half of all banks in Africa are foreign-owned, which has helped financial systems in SSA overcome problems associated with undiversified economies, small size, a lack of access to domestic financial markets, and a shortage of knowledge about best financial practices. While many of these are developed country banks with large international presences, such as Barclays or Société Générale, some of them are foreign banks from other emerging market economies. For example, Standard Bank of South Africa (Stanbic), which is the largest African bank, operates in 16 African countries. The Industrial and Commercial Bank of China, the largest emerging economy bank in the world, has been expanding its operations in Africa and bought a 20 percent stake ($5.5 billion) in Stanbic in 2011.[22]

One of the most important aspects of financial liberalization has been a significant improvement in macroeconomic policy in SSA. Table 9.1 presents average macroeconomic statistics for SSA between 2004 and 2012 (estimated). In addition to strong real GDP growth, inflation across the region is lower and has become more stable, averaging 8.1 percent in 2011. Only six SSA countries had inflation rates greater than 10 percent in 2011. Government budget deficits have been falling and are below historical averages. Current accounts have generally been positive, primarily because of growth in exports (particularly commodities) to other fast-growing emerging economies such as China. Foreign reserves are also at historic highs, helping to provide a buffer against sudden capital outflows. Overall, the macroeconomic environment for finance in SSA is vastly better than in previous decades and is currently at levels that are sustainable over the long run.

Unlike other regions of the world, financial liberalization has not led to an increase in the number of asset bubbles, banking crises, sovereign debt crises, or currency crises. Between 1980 and 2010 there have been 40 bank crises in 32 SSA countries, but in most cases these crises have been the result of corruption, political turmoil, or government defaults, not the result of excessive credit expansion and moral hazard lending. Because most countries in SSA are debt

Table 9.1 Macroeconomic performance in Sub-Saharan Africa

	2004–2008	*2009*	*2010*	*2011*	*2012 (est.)*
Real GDP growth (%)	6.6	2.8	4.9	5.5	5.9
Inflation (%)	8.7	8.3	7.0	8.1	6.7
Budget surplus, % of GDP	0.1	−7.2	−5.6	−3.2	−2.3
Current account balance, % of GDP	0.8	−2.3	−2.2	0.5	0.5
Foreign reserves, % of GDP	4.6	5.0	4.5	5.0	5.5

Source: IMF (2011d).

intolerant, liberalization has not led to rapid growth in external debt despite the strong growth in private capital inflows (primarily foreign direct investment) to the region (refer back to Figure 6.4). As a result, currency mismatch has not been as big a problem as it has been after liberalization of financial systems in Asia, for example.

Of course, what seems to be good news about liberalization in Africa is actually fundamentally bad news: two decades of sustained reform and liberalization has not resulted in any significant deepening of financial development. Numerous empirical studies have concluded that financial liberalization in SSA has had no measurable impact on real interest rates, savings and investment rates, or credit expansion on the continent.[23] The reason for this leads us back to the continuing theme of this chapter: despite lower risks today, SSA remains an environment with low investment productivity, high credit risk, insufficient information, high costs, and weak legal protections for creditors and property. As a result, even when they have the resources, banks and other lenders are reluctant to extend loans and instead credit ration all but the highest-quality borrowers.

Technology could eventually change this in Africa. In Chapter 2 we talked about the incredible success of Kenya's M-Pesa mobile banking program, which uses text messaging and street vendors to provide loan, deposit, and cash flow management services to nearly 70 percent of Kenya's population, most of which has never had access to formal financial services before. Also helping is the spread of smart cards (or stored value cards), which can be used to facilitate cash flows and ease electronic purchases, and mobile banking units, which are branch banks based in vehicles that can be used to help provide financial access to those in isolated rural communities. Because of its high transaction costs and limited transportation and communication infrastructure, Africa stands to gain more from these technologies than any other region in the world, potentially allowing Africans to climb many rungs on the financial development ladder in one giant leap. Largely because of these innovations, credit has been growing at 20 percent a year over the last five years in Kenya as well as other SSA countries, such as Zambia, where mobile banking is taking off.[24]

Central banking in Sub-Saharan Africa

Two monetary unions currently exist in SSA, with possibly more to come in the future. Currency unions make a great deal of sense for SSA countries considering the relatively small size of most African economies, the importance of trade linkages with close neighbors, and the historical legacies of disastrous monetary policy during which many central banks were forced to monetize government budget deficits. Monetary unions have effectively served as commitment mechanisms that have tied central banks to lower and more stable currencies, with positive effect. The West African Economic and Monetary Union (WAEMU) is composed of seven francophone countries with its central bank located in Dakar, Senegal.[25] The Economic and Monetary Union of Central Africa (CEMAC) consists of six central

African countries with its central bank in Cameroon.[26] Both monetary unions essentially operate under an Argentinean-style currency board in which their currencies, the West African CFA Franc and the Central African CFA Franc, are pegged to each other and guaranteed by the French treasury to be convertible into euros at a fixed rate. In return for this privilege, member central banks hold 65 percent of their foreign reserves in France's central bank. There are plans for the English-speaking West African countries to form their own currency union in 2015 and possibly merge with the WAEMU in the future.

Southern Africa has no monetary union, but they do have a Rand Monetary Area where multiple currencies in the region are either fixed or fully convertible to the South African rand with no exchange controls between these countries.

Table 9.2 breaks SSA countries into two categories: countries that follow some type of hard or soft exchange rate pegging policy, and countries that float while targeting either money growth or inflation. SSA is split almost evenly between those adopting some form of a fixed exchange rate and those adopting some form of floating or managed float exchange rate. For most of the other countries that fix, pegged exchange rate strategies are associated with either being a part of a monetary union or monetary area or the fact that the country is an oil exporter, which encourages pegging to the dollar because oil is primarily sold in dollars and is such a large part of the GDP of these economies.

For those countries that follow independent discretionary policy, an important question should be asked: can independent monetary policy be successful within the African macroeconomic environment? There are two good reasons to think that it cannot. First, the lack of political independence and fiscal dominance suffered by many central banks means that monetary policy is too easily used to achieve political and fiscal objectives, not objectives traditionally associated with monetary policy such as price stability and output stabilization.

Second, weak or non-existent financial systems eliminate the primary means through which monetary policy impacts the real economy. One of the primary

Table 9.2 Sub-Saharan exchange rate regimes, 2010

Fixed/crawling peg exchange rate		*Float/managed float/inflation target*	
Angola	Equatorial Guinea	Burundi	Mozambique
Benin	Gabon	DR Congo	Nigeria
Botswana	Guinea-Bissau	Ethiopia	Republic of Congo
Burkina Faso	Lesotho	Gambia	Rwanda
Cameroon	Mali	Ghana	São Tomé and Príncipe
Cape Verde	Namibia	Guinea	Sierra Leone
Chad	Niger	Kenya	South Africa
Central African Republic	Senegal	Liberia	Tanzania
Comoros	Seychelles	Madagascar	Uganda
Côte d'Ivoire	Swaziland	Malawi	Zambia
Eritrea	Togo	Mauritius	

Source: IMF (2010a).

channels by which monetary policy works is through its effect on interest rates and the demand for credit. But in a financial system where credit rationing is endemic and banks regularly hold excess liquidity because of high perceived risk, expanding reserves and reducing interest rates will not necessarily lead to more lending. In other words, it is not the demand for credit that is the constraint, but the supply of credit. Evidence of this credit rationing effect at work can be found in the relatively low *money multiplier* (the change in the money supply from a change in new reserves created by the central bank), which is only three in SSA but typically around ten in developed countries.[27] With such a low multiplier, any change in reserves by the central bank will have a limited impact on the overall amount of credit and economic activity. To illustrate this point, Figure 9.2 presents data on excess reserve holdings and credit growth for 30 SSA countries, where countries are divided into two groups based on whether they have low or high levels of non-performing loans (NPLs). What becomes clear is that countries with fewer bad loans, and presumably lower systemic risk, hold less excess reserves and extend more credit.

Monetary policy can also work through a financial market channel by pushing up yields on bonds, the returns on stocks, and real estate prices. As asset prices rise, wealth increases as does the value of assets that can be used as collateral to back a loan, stimulating economic activity. But in countries where financial markets are limited and where assets are difficult to collateralize, this channel is eliminated as well.

Finally, monetary policy could have important macroeconomic effects in emerging economies through the exchange rate channel, in which an increase in the money supply can temporarily reduce nominal and real exchange rates, stimulating export growth and discouraging imports which can, in turn, accelerate

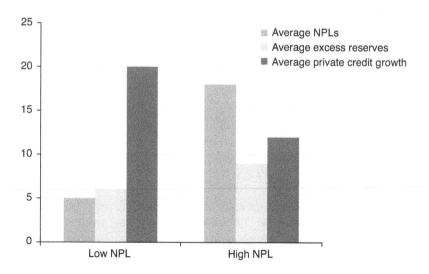

Figure 9.2 NPLs, excess reserves, and credit growth in SSA (source: IMF (2010a)).

economic activity in the economy. The strength of this channel depends upon how flexible wage and product markets are in response to a change in the money supply. If prices and wages adjust quickly to changes in the money supply, then a change in the nominal exchange rate will not necessarily lead to a change in the real exchange rate. Under these circumstances, monetary policy will have a limited ability to stimulate net exports and other sectors of the economy. Empirical evidence suggests that countries in SSA with floating exchange rates have higher average inflation but less volatile changes in their current account balances. This suggests that monetary policy does not have a strong impact on net exports and that the exchange rate channel in SSA countries is weak.[28]

In summary, both theoretical arguments and empirical studies suggest that monetary policy has weaker real effects on the macroeconomy in SSA than elsewhere.[29] Only with financial development, an overall reduction in systemic risk, and a lessening of fiscal dominance can monetary policy become a powerful and consistent tool for macroeconomic stabilization in the region. However, this does not mean that central banks do not have any power. Certainly they have the power to keep average inflation low and to provide exchange rate stability within reasonable ranges. Most importantly, to the extent that central banks are also engaged in supervising prudential regulation and monitoring the health of their financial systems, central banks have an important role to play in reducing overall risk and creating sustainable levels of credit growth in SSA.

Financial development in Nigeria

Nigeria is the most populous country in SSA with 215 million people. It has the second-largest economy in SSA with a GDP of $377 billion in 2010, giving it a per-capita GDP level of roughly $2,500. Nigeria grew at an impressive 7.5 percent in 2011. However, given Nigeria's wealth of natural resources (it is the world's seventh-largest oil exporter) and a highly educated segment of the labor force, these statistics can only be viewed as disappointing. Despite its growth, 70 percent of Nigerians continue to live on less than $2.50 a day. Nigeria's inefficient and unstable financial system has played an important role in its underwhelming performance over the four decades since its independence.

Some aspects of Nigeria's financial system resemble those in the most developed emerging market economies. Its stock market has been in existence since the 1960s and is the second largest in Africa, trading approximately 300 companies with a total capitalization of 35 percent of GDP. Its bond market trades in bonds with maturities of up to 20 years. It also has roughly 50 insurance firms in operation.[30]

Nigeria has 24 domestic banks, the oldest in operation since 1892. The Nigerian banking system is unlike others in SSA for three reasons. First, its banks are not predominantly foreign-owned but Nigerian; 21 are privately owned, three are state-owned. This is in large part due to government-created barriers to foreign entry. Second, Nigeria is one of the last SSA countries that has not liberalized its capital account and still engages in a dual exchange rate system to control capital flows, which creates a black market for its exchange rate. In other words, Nigeria has not fully abandoned the financial repression policies of the 1970s, unlike many of its neighbors. Third, Nigerian banks do not suffer from an excess of liquidity but a shortage of liquidity. Nigerian banks struggle to attract funds; deposits are only 19 percent of GDP. This is the consequence of the fact that Nigeria is largely a cash-based economy and that 74 percent of Nigerians participate in no formal banking services.[31] Too little liquidity limits credit growth; private credit is only 24 percent of GDP in Nigeria, which is somewhat above average for SSA but significantly below the most developed financial system on the continent in South Africa (where it is above 100 percent).[32]

According to the Financial Development Index created by the World Economic Forum (see Table 1.1), Nigeria ranked dead last among the 60 countries evaluated. This lack of formal financial intermediation in Nigeria is a significant drag on investment and growth. The depressing lack of capital and infrastructure in Nigeria—be it in the form of roads, bridges, buildings, housing, communications, etc.—is the most important fact of economic life in the country and becomes instantly apparent on any visit. Only 10 percent of all bank credit goes to home mortgages.[33] Only 5 percent of SMEs in Nigeria receive bank loans, despite the fact that 80 percent report that they are seeking financing for investment. Despite the facts that two-thirds of all Nigerians are subsistence farmers and that agriculture is responsible for 42 percent of Nigerian GDP, agricultural loans constitute less than 2 percent of all bank credit.[34] Most credit in Nigeria flows to the oil, mining, and telecommunications industries.

Why is financial intermediation so rare when, on the surface, the Nigerian financial system appears to be relatively developed? The primary reason is Nigeria's poor financial institutions, particularly those affected by corruption. Nigeria consistently ranks among the most corrupt countries in the world. Transparency International (2010) ranks Nigeria 134 out of 178 countries in terms of perceptions of corruption.[35] To make matters worse, Nigeria's weak government means that most of this corruption is decentralized, which is particularly costly (see Chapter 3). Stories of corruption in Nigeria are endless, but what is most shocking about these stories is not what is illegal, but what is considered perfectly legal.[36] For example, elected public officials have to personally approve many property transfers, typically for a personal fee (which is the reason the World Bank ranks Nigeria 178 out of 183 countries in terms of ease of transferring property). Many elected representatives are paid more than $2 million a year—legally. State-owned development banks in Nigeria regularly suffer default rates of 9 percent a year after making regular loans to elected officials and other elites. Nigeria's export bank suffered bad loans equal to 99.7 percent of its portfolio after its first six years, while its education bank never made a single loan after seven years of existence (despite employing 261 staff).[37] In sum, it is estimated that between $4 billion and $8 billion is stolen from Nigeria's government every single year, yet not one politician is currently serving jail time on corruption charges in the country.[38]

Corruption has polluted the banking system as well. In 2009, the government provided a $4 billion bailout to clean up the bad loans of nine Nigerian banks that held 40 percent of all deposits in the country. The sources of these bad loans were large numbers of connected loans to political elites. In 2010, a crisis in confidence spread to more banks, leading to capital flight out of the country and rapid disintermediation by depositors. In order to prevent a full banking crisis, the government established a $20 billion fund (slightly less than 10 percent of GDP) to purchase bad loans and recapitalize banks.[39] This crisis occurred only ten years after a similar banking crisis in 1999.

In this environment, it is easy to understand why many Nigerians might choose to stay out of the formal financial system and remain in the cash economy—in other words, why the lack of financial access in Nigeria might be voluntary, not imposed. Trust (based on information) is the foundation of all finance, and without it there are no incentives to borrow or lend. Instead, Nigerians have developed many informal arrangements that provide a variety of ways to save and invest with people they do trust. For example, ROSCAs have existed in Nigeria since the sixteenth century. Today, most Nigerians belong to at least one, often times many of these associations. Microfinance is also booming in Nigeria and there are now more than 800 microfinance institutions operating in Nigeria.[40] Unfortunately, microfinance in Nigeria is inhibited by many of the same factors that limit formal finance, particularly corruption and unnecessary regulation.

Nigeria has undergone many past attempts at reform that have included many of the policies typically adopted during financial liberalization programs. Studies reviewing these reforms have found that this liberalization has not facilitated financial development because of policy reversals, corruption, and a lack of reform in the real sector of the economy.[41] A recent move by the Central Bank of Nigeria to ban cash payments of more than a few thousand dollars—in an effort to encourage more bank deposits—is indicative of the continuing belief that financial repression can solve the country's financial problems.[42] Ultimately, until Nigerians can find reasons to trust their financial system, they will continue to find that their financial system is more of a hindrance than a help to its economic development.

Financial success: Botswana

Few countries have ever had seemingly less going for it than Botswana did at the time of its independence in 1966. Botswana had 12 km of paved road, 22 university graduates, 100 secondary school graduates, and the incredible disadvantage of being landlocked in the middle of the Kalahari Desert and surrounded by countries in political turmoil.[43] Since that time, however, Botswana has had the highest growth rate in the world at 9 percent a year and today its per-capita GDP of $14,000 puts it squarely in the range of middle-income countries.

Economic growth has coincided with the development of a small but thriving financial system in Botswana. Its banking system comprises six large foreign-owned banks and two state-owned development banks. These development banks conduct directed lending for the government, particularly to the state sector of the economy that is heavily involved in the mining and diamond industries, which accounts for 40 percent of Botswana's GDP. Credit, which was only 9 percent of GDP in 1997, has risen to 21 percent of GDP in 2011. This growth in credit has coincided with the creation of a credit bureau that distributes financial information publicly and that covers more than 50 percent of the adult population.[44] Botswana's stock market, founded in 1989, has 40 companies listed with a market capitalization of 90 percent of GDP.[45] The bond market is small and primarily comprises issuances from banks and the government. However, Botswana became the first country in Africa to have its government bonds, both domestic and external bonds denominated in dollars, ranked as investment grade by credit rating agencies.

How did a small, sparsely populated, and seemingly nondescript place such as Botswana achieve success while its seemingly better-off neighbors, such as Zimbabwe, have fallen behind? Acemoglu *et al.* (2001b) tell a story of a country that, despite the odds, was able to take the outlines of a quality institutional framework and build it into a system of institutions that align incentives with productive behavior as well as any country in SSA. Acemoglu and his co-authors point to five factors that explain why Botswana institutions work so well. First, the tribal institutions that existed in Botswana encouraged cooperation and participation. Particularly important is the *kgotla* system, in which chiefs governed in conjunction with the input of public assemblies. These assemblies limited the power of elites, but they also encouraged the sharing of information, key to a functioning financial system. Second, because the vast majority of the population was historically cattle herders, the elites and chiefs had incentives to protect and enforce property rights for everyone so that everyone had property rights to both individual and community land. Third, colonization in Botswana was not intrusive, leaving traditional institutions, such as tribal courts that effectively adjudicated property rights disputes, in place. Fourth, diamond resources were discovered following independence and after many of the institutions needed to protect these resources from exploitation were already in place. As a result, the revenues generated have gone toward building the country's infrastructure, not corrupt leaders. Finally, the leadership of Seretse Khama was crucial. Khama was the chief of the largest tribe in Botswana who studied in the United Kingdom and eventually married a white woman there. For a time banned from returning to Botswana by the apartheid government in South Africa, he eventually became Botswana's first president and played a crucial role in creating an egalitarian, race-neutral society.

Today, because of these institutions, Botswana has created an economic environment that is conducive for conducting business and making financial transactions. Botswana consistently ranks as having the lowest levels of corruption in SSA. In the World Bank's (2011) Ease of Doing Business index, Botswana ranks 52 overall, 46 in the ease of getting credit, and 44 in protecting investor's rights—all the highest rankings in SSA. One of the most important ways that

Botswana has contributed to a positive financial and business environment is through the effective management of its exchange rate by the Central Bank of Botswana. Small countries that heavily rely upon a single export good, such as diamonds, are vulnerable to what is referred to as the *Dutch disease*, or an appreciation of their real exchange rate associated with the growth in exports of this single good. This higher exchange rate can price other export industries out of their markets and eventually lead to an undiversified and generally unproductive economy. The Central Bank of Botswana has traditionally held large amounts of foreign reserves to protect against unexpected capital outflows and to smooth appreciations in its currency. They do this by maintaining a crawling peg with their primary trade partner, South Africa.

Of course, Botswana faces a number of significant challenges going forward. It has the highest incidence of HIV/AIDS in the world with an estimated 25 percent of all adults between the ages of 19 and 45 infected with the disease. This has reduced life expectancy in the country to 55 years, not only significantly reducing human capital but also significantly increasing credit risk and contributing to additional credit rationing. The economy remains relatively undiversified, which also increases credit risk. In rural areas, transaction costs are extremely high because of low population density and difficulties in traveling in the Kalahari Desert. Largely because of this, 40 percent of the population lacks access to formal finance. Most of the rural population still lives on tribal land that is difficult to collateralize for accessing formal credit.

Botswana is no financial Eden. To live in Botswana is to be consistently frustrated by the days wasted paying for bills in cash because there was no electronic financial transfer system. Hours can be spent filling out paperwork to open a bank account and weeks are lost waiting for that paperwork to be processed. Seeming lifetimes are spent waiting in lines to withdraw money because of a lack of ATM machines. Even senior officials cannot get a credit card if they are older than 55. It still is far short of the financial system those who live in developed economies might expect, but Botswana is much closer to that goal than anyone would have thought possible 45 years ago, thanks largely to its unique and effective institutions.

Financial disaster: Democratic Republic of Congo

The Congo provides an extreme contrast with Botswana: a country loaded with natural resources and strategic advantages, it suffered through oppressive colonization that significantly weakened its traditional institutions, which were already corrupted by a devastating slave trade industry that had been in operation since at least the fifteenth century. The Congo then suffered through a disastrous transition to independence that undermined these institutions even further. As political instability in the Congo continues, caused by both conflict from within the country and also by conflicts spilling over from neighboring countries, the Congo has come to represent the prototypical failed state and failed financial system.

The Congo is the perfect example of the argument made by Acemoglu *et al.* (2001a) (and summarized in Chapter 3) that colonial strategies adopted in different countries can lead to long-lasting effects on institutions and, in turn, on financial and economic development. According to their theory, those countries that had lower settler mortality rates adopted colonization strategies that focused on establishing quality institutions that facilitated long-run economic growth and financial development. This included establishing representative political systems and legal systems that protect property rights. But in countries in which settler mortality was high, the economic incentives faced by colonists encouraged extractive colonization policies, such as mineral exploitation and slavery, which were not consistent with the creation of quality institutions.

The exploitation of the Congo by its Belgian colonizers is notorious even by Sub-Saharan African standards.[46] Between 1884 and 1908, the entire country—one-fourth the size of the continental US—was owned by a single individual: King Leopold of Belgium. Acts of incredible brutality (beatings and the removal of body parts) were commonplace as Belgian officials rushed to extract the abundant natural resources of the Congo—first ivory, then rubber, then minerals—before they died. Roughly one-third of all Belgian officials died between 1884 and 1960, taking an estimated 13 million Congolese with them.[47]

When the Congo became hurriedly independent in 1960 (and renamed Zaire), the Belgians left few institutions to build upon, having not only failed to build any but also destroyed most traditional tribal institutions. Only 17 people had a university education in a country of 64 million people. After a chaotic transition, Mobuto Sese Seko came to power, beginning a 30-year rule that set historical standards for corruption. Mobutu himself said, "Everything is for sale and everything can be bought in this country. And in this trade, the slightest access to power constitutes a veritable instrument of exchange." Mobutu personally directed cash flows from the central bank, ordering all revenue from the country's large state-owned copper industry deposited directly into his personal bank accounts. Mobutu's personal security and travel expenses accounted for 15 to 20 percent of the entire government budget. When copper sales were no longer sufficient to pay the bills, the central bank began printing money to finance Mobutu's corruption. Inflation reached nearly 10,000 percent a year by the mid-1990s. In one notorious incident, when one plane-load of new currency was ordered from abroad by the central bank, two plane-loads of bills were actually delivered. After being confiscated by international authorities, this second load of currency (nearly 30 tons of bills) mysteriously disappeared within the country.

During much of this time, Zaire continued to receive support from the IMF and World Bank under structural adjustment programs, in large part because of pressure from the United States because of Mobutu's perceived importance as an ally during the Cold War. The loans arrived, but the structural adjustment never did. In Mobutu's words, "You cannot eat austerity."

As the expropriation worsened, the economy collapsed. In 1955, 55 percent of the economy worked in the formal sector. By the 1990s, only 5 percent did, and per-capita GDP had fallen to $120. A local joke goes: "Q: How did you light a room before candles? A: Electricity." Traditional methods of pricing goods in the local currency disappeared. Either you paid in dollars, or you paid for goods based on the category they were grouped in. Goods in the same category were charged the same price, allowing for easy price adjustment in an environment where prices were rising daily.

When Mobutu's regime fell in 1997, the newly christened Democratic Republic of Congo (DR Congo) had few economic or political institutions to build upon. As a result, things have generally not improved. According to the World Bank, if firms paid all of the taxes they are legally required to pay in the DR Congo, they would have to pay 230 percent of their profits.[48] These sorts of policies force people to cheat in order to survive. The DR Congo ranks 175 out of 183 countries in the World Bank's Ease Of Doing Business, 118th in registering property, 168th in the ease of getting credit, and 154th in protecting investor's rights. Despite substantial wealth in natural resources, the UN has named DR Congo as the least-developed country in the world. Per-capita GDP was only $328 in 2010 (half of what it was at independence in 1960), much of it created through rogue mining operations run by militias and the army, often exploiting local populations for cheap labor. The economy is 70 percent dollarized and all dollar transactions take place outside of the formal banking system. While 18 banks currently operate in the country, there are only 60,000 bank accounts for a population of 71 million people, almost all denominated in foreign currencies. Private credit is only 3 percent of GDP. There is no insurance industry, no stock market, and while there is a government bond market, its longest maturity is only 28 days.[49]

But within this failed state, informal finance still manages to thrive. ROSCAs and moneylenders are common, as are cash transfers between moneylenders via text messages or verbally over the phone. The fact that these informal transactions continue to take place within an environment in which risk is so rampant is a testament to the power of finance. It illustrates the importance of trust, and the fact that trust is often a function of mutual need.

The impact of the 2007 global financial crisis on Sub-Saharan Africa

Because of its relatively low levels of financial development, the general consensus during the early stages of the 2007 global financial crisis was that Africa would be fairly isolated from the impacts of the crisis. The chances of financial contagion spreading to the economies of SSA seemed limited because most SSA banks are not closely integrated with banks in the rest of the world. In addition, African banks have limited business in more technical financial instruments such as derivatives and mortgage-backed securities. Finally, most SSA banks are highly liquid, have low leverage, and are not highly dependent upon foreign capital.

In fact, SSA suffered more than any other emerging market region during the global financial crisis. Stock markets in Nigeria and South Africa fell by between 40 and 50 percent during the early stages of the crisis. The IMF estimates that growth fell by 5 percent (from 6 percent to 1 percent) in 2009, by 2 percent in 2010, and by 0.5 percent in 2011 because of the crisis.[50] As a result of this slow-down, an additional seven million people were pushed into extreme poverty in SSA in 2009, followed by three million more in 2010.[51]

Why did this crisis have such a large impact on Africa? In part, the slowdown was driven by a large negative shock to African exports. World trade fell by 11 percent in 2009 and exports from Africa fell by even more than this.[52] In addi-tion, falling demand for raw materials and minerals reduced prices and incomes in many SSA economies.

But Africa was also significantly hurt by a disruption in the "hidden" financial linkages between it and the developed world, many of which are just as impor-tant as the linkages between financial institutions and financial markets that are typically focused on. The first of these hidden linkages is the financial remit-tances that SSA receives from Africans working in the developed world. The IMF estimates that remittances to Africa fell by up to 14 percent. While most African countries do not rely heavily on remittances, in those countries that do (such as Nigeria), GDP growth may have been reduced by up to 2 percent in 2009.[53]

Second, because African banking systems are dominated by foreign banks, any international crisis that impacts these banks is likely to result in broad delev-eraging across all of the countries that they do business in, including in Africa. As a result, these financial linkages essentially spread contagion to Africa. SSA saw a significant reduction in foreign capital flows, falling by 26.7 percent in 2009 relative to their 2008 levels. Particularly hard hit was foreign portfolio investment, which went from a net inflow of $18.7 billion in 2006 to a net outflow of $16.6 billion in 2009.[54]

Finally, because of its poor domestic financial systems, African firms are more reliant on trade credit through the use of accounts payable loans and *letters of credit*, where one firm guarantees payment by another firm. During good times, developed country firms are likely to be more generous regarding the terms of trade credit they extend to their African customers when they them-selves have easy access to financing. But when these developed firms become credit constrained, they begin to restrict trade credit to their suppliers and cus-tomers, either by restricting its quantity or increasing its price. What is at work here is a credit chain; African companies, who have little access to their own domestic finance, often find themselves at the end of these chains and vulnerable to a break in any single link. Berman and Martin (2010) find empirical evidence that the African reliance on trade credit coupled with the significant contraction in exports explains why this crisis impacted SSA more than other emerging market regions. Thus, contrary to the claim of some, financial backwardness has no advantages for Africa, even when it comes to being protected from financial instability in developed financial systems.

Conclusions

Our discussion of the financial systems of SSA once again raises the "chicken and egg" question about development discussed in Chapter 1. Does financial development foster economic development, or is economic development a prerequisite for financial development? While there are empirical and theoretical reasons to think that both are true, the bulk of the evidence suggests that it is primarily financial development that leads and fosters economic development. In that case, it is also clear that one of the primary reasons that SSA continues to lag behind other emerging regions of the world—despite more than a decade of rapid growth across the continent—is that most Africans continue to lack access to formal financial services. As a result, their savings earns low returns and is not funneled into productive activities; their borrowing is rationed, is short term, and is much more costly than it needs to be; their lives are riskier and less productive than they should be.

There are two fundamental causes of this lack of financial development. First, most SSA countries have financial environments that are too risky for rapid credit expansion. Because of a lack of investment opportunities, a lack of collateral, and a persistent lack of information, financial systems in SSA are best characterized as systems for credit rationing. Until the real sectors of these economies are reformed, credit bureaus and other means of disseminating information are created, and legal systems for registering and transferring property are improved, financial development will continue to lag behind economic growth.

Which leads to the second large problem with finance in SSA: governments continue to be a bigger part of the problem than they are of the solution. Legal and political systems in SSA are consistently the weakest of any region of the emerging world, particularly in regard to establishing property rights that expand the amount of collateral available for lending and in protecting creditor rights in a timely manner. Until these cornerstones of quality financial institutions are in place, other improvements that have taken place in Africa—such as improved macroeconomic management and increased political stability—will not translate into the kind of financial deepening that will help bridge Africa's development gap.

10 Financial systems in the Middle East and North Africa

Overview

The Middle East and North Africa (MENA) region has only 5 percent of the world's population and 3 percent of the world's GDP. However, the influence of its 22 countries far outweigh these numbers because of its important geopolitical location, its wealth of energy resources, and the fact that it has the fastest-growing (and youngest) population in the world.[1] Unfortunately, MENA has also been the slowest-growing region of the emerging world over the last decade. In 2011, GDP within MENA grew at only 3.9 percent, compared to 6.5 percent for emerging economies in general. Inefficient financial systems have played an important role in this regional failure to match the overall pace of emerging market growth.

Describing financial systems in MENA

Six characteristics define MENA financial systems.

There is great variation in financial development within MENA. This variation largely, but not exclusively, breaks down according to which countries are oil importers and oil exporters. Oil exporters are richer and are faster growing.[2] Over the last decade, oil-importing countries in MENA grew at only 3 percent as compared to the 6 percent growth rate in oil-exporting countries and the 6.5 percent growth rate in emerging economies overall. Per-capita GDP in oil-exporting MENA countries averaged roughly $23,000 in 2009, compared to only $4,000 in oil-importing countries.[3] Within this group of oil exporters, the most financially developed countries are the Gulf Cooperation Council countries (GCC), which are the countries with the largest energy reserves.[4] These GCC countries have only 11 percent of MENA's population but nearly half of its GDP. GCC countries grew at 7.8 percent in 2011, aided in large part by rising oil prices.

While there is a positive correlation between oil revenues and financial development in the region, there are also countries that are exceptions to this rule. Figure 10.1 plots credit-to-GDP ratios against oil production-to-GDP ratios for MENA countries. In theory, greater oil production facilitates greater finance in two ways. First, oil trades are largely conducted in dollars, the capital needs in oil production are large, futures trades are common, and drilling projects are long term. As a result, oil-intensive economies will typically demand more financial transactions than other economies, *ceteris paribus*. Second, oil production contributes to GDP, and richer countries in general demand a greater amount of finance. However, in Figure 10.1, note that this relationship is not perfect and outliers exist. Iraq and Libya stand as significant outliers in which high levels of oil production have facilitated neither financial development nor economic development in general.

Access to formal finance is limited. As in Sub-Saharan Africa, the vast majority of MENA households and small businesses do not have a reliable source for savings and lending services from banks or other financial institutions. The World Bank Enterprise Survey reports that only 30 percent of MENA firms have access to bank loans, while 35 percent of businesses identify access to credit as a major obstacle to their operations.[5] Figure 10.2 presents cross-regional data on the percentage of firms that have access to formal bank loans or lines of credit. The MENA region ranks lowest, with only 25 percent of firms having access to bank finance.

Regarding households, only 21.3 percent of MENA households report having access to bank services, but this number is as low as 10.4 percent in the least financially developed countries such as Yemen.[6] Referring back to Figure 9.1, which presents data on bank loans and deposit accounts across emerging market regions, MENA countries do only slightly better in creating loans than Sub-Saharan Africa and South Asia and much worse than other regions. MENA countries do relatively better in generating bank deposits. However, these aggregate numbers mask a great deal of cross-country variability in the region. While Syria generates only 191 deposits and 99 loans per 1,000 residents, Lebanon

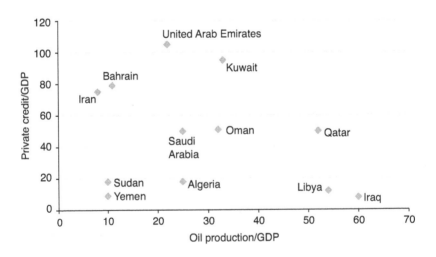

Figure 10.1 Oil production/GDP vs. credit/GDP (source: IMF (2010b)).

generates 1,750 deposits and 566 loans.[7] This same variability exists across other measures of financial access as well. Jordan has more than 18 bank branches and 26 ATMs per 100,000 residents, while Syria has only three branches and three ATMs.

This lack of access creates a paradox for MENA financial systems. By many measures, MENA financial systems appear to be well developed relative to the financial systems in other emerging market economies. For example, the average credit-to-GDP ratio in MENA countries averages 45 percent, which is greater than average (38 percent) for all emerging market economies.[8] However, these aggregate statistics camouflage the problems associated with a lack of access. Because of its lower rates of access, the IMF estimates that financial development impacts economic development in MENA countries by one-third less than it does in the average emerging market economy.[9] As a result, financial development is bypassing the vast majority of MENA households and SMEs that play a crucial role in fostering economic growth.

Non-bank financing is limited. Stock markets, bond markets, and non-bank financial institutions such as insurance firms are scarce, and where financial markets do exist they tend to have low volumes, few companies participate, and secondary markets are thin. Stock markets are most developed in the oil-rich GCC countries, such as Saudi Arabia. But outside of the gulf, measures of stock market development, such as the percentage of stock market capitalization that is traded each year, are typically significantly below averages for emerging market economies in general.

Governments play a large role in banking systems that are generally uncompetitive. As in other emerging market economies, banks dominate

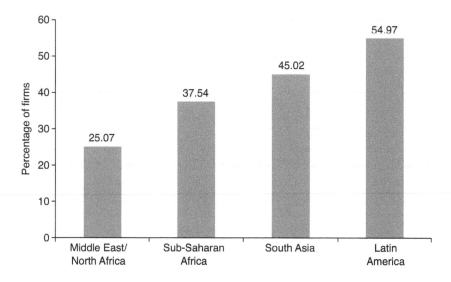

Figure 10.2 Firm's access to line of credit or formal loan (source: de la Campa (2011)).

formal financial systems. However, banks are even smaller and competition is even lower in MENA than in other regions.[10] Banks are small relative to their global peers: the largest MENA bank, NCB from Saudi Arabia, is only the 121st-largest in the world. The 100 largest MENA banks have only 130 percent of the assets of the Bank of America.[11] Competition in the banking industry is limited by small financial markets and a relatively low number of private banks because of government-created barriers to entry. In eight of 20 MENA countries examined, Creane *et al.* (2007) find that three banks hold more than 70 percent of total assets. This lack of competition creates relatively little competition for customers. This is one of the reasons that access to lending is so limited in MENA; banks account for only 8 percent of the lending to SMEs in the region.[12]

Bank competition is also limited by the importance of state-owned banks in many countries. State-owned banks (either wholly or partially owned by the government) hold a majority of bank assets in more than half of all MENA countries.[13] These state-owned banks primarily engage in directed lending, leading to many of the inefficiencies that go along with financial repression: high levels of non-performing loans, large interest rate margins, and a lack of bank profitability. Fazari *et al.* (2011) find that state-owned MENA banks have higher costs, lower profitability, and lower loan quality than private banks. In addition, there is no empirical evidence that these state-owned banks provide greater financial access for households or small businesses.

Microfinance is undeveloped. In every MENA country except Morocco and Jordan, microfinance provides service to less than 2 percent of the working-age population despite the persistent lack of access to formal finance in the region. In Syria and Yemen, microfinance serves less than 0.2 percent of the population. The vast majority of microfinance in MENA takes place in only two countries: Egypt (47 percent) and Morocco (33 percent). Microfinance services are also provided by only a small number of firms, with 20 microfinance institutions providing 75 percent of the lending.[14] Like the mainstream banking sector, microfinance institutions are typically government run or, in many countries, run by non-profit NGOs.

The provision of microsavings or microinsurance programs in the region is limited, with most of the focus exclusively on credit. In other words, microfinance in the region appears to be at least a decade behind where it has evolved to in South Asia or even parts of Sub-Saharan Africa. Microfinance growth has been slowed primarily by regulatory barriers and a reluctance of dominant state-owned banks to evolve into microfinance. These same barriers have slowed the growth of mobile phone banking in the region despite a high rate of mobile phone ownership in some countries (for example, 65 percent of Egyptians own mobile phones).[15] What little mobile phone banking there is is almost exclusively focused on transactions, not on savings and credit services. On the positive side, microfinance in MENA does a relatively good job of reaching women (63 percent of total clients), meaning that those that do receive microfinance are those that are most likely to be credit constrained.

Fixed exchange rates to the US dollar are common. With few exceptions, central banks follow hard or soft exchange rate pegs either to the US dollar or to a basket of currencies in which the dollar is heavily weighted. This primarily reflects the importance of oil in the region's economies and the fact that oil trades are primarily in dollars. Even oil-importing economies are implicitly tied to the dollar because of the importance of trade with oil-exporting MENA countries and the size of remittances from expatriates working in oil-exporting countries. The IMF estimates that for every 1 percent increase in GDP in GCC countries, growth rises by one-third of a percent in non-GCC MENA countries.[16]

One of the primary dangers of fixed exchange rate regimes is that they encourage borrowing in foreign currencies which can foster currency mismatch and increase exposure to exchange rate risk in the financial system. However, one of the big advantages that oil-exporting MENA countries have is that they have a dependable source of dollar revenues that can be used to repay any external dollar debt. As a result, foreign capital flows and the fixed exchange rate regimes of oil-exporting countries in the region have been historically stable, with currency and banking crises relatively rare.

Reforming MENA financial systems

What explains the relative financial underdevelopment in MENA and what reforms might address these shortcomings?

Financial access must be expanded, particularly for small and medium-sized firms. As mentioned earlier, financial development in MENA will not significantly speed economic growth without first broadening financial access across all sectors of the economy, particularly those that are the most credit rationed: the poor, the young, women, small firms, and newer firms. These groups are the most likely to be credit rationed because they are the ones that are most deficient in collateral and lack the quality information needed to attract credit. According to the World Bank, 85 percent of MENA banks say that a lack of information is a significant barrier to expanding credit.[17]

Information is limited in MENA financial systems for many of the same reasons that we have discussed throughout this book. The creation and expansion of credit bureaus have been stalled by concerns about privacy and security. Bureaucratic systems for providing this information are often slow, politicized, and corrupt. Other forms of information are difficult to obtain because of the prevalence of people living and working outside the formal economy. Barriers to entry and a lack of competition in the banking sector have also limited the incentives banks have to seek out new customers, forcing many borrowers to remain in the informal sector where they cannot build a credit history. Without this credit history, borrowers find it more difficult to gain access to formal finance, trapping them in a vicious cycle.

A lack of collateral is also a huge barrier to expanding credit. Borrowers with collateral receive nine times more credit than borrowers without collateral.[18] Yet many of the assets of households and small businesses are difficult to collateralize because of poor property laws, slow and convoluted legal systems, and corruption. According to one study, only three MENA countries rank as having high levels of property rights protection: Bahrain, Saudi Arabia, and Kuwait.[19] In the case of default, creditors find it difficult to recover their debts. The World Bank's *Doing Business 2011* reports that the recovery rate on debts in MENA countries is half of what it is in developed countries, while the time it takes to close a business is twice as long. Only two MENA countries—Tunisia and Jordan—come close to the average of emerging Asian economies when it comes to overall rankings on the ease of doing business.

Why have these institutional reforms not occurred before now? In Sub-Saharan Africa, it is easy to point to a lack of political and social stability in many countries that makes reform difficult to implement and sustain. In MENA, the problem is exactly the opposite: too much stability that has been sustained by strict limits on political participation. The lack of representative democracies in the region has reduced government accountability to the public and served to protect the interests of elites. The social and political upheaval associated with the "Arab Spring" uprisings in 2011 indicate that this era of limited political participation in MENA countries may be on the wane, but whether these new governments will be more democratic—and whether they will better provide and protect economic and financial institutions—remains to be seen.

Risk in the banking sector is too high, so lending is too low. While financial liberalization has lagged behind in MENA, so has prudential regulation. Many banking systems in the region are highly regulated, highly risky, but also highly liquid. In 2008, the average level of non-performing loans in non-GCC countries was 20.5 percent. In 2009, as a result of a concerted effort by many MENA governments, bad loans were written off and banks recapitalized. However, non-performing loans still remained greater than 10 percent in 8 of 22 countries.[20]

Because of these high default rates, banks find themselves caught in a trap of needing to hold lots of liquidity because they have to be ready to cover loan losses. As long as these bad loans are on their balance sheets they must hold liquidity because they cannot accept further risk by making additional loans. The first step in breaking out of this trap is to improve legal systems so that property and creditor rights are better protected and more collateral is created. MENA countries with better legal systems have more developed financial systems and lower levels of non-performing loans, indicating once again that lower risk and greater credit expansion go hand in hand.[21]

MENA banks can also reduce risk by conducting further recapitalization of banks with the help of governments in return for extensive and rigorous writing off of non-performing loans. One of the best ways to raise this capital is through the privatization of state-owned banks.

State-owned banks should be prudently privatized. Reducing the profile of state-owned banks would help achieve many objectives. First, as discussed before, empirical evidence suggests that these state-owned banks are inefficient and make low-quality loans. Privatizing these banks in a prudent way is a means of increasing financial efficiency and reducing bank risk. It would also help create competition among banks for new customers, which should improve financial access for households and SMEs. Finally, privatizing these banks will increase the capitalization of stock markets and help foster a non-bank means of finance for larger firms.

Bond market development needs to be fostered. Bond markets are needed to not only provide firms with an alternative source of financing but also in order to provide competition for MENA banks. Secondary bond markets in MENA countries are thin, in large part because governments sell their sovereign debt directly to banks who then buy and hold it until maturity. This essentially leads to a crowding-out of lending to the private sector. Governments must be encouraged to sell their sovereign debt on the open market, even if this exposes them to more risk and possibly higher financing costs. Central banks also need to be encouraged to conduct their monetary operations through buying and selling bonds on the secondary bond market, which will increase the depth of these markets, and not through direct lending to banks, which only encourages banks to hold more liquidity.

Financial development in Egypt

Egypt exemplifies many of the opportunities and challenges that face financial systems in the MENA region, particularly for oil-importing nations. Egypt has the region's largest population, with more than 78 million people, and its third-largest economy. However, per-capita GDP was only $2,800 in 2010 and has stagnated since the global financial crisis and the Arab Spring uprisings in 2011.

Egypt has a long and storied history, and the same can be said of its financial development. The modern Egyptian state can be dated back to a debt crisis experienced in 1869, the result of the costs associated with building the Suez Canal. A great deal of this debt was owed to British investors. Britain seized control of the country in 1882 to protect these investments and remained in control of Egypt until 1952. After independence, Egypt and its autocratic leader Gamel Nassar nationalized a large proportion of the economy, including the banking sector. Until the 1990s, Egypt in most ways had the quintessential state-owned, repressed financial system that was characterized by directed lending, market controls, a lack of financial access, and general inefficiency. By 1988, Egypt was the verge of multiple financial crises. Debt levels had reached 175 percent of GDP, among the highest in the world, while inflation was consistently above 20 percent a year. In part because of this high inflation, banks were saddled with high levels of non-performing loans—20 percent or more—and credit rationing was rampant.[22]

Egypt's first stage of financial liberalization began in response to this impending financial crisis as part of an IMF structural adjustment program that focused on restoring macroeconomic stability through austerity. Deficits were reduced from 17 percent of GDP to 0.9 percent of GDP and inflation was lowered to less than 4 percent (although it has since risen once again to an average of between

15 and 20 percent a year). Egypt's capital account was also liberalized by eliminating its system of foreign exchange limits and dual exchange rates.

One of the most important aspects of financial liberalization in Egypt has been the privatization of banks, which began in the 1990s but which accelerated in 2005. Smartly, Egypt used much of the proceeds from these privatizations to fund a badly needed recapitalization of banks. Before this recapitalization, banks had non-performing loan rates of 25 percent, an unsustainable level that explains why banks remained very liquid and reluctant to lend. In 2008 the Egyptian government forced banks to settle 90 percent of these non-performing loans while at the same time merging banks in an effort to enhance stability.

While recapitalization and mergers have increased bank capital, they have also served to limit competition in the banking industry. The number of banks in Egypt fell from 59 to 39. Today, 30 of these banks are private, 25 of which are foreign-owned. As a result, the state-owned monopoly before liberalization has been replaced with privately owned oligopolies after privatization, which is an improvement, but not a dramatic one.

Bank privatization has helped to foster non-bank finance in Egypt. The Egyptian Stock Exchange is one of the oldest in the world, dating back to 1885. By 2009, over 250 corporations were listed and trading volume has increased significantly. Maturities in the bond market rose from an average of 120 days to 2.1 years. But bond market development is still stunted by banks that continue to smother the expansion of a secondary market in their desire to possess liquidity. Banks hold over 90 percent of all short-term treasury bonds and 70 percent of long-term treasury bonds.[23]

Financial liberalization in Egypt—particularly the privatization and recapitalization of banks—has had some positive effects on financial access. Between 2006 and 2009, the number of deposits rose by 15 percent while the number of loans rose by 165 percent. However, financial liberalization has been no panacea. Despite this growth, financial access remains very limited, primarily because the Egyptian banking industry remains highly concentrated, creating few incentives for banks to expand their customer base. Only 17.4 percent of Egyptian households and 13 percent of small firms have access to formal finance. Only 7 percent of new investment in small businesses is financed through banks, while 70 percent of lending goes to large and connected corporations.[24]

Financial access continues to be a problem in Egypt because of a lack of quality financial institutions. Legal systems for enforcing contracts and dealing with bankruptcies remain unreliable and very slow. While Egypt does have a credit registry bureau, it can only be accessed by banks and its coverage of the population is poor. Most importantly, systems for legalizing collateral are not efficient, yet collateral is paramount in Egyptian lending because of the high amounts of risk in the system. Roughly 90 percent of all loans in Egypt require collateral averaging over 120 percent of the value of the loan. This is a high hurdle that creates a significant barrier to finance for all but the wealthiest Egyptian households and firms. These collateral barriers are particularly harmful to women; there is extensive evidence that there is a lending bias against them based on the fact that they are regularly required to provide more collateral than men. This is an important part of the reason why women have higher loan rejection rates than men and constitute less than 25 percent of all bank clients in Egypt.[25]

In place of bank finance, households use informal methods of finance, particularly postal savings accounts such as those offered by Egypt Post. These postal accounts are popular in many emerging market economies, particularly in former British colonies because of the British emphasis on postal system development. Postal accounts allow people to easily open savings accounts that pay very low, or non-existent, rates of return as well as make payments and transfers between other postal accounts in order to pay bills (such as utilities) or to contribute to pension and insurance funds. The advantages of postal accounts are that they allow very small transactions and that postal branches are widely available throughout the country. Egypt Post has over 3,600 branches and is able to serve over 17 million clients in Egypt. However, Egypt Post accounts do not extend credit, they cannot make transactions except with other postal accounts, few are connected by high-speed communication systems for use in international remittance payments, and they fail to establish the same information and credit history trail that formal financial transactions create.

Postal accounts do offer one additional, and often overlooked, advantage: they require little education to use. The World Bank reports that postal savings accounts are twice as likely to be used by illiterate Egyptians.[26] Less than 7 percent of households headed by an adult with less than a secondary school education have formal savings accounts, often because they require the ability to read and understand complex account statements. For these Egyptians, postal accounts offer a simple alternative.

Microfinance also offers financial alternatives for some poor Egyptians. Nearly one million Egyptians—43 percent of all of the microfinance clients in MENA—use microfinance in Egypt. Still, this is less than 2 percent of the Egyptian population.[27] Microfinance organizations continue to be hampered by the fact that they are generally run by the government or NGOs and are not private, for-profit institutions. This limits their competitiveness for new customers as well as their ability to attract resources to lend. It also limits their incentives to evolve, as new developments such as microsavings or microinsurance are rare in Egypt outside of postal accounts. Regulatory restrictions also prevent outreach to new customers and expansion into new services.

Despite worries about capital flight, financial panic, and financial crises during the Arab Spring uprisings, the Egyptian financial system withstood the tumult in good form, in part because Egypt has enacted many difficult financial reforms over the last two decades, particularly reducing its external debt levels and privatizing its inefficient and NPL-laden state-owned banks. With these historic events behind it, Egypt seems destined to change quite dramatically over the next few years. The question now is whether these changes will be for the better or for the worse. Will Egypt continue to privatize and liberalize its financial system and its economy? Can the next phase of liberalization focus on improving institutions specifically aimed at enhancing access to formal finance for more Egyptians? Or could Egypt return to its economic past of centralized economic control and renewed bank nationalization; a past that failed to serve the financial needs of the vast majority of Egyptians?

Islamic finance

Islam is practiced by one-fifth of the world's population, more than 1.3 billion people. As the religious, cultural, and population center of Islam, every aspect of life in MENA countries is profoundly influenced by Islamic principles. Finance is no different. *Shari'a* law, or Islamic law laid out in the Muslim holy book the *Qur'an*, prohibits a number of activities including the consumption of certain foods, alcohol, and smoking. It also forbids two types of financial activities. The first is *riba*, which roughly translates to the charging of monetary interest, otherwise known as usury. The second is *gharar*, which toughly translates as the making of uncertain, or speculative, investments.

Charging interest and dealing in risk are cornerstones of modern financial intermediation. However, Islamic jurists have developed rules, known as *Islamic finance*, that must govern financial transactions if they are to be consistent with *Shari'a* law. The primary characteristic of Islamic finance is that in place of speculation and interest, profit sharing must be the key principle that governs all financial transactions.

Islamic finance traces its roots back to Islamic traditionalist movements in Saudi Arabia in the 1950s and Egypt in the 1960s. The principles of Islamic finance are meant to govern the financial transactions of banks, stocks, bonds, and insurance markets as well as the informal financial transactions of all observant Muslims. The growth in Islamic finance, particularly in Muslim-majority countries, has been remarkable. It is expected that Islamic finance will double in size from roughly $900 billion in 2011 to $1.8 trillion by 2016.[28]

The cornerstones of Islamic banking are two types of liabilities that banks can issue and two types of assets that they can create. On the liabilities side, Islamic banks can issue *transactions deposits*, which are demand deposits that pay no interest and usually charge maintenance fees (meaning they pay negative interest rates) but have a fixed nominal value so that there is limited risk for the saver. The other type of liability they can issue is *investment deposits*, which essentially grant the depositor a share of the profits or losses of the bank. Investment deposits are allowed under Islamic law because they are considered ownership, not speculation.

Regarding the assets Islamic banks can create, the first type is *mudarabah* finance. Here, a bank receives a share of the profits or losses of the business accepting the loan in lieu of interest. Once again, this is considered investment, not speculation, under *Shari'a* law. Payments made to the bank are more akin to dividends than interest. The second type of asset is *murabaha* financing, in which the bank purchases an asset for the borrower, such as raw materials or goods, and the borrower then repays the bank in installments at a profit.

Murabaha financing is often referred to as Islamic leasing, but it is also similar to trade financing conducted through banks. Because the returns from *murabaha* financing are tied to trade in goods, they are not considered speculative transactions as long as the financial obligations are not sold to third parties.

There are many other forms of Islamic financing outside the banking system as well. So-called *Shari'a stocks* are stocks of companies that do not hold excessive levels of debt and also are not involved in prohibited activities, such as producing alcohol, running casinos, etc. *Musharakah* (meaning "sharing" in Arabic) is a commercial enterprise in which the partners that operate the firm share profits as agreed upon and any losses in proportion to the capital each investor has contributed. *Injara* is the leasing of capital equipment under *Shari'a* law. *Sukuks* are investment certificates that represent partial ownership of an asset or business in which the cash flows from the rent are structured to resemble those of a traditional bond. Finally, *takaful*, or Islamic insurance, takes advantage of the fact that the sharing of risk (as opposed to the selling of risk) is allowed under *Shari'a*. As a result, individuals can contribute to pools of assets in return for commitments for compensation from others in the pool in the event of a loss.[29]

In many ways, Islamic financing can be thought of as a branch of structured financing, or financing that manages cash flows so that risk is transferred in specific ways between agents. For example, the process of mortgage securitization involves selling and pooling mortgages, then distributing the cash flows in ways that redistribute risk. This is not dissimilar from *murabaha* financing (or Islamic leasing) in which banks allocate goods and the cash flows from the resulting installment payments in ways that redistribute risk. From this perspective, Islamic finance is simply structured finance under specific constraints. As a result, many conventional financial practices can be made *Shari'a*-compliant. But once again, the principle that all forms of Islamic finance share is the idea of profit sharing in place of interest and speculation.

All of this said, Islamic finance does impose some real constraints relative to conventional finance. It essentially requires a substitution of debt for equity financing and as a result has a real impact on the incidence of risk in any financial transaction. It also makes purely speculative transactions or financial transactions that do not involve the transfer of real assets very difficult. As a result, many types of financial transactions such as derivatives or the trading of one form of debt for another form of debt are not possible under Islamic finance.

The impact of Islamic finance on financial development and efficiency is not completely clear. On one hand, external constraints on markets always impose costs that discourage intermediation. Islamic finance increases the costs of finance by adding an extra layer of supervision and uncertainty. This is one of the reasons that so little microfinance is *Shari'a*-compliant—the costs that are incurred to ensure conformity are prohibitively large relative to most small microfinance transactions. Less than 5 percent of all microfinance in MENA countries is *Shari'a*-compliant.[30] In addition, Islamic finance tends to be less transparent because of the complexity of the financial transactions that are involved. Finally, Islamic principles largely prohibit borrowing to finance consumption. As discussed in previous chapters, the need to smooth consumption in the face of volatile incomes is one of the most pressing needs for those living in poverty. By prohibiting the finance of consumption with debt, one of the primary advantages of finance in general, and microfinance in particular, is forbidden.

It is possible to argue that Islamic finance has potential economic advantages, however. First, by forcing both borrowers and lenders to share in the risk of profits and losses, Islamic banking creates more market discipline and potentially reduces the problems of adverse selection and moral hazard that are inherent in all forms of finance. Also, by discouraging outright speculation and short-selling, excessive risk taking that is not tied to real assets is discouraged. As a result, an argument could be made that Islamic finance is inherently less risky than many conventional financial arrangements. Given the fact that finance in emerging markets is inherently volatile, *Shari'a* constraints on risk taking could be viewed as a form of needed prudential regulation.

The counterargument to this line of thought is that one person's risk-taking activity is often another person's method of reducing risk. The hedging of risk is a crucial function of financial systems, and by limiting the ways that people can transfer risk the overall financial system may be made riskier. For example, *mudarabah* and *murabaha* financing transfer more risk to banks and away from borrowers because they are more like equity than debt, meaning that payments the bank receives are not fixed and will be more volatile. This increase in the risk faced by banks could make the banking system less volatile. It could do this by discouraging excessive credit growth through the removal of moral hazard incentives banks face given the existence of deposit insurance and government bailouts. On the other hand, from a depositor's point of view, the greater the risk that banks are exposed to, the greater the risk that depositors are exposed to, making them less confident in the banking system and increasing the frequency of bank runs. As a result, the overall impact of Islamic finance on systemic bank risk is very difficult to predict.

In the most extensive empirical study of Islamic finance to date, Beck, Demirgüç-Kunt, and Merroche (2010) find few significant differences between conventional and Islamic banks in terms of the types of businesses they lend to, efficiency, asset quality, and overall stability. The key difference they identify is that Islamic banks tend to hold more capital and have higher liquidity than conventional banks, which makes them less volatile but also limits their ability to expand credit. Likewise, Ali (2011) finds that Islamic and conventional finance tend to develop at similar rates within countries and their levels of development also vary similarly across countries. The author also finds that the rates of return on equity and assets are converging between Islamic and conventional banks over time, indicating that the differences between the two are increasingly becoming more superficial than real as the Islamic finance industry matures.

One of the difficulties in evaluating the performance of Islamic finance is that it primarily takes place in countries with weaker financial institutions. Some historians and economists argue that this is not a coincidence and that many of the tenets of *Shari'a* law are, at least historically, inconsistent with efficient institutions.[31] The first problematic institution in Islam is the prohibition on usury and speculation, which is argued to have limited financial development, particularly before the growth of Islamic finance. Second, difficulties in forming corporations and business partnerships posed by the nature of Islamic inheritance laws has tended to make it difficult for commercial enterprises to sustain themselves over time and expand in size.[32] Third, arbitrary expropriation and a lack of property rights protection have been common in many Islamic countries, particularly in regard to non-Muslim residents. Fourth, as opposed to many Western countries where a dual system of secular and religious law developed, no secular law was permissible in Islamic societies, only *Shari'a* law. This has limited the participation of many Muslims in certain activities, such as finance. However, it also allowed minorities that were not bound by *Shari'a* law to specialize in these prohibited activities. Minorities, such as Jews, achieved economic success in many Islamic countries by essentially trading the right to engage in certain business practices (such as finance) under their law in return for paying higher taxes and sacrificing some of their political rights.

Islamic finance is not a means of looking backward toward restoring traditional prohibitions, but a way to look forward toward finding ways for Muslims to engage in much-needed financial intermediation that is consistent with their religious beliefs by emphasizing profit sharing. As a result, Islamic finance is one of the most exciting financial developments in emerging market economies in the last two decades. Its potential for spurring financial development among populations not traditionally served by formal finance is large anywhere significant Muslim populations live, particularly in MENA and South Asia. However, Islamic banking is still in its relative infancy and, as such, promises significant unknown risks as well as rewards as it matures.

Financial disaster: Iran

Iran is the second-largest economy (after Saudi Arabia) and the largest financial system in the MENA region. Iran also has the largest Islamic financial markets in the world with over $300 billion in assets in 2011, which is one-third of global Islamic financial assets.[33] The Islamic Revolution in Iran in 1979 established a country governed wholly by *Shari'a* law and all formal finance in the country is legally required to be consistent with the principles of Islamic finance.

After the Islamic Revolution, all banks and insurance companies in the country were nationalized. Since the revolution, money growth in Iran has regularly been greater than 40 percent a year and inflation has consistently averaged between 10 and 20 percent a year. The primary cause of this currency debasement has been the fact that Iran's central bank, Bank Markazi, is not independent from the government. As a result, it suffers from fiscal dominance, setting its policies primarily based upon fiscal and political priorities and not money and price stability.

Iran's revolutionary government imposes strict financial repression on the banking system in the form of interest rate and quantity controls on lending. For example, the government sets the rate of profit allowable on financial contracts at less than the 10 to 20 percent inflation rate that currently exists in Iran. This leads to negative real interest rates that create significant disincentives for saving in bank deposits. Households regularly hold a great deal of their savings in assets outside of the financial system, such as in real estate, gold, and foreign exchange. Negative real interest rates also create no incentives for banks to engage in lending. As a result, a great deal of lending conducted by banks is mandated by directed lending requirements set by the government. Most directed lending is aimed at SMEs and at low-income housing. However, this directed lending is generally unprofitable and has high rates of default. In 2010, non-performing loans in the Iranian banking system were estimated at 23 percent, only 12 percent of which could be covered by bad-loan provision set aside by banks. After an aggressive bank recapitalization program in 2011, Iran has been able to improve these numbers to 16 percent and 32 percent, respectively, although these levels are still not sustainable over the longer term without an eventual banking crisis.[34]

Iran has gradually taken steps to decentralize its banking system. Over the last decade, Iran has privatized a majority of its banks. Today, 20 of 26 Iranian banks are private. These private banks also hold over half of all bank assets. After this privatization, the credit-to-GDP ratio in Iran has doubled to a respectable 90 percent of GDP. However, the government's tight control over the banking system, particularly in regard to stringent requirements for directed lending goals and interest rate ceilings, has only been marginally loosened. According to one IMF study, Iran ranks below MENA averages across every measure of the quality of its financial institutions.[35] As a result of these poor institutions, Iranian banks are generally unprofitable and are exposed to high levels of risk.

Another factor stifling the Iranian financial system is widespread corruption. Transparency International ranks Iran 142 out of 178 countries and falling in terms of perceptions of corruption.[36] The growth of Islamic finance may contribute to this by granting power to a limited number of Islamic scholars and experts who, even when honest, slow the process of Islamic finance and when not honest, have a great deal of leverage to generate bribes. In one recent example, a $2.6 billion bank embezzlement case was brought in 2011 against 36 people associated with Bank Melli, the largest Iranian bank.[37]

One area of Iranian finance that has been thriving is its stock markets, which currently list more than 500 firms. Stock market capitalization has doubled since 2009 and now has risen to 20 percent of GDP. The seven largest private banks in Iran are now publicly traded on these exchanges. Equity has the significant advantage that it is readily permissible under Islamic finance and, as such, does not suffer from the same degree of regulation and repression by the government.

One of the most significant challenges facing Iran is the financial sanctions imposed on it by the United States and other Western countries. These sanctions were first applied in response to the Islamic Revolution but have been tightened recently in response to Iran's covert nuclear weapons development program. These sanctions have frozen some Iranian assets abroad and limited capital flows into Iran, in many ways forcing Iran to become a closed financial system. In 2010, the situation worsened for Iran when the United States passed a law barring any firm from participating in the US financial system that is found to do business with 12 sanctioned Iranian banks as well as a list of other Iranian firms. In 2011, 90 US senators called for banning Bank Markazi from the international financial system in response to a charge that it was engaged in illegal financial transfers in support of Iran's nuclear program. Such a restriction, if imposed, would make it very difficult for Iran to transfer the billions of US dollars it earns every year in oil revenue.[38] In this atmosphere, it is hard to see how financial development can progress at a rate that can support and not hinder economic development in Iran.

The United Arab Emirates and the rise of sovereign wealth funds

The United Arab Emirates (UAE) is a loose federation of seven principalities each governed by a hereditary emir. The UAE has become the sixth-richest economy in the world with a per-capita GDP of nearly $44,500 in 2010. It has 10 percent of the world's oil reserves (sixth largest in the world) and 4 percent of the world's natural gas reserves; all of this for a small country of five million people, four million of whom are expatriates. But what makes the UAE most interesting is its free market approach to economic development. Instead of following the typical model followed by other MENA countries of financial repression and limited economic freedom, the UAE—and particularly the city/ principality of Dubai—has tried the other extreme by emphasizing hyperactive, laissez-faire capitalism.

Long before the oil boom, Dubai was a financial center of the Middle East. The *hawala* banking system, which has been centered in Dubai for over 4,000 years, is a network of traders in different cities that have specialized in exchanging debts between individuals over long distances. The *hawala* system exists today in a more modern form in the series of brokers spread throughout the world that migrants use to send remittances back to their home countries. The *hawala* system was one that was built primarily on trust, with little paperwork required in order to make things as simple as possible.[39] Dubai has built upon this tradition to build what has been ranked as the top financial center in the MENA region and one of the largest in the world.

The banking sector of the UAE is dominated by five large banks. Roughly half of all banks are domestic and half are foreign owned, but all of them are private. Management of the largest banks is widely regarded as being financially sound and competitive with the largest international banks.[40] For example, non-performing loans have consistently been lower than 3 percent and can be more than covered by loan-loss provisions in the banking system. The Central Bank of

UAE has adopted a currency board system to the US dollar that is regarded as very stable, in large part because of the UAE's ability to earn large amounts of dollars through its oil exports.

Awash in oil revenues and relatively easy credit from its laissez-faire banking system, during the early 2000s Dubai pursed its dream of becoming the "playground of the Middle East." Dubai became home to the iconic Burj Al Arab, the world's most expensive (and second-tallest) hotel, Burji Khalifa, the world's tallest building, the Palm Island project, composed of a vast network of man-made islands in the shape of a giant palm tree, as well as world-renowned shopping malls and even indoor skiing. By 2007, Dubai had become the eighth most visited city in the world.[41]

Dubai's banks by themselves were not large enough to finance all of this investment. Instead, Dubai primarily relied upon three sovereign wealth funds, the largest being Dubai World which was established in 2006. A *sovereign wealth fund* (SWF) is a state-owned investment fund of asset holdings. The resources for these SWFs in Dubai came from its oil revenues, with the emir of Dubai personally holding a majority stake. These three SWFs, particularly Dubai World, invested heavily in local real estate and construction projects in addition to other ventures such as airlines, casinos, and shipping ports.

In a story as old as the existence of asset bubbles, economic growth and a rapid expansion in credit led to a real estate boom in Dubai of historic proportions. The boom, which occurred between 2003 and 2008, began with a legalization of foreign ownership of land in Dubai. The immediate impact was an influx of foreign investment in real estate driven primarily by speculation, as few foreigners actually resided in Dubai for more than a few days of the year. Real estate was often bought one day and "flipped" weeks later. Real estate prices grew at between 20 and 30 percent a year on average during the boom, with some estimates suggesting that prices rose by nearly 80 percent in some years. A construction boom financed by Dubai's banks and SWFs took place at an equivalent pace.

This all came crashing down in 2008 after the global financial crisis struck. As credit dried up and foreign investors tightened their risk assessments, property prices in Dubai dropped precipitously, falling by 47 percent in 2009 and eventually dipping to levels 80 percent below peak prices.[42] Many real estate developers and banks suffered huge losses, but the biggest were incurred by Dubai World, the largest SWF in the world at the time. In November 2009, Dubai World announced that it could not meet its debt payments of roughly $26 billion. Eventually (although unclear at the time) it became clear that Dubai World was responsible for $60 billion of the UAE government's $80 billion in total debt, an amount equal to 150 percent of the UAE's GDP. However, at the time it was unclear how much of Dubai World's debt the government and the emir of Dubai was responsible for, how much the federal government of the UAE was responsible for (other emirs made it clear that they would not assume any of Dubai World's debt), and how much UAE banks were responsible for, given that they had lent extensively to all of Dubai's SWFs. World markets dropped sharply and many investors feared a significant banking crisis in Dubai and beyond.

Eventually, the broad outline of a rescue plan was announced for Dubai World. Under the plan made public in December 2009, the Dubai government and Emir Khalifa of the Emirate of Abu Dhabi (who personally contributed $10 billion and became the man after whom the largest building in the world in Dubai was later renamed) provided bailout funds to Dubai World. In return, banks would take losses by rescheduling payments at longer maturities and lower interest rates while bondholders were completely repaid, albeit over a longer period. While an outright banking and financial crisis was avoided, the boom times for Dubai's real estate and financial industries are over for the foreseeable future and economic growth has slowed dramatically.

The crisis in Dubai has brought increased attention to SWFs. SWFs are playing an increasingly prominent role in the financial systems of emerging market economies. In 2011 SWFs are estimated to hold over $5.8 trillion in assets and the IMF estimates that by 2015 SWFs will hold more than $12 trillion in assets.[43] Table 10.1 presents data on the 20 largest SWFs in the world, 14 of which are associated with a government of an emerging market economy. The resources to create these SWFs come from two sources. The first is the sale of commodities such as oil and other raw materials. This explains the preponderance of MENA countries on the list. In 2012, the IMF expects oil-exporting countries to run current account surpluses of nearly $740 billion (more than three times the size of China's current account surplus), the majority of this coming from MENA. In Saudi Arabia, Qatar, and Kuwait these surpluses are more than 20 percent of GDP.[44] The second source is the foreign exchange resources earned by countries running trade surpluses, often as a result of maintaining overvalued exchange rates. The growing popularity of this export-promotion strategy was discussed in Chapter 8 and explains the existence of multiple SWFs from China and Singapore on this list.[45]

SWFs are useful for emerging market economies for a number of reasons. Emerging economies have a desire to build reserve funds that can be used to provide insurance against balance of payment or fiscal shortfalls. As discussed before, this is particularly valuable for emerging economies because they are more vulnerable to economic shocks, are poorer, and have less diversified economies. However, holding these resources in foreign exchange or low-yielding US government T-bonds does not make financial sense. SWFs allow emerging market economies to diversify their wealth while also maximizing returns.

However, many concerns have been raised about the growing size and importance of SWFs. Many developed countries have worried that SWFs could be used to pursue political objectives. Countries could use their SWFs to destabilize financial markets in rival countries or manipulate asset prices in ways that could further their economic or military objectives. For example, many politicians in the United States and Europe have publicly worried about the leverage Chinese SWFs have over the United States by holding so many US assets, particularly US government debt. The fear is that if Chinese SWFs were to sell all of these assets at the same time, asset prices would plummet and interest rates would spike to such an extent that a financial crisis or economic slowdown in the

Table 10.1 20 largest sovereign wealth funds by assets, March 2012

Country	Fund name	Assets ($ billions)	Origin	Lindburg–Madwell transparency index
UAE – Abu Dhabi	Abu Dhabi Investment Authority	627	Oil	5
Norway	Government Pension Fund	611	Oil	10
China	SAFE Investment Co.	567.9	Non-commodity	4
Saudi Arabia	SAMA Foreign Holdings	532.8	Oil	4
China	China Investment Corp.	439.6	Non-commodity	7
Kuwait	Kuwait Investment Authority	296	Oil	6
China – Hong Kong	Hong Kong Monetary Authority	293.3	Non-commodity	8
Singapore	Govt. of Singapore Investment Corp.	247.5	Non-commodity	6
Singapore	Temasek Holdings	157.2	Non-commodity	10
Russia	National Welfare Fund	149.7	Oil	5
China	National Social Security Fund	134.5	Non-commodity	5
Qatar	Qatar Investment Authority	85	Oil	5
Australia	Australian Future Fund	73	Non-commodity	10
UAE – Dubai	Investment Corp. of Dubai	70	Oil	4
Libya	Libyan Investment Authority	65	Oil	1
UAE – Abu Dhabi	Int'l Petroleum Investment Co.	58	Oil	9
Algeria	Revenue Regulation Fund	56.7	Oil	1
South Korea	Korea Investment Corp.	43	Non-commodity	9
US – Alaska	Alaska Permanent Fund	40.3	Oil	10
Kazakhstan	Kazakhstan National Fund	38.6	Oil	8

Source: SWF Institute (2011), available at: www.swfinstitute.org/fund-rankings.

United States could occur. However, such a strategy seems highly unlikely given that it would lead to large losses for China in addition to China abandoning a key component of its export promotion strategy that has fueled Chinese economic growth.[46]

Another concern regarding SWFs is their lack of regulation and direct oversight. Because SWFs often operate outside of domestic financial systems and in many cases do not have to directly report to their central bank or other regulators, there is no clear supervision of many SWFs and little prudential regulation (as was obviously clear in the case of Dubai World). In this sense, SWFs in some countries appear to operate in a financial gray area.

One final concern about SWFs is their lack of transparency. In many cases, such as Dubai World, it is unclear who is actually in charge of the SWF (the Emir? Government officials? The administrators of the fund?), who is the ultimate owner of the SWF (the Emir? The Government? Taxpayers/residents? Citizens?), and who is ultimately responsible for any losses incurred by the SWF. Finally, because their financial statements do not have to be made public, it is often unclear what investment objectives each SWF are following and what trades they are engaged in. The final column of Table 10.1 presents one measure of transparency published by the SWF Institute, the Lindburg–Madwell Index. According to this measure, countries that are not democracies tend to have SWFs that are less transparent.

In order to address some of these transparency issues, 25 nations signed the Santiago Principles outlined by the IMF in 2008. These nations pledged to follow 24 guidelines aimed at ensuring that SWFs make investment decisions based on economic, not political, goals as well as committing SWFs to certain governance and transparency standards. However, these commitments are only voluntary at this time.

SWFs continue to make important economic news in a variety of different ways. During the global financial crisis, Chinese, Singaporean, and Persian Gulf SWFs were active participants in contributing new capital to faltering US and European banks; this was a phenomenon never considered by critics who charged SWFs with having nefarious political purposes. On the other hand, in October 2011, Chinese SWFs began buying stock of four of the largest Chinese banks in an effort of prop up their stock prices, which had fallen by one-third during the year over worries about excessive bad debts and a real estate bubble. The fact that these Chinese SWFs were supposed to focus on offshore holdings revived concerns about the manipulative uses SWFs can be put to. Finally, there is the case of Libya's SWF, which had $70 billion in assets, or more than $10,000 per Libyan, at the time of the collapse of the Qaddafi government in August 2011. Since that time, the new Libyan government and other international officials have been desperately trying to identify its assets and see what can be recovered given that few people outside of Qaddafi's immediate circle knew all of the SWF's activities. There are significant worries that few of these assets will ever be found and that Libya's SWF was simply a vehicle for expropriation from the Libyan people.

Conclusions

This is a time of change in the Middle East and North Africa. The region's political systems are changing after the events of the Arab Spring and popular uprisings in Egypt, Tunisia, Libya, Yemen, and Syria. The region boasts the youngest population in the world. Its economies have also rapidly become more integrated with the rest of the world over the last 25 years.

Financial systems in the MENA region are changing as well. The privatization of state-owned banking systems has gradually taken place. This movement has increased the efficiency of MENA banks and reduced their levels of non-performing loans, although it has not greatly expanded financial access because government-owned bank monopolies were only replaced with privately owned bank oligopolies. In most countries there has also been a movement away from the financial repression policies of directed lending and interest rate controls that has reduced loan quality and encouraged more credit rationing. Although the results have not yet been dramatic, the primary focus of these and of future reforms must be on dealing with the largest financial problem in the region: the lack of formal financial access for households and particularly small and medium businesses. This lack of access has been driven by three factors: poor institutions that limit collateral and increase risk, a lack of competition in MENA banking systems, and credit rationing resulting from financial repression and a lack of information. Until financial access improves, financial development will contribute less than it could to broader economic development.

Finance in the MENA region is also changing dramatically because of growth in Islamic finance, which is becoming an avenue through which traditional Islamic beliefs can be reconciled with modern finance. Islamic finance should not be viewed as a means of excessively regulating finance so that it is too costly or difficult to conduct. Instead, it is a way to bring access to those who have previously been excluded from formal financial systems because of their religious beliefs.

Finally, finance is changing in MENA because of the growth of sovereign wealth funds. These funds have allowed many countries to put their accumulated wealth to more productive and profitable uses as they save for a "rainy day." However, sovereign wealth funds also bring with them many of the dangers associated with concentrated power, namely political manipulation and corruption. Whether these funds bring greater prosperity to the average citizens of MENA depends upon whether prudential governance and financial transparency can be brought to bear on SWFs by the political systems of each country.

Overall, in contrast to the preconceived biases of many, MENA is a region that is aggressively moving forward, not stuck in the past, and facing many of the challenges and opportunities that always accompany progress.

11 Financial systems in Asia

Overview

When most people think of emerging market economies, they reflexively think of Asia, and with good reason. Not only is Asia home to over 60 percent of the world's population, but it is also the source of a significant fraction of world growth. All emerging market economies accounted for 63 percent of global growth in 2010; emerging economies in Asia accounted for two-thirds of this growth. This trend is likely to continue well beyond 2010. Overall growth in Asia is expected to be 8 percent in 2011 and 2012, but higher than this in many countries, particularly the two dominant economies in the region: China and India.

Of course, in many ways it is difficult to talk about Asia in general when in fact there are many different Asias.[1] The lower-income countries in Asia (Bangladesh, Cambodia, Laos, Mongolia, Myanmar, Nepal) have quite different financial systems from the East and South East Asian economies (South Korea, Indonesia, Malaysia, Philippines, Thailand, Vietnam), while both China and India are large enough to each be considered a separate region of their own.

However, it is also true that there are a great many similarities between the economic and financial development strategies followed by most Asian countries. In fact, Asia's prominence among emerging market economies has not only been driven by its economic performance but also by the power of its shared ideas relating to economic development. The "Asian Model" has become a commonly used term to describe a similar set of policies that have been followed across the region. In the prototypical Asian Model, exports and high domestic investment are the principal engines behind economic growth. Export promotion is encouraged by maintaining undervalued exchange rates funded by the rapid accumulation of foreign reserves. High levels of investment are funded with high private savings (and correspondingly low levels of private consumption) and government surpluses. In regard to its financial systems, the Asian Model is characterized by large, domestically owned banks that dominate overall finance, while equity and particularly bond markets are relatively underdeveloped. It also incorporates an important role for directed lending by the government (particularly to export industries and public investment projects) and connected lending between banks and large corporations.

Figure 11.1 presents data on bank credit, stock market capitalization, and bond market capitalization for a selected group of Asian and OECD countries. Banks and/or stock markets play the largest role in financial intermediation across these countries. However, most Asian countries have levels of bank credit that are less than half that of the OECD average. The exceptions are China, Thailand, and Malaysia, which have closed the gap in bank lending with the OECD. In regard to stock and bond markets, no country in Asia has more than three-fourths the capitalization of the OECD average, with the exception of India and Malaysia. The difference between Asian and OECD financial systems is greatest in bond markets, which are the least developed sector of Asian financial systems. With the exception of Malaysia and Thailand, no country has more than half of the bond market capitalization of the OECD average.

While Asia lags behind developed countries in terms of levels of financial development, financial depth has increased in Asia over time. While there is quite a bit of variation across countries, bank credit has increased in Asian economies by roughly 10–30 percent per year since the 1990s; in East Asia bank assets doubled as a percentage of GDP between 2000 and 2008.[2] The growth rate of stock market capitalization has been even greater, allowing Asian stock markets to progress relative to banks in their own countries as well as against OECD stock markets. However, bond market development has lagged behind and the gap between Asia and the OECD remains large.

Asian banks remain the principal method of formal finance in Asia, and they also played a crucial role in driving the East Asian financial crisis of 1997–1999 (see Chapter 8). Many studies of Asian banks since the crisis have found that Asian banking systems are deeper and more diversified than they were before

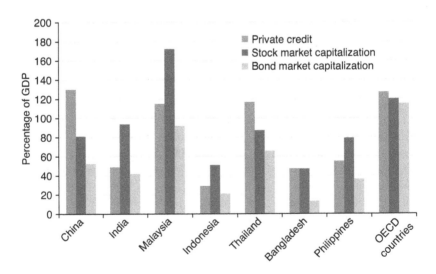

Figure 11.1 Measures of financial depth in selected Asian countries, 2010 (source: World Bank, World Development Indicators (2012)).

the crisis.[3] Across the region, bank capital as well as various measures of profit-ability and balance sheet strength have improved while levels of non-performing loans (NPLs) have fallen. In part this has been achieved by increases in foreign ownership of banks and the privatization of some state-owned banks. In addition, prudential regulation and transparency have improved in many Asian countries.

However, Asian financial systems still lag behind in a number of important areas. In addition to slow bond market development, access to financial services for households and particularly small and medium-sized firms remains limited. Only between 25 and 50 percent of Asian households had access to deposit accounts in 2010.[4] Referring back to Figure 9.1, note that East Asia almost matches the OECD in the average number of deposit accounts, but it lags far behind in loans, while South Asia lags behind in both measures to a much greater extent. Financial access is hampered in all regions of Asia by a lack of physical access to branch banks and ATM machines. The lack of finance for SMEs is just as pronounced. Only 32 percent of SMEs have access to formal external finance in Asia, compared to 56 percent for large Asian firms. In some Asian countries, such as Indonesia and India, SMEs receive less than 10 percent of total bank loans.

Overall, this general description paints a picture of financial systems in the region that, while growing, has been uneven and has not kept pace with overall economic growth. Why hasn't financial development, particularly in regard to bond markets and financial access, been more pronounced? The answer should not be surprising to the reader who has reached this point in the book: in those Asian countries where financial institutions are approaching those that exist in developed countries, financial development is converging to that of the developed world. But where reform of financial institutions is lagging, so too is financial development. Those countries that have reformed their legal and accounting systems, increased financial openness (particularly to foreign competition), improved transparency, and strengthened prudential regulation and supervision have seen convergence with the financial systems of the developed world. Interestingly, some of the countries that have been most successful at these reforms over the last decade—namely South Korea and Malaysia—are countries that suffered the most during the East Asian crisis, where the costs of financial growth without having the proper financial fundamentals in place were most strongly felt. However, in many other countries reform has been much more sporadic, in part because many of these same countries were protected from the crisis by a lack of financial integration and development, but now (as before the crisis) find themselves lagging behind in both financial and economic development.

Many critics have begun to raise questions about the benefits of the Asian Model in general, particularly as a larger number of Asian economies begin to reach the ranks of middle-income countries and beyond. One criticism of the Asian Model is that it emphasizes export promotion over domestic consumption. Doing this has two costs. First, it forces countries to rely on external demand that can expose countries to destabilizing shocks, such as during the global financial crisis of 2007 when GDP growth in India and China fell by roughly 10 percent combined. Exports are estimated to generate more than 40 percent of output growth in Asia, making it particularly sensitive to global economic conditions.[5] Potential shocks are created not only by changes in foreign demand for goods and services but also from the financial linkages created by trade and undervalued exchange rates. When credit tightens in the rest of the world, Asian countries not only see a decline in cross-country capital flows but they also see a decline in their wealth as foreign asset prices fall and the value of their extensive foreign reserve holdings decline.

The second cost of the Asian Model is that it limits consumption and relies too heavily on investment. Figure 11.2 presents data on consumption and investment as a percentage of GDP across a selection of Asian countries. Consumption varies quite a bit in the region, from 70 percent of GDP in the Philippines to only 38 percent in China. Low rates of consumption keep household standards of living depressed relative to their aggregate income levels. But it also keeps investment rates at levels that are not sustainable over the long term. For example, China invests nearly 45 percent of its GDP (recently nearly 50 percent), twice the level of developed countries. In many Asian countries, vast amounts of savings are chasing investment projects that are declining in profitability (often having negative real rates of return) as these countries become richer and diminishing marginal returns to investment become stronger. The results of excessive investment are reduced financial efficiency and higher default rates; together these threaten financial stability. There is a pressing need in many Asian countries to rebalance their aggregate demand away from excessive, unproductive investment and toward consumption.

A big part of achieving this rebalancing is for financial systems in Asia to focus on providing more consumption finance to households and increased lending to entrepreneurs and SMEs, as opposed to directing lending only to large corporations to fund large investment projects. One important way of doing this is to encourage financial reform in the ways already discussed because financial repression in the region is often aimed directly at discouraging consumer lending. Abiad *et al.* (2008) find that increases in an index measuring financial reform in Asia are correlated with increases in household consumption rates. According to their estimates, increasing the measure of financial reform in China to that of South Korea would increase consumption in China by 2.4 percent of GDP.

Another problematic aspect of the Asian Model is its reliance on large domestic banks that engage in connected and/or government-directed lending. The rationale is that large banks can increase the scale of lending, while connected lending allows for a better flow of information so that credit rationing can be mitigated. Directed lending ensures that resources go to the most strategically important industries and investment projects. During the early stages of development in the region, this approach was effective in Asia at mobilizing resources, encouraging investment and allowing firms to increase productivity by taking advantage of economies of scale.

However, this approach has never been a strategy to maximize the efficiency of financial resources. Asian banks have the lowest returns on assets of any region of the emerging market world at less than 1 percent (compared to between 2 and 2.5 percent in Latin America and the Middle East). Asia also has the lowest capital ratios (at less than 7 percent), foreign bank ownership (at less than 10 percent), and highest rates of NPLs of any region (at roughly 5 percent of loans in 2007).[6] This is despite the fact that all of these measures have improved significantly since the East Asian crisis. Unless Asian banking systems become more efficient in the future and move toward ensuring that financial resources are flowing to those that have the most productive uses for them, its financial

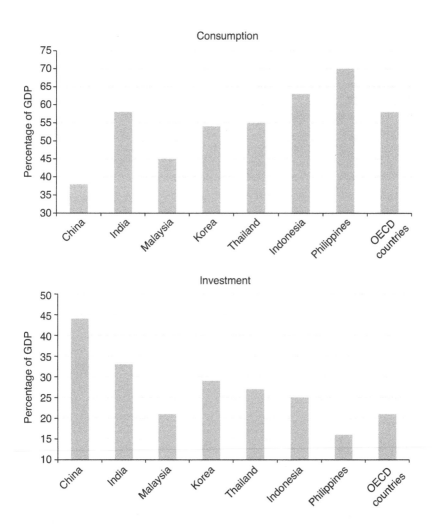

Figure 11.2 Consumption and investment as a percentage of GDP, 2004–2008 average (source: IMF (2010c)).

systems will be a long-term drag on economic growth and a future source of economic volatility. In order to become more efficient, Asian countries must move away from financial repression and connected lending and toward more market-oriented lending in conjunction with improved competition and prudential regulation. Transparency and information must also improve, while risk must be priced more appropriately. During the transition, governments must reduce NPLs by privatizing and recapitalizing banks. These reforms have happened more quickly in certain Asian countries, such as South Korea and Malaysia, but have not been happening quickly enough in other Asian countries that will be examined later in this chapter.

International capital flows and monetary policy

Another important component of the Asian Model is attracting foreign capital inflows in order to fund investment and to facilitate technology and human capital transfer. Six of the world's ten largest recipient countries of foreign capital are in Asia. Table 11.1 presents the aggregate balance of payments for the eight largest economies in Asia between 2009 and 2012 (estimated). Net private inflows to emerging market Asia amounted to more than $500 billion in 2011 (more than 4 percent of GDP), which is half of all capital flows to emerging

Table 11.1 Balance of payments for emerging Asia ($ billions)*

	2009	2010	2011	2012 (forecast)
Capital inflows				
Total inflows, net	388.7	503.5	502.1	485.2
Private inflows, net	371.4	478.3	491.7	475.8
Equity investment, net	254.5	286.3	252.8	264.8
Direct investment, net	168.4	159.5	182.2	175.7
Portfolio investment, net	86.0	126.8	70.6	89.1
Private credit, net	116.9	192.0	238.9	211.1
Commercial banks, net	72.0	110.9	125.6	117.4
Non-banks, net	44.9	81.1	113.4	93.7
Official inflows, net	17.4	25.2	10.4	9.4
Int'l financial institutions	5.4	4.8	2.6	2.0
Bilateral creditors	12.0	20.4	7.7	7.4
Capital outflows				
Total outflows, net	−717.9	−849.6	−822.6	−827.1
Private outflows, net	−136.5	−253.1	−211.1	−259.4
Equity investment abroad, net	−157.5	−135.2	−168.2	−193.9
Resident lending/other, net	21.1	−117.9	−42.9	−65.5
Foreign reserves (− is increase)	−581.5	−596.5	−611.5	−567.8
Current account balance	329.2	346.1	320.5	342.1

Source: *Institute for International Finance Research Note*, September 25, 2011.

Note
* For the seven largest economies in emerging Asia: China, India, Indonesia, Malaysia, Philippines, South Korea, and Thailand.

market economies. Of this amount, more than half went to equity investment, with foreign direct investment outweighing foreign portfolio investment. Commercial banks received the majority of the $240 billion in private credit. Of total private inflows to Asia, 60 percent went to China and 20 percent went to India.[7]

Asia's current account surplus was $320 billion in 2011, which is the direct result of the region's emphasis on export promotion. As a result, net capital outflows must be even larger than inflows. In 2011, net capital outflows from Asia stood at nearly $822 billion, $611 billion of which came from growth in foreign reserve holdings. Once again, this immense growth in foreign reserve holdings has been driven by the strategy of maintaining undervalued exchange rates to facilitate export growth. At the end of 2011, most Asian currencies were undervalued by an estimated 10–40 percent against the dollar.[8]

Of course, not all countries in Asia are equally responsible for this situation in the region's balance of payments. Of the $320 billion capital account surplus in the region in 2011, $290 billion of it was from China. China's net capital inflows were roughly $280 billion, balanced with $570 billion in net capital outflows (6 percent of its GDP), over $500 billion of which came in the form of increases in foreign reserve holdings by the Chinese government. Since 2007, net capital inflows to China have fluctuated greatly but have consistently been roughly 4 percent of GDP (refer back to Figure 6.3).

Capital flows to the low-income Asian countries are different from those to the rest of Asia. While overall capital inflows to these countries are small, only $10 billion in 2010, they amount to nearly 5 percent of GDP in these countries. However, 86 percent of these inflows come in the form of either aid or remittances (compared to 32 percent of inflows for the rest of Asia).[9] As you would expect given the volatile nature of these economies and their weaker financial markets, capital inflows are also much more volatile across time.

One thing that is much different regarding capital inflows to Asia now as compared to before the East Asian financial crisis is that most countries in the region have taken extensive actions to protect against future currency crises. Asian countries are restricting the flow of short-term dollar-denominated debt ("hot money"), adopting more flexible exchange rate regimes (such as inflation targeting or pegging to a basket of currencies), and holding more foreign reserves.[10] In 2009, the ratio of foreign reserves to short-term debt was as high as 7.6 in the Philippines and over 3 in many Asian countries.[11]

High levels of capital inflows to Asia place great pressure on monetary policy and central banks in the region. Greater inflows encourage credit growth, put upward pressure on prices (particularly on asset prices), and reduce domestic interest rates. If a central bank is worried about the inflationary effect of these inflows—and the fact that their grip on domestic interest rates is loosening—they are forced to respond in one of two ways. First, they could allow their exchange rate to appreciate, which will stem the amount of capital inflows. However, this also discourages exports and means abandoning part of their export promotion strategy. The second option could be to tighten domestic monetary policy and raise domestic interest rates through sterilization. However, in the face of strong capital inflows, it is often difficult for central banks to tighten enough and withdraw sufficient amounts of excess reserves to offset the funds that are pouring into the banking system.

These realities have forced many central banks to tighten monetary policy not only through open market operations and by restricting their lending to banks, but also through tightening restrictions on credit and increasing required reserve ratios. For example, required reserve ratios peaked in China at 21 percent in 2011. Such high reserve ratios are a form of financial repression; they not only reduce the efficiency of financial intermediation but also severely restrict the impact of monetary policy by reducing the money multiplier. However, by doing this, Asian economies, including China, have to this point been able to maintain their undervalued exchange rate targets without large increases in inflation. Inflation in the region has remained between 2 and 4 percent in most countries, although it did rise above 5 percent in China and 8 percent in India in 2011.

The financial system of China

It is impossible to talk about finance in Asia, and financial development among emerging market economies in general, without talking extensively about China. More than 440 million people have been raised out of poverty in China over the last 30 years, more than in any country over a similar time period in history. Today, China is the second-largest economy in the world, accounting for 20 percent of global GDP and 11 percent of international trade. Its financial system is disproportionally important to the global financial system: China accounts for nearly 30 percent of total financial assets and holds 60 percent of the world's foreign reserves.

The Chinese financial system is as convoluted and opaque as any in the world. Only a Chinese engineer could understand it (which is exactly the training of most of the leaders of the Chinese Communist Party that designed this system). The complexity of its financial system does not reduce China's importance, just the difficulty of understanding how China has achieved such growth with such an inefficient financial system that has not—as yet—experienced a major financial crisis.

There are two cornerstones to the Chinese financial system. The first is an unbending commitment to an extreme version of the Asian Model: export promotion, undervalued exchange rates, high rates of investment, low rates of consumption, managed capital inflows, and bank-led financial development. But the Asian Model in China looks different than elsewhere because of the other, and most important, cornerstone of the Chinese system: the Communist Party's unchallenged control over banks and financial markets. In the words of Dai Bingguo, China's most senior foreign policy official, the Communist Party's "number one core interest is to maintain its fundamental system and state security."[12] In order to maintain these two cornerstones, a carefully designed system of financial repression exists in China organized around sustaining an undervalued exchange rate while at the same time maintaining stability and the Communist Party's control of the financial system.

The Chinese banking system

In order to understand the nature of financial repression in China, it is important to first understand China's banks—particularly the four largest state-owned banks—which largely are China's financial system.[13] China essentially did not have a financial system in 1980 and these "Big Four" banks—each of which are controlled by a separate sphere of influence within the Communist Party—have been the overwhelming force behind financial development in the country since that time. In many ways these Big Four banks operate like public utilities, taking advantage of financial economies of scale through funneling the huge levels of domestic savings generated by Chinese households into state-owned corporations with little emphasis on economic returns. These corporations in turn conduct the domestic investment that, as mentioned in the previous section, is a cornerstone of economic growth in the Asian Model. Chinese banks do little lending to private firms or consumers; while in the United States there are five credit cards per person, in China there are 33 persons per credit card.[14]

Today these Big Four banks are each among the largest 25 banks in the world (in total assets) and hold over 70 percent of all assets in the Chinese financial system (in 2011 this amounted to nearly $6 trillion).[15] However, even these numbers underestimate the effective influence of the Big Four as these banks also are the owners of large amounts of equity in Chinese corporations and hold over 70 percent of all bonds issued in China.

Of course, size alone does not measure the strength of a banking system; asset quality also matters, and on this score China has one of the weakest banking systems in the world. Reported NPLs in China's financial system have fallen from 12.5 percent of loans in 2005 to less than 1 percent in 2011. But few objective observers believe these numbers, however, particularly given that the total number of loans outstanding in China has nearly tripled during the same period.[16] Chinese banks primarily lend to the large state-owned sector of the Chinese economy at highly subsidized rates.[17] While SOEs produce only one-third of Chinese GDP, they receive two-thirds of total credit and total investment.[18] These SOEs—just like the state-owned banks that lend to them—are run by political appointees of the Communist Party. While state-owned banks and corporations superficially operate under Western institutions that guarantee property rights, legal protections, accounting standards, and transparency, it is generally true that political influence and organized corruption are the primary influence behind most decisions.[19] For example, bank loans of more than $500 million must be directly approved by an official at the highest level of the Communist Party.[20] According to one journalist, a red phone sits on the desks of chief executives designated only for the party to communicate its orders to all the largest banks and SOEs.[21]

Because business decisions are largely politically driven and not profit-driven, Chinese SOEs are unprofitable despite their high levels of investment and fast growth. A 2009 study by Hong Kong's Institute for Monetary Research found that profits in Chinese SOEs would be below zero if they had to pay market interest rates.[22] In this environment—where growth takes place without profit-ability—the potential level of hidden NPLs could be staggering. One estimate by Credit Suisse bank is that the actual level of NPLs in the Chinese banking system is between 8 and 12 percent of total credit, representing a potential loss of between 65 and 100 percent of the total equity in the banking system.[23] These NPLs are particularly dangerous because Chinese banks are among the most weakly capitalized in the world, with capital-to-asset ratios of only 6 percent.

The Big Four banks, like many of the SOEs in China, are partially owned by the public. Approximately 30 percent of the shares of these banks are publicly tradable.[24] Purchasing stock in Chinese banks is the primary way that foreign banks can enter the Chinese banking system. Private capital in these banks has been growing rapidly in order to support China's huge growth in lending. However, Walter and Howie (2011) point out that between 2004 and 2008 the amount of new capital in the Chinese banking system was equal to the total amount of dividends distributed by Chinese banks. Coupled with the almost complete lack of transparency regarding the lending activities of these banks, there are real questions about whether any real value is being created in the Chinese banking system or if, in fact, the entire system is an elaborate Ponzi system for moving resources from households to state-controlled enterprises and with old stockholders receiving dividends generated by the contributions of new stockholders.

Financial repression in China

Chinese banks are not just inefficient because of a lack of profit-motive incentives in their decision making, but also because of the financial repression policies imposed by the Chinese government. Financial repression in China takes place in many different forms but primarily through the distortion of two prices: the exchange rate and interest rates. We have talked extensively about China's undervalued exchange rate policy and its importance in China's export- and investment-led economic development strategy. As discussed in more detail in Chapter 8, in order to maintain this undervalued exchange rate, China's central bank, the People's Bank of China (PBOC), must buy enormous quantities of foreign reserves (primarily dollar assets) and sell RMB (the Chinese currency).

Maintaining this undervalued exchange rate without generating high levels of inflation would not be possible without extensive sterilization of the RMB created. The PBOC tries to sterilize RMB growth and stabilize inflation through two methods. First, they limit money growth through massive open market sales by requiring banks to hold large amounts of sovereign bonds. Second, the PBOC attempts to reduce the money multiplier by setting the reserve requirement ratio at a high level so that the banking system's ability to lend reserves is limited. In October 2011 the PBOC had raised the reserve requirement ratio on deposits to 21.5 percent of deposits, which is 2–3 times what it is in developed countries. While these repressive policies have managed to limit inflation in China to less than 5 percent, it has also severely reduced the profitability and efficiency of

Chinese banks, which are forced to hold the vast majority of their assets in government bonds and required reserves.

At the same time that the PBOC is dampening credit growth, it enforces ceilings on all types of nominal interest rates. Nominal interest rate ceilings on bank deposits are at or below the rate of inflation, reducing the real interest rate below zero. This deposit interest rate ceiling helps banks raise vast pools of money cheaply and guarantees them profits, even when the money is distributed inefficiently, because the interest rate ceilings on sovereign bonds and loans are greater than on deposits. These interest rate ceilings aim to encourage domestic investment, which is one important reason that investment in China was 44 percent of GDP in 2010—an incredible 18 percent of global investment.

So while the PBOC enhances the profitability of banks on one hand with interest rate ceilings, it reduces the profitability of banks on the other hand through their exchange rate sterilization measures that limit credit growth. The overall impact of these policies is to make financial intermediation very inefficient. The Chinese system of financial repression creates no mechanisms to ensure that finance is flowing to those firms that have the most productive uses for it. Nor is there any mechanism to ensure that financial risk is priced appropriately, i.e. that riskier borrowers pay more for credit. Instead, this system of interest rate ceilings and limited credit only magnifies the extent of credit rationing and reduces access to formal finance for households, SMEs, and the private sector of the economy.

The financial repression of banks in China also plays a large role in the underdevelopment of bond and stock markets in the country. In the bond market, the government sets interest rate ceilings for all bonds, which distort both their returns and their risk while eliminating incentives for private individuals to hold bonds. However, because the interest rates on sovereign bonds are greater than interest rates on deposits, banks have an incentive—as well as a mandate—to not only purchase government bonds but to hold them until maturity. (Given that the government is both the issuer of the bonds and the majority owner of banks, banks holding bonds is much like the left hand lending to the right hand.) As a result, banks hold more than 70 percent of all bonds issued, while households hold less than 5 percent. Liquidity is very thin in bond markets (0.25 percent of the number of transactions in US Treasury bond markets), leading to large liquidity premiums in the secondary bond market that discourage private purchases of bonds and also deter private companies from issuing bonds to finance their capital.

Bank deposits and bonds offer minimal returns to savers and almost no diversification because they are all tied directly to the performance of the state-owned sector of the economy. In order to achieve higher returns, vast amounts of funds—both domestic and foreign—have poured into China's stock markets. China now has the second-largest stock market in the world with nearly $4 trillion in total capitalization in 2011 (more than 40 times what it was in 1999). Initial public offerings (IPOs) have become the way that China's SOEs—including its banks—have partially privatized. In 2009 alone Chinese companies raised more than $100 billion in new capital.[25] However, the state remains the majority owner of most corporations, meaning that decisions are driven by politics and not by profits. Coupled with a general lack of transparency, it is unclear how Chinese shares should be valued by investors. Instead of fundamentals-based prices, Chinese stock markets are largely driven by speculation and insider information. Only the most privileged party officials earn the right to participate in IPOs. Some of the biggest speculators in the stock market are other SOEs. Walter and Howie (2011) estimate that 20 percent of corporate profits in China come from stock trading in the stock of other firms!

As we have discussed, excess liquidity coupled with a lack of transparency and rampant speculation are prerequisites for destabilizing asset bubbles to occur. Asset bubbles may not only be building in Chinese stock markets, but as we discussed in Chapter 5 may also be occurring in China's real estate market as large amounts of savings chase a limited range of speculative assets that can offer positive real rates of return—something that bonds and bank deposits do not offer because of interest rate ceilings.

The private sector and underground lending

While the state-owned sector receives the vast majority of credit and foreign investment, it is the private sector that attracts the most talent, technology, and entrepreneurship in the Chinese economy. These private firms are also those that are the most export-oriented and most competitive in international markets. Given that exports generate roughly 40 percent of Chinese growth, private firms now account for 70 percent of employment and two-thirds of total GDP growth in China.

Only 20 percent of private firms have access to formal finance through banks in China, which is roughly equivalent to countries such as India, Nigeria, and Bangladesh.[26] In the search for credit, households and SMEs resort to extensive underground lending markets that have developed in China, often illegally (although often ignored by local government officials). The largest underground lending markets are centered in the coastal city of Wenzhou, which was also home to the first private enterprises established in China after the reforms of 1978.[27] This underground lending takes place through middlemen, collateralized trade credit, and credit cooperatives (often called "lending houses"). It also takes place through ROSCAs, which are much larger and more developed in China than the African versions discussed in Chapter 9. For example, in "bidding ROSCAs" (often referred to as *hui* in China), participants can make bids to increase their chances of receiving the pool of savings, with these bids essentially serving as interest earned for the entire pool.

In these underground lending markets, interest rate ceilings are ignored and party influence is negligible. In fact, most underground loans are made indirectly by individuals or companies—often branches of SOEs and even local governments—that have access to formal finance and can take these loans and recycle them to those without access to formal credit but at significantly higher interest rates (often at rates as high as 6 percent *a month*). When private firms pay exist-ing SOEs in order to use their name to get a loan, it is referred to in China as "wearing a red hat." Experts claim that 80 percent of SMEs use some form of underground lending.[28] Estimates are that underground lending in China was more than $630 billion in 2011 (up more than 40 percent) and accounts for more than $2.6 trillion in total loans outstanding, or one-third of all lending in the country.[29]

Underground lending thrives in China for the same reasons that informal finance thrives wherever large numbers of individuals do not have access to formal finance. According to Anderson (2006), 66 percent of Chinese firms that do not have access to formal finance cite a lack of collateral as the reason. However, because underground loans are often made based on relationships (*guanxi*), physical collateral is not as important. In addition, better information is often available in informal lending that helps to overcome credit rationing and the costs of credit intermediation. Tsai (2002) finds empirical evidence that those that are most likely to be credit rationed—the poor, women, migrants, smaller businesses, and those that lack political ties—are most likely to rely on under-ground lending. Underground lending markets also allow lenders to avoid rate ceilings and charge higher interest rates, which also helps mitigate credit ration-ing. Finally, there is the attractiveness of using underground lending to avoid regulation, party scrutiny, and corruption by obtaining finance through informal channels. According to a popular Chinese proverb, "The mountains are high and the emperor is far away." This is particularly true when it comes to underground lending markets.

Of course, the lack of transparency in underground markets coupled with the increased riskiness of firms that are smaller, newer, and without political con-nections means that these informal loans are much higher risk.[30] Estimates of NPLs in the Chinese banking system of between 8 and 12 percent are predicated on the fact that defaults in the underground market will eventually lead to defaults in the formal banking systems because of loan recycling, particularly by local governments that receive one-fifth of all loans but are responsible for about half of all NPLs (roughly 20 to 30 percent of the loans SOEs make are non-performing).[31]

The lack of transparency coupled with the lack of regulation of underground lending raises the specter of a future banking crisis building within China. Banks have little idea of the actual risk they are exposed to given that they have no idea to whom many of their formal loans are being re-lent.[32] Likewise, there is little idea as to the quality of the collateral that is backing many of these loans. Many underground loans are used to finance real estate and stock purchases that may be experiencing bubbles in China. Fitch Ratings agency estimates that a banking crisis triggered by a spike in NPLs in the underground lending market could necessitate a bailout of the Chinese banking system that could cost upwards of 30 percent of GDP.[33]

Regardless of the quality of the specific underground loans, there is also signifi-cant concern that the growth of overall domestic lending and debt in the Chinese economy is unsustainable. Fueled largely by this underground market, total credit in China has grown by over 15 percent a year in the last decade and reached a high growth rate of 35 percent in 2009. Household debt has risen to nearly 55 percent of disposable income in 2010. In addition, the stated debt of the central government is roughly 20 percent of GDP. To these debts must also be added other "hidden debts." Walter and Howie (2011) estimate that these hidden debts include the debt of banks (because they are state-owned, making it unlikely that they would be allowed to fail by the government) which is roughly 23 percent of GDP, local government debt (largely involved in the underground market) of roughly 28 percent of GDP, and NPLs in the banking system (past and future) of roughly 15 percent of GDP. Together, the total public debt obligations of China sum to 76 percent of GDP, well above average for emerging market economies. It is important to note that all of this debt, both private and public, is domestic and not external debt.[34] As a result, the Chinese financial system is largely protected from capital flight and exchange rate risk in ways that other emerging market economies are not. Still, China has accumulated a remarkable amount of debt in a short period of time, and the idea that China is protected from a financial crisis simply because it is a low-debt country does not withstand closer scrutiny.

The 2007 global financial crisis: is China next?

The two decades preceding the 2007 global financial crisis were generally a period of slow but progressive financial liberalization in China. The country's two primary stock exchanges—in Shanghai and Shenzhen—were established. The PBOC was granted a measure of independence. The largest state-owned banks were liberalized as directed lending requirements were reduced and the banks were partially privatized. When the East Asian financial crisis struck in 1997, China was able to largely avoid the crisis primarily because of their adoption of capital controls and a non-convertible currency. In fact, the East Asian crisis may have been a net benefit for the country as reformers in China were able to use the crisis as an opportunity to push forward further financial reforms, including a $625 billion recapitalization of Chinese banks (and remove nearly half the loans in the banking system from bank balance sheets because they were non-performing) funded by the Chinese government (nearly 28 percent of GDP).[35] This was followed by a massive partial privatization of Chinese banks to raise more capital. In 2005, the PBOC even began to loosen the cornerstone of Chinese financial policy: the strict undervalued peg of the RMB to the dollar. As a result, the RMB appreciated against the dollar by nearly 20 percent. In 2007, the PBOC gradually began to raise interest rate ceilings.

However, the tide of reform began to ebb beginning in 2005, and since that time reformers in China have begun to lose more inside political fights within the Communist Party than they have won. The biggest impact of the 2007 global financial crisis in China has been to strengthen the hand of the anti-reform elements within the party and weaken proponents of liberalization and "American"-style financial systems. Beginning in 2008, the RMB was re-linked to the dollar, interest rate ceilings re-established, and financial repression poli-cies were frozen in place. As a result, financial institutions in China remain, as argued in Chapter 3, among the worst in the emerging market world in de facto terms (if not *de jure*).[36] A good example of this is the state of financial regulation in China, which is highly fragmented among eight different regulatory bodies in addition to intervention by party insiders. There is little coordination between these regulators and little transparency regarding their actions.

Given the weakness of Chinese financial institutions, history tells us that a future financial crisis in China is a real possibility. In our discussion here we have highlighted a number of areas where China could be approaching a tipping point toward financial crisis.

First, a banking crisis could be triggered by a spike in NPLs in China, most likely from within its vast, unregulated, and opaque underground lending market.[37] Any spike in NPLs would immediately threaten a banking crisis because China's banks are weakly capitalized.

Second, a banking crisis could be triggered by the general inefficiency of the system caused by financial repression. For example, a spike in inflation in China (which rose above 5 percent in 2011) could reduce real rates so far below zero that rapid deposit disintermediation could take place and bank runs could occur. High inflation could also reduce bond prices and create large capital losses for banks given that bonds are 20 to 30 percent of banks' total assets. This rise in inflation could be the result of China's inflexible commitment to its undervalued exchange rate. There is some evidence that more sophisticated depositors, such as larger Chinese firms, have already moved many of their deposits and bond purchases overseas in search of higher returns.[38]

Third, the bursting of potential asset bubbles in the stock market and real estate market could also lead to a spike in bankruptcies that could initiate a banking crisis. These potential bubbles are fueled by excessive domestic savings, financial repression policies that limit the returns on other types of less specula-tive financial assets such as bank deposits and bonds, and a general lack of infor-mation and transparency that encourages speculation.

Fourth, a domestic debt crisis could occur in which the Chinese government finds itself unable to pay its debts. While the official public debt is quite low (approximately 20 percent of GDP), there are many hidden debts: debt incurred by local governments, debt issued by government-owned banks, and the recapi-talization costs of banks from hidden NPLs. In addition, the government also has ignored future obligations that will result from the drastic demographic changes that are taking place within China because of its one-child policy. China is in the unprecedented situation of growing old before it becomes developed. By 2050, one-fourth of the Chinese population will be older than 65 and its labor force will shrink by more than 10 percent. As the population rapidly ages, the govern-ment is likely to see GDP growth slow, its social safety-net obligations grow, and household savings decline significantly. Each of these factors will put upward pressure on future debt levels in China. Currently, unfunded pension liabilities for the government stand at 150 percent of GDP.

Fifth, a financial crisis could be sparked by a crisis of confidence caused by endemic corruption—both political and venal—throughout the financial system and the state-owned sector of the economy. As growth eventually slows in China, the costs of this corruption coupled with the problems of the state being both the owner and the regulator of the financial system may cause many foreign and domestic investors to flee the country, creating capital flight that could depress economic growth and initiate a financial crisis.

The possibility of all of these potential crises certainly does not mean that any of them are going to happen. In fact, during the 2007 global financial crisis and its aftermath many observers have continued to point to China as a model of financial stability. Credit growth has been nearly 20 percent a year post-crisis, China's bank profits rose by 20 percent in 2010, and *reported* NPLs remain low. But even if China does manage to avoid a financial crisis, its financial system remains a drag on its economic growth.

For China to have a financial system that is not a hindrance to its growth, it is going to have to gradually move away from its arcane and idiosyncratic system and toward a more modern and transparent system. This primarily involves enacting reforms that increase transparency, developing a better system of independent prudential regulation, and using market forces to generate prices that convey better information and more accurately reflect true risk.

However, the most important reforms of the Chinese financial system that could be implemented would be the gradual elimination of its reliance on undervalued exchange rates and interest rate ceilings, both of which reduce the efficiency of financial intermediation and stunt financial development. Over the long run these distortions destabilize the Chinese financial system by increasing NPLs, encourage an over-reliance on SOE investment and exports, and create incentives for asset bubbles to grow in more speculative asset markets such as stocks and real estate. By allowing greater market influence over interest rates and the exchange rate, China would also be able to achieve another critical objective: rebalancing its aggregate demand by encouraging more domestic consumption and investment by private firms and relying less on SOE investment and exports. When interest rates reflect the true price of loanable funds, households and SMEs will be able to gain more access to formal credit, increasing consumption and private investment. If the exchange rate was allowed to better balance the flow of goods and capital across its borders, Chinese households will also be able to import more goods and improve their standards of living. Moving to a convertible, flexible currency might also allow the RMB to eventually become a reserve currency that could rival the dollar, providing many different financial privileges to China that the United States currently enjoys all to itself. But as things stand now, the RMB will not become a dominant reserve currency because it is not fully convertible and because it is undervalued, meaning that it can only appreciate in the future. There is little incentive to borrow (only lend) in a currency that only appreciates, and an international currency must be one that is liquid enough to both borrow and lend in.[39]

There is a group of reformers within the Chinese government, many of them at the PBOC, who believe such reforms are necessary. In early 2012, the PBOC released a study calling for staged capital account liberalization over the next decade in the following order.[40] First, restrictions on capital outflows would be phased out. Second, controls on international lending, including lending in RMB, would be phased out. Third, restrictions on capital inflows to Chinese stock, bond, and property markets would be eased (retaining restrictions on hot money). However, history tells us (see Chapter 6) that to conduct such capital account reforms without first reforming the domestic financial system—particularly eliminating interest rate controls and allowing the exchange rate to appreciate—risks capital flight and an eventual financial crisis. Unfortunately, the lesson that many Chinese policymakers outside the PBOC learned from the 2007 global financial crisis is that China cannot afford to liberalize because to do so would lead to a similar financial crisis in China. In the analogy of one Communist Party official, the Chinese economy is a "bird in a cage," where the party's control is the cage and must be expanded as the bird grows, but cannot be opened lest the bird fly away.[41] However, the fact of the matter is that China cannot afford to remain stagnant as its financial system gets larger and the imbalances grow more extreme. To fail to do so is costly not only in terms of slower growth, but because of the increased risk of a future financial crisis that could make the 2007 global financial crisis pale in comparison.

The financial system of India in comparison with China

China and India are tied together, both economically and in our psyches. In addition to being the two fastest-growing economies in the world, they are the two most populated countries with over two billion people between them. Interestingly, however, their approaches to financial development are quite different while at the same time sharing a number of important characteristics.

The similarities between the financial systems of China and India

The banking system, bond markets, and stock markets in India and China are alike in four important ways. The first is that the banking systems of each country are dominated by state-owned banks that suffer from extensive financial repression. While there are a large number of private banks in India, only three of the top 20 banks are private and only one is foreign.[42] Financial repression of the banking system takes many different forms. In India, one of the most important is through excessive requirements placed on banks to hold government bonds. All banks are required to hold at least 24 percent of their assets in government bonds. This provides the government with a cheap form of finance, but also serves as a tax on banks that limits diversification and increases the cost of credit.[43] By forcing banks to hold so many bonds, banks engage in relatively little lending and secondary bond market development in India is as stunted as it is in China. In addition, strict limits on foreign capital inflows and foreign bank entry reduce competition and the overall efficiency of the Indian banking system, just as they do in China.

The second important similarity between India and China is that their financial institutions are weak and corruption within their systems is endemic. As discussed in Chapter 3, weak institutions in both China and India are a significant hindrance to their financial development. In each country, legal systems, protection of property rights, and prohibitions on corruption appear to be good on paper (*de jure*) but are lacking in practice (de facto). As in China, state regulators and politicians play an important role in shaping the financial decisions of Indian banks. In the words of Shah and Patnaik (2011: 7), "The structure of legislation and regulation is one where everything is prohibited unless explicitly permitted." This attitude limits financial innovation, limits the efficacy of prudential regulation, and also grants inordinate power to regulators that increases the possibilities for graft. Corruption in India tends to be more decentralized—meaning unorganized and largely taking place by individuals—and not centralized and organized as it is in China. As discussed in Chapter 3, this actually increases the costs of corruption and makes it more harmful to financial development because it increases the quantity of corruption.

The third similarity is that within both countries access to formal finance is severely limited. As in China, most formal finance in India flows to SOEs, not private firms. Private companies receive only 43 percent of formal credit in India (compared to 25 percent in China). While this lack of access has led to a booming underground lending market in China, in India it has led to growth in microfinance and also to the popularity of family-owned firms that rely heavily on internal finance.[44]

Because they suffer from financial repression, low profitability, and corruption, India and China also share a final similarity: high levels of non-performing loans. While reported NPLs in India were 2.5 percent of total loans, some analysts believe that the loans close to default in India may be as high as 17 percent.[45]

Taken together, the similarities between India and China mean that both financial systems are inefficient and resources do not always go to the most productive uses. As a result, both countries would benefit greatly from financial liberalization. According to a McKinsey study, reform of the Chinese financial system so that it achieved efficiency levels similar to those found in other emerging market economies would increase GDP in China by an incredible 17 percent and in India by 6.7 percent.[46]

The differences between the financial systems in China and India

There are clearly some important differences between these two countries as well. The most obvious is that financial depth is much greater in China than it is in India. The commercial banking system in China is eight times the size of India's.[47] The ratio of private credit to GDP in China was 130 percent in 2010, compared to only 50 percent in India.[48] In large part this difference reflects

China's commitment to the Asian Model of investment and export-led development which has generated an incredible amount of savings. While the total savings rate in India is high at 35 percent of GDP, China's has reached an astounding 50 percent of GDP. Even more interesting, China has managed to use their system of financial repression, undervalued exchange rates, and a lack of a social safety net to generate these extraordinary levels of savings while keeping the real returns on many financial assets below zero. This creates greater financial depth in China relative to India, where the costs of credit are much higher (and closer to true market prices). However, it also means that India is much less reliant on investment and exports to sustain aggregate demand than China.

A second, but related, difference between China and India is that while China's financial system is dominated by state-owned banks, the Indian financial system is dominated by its large and rapidly growing stock markets. India is often referred to as having a "stock culture," in part because its stock markets have a long history dating back to the British colonial period which also established a reasonable system of legal protections for equity investors in common law. Indian stock markets were liberalized beginning in 1993 making prices more likely to reflect real underlying value. Stock market capitalization in India has grown from 3.5 percent of GDP in the 1980s to more than 90 percent of GDP today (but down significantly from 2007 highs). India has two of the five largest stock exchanges in the world, the National Stock Exchange and the Bombay Stock Exchange. Incredibly, equity accounts for 75 percent of all financial assets in India, reflecting both the importance of stock markets but also the relative weakness of Indian banks and the bond market.

The importance of equity in Indian finance has a number of implications. One of the most important is that Indian firms and banks do not tend to be highly leveraged because they have little debt and a great deal of equity. This reduces default risk in the economy and may mean that high levels of NPLs in India may not pose as great a threat to banking stability as elsewhere. In addition, because only a relatively small number of Indian firms dominate the stock market, these corporations tend to "sprawl," meaning that they operate in a wide variety of areas as opposed to outsourcing parts of their business. The extensive vertical and horizontal integration of Indian firms also helps to keep more transactions internal, limiting the opportunities for corruption or for having to deal with the legal system. Of course, such integration also means that firms are much less specialized in India, reducing overall economic efficiency. For Indian savers, the excessive reliance on stocks reduces returns on equity and increases the risk of stock market bubbles. However, Indian savers do have the advantage of being able to get much higher returns on their savings than most Chinese savers because of open access to equity markets and the fact that rates on bank deposits (and, as a result, loans) are higher in order to compete with equity.

One final difference between India and China is in how India chooses to manage its exchange rate and its balance of payments. India has rejected an important part of the Asian Model by allowing its exchange rate to float, although the Central Bank of India has managed the rupee to different degrees over time. As a result, India is one of the few Asian countries that runs a current account deficit and a capital account surplus. The current account deficit in India was high in 2011 at 3 percent of GDP, largely driven by imports of consumer goods that help increase standards of living in India.

One of the reasons that the Indian current account deficit is not larger than this is that India has long placed controls on foreign capital inflows. Restrictions take many forms, including limits on the entry of foreign banks into India, the number of branches foreign banks can open, and foreign holdings of government bonds. However, as argued by Prasad (2009), many of these *de jure* restrictions are circumvented on a de facto basis, making India's capital account not as closed as it might appear on paper. Even accounting for this, however, India still lags behind other emerging market economies in terms of de facto measures of openness. While Indian capital inflows grew steadily in the 1990s and 2000s, peaking at nearly 9 percent of its GDP in 2008 (before falling significantly during the global financial crisis), on average India only attracts 5 percent of all capital inflows to emerging market economies, which is less than its share of total emerging market GDP of roughly 7 percent.

The stated purpose of Indian capital controls is to limit potentially destabilizing foreign capital inflows, particularly short-term foreign-denominated debt. These restrictions on hot money have kept India's external debt low—at roughly 20 percent of GDP—as well as allowed it to avoid holding the massive amounts of foreign reserves that many countries feel they have to hold as insurance against sudden capital outflows. However, in return India has given up many other advantages that higher levels of foreign capital offer: higher productivity, external discipline on macroeconomic policy, incentives to adopt international institutions and prudential regulations, increased competition, and improved diversification. Whether this has been a good tradeoff or a bad one for India is not completely clear. However, just as in China, the lesson that many Indian policymakers seem to have taken away from the 2007 global financial crisis is that the potential instability created by financial liberalization makes it too dangerous to adopt in the foreseeable future. Instead, the question Indian policymakers should be asking is whether a country in which nearly one-fourth of its citizens live in extreme poverty can afford slower growth in the long term for the uncertain hope of more financial stability in the short term.

Evaluating the Indian and Chinese financial models

In summary, while superficially similar in many ways, India and China in fact represent two very different models of how to pursue financial development. India represents many of the pros and cons of having a long-established system of institutions that have incorporated many elements of market-based development—such as the recognition of private property rights and liberalized stock markets—but is also struggling to shake off the heavy hand of a state that has traditionally played a large role in the economy. India is the world's largest democracy and the potential chaos that accompanies democracy can be seen in its erratic pursuit of liberalization and in the decentralized corruption that threatens to undermine every step it makes toward progress.

China, on the other hand, had the luxury of starting a financial system essentially from scratch in the 1980s but has been weighed down with a political obsession for control and stability that has locked them into an ideological and idiosyncratic system. This system has managed to funnel an immense amount of resources toward investment, export promotion, and economic growth over the last 20 years, but is undermined by its inability to ensure that these resources are going toward their most productive uses. The question that will define much of the future of the emerging market development is which model will be most successful: one characterized by chaos and flexibility or one characterized by stability and oppression.

South East Asia and the aftermath of the East Asian crisis in Indonesia and Malaysia

In contrast to the very large economies of China, India, and South Korea, the economies of South East Asia receive relatively little attention. This is likely because of the larger number of relatively smaller countries that populate the area (although Indonesia is home to nearly 240 million people). However, these countries together would be the ninth-largest economy in the world, accounting for almost $2 trillion in GDP in 2010.

Unfortunately, South East Asia's biggest moment in the economic limelight was the East Asian crisis between 1997 and 1999. Three of the four countries that suffered the worst crises—Thailand, Malaysia, and Indonesia—were in the sub-region. During the crisis, nominal GDP per capita fell among these three countries by an average of more than 25 percent in 1998. Real GDP per capita was still lower in these countries in 2006 than it was in 1997.

One of the reasons that these countries suffered similarly during the crisis is that they had largely adopted the same set of macroeconomic policies before the crisis. As discussed in Chapter 8, these countries adopted rigid pegs to the dollar that led to overvalued exchange rates, capital account deficits, and rapid foreign capital inflows in the period leading up to the crisis. These countries also had weak prudential regulation, legal systems, and transparency requirements. This was particularly true in regard to their concentrated banking systems, where little attention was paid by regulators to improving the quality of information and limiting moral hazard. Instead, each banking system was dominated by government-directed lending and connected lending (sometimes crony capitalism) between banks and their clients.

Given their similarities before and during the crisis, it is valuable to examine how these countries have performed in the decade or more since the crisis. In order to narrow our focus, the discussion here will focus on comparing and contrasting two South East Asia countries in particular: Malaysia and Indonesia.

Indonesia and Malaysia have significantly adjusted both their macroeconomic policies and their financial institutions since the crisis. Regarding macroeconomic policy, both countries have tried to minimize the dangers of speculative over-valued exchange rates and short-term capital inflows. Both Indonesia and Malaysia, along with their South East Asian neighbors, have been careful to maintain undervalued exchange rates (and accumulate foreign reserves) in order to discourage future currency crises and also to encourage export growth. As a result, these countries have been consistently running current account surpluses and have high export-to-GDP ratios of between 30 and 60 percent of GDP. Malaysia's current account surplus was 14 percent of GDP in 2010, while Indonesia's was nearly 2 percent. In other words, these countries have been adapting their macroeconomic policy toward export promotion in similar ways to many other Asian emerging market economies.

Malaysia and Indonesia have also tried to limit foreign capital inflows, with mixed success. Figure 11.3 presents external short-term debt in South East Asian countries. After an incredible buildup and crash before and during the East Asian crisis, short-term debt levels have once again been building in Indonesia and Malaysia (as well as Thailand and Vietnam), largely in response to solid growth in the region and also relatively high interest rates. However, the situation is not as precarious as it was in the mid-1990s because these countries are now running current account surpluses, not deficits as they were in the 1990s, and their currencies are now undervalued, not overvalued. In addition, these countries now hold very large amounts of foreign reserves, with the ratio of foreign reserves to short-term debt being roughly three to one in both Indonesia and Malaysia.[49]

In regard to prudential regulation, both countries have also taken measures to improve financial institutions and to prevent a financial crisis from

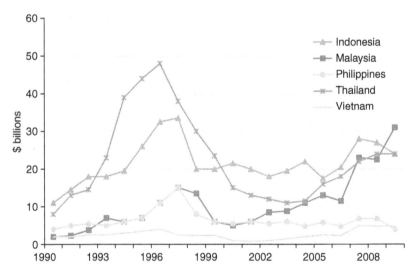

Figure 11.3 External short-term debt in South East Asian countries (source: Shimada and Yang (2010)).

occurring again. Reform began with extensive bank bailouts and recapitalizations in the immediate aftermath of the crisis, which cost roughly 5 percent of GDP in Malaysia and more than 50 percent of GDP in Indonesia. The bailout was so much larger in Indonesia because of their weaker financial fundamentals, higher levels of NPLs, and a larger devaluation (75 percent in Indonesia as compared to 40 percent in Malaysia). Following these bailouts, Indonesia and Malaysia enacted an extensive series of reforms, although the exact structure and detail of these reforms did differ across countries. Prudential regulations on banks that were added included (1) increased capital ratios for banks, (2) more transparency requirements and increased supervision, (3) opening the banking system to more foreign entry, (4) increased consumer regulation to reduce "predatory lending," and (5) expanded deposit insurance. Broader institutional reforms exacted also included legal reform and enhanced payment systems to aid stock and bond market development. Finally, more cooperation between countries in the region was encouraged through improved lending programs between central banks and an initiative to develop an Asian bond market.

Improvements in the quality and stability of the financial systems in the region since the crisis have been significant. NPLs in Indonesia and Malaysia have fallen from 49 and 18 percent in 1998, respectively, to 3.8 percent in both countries in 2009, which is roughly at the OECD average. Leverage ratios have also fallen, capital ratios are above international standards, and returns on equity and assets are strong.[50] Finally, foreign ownership of banks as well as foreign borrowing have risen, meaning that the banking system is both more competitive and more diversified, although, as stated before, this increased foreign borrowing is mildly ominous.

All of this good news masks some real difficulties that still exist in these countries, however. A significant challenge remains across the region in regard to not just reforming macroeconomic policy, but also conducting microeconomic reforms that increase the role that individual profit incentives play in decision making. Indonesia is a good example of a country that has not reformed at the microeconomic level, while Malaysia has made much more significant progress toward having a truly market-driven financial system.

An example of this is the different approach that each country has taken toward dealing with the corruption and connected lending that existed within their economies before the East Asian crisis. While the state has always played a large role in both of these economies, Malaysia is a parliamentary democracy where the state's control over the economy has gradually declined over time. Because Malaysia is much smaller than Indonesia (roughly one-tenth of its size in terms of population), it also has been forced to have a more open economy and financial system. On the other hand, Indonesia's size has allowed it to more easily rely on inefficient import substitution policies and domestic finance. Indonesia has long been an autocracy where elites control an inordinate amount of power and patronage and nepotism are rampant. Autocracy in Indonesia has been justified as a means of keeping a very ethnically diverse country from fracturing.

Autocracy in Indonesia has also led to some of the worst corruption in the world. According to Transparency International's corruption perceptions index, Indonesia ranks 110th out of 182 countries in terms of corruption.[51] Extensive corruption has created political instability (which contributed to magnifying the size of the East Asian crisis in Indonesia). It has also undermined other crucial institutions as bureaucrats and politicians have created extra regulations and procedures to maximize their opportunities for bribery. Evidence for this can be found in the World Bank's *Doing Business 2011* report, where Indonesia overall ranks 121st out of 183 countries. Indonesia does particularly poorly regarding measures of excessive regulation and the costs related to starting a business (155th), the ease of closing a business (144th), and the costs of enforcing contracts (154th). In Indonesia, thanks to its poor laws and legal system, enforcing a loan contract takes on average 5.5 years and costs 123 percent of its value! Likewise, financial regulation is not transparent and is routinely influenced by political connections.[52]

On the other hand, Malaysia ranks a mediocre 56th in the world in terms of corruption perceptions but 21st in the world in the ease of doing business. Malaysia's ranking in the ease of doing business is primarily driven by its particularly strong scores relating to the ease of getting credit, where it ranks an incredible first in the world thanks to its strong legal system, investor protections, and transparency requirements. A great deal of this ranking is attributable to Malaysia's private credit registry bureau that provides extensive credit information on all of Malaysia's citizens.

The superior financial institutions and limited cronyism and corruption in Malaysia have led to a much deeper and more efficient financial system. According to the World Economic Forum rankings of financial development in Table 1.1, Malaysia is the highest-ranked emerging market economy in the world (16th of 60 countries). Indonesia, on the other hand, only ranks 51st out of 60 countries in the same ranking. Referring back to Figure 11.1, the private credit-to-GDP ratio in Malaysia stood at 115 percent in 2010, but only 30 percent in Indonesia. Likewise, stock and bond market capitalization was 172 and 92 percent of GDP in Malaysia in 2010; in Indonesia these numbers stood at 51 and 21 percent.[53] Indonesian financial development has been severely hindered by the fact that many Indonesians save offshore (particularly in Malaysia) in order to protect against corruption and political instability. These factors also keep risk premiums and interest rates higher in Indonesia than in other countries in the region.

Deeper and more efficient financial systems have also led to broader access to formal credit in Malaysia. Table 11.2 presents information on different measures of financial access for Malaysia and Indonesia. Malaysia outperforms Indonesia on every measure. Most remarkable is the minimal amount of lending to SMEs in Indonesia, which is an important driver of economic growth. This broader and deeper access to credit is an important reason why Malaysia is much richer than Indonesia on a per-capita basis ($15,600 vs. $4,700 at PPP exchange rates in 2011) and also why income is distributed much more equally.

Table 11.2 Measures of financial access

	Malaysia	Indonesia
Access to deposit accounts (%)	60	40
SME finance/GDP (%)	18	2
Deposit accts./10,000 people	2,063	504
Loan accts./10,000 people	963	197
ATMs/100,000 people	54	14

Source: CGAP/World Bank (2010).

The difference in financial system development between Indonesia and Malaysia reflects more than just the impact of corruption and excessive state influence, however. It also reflects a difference in development strategy. Malaysia has chosen to focus on its financial system as a leading sector in its overall economic development; the financial sector contributed an exceptional 12 percent of GDP in Malaysia in 2010.[54] In Indonesia, the financial system is viewed as something that must accompany economic development and as a source of influence for politicians.

This difference in strategy is most evident in Malaysia's approach to its rapidly growing Islamic banking business. Instead of viewing Islamic banking as a necessary evil, Malaysia has striven to become the world's leader in Islamic banking and also an important export sector. Malaysia has 17 Islamic banks, three of which operate internationally. Malaysia also has the largest bond market in South East Asia, roughly two-thirds of which are *sukuks*, or Islamic bonds. As discussed in Chapter 10, *sukuks* are investment certificates that represent partial ownership of an asset or business (so they are not debt, which is prohibited according to *Shari'a* law). The cash flows from the rent associated with *sukuks* are structured to resemble those of a traditional bond. While *sukuks* have not been ruled S*hari'a*-compliant in many countries, they have been allowed in Malaysia and have become extremely popular both domestically and internationally. Malaysia's *sukuk* market has been growing at more than 10 percent a year and now constitutes nearly three-fourths of all *sukuks* issued worldwide.[55] In large part the attractiveness of these *sukuks* has been fostered by an extensive regulatory framework, both in terms of secular and *Shari'a* law, that Malaysia has developed around them.

Malaysia has also become a leader in the *takaful*, or Islamic insurance, business. Because, the sharing of risk (not the selling of risk) is allowed under *Shari'a* law, the *takaful* ("guaranteeing each other" in Arabic) business involves individuals that contribute to a pool of assets and in return for a commitment to receive compensation from others in the pool in the event of a loss. Any profits generated by the pool are shared among the contributors. Malaysia's *takaful* industry has been growing at nearly 20 percent a year since 2005 and now constitutes roughly one-tenth of the total insurance market in the country.[56]

Conclusions

The conventional wisdom is that Asia defines what it means to be a successfully developing emerging market economy. Its growth over the last three decades has been unprecedented and, except for the rather large bump in the road created by the East Asian crisis, growth has also been remarkably stable. However, it is interesting to note that while some aspects of the Asian Model have been widely adopted among emerging countries—such as undervalued exchange rates and export promotion—many other aspects of the model have not caught on. The dominant trend today among emerging economies is away from state-controlled banks, closed banking systems, foreign capital controls, financial repression, and investment-dominated development; this is slowly becoming true even within Asia itself, with the important exception of China.

In various ways, many Asian financial systems actually appear to be lagging behind the financial systems of other emerging economies. Their remarkable economic growth rates, which have been fueled by the mobilization of vast latent resources, have hidden the growth drag that their financial systems create. These financial systems have experienced significant financial deepening in recent years, but not growth in financial efficiency. However, as the region gradually becomes middle income, growth will inevitably slow and a transition will have to be made away from input-led development and toward productivity-led development. Historically, this transition occurs somewhere around $15,000 a year per-capita GDP. Given China's current per-capita GDP of $8,300 (at PPP), they could reach this tipping point within the next 15 years at current growth rates. While many other Asian countries are poorer than China and growing more slowly, the important point is that it is not too early to begin to plan for this transition.

Asia faces a fork in road. One path is to maintain government control and financial repression out of fear of markets and a desire for stability. The result is likely to be stagnant productivity growth and financial systems that are a hindrance to growth. Another consequence is future financial crises, which are more likely when risk is not priced appropriately. The other path is to continue to liberalize financial systems and rely on market-based decision making, making sure to first have in place a comprehensive system of prudential regulation and credible financial institutions. Although this path comes with risks of financial instability as well, it also creates the possibility that financial development can become a driving factor for broader economic development. China, Indonesia, and possibly India have chosen the former path. Malaysia and South Korea have chosen the latter. The ramifications of this decision as to which financial path each Asian country chooses to follow is likely to be the most important financial and economic development story in emerging market economies over the next few decades.

12 Financial systems in Latin America

Overview

Despite being the fourth-largest continent in terms of population and third-largest in land area, Latin America (which here is defined to include Mexico, Central America, South America, and the Caribbean) is often the forgotten region of the emerging world. This may be because it is neither the slowest-growing region nor the fastest. Real per-capita income in Latin America has doubled over the last 45 years, which looks good relative to many countries in Sub-Saharan Africa where incomes have been stagnant, but pales in comparison to many Asian countries such as South Korea where per-capita incomes have increased by a factor of 15. Latin America continues to grow but at a rate slower than emerging market economies in general. In 2011, it grew at a rate of 4.2 percent, smaller than the 6.3 percent average rate among all emerging market economies.

While more developed than in Africa and the Middle East, Latin American financial systems significantly lag behind most Asian countries and are far behind those in developed countries. Upon closer inspection, there are three important ways that Latin American financial systems are different from those in most emerging economies.

Banks are the primary source of financial underdevelopment in Latin America. Banks do not dominate finance in Latin America to the extent they do in most emerging market economies. This is because banks in Latin America are relatively underdeveloped, not because its bond and stock markets are more developed. Figure 12.1 presents data on financial depth as measured by bond capitalization, stock capitalization, and bank assets as a percentage of GDP between 1990 and 2010 for the seven largest Latin American economies as well as for emerging Asia, China, India, and G7 economies. Latin American countries have bond markets and stock markets that are somewhat behind Asian economies (but roughly on par with African and Middle Eastern averages), but bank assets that are roughly half of Asian peers (excluding India).[1] The shallowness of Latin American banking systems persists despite credit growth in the region that has averaged between 20 and 25 percent a year between 2000 and 2008. After a decline in lending associated with the global financial crisis, credit growth in most Latin American economies has rebounded in most countries to between 10 and 15 percent in 2010.

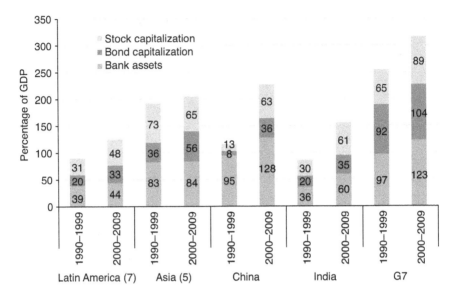

Figure 12.1 Structure of emerging market financial systems, 1990–2010 (source: Didier *et al.* (2011)).

Latin American banking systems are underdeveloped by other measures of financial development in addition to those simply capturing financial depth. High levels of returns on assets (of 2 percent), returns on equity (of 20 percent), risk-weighted capital (of 15 percent), net interest margins (the difference between lending and deposit interest rates), and low non-performing loans (of 2.5 percent) in the region all point to a banking system that is profitable and stable.[2] However, many of these statistics are also symptomatic of banking systems that are not highly competitive. Competition is limited by the high concentration of Latin American banking systems. In many countries, the ten largest banks control over 90 percent of banking assets. The excessive concentration of banks in Latin America creates few incentives for banks to compete for new customers in commercial and consumer loans market.

Financial efficiency in Latin America is also diminished by high required reserve ratios that are imposed on banks (such as in Brazil where the reserve ratio is between 32 and 55 percent depending upon the type of deposit). Banks also hold a large percentage of their assets in government bonds, either because of explicit requirements imposed by the government or because of a lack of alternative liquid assets. Government bonds constitute one-quarter of bank assets in the region's largest economies of Brazil, Mexico, and Argentina, and more than one-third in countries such as Columbia.[3] Together, high required reserves and government bond holdings not only increase the cost of credit, but reduce its supply by crowding out private lending. As a result, private credit is only two-thirds of total deposits in Latin America, well below average for emerging economies.[4]

A lack of competition and reduced incentives to make loans significantly impact financial access for households and SMEs. SMEs play an outsized role in Latin American economies. In fact, 98 percent of all companies in Latin America are SMEs, accounting for upwards of 50 percent of GDP. Over 70 percent of the poor in Latin America are owners or employees of microenterprises. Unfortunately, however, according to one survey, nearly one-fifth of these small firms consider the lack of finance to be a severe obstacle to doing business. Regarding households, only 42 percent of Latin American households have access to formal finance, slightly less than East Asia and the MENA region (although higher than in South Asia and Sub-Saharan Africa). In addition, Latin America has the highest annual banking fees of any emerging market region.[5] These statistics suggest that SMEs and households are severely underfunded relative to their importance in the economy.

As discussed in Chapter 3, financial access in Latin America is also limited by a lack of collateral created by insufficient property rights, particularly in regard to the ability to obtain legal title on formal property. Hernando de Soto's (2000) research suggests that more than $9 trillion of deal capital exists in Latin America that cannot be used as collateral for credit.

Financial access is even a problem for larger corporations in Latin America. According to one survey, only 40 percent of corporate executives say that they have adequate access to formal finance, while 31 percent say that they expect a lack of finance to limit their future investment and growth. As a result, Latin American firms tend to rely more heavily on trade credit and retained earnings than firms in other emerging economies.[6]

The lack of access to banking services for corporations has not been substituted with bond and stock market development in Latin America. Bond capitalization in Latin America has grown from 23 percent of GDP in 2000 to 35 percent in 2009, but still lags significantly behind Asia (excluding India). While public borrowing in the region is down significantly since the 1990s, it is still the case that two-thirds of bonds are issued by the government, much larger than in any other emerging region.[7] Such high levels of public debt means that crowding out plays an important role in Latin American financial systems, driving up interest rates and reducing the quantity demanded for private bonds. Likewise, stock market capitalization growth in Latin America over the last decade has been rapid, rising from 26 percent of GDP in 2000 to 41 percent in 2009. However, this fast growth has only narrowed, not eliminated, the gap between domestic stock capitalization in Latin America and its emerging economy peers.

Foreign banks and foreign capital flows play a larger role in Latin American finance. Foreign finance has always played an important role in Latin American finance. For example, foreign banks own 46 percent of total assets in Latin American banking systems, much higher than in other emerging market regions.[8] There are a number of reasons for this. First, the history of colonization in Latin America created institutions that discouraged domestic finance (such as a lack of legal systems that generated legal titles for informal property) and encouraged reliance on finance from European colonizers and the United States. Second,

Latin America has traditionally been heavily reliant on exports that necessitate international finance. In Central America and the Caribbean the importance of exports is the result of their proximity to the economic hegemon of the United States. In South America it is the result of a heavy reliance on the production of raw materials and agricultural goods.[9] Finally, the weakness of domestic finance across the region itself has necessitated more foreign borrowing and lending.

Table 12.1 presents the combined balance of payments account for the eight largest Latin America between 2009 and 2012 (forecasted). Net capital inflows to the region were a record $280 billion in 2011, or 4.5 percent of regional GDP (at purchasing power parity), which is greater than average among emerging economies. The largest portion of private inflows was in the form of foreign direct investment, with private credit (primarily from banks) making up most of the rest. Foreign portfolio investment contributed only $25 billion in capital inflows, reflecting the weakness of Latin American bond and stock markets. Overall, the growth in foreign capital inflows to Latin America has been driven by faster economic growth, better macroeconomic policies, and more political and economic stability in the region.

The majority of capital outflows from Latin America have come from central banks increasing their foreign reserve holdings, a change of $121 billion in 2011, leading to a total accumulation of reserves roughly equal to 10 percent of the

Table 12.1 Balance of payments for Latin America ($ billions)*

	2009	*2010*	*2011*	*2012 (forecast)*
Capital inflows				
Total inflows, net:	171.3	277.9	280.3	276.2
Private inflows, net	147.9	258.8	256.8	254.2
Equity investment, net	108.6	134.6	145.7	152.2
Direct investment, net	62.4	91.4	120.8	119.5
Portfolio investment, net	46.2	43.2	24.9	32.7
Private credit, net	39.3	124.2	111.1	102.0
Commercial banks, net	0.0	29.2	29.9	36.6
Non-banks, net	39.3	95.0	81.2	65.4
Official inflows, net	23.4	19.1	23.5	22.0
Int'l financial institutions	8.8	6.1	4.4	4.0
Bilateral creditors	14.5	13.0	19.1	18.0
Capital outflows				
Total outflows, net	−158.5	−232.8	−232.3	−188.6
Private outflows, net	−118.4	−148.3	−110.7	−122.9
Equity investment abroad, net	−43.9	−67.0	−47.0	−48.4
Resident lending/other, net	−74.5	−81.3	−63.7	−74.5
Foreign reserves (− is increase)	−40.1	−84.5	−121.7	−65.8
Current account balance	−12.7	−45.1	−48.0	−87.5

Source: *Institute for International Finance Research Note*, September 25, 2011.

Note
*For eight largest economies in Latin America: Argentina, Brazil, Chile, Columbia, Ecuador, Mexico, Peru, and Venezuela.

region's GDP. This is less than half of the average for all emerging economies, but still large and growing rapidly.[10]

One of the important changes in Latin America over the last decade has been a movement away from fixed exchange regimes—such as the disastrous currency board in Argentina—and toward more flexible exchange rate regimes. Unlike other regions of the emerging world, Latin American countries in general are not accumulating foreign reserves as a result of maintaining undervalued exchange rates (as evidenced by the small current account deficit the region has at less than 1 percent of GDP). Instead, foreign reserves are being accumulated in an effort to smooth exchange rate movements and provide insurance against capital flight. Recently, as exchange rates in the region have been rapidly appreciating—particularly in the commodity intensive countries of South America— the focus of monetary policy has been to "lean against the wind" and try to slow the rate of exchange rate appreciation (and fight "Dutch disease") with regular foreign exchange purchases.[11] At the same time, central banks are trying to stabilize domestic inflation by sterilizing these foreign exchange interventions with bond sales to limit money growth. According to the IMF, one-third of central banks intervene in foreign exchange markets on a daily basis, often according to predetermined rules.[12] However, based on the size of capital inflows to the region, both inflation and exchange rate stability remain a huge challenge for monetary policymakers.

While foreign capital brings benefits in the forms of investment, diversification, and technology transfer, it also brings dangers, as Latin American countries know only too well. Capital flows to Latin America have always been volatile, in part because of bad policy, domestic instability, a reliance on exports (particularly to the United States), and frequent terms of trade shocks that can affect the price of commodity exports. Given Latin America's high rate of financial exposure to the United States, it is not surprising that the global financial crisis of 2007 generated a great deal of capital flow volatility in Latin America. After a significant drop in inflows in 2008, a strong recovery in regional inflows has largely been driven by historically low interest rates in the United States. So sensitive are capital flows to financial conditions in the United States that the IMF estimates that a decrease in real interest rates of only 0.05 percent in the United States can increase capital inflows to Latin America by as much as 1 percent of GDP within two years.[13]

However, while foreign capital flows to the region continue to grow, these flows are different in important ways than they were before the 2000s. Much less of it is debt and much less is denominated in foreign currencies. In the mid-1980s, Latin America had the highest levels of external sovereign debt of any emerging market region—today it has the lowest. In addition, more than 85 percent of total debt in Latin America is denominated in domestic currencies now as compared to 67 percent in the mid-1990s.[14] Even foreign banks now do more than half of their lending in domestic currencies. This has significantly limited currency mismatch and exchange rate risk in Latin America. This important change has been driven by a number of factors, such as improved confidence in the macroeconomic management of Latin American countries, lower political instability, and larger domestic bond markets. Most importantly, foreign-denominated debt is less attractive because more flexible exchange rates have discouraged moral-hazard-fueled capital inflows by forcing markets to incorporate exchange rate risk in their decision making.

A long history of financial instability continues to play a large role in shaping Latin American financial systems. For most of its history, Latin American development has been largely synonymous with financial crises. Table 12.2 presents data on the number of different types of financial crises within Latin America, Asia, G7, and other advanced countries. Clearly, Latin America is an outlier among these groups, experiencing the largest number of debt crises (external and domestic), banking crises, and currency crises. There is strong empirical and theoretical evidence that past crises have had lingering effects and negatively impact finance in the region today. Testing for the impact of financial crises on Latin American finance, de la Torre *et al.* (2011) find that past financial crises play a significant role in explaining the "banking gap" between Latin America and other emerging market economies.

The historical legacy of past financial crises has had long-lasting effects on financial systems in Latin America in four important ways. First, it has created a vicious cycle in the region. Weak domestic financial systems have increased the need for foreign finance. Because foreign finance is more volatile due to the potential for capital flight and currency mismatch, financial crises have been more common in Latin America which, in turn, weakens domestic financial systems, increasing the need for foreign finance, etc.

Second, a history of financial instability has weakened confidence and increased perceived risk in the region. It is a widely held belief among Latin Americans, even in the wealthiest and most stable economies, that the next financial crisis is just around the corner. This mindset often dominates borrower-specific information and

Table 12.2 Number of crises by type, 1970–2007*

Country or region	External debt crisis	Domestic debt crisis	Banking crisis	Currency crisis	Any type of crisis
Asia (5)	5	0	14	17	27
China	0	0	3	2	5
G7	0	0	16	1	17
India	0	0	1	1	2
Other developed countries (7)	0	0	9	10	18
Latin America	47	13	53	72	149
Caribbean (5)	7	1	4	7	17
Central America (6)	11	2	13	14	33
Largest economies (7)	16	7	21	36	63
Other South American (4)	13	3	15	15	36

Source: Broner *et al.* (2010).

Note
* Number of countries in parenthesis.

encourages credit rationing that limits access to formal finance (particularly for SMEs and households). This "gun shy" mentality explains many of the stylized facts described earlier, such as the facts that banks in the region stay very liquid, do relatively little lending, hold lots of capital, have high risk premiums, and keep their lending short term. Only 31 percent of bonds have fixed interest rates in Latin America, compared to 66 for all emerging market economies, indicating that fears of unexpected inflation in the region remain high despite the fact that inflation has been generally stable over the last decade.

Third, past financial crises have led to persistent dollarization in Latin America that has hampered both financial development and the effectiveness of monetary policy. More on this in a later section of this chapter.

Finally, past crises impact current finance because the root cause of financial instability has not changed in many Latin American countries: its poor institutions. Latin America continues to perform poorly on most measures of institutional quality, leading to the mismatched incentives that can fuel financial crises and discourage growth. In regard to corruption, according to Transparency International's corruption perceptions index, only two Latin American countries score in the top 15 percent of all countries (Chile at 21 and Uruguay at 24) while the majority fall in the bottom half of countries.[15] Regarding measures of legal and regulatory institutions, the World Bank scores Latin America as the worst region in the world in regard to investor protections, ease of shareholder lawsuits, and a disclosure index that measures the quality of information (such as the existence of credit bureaus). In the World Bank's (2011) Ease of Doing Business Index, Latin America had the slowest rate of reform in 2011.

On the more positive side, Latin America has made slow improvements in eliminating financial repression. For example, directed lending and the government ownership of banks have fallen in the region, although bond holding requirements and high required reserve ratios still exist in many countries. Prudential regulation has significantly improved; the best evidence of this is that the region withstood the 2007 global financial crisis relatively well with no major bank, currency, or sovereign debt crises of any kind.[16] Macroeconomic and political stability have also improved in Latin America. Since 2000, inflation in most countries has averaged between 5 and 10 percent, debt ratios have fallen, and current account balances have remained close to zero. Monetary and fiscal policy has generally been much more countercyclical, where historically it has been highly procyclical, fueling financial booms and busts.

Overall, not only has financial development been stronger in the 2000s as a result of these institutional improvements, but economic growth has been faster and steadier. Per-capita GDP growth in the 2000s averaged 3.3 percent a year, up from the 0.3 percent a year averaged in the region between 1980 and 2000. But those who have lived through past financial crises—which is most everyone in Latin America—tend to have long memories, and rightly so. It will take many more years of stable growth and increased institutional reform before Latin American financial systems are willing to forget their history and begin to accept more risk again.

Offshore financial centers in the Caribbean

An important and well-known aspect of finance in Latin America is the rapid growth of *offshore financial centers* (OFCs), particularly in the Caribbean. OFCs are subsidiaries of large international banks and corporations that provide a wide range of financial services to foreign clients, including commercial banking, investment banking, and insurance services. These financial transactions are typically conducted in dollars at zero, or near zero, tax rates. OFCs are infamous in the developed world for being conduits for tax evasion, regulation avoidance, and money laundering.[17] In fact, intense international pressure from international organizations such as the IMF has recently been placed on host countries to improve regulation and disclosure of the activities of OFCs and their clients.

The Caribbean is home for more than half of all OFCs in the world. To understand how large a business this is, consider that the total assets held in Caribbean OFCs were roughly \$4 trillion in 2007, half of the amount of the cross-border assets held in the United States, France, and Germany combined.[18] The most popular home for OFCs in the Caribbean is the Cayman Islands with nearly 75 percent of OFC assets in the region.[19]

From the perspective of Caribbean countries, OFCs provide a source of foreign capital that can help stimulate financial and economic development. Countries in the region that host OFCs have twice the level of financial depth as the average Latin American country (financial assets for OFC countries averaged 87 percent of GDP in 2009). Proponents also argue that OFCs offer many indirect benefits by encouraging tourism, the development of telecommunications systems, improved transportation infrastructure, and some employment opportunities for domestic residents. Finally, proponents of OFCs argue that increasing financial openness increases incentives in these countries to improve prudential regulation and adopt better financial institutions. There is evidence that Caribbean countries that have adopted international regulatory standards received more capital inflows between 2000 and 2008.[20] These improved institutions could eventually contribute to greater domestic financial development and faster economic growth.

On the other hand, critics charge that most of these indirect benefits are small and that most of the business OFCs conduct facilitates foreign financial intermediation, not domestic finance. As a result, there is good reason to think that OFCs contribute little to domestic growth but at the cost of exposing these financial systems to a great deal of risk from volatile foreign capital flows and unregulated financial dealings. In addition, because many Caribbean governments offer deposit insurance and other guarantees to OFCs, rapid expansion in OFCs has exposed these governments to huge potential liabilities in the event of a financial crisis. A recent example comes from Trinidad and Tobago, where the failure of CL Financial Group in 2010 (whose failure was tied to the global financial crisis) necessitated a bailout of various insurance subsidiaries that cost the government 4 percent of GDP. Potential future claims from this failure could push the cost of this bailout toward 10 percent of GDP.[21]

As an empirical matter, a recent IMF study finds that increased capital flows to OFCs have had a small, but positive, effect on economic growth in the Caribbean.[22] However, even under the best-case scenarios, OFCs are no panacea for Caribbean countries. First, they tie these economies even more closely to the United States than they already are because of their reliance on tourism. As a result, the 2007 global financial crisis was more severe and lasted longer in the Caribbean than it did even in the United States. Second, the growth of OFCs have contributed to the growth in public debt in the region. In 2010, 5 of 13 Caribbean countries had debt-to-GDP ratios of greater than 100 percent and four more had ratios of greater than 70 percent; these are well above sustainable levels for most emerging economies and threaten future sovereign debt crises. In addition, this growth in public debt encouraged profligate spending before the global financial crisis that limited these countries' abilities to provide social safety net spending to the poor during the crisis. In sum, the evidence suggests that hosting OFCs is a highly risky strategy for encouraging financial and economic development, with uncertain benefits and potentially large costs.

Financial development in Brazil and Mexico

A comparison of the financial systems in the two largest economies in Latin America—Brazil and Mexico—illustrates many of the financial challenges that Latin American countries face in general. The most important similarity between these countries has been their successful recovery from disastrous financial crises in the 1990s. The Mexican Tequila crisis in 1994 was discussed in Chapter 5. In 1995, Mexico implemented a large bailout of banks in the aftermath of the crisis that also involved privatizing national banks and allowing foreign investors to purchase domestic private banks. In addition, Mexico embarked on an aggressive liberalization program that eliminated all barriers to entry for foreign banks operating in the country, reformed bankruptcy laws, created credit information bureaus, required more financial transparency, increased capital requirements, and encouraged bond market development. This liberalization has spurred growing bond markets and led to much higher returns on assets, lower leverage, and lower NPLs in the banking system.

The problem is that these indicators of bank strength are also indicators of a banking system that is still not competitive. Market concentration is a problem in Mexico as the five largest Mexican banks own 75 percent of all assets. This lack of competitive pressure has limited incentives to expand outreach to new customers: only 25 percent of the population has access to formal finance. Of those that do not have access, 70 percent say that the fees and minimum balances associated with formal banking are too high.[23] As a result of a lack of access and competition, bank credit was less than 20 percent of GDP in Mexico in 2011, well below the emerging market average of 75 percent (and lower than where it stood before the crisis at 40 percent).[24]

Brazil's story is quite similar. After a disastrous sovereign debt crisis and hyperinflation in the early 1990s, Brazil attempted a series of fiscal and monetary reforms. In 1994, it adopted the *real* plan, under which the Brazilian currency (the *real*) was hard-pegged to the dollar in an attempt to reduce money growth and expected inflation. In the short run, this policy led to huge spikes in real interest rates, the real exchange rate, and precipitous falls in Brazil's current account. However, inflation fell from over 2,000 percent in 1994 to 7 percent in 1997 (see Figure 12.2). The East Asian crisis in 1997 once again threatened to create a currency crisis in Brazil and put upward pressure on inflation, but a bailout from the IMF and an early abandonment of its strict peg with the dollar allowed Brazil to weather the storm and sustain growth of over 5 percent a year during the last decade.

Brazil is now the seventh-largest economy in the world. While its economy is roughly twice the size of Mexico's, its financial system is three times larger.[25] The most highly developed sector of Brazil's financial system is its stock market, which is now the fourth largest among emerging markets and accounts for 55 percent of total equity in Latin America. Like Mexico, its bond market has also experienced growth, primarily in the public bond market. However, also like

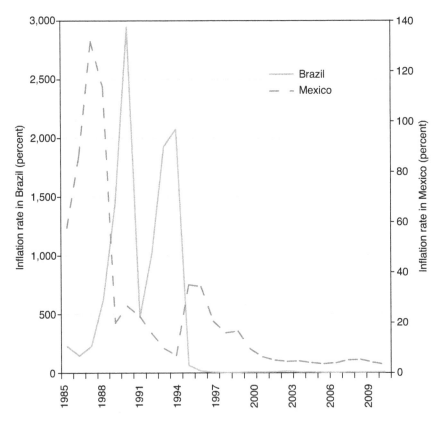

Figure 12.2 Inflation in Brazil and Mexico (source: IMF, *World Economic Outlook Database* (2011a)).

Mexico, its banking system is superficially strong but structurally weak. Bank credit-to-GDP has doubled over the last decade (to nearly 50 percent); returns on assets and capital ratios are high while NPLs are low. But this apparent financial strength is primarily a function of limited competition. Brazilian banks are highly concentrated: the five largest banks hold 80 percent of total assets. Without the appropriate incentives to compete for customers, only 42 percent of the population has access to formal finance and total credit is only 57 percent of GDP. While these numbers are better than Mexico's, they are not impressive relative to other emerging market economies or relative to its own levels of economic development.

The largest contributor to improved financial development in Brazil and Mexico is their improved macroeconomic environment. Most importantly, referring back to Figure 12.2, there has been a remarkable reduction in both the level and the variability of inflation in both countries. This recent success in moderating inflation has come about as the result of strict fiscal discipline and the adoption of inflation targeting regimes in both countries. In 1999, Brazil adopted their stated target of inflation at 4.5 percent plus/minus 2 percent. Empirical work by Barbosa-Fiho (2008) and Kamal (2010) indicates that Brazil's central bank has consistently followed its stated inflation target and that doing so has reduced the level, the volatility, and the persistence of inflation. Output has also been more stable during the inflation-targeting period, but Brazil's exchange rate has been more volatile. Mexico adopted their inflation target of 3 percent plus/minus 1 percent in 2002, but actual inflation has been regularly 1 to 2 percent higher than this. While Mexico's inflation target was adopted after inflation levels had already declined, Carrasco and Ferreiro (2011) find that adopting an inflation target helped lock in and stabilize inflation expectations and reduce real interest rates.

There are some important differences between Brazil and Mexico which portend different paths for their future financial development. First, foreign banks play a much bigger role in Mexico than Brazil; at the same time, state-owned banks play no role in Mexico but a large role in Brazil. As mentioned earlier, the privatization of public and private banks to foreign owners was an important part of Mexico's post-crisis bank recapitalization plan. Today foreign banks own 82 percent of total bank assets in Mexico. In Brazil, which has traditionally been much more closed to trade and finance, foreign banks own only 25 percent of total assets. The Brazilian government owns more than one-third of the equity in the banking system and is the majority owner of three of the ten largest banks.[26]

This attitude toward foreign finance in the two countries is also evident in their attitude toward foreign capital flows. Mexico has a much more open capital account (in part because of its participation in the North American Free Trade Agreement with the United States and Canada). Brazil currently imposes a number of targeted capital controls, such as a 6 percent tax on residents borrowing from abroad for less than two years as well as a tax on non-resident bond inflows.

The costs of state-owned banks and of a relatively closed financial system in Brazil are that they lessen competition, limit diversification, and restrict the availability of external financial expertise, together reducing the overall efficiency of financial intermediation. As an example of how much efficiency has improved in Mexico as a result of its liberalization, Sidaoui (2008) reports that the transaction costs on government debt has fallen in Mexico from 55 basis points in 2001 to only 1–2 basis points currently, while at the same time bond maturities have increased.

Openness has also forced Mexico to more quickly reform and adopt the institutions of its international trading partners. For example, in the World Bank's Ease of Doing Business report, Mexico ranks 35th, Brazil only ranks 127th. Mexico does particularly well in measures of the ease of getting credit, protecting investors' rights, and opening/closing a business; each of these institutions are directly influenced by international pressure and are also areas where Brazil scores poorly.

Brazil does have a widely admired *de jure* legal system when it comes to protecting property rights and transparency and it has one of the highest numbers of lawyers per capita in the world at one lawyer per 255 people.[27] But de facto, a legal system of Kafkaesque complexity has developed. According to one observer, "Bringing a lawsuit to right a wrong or repair some damage is invariably complex and expensive.... In some cases the situation borders on the absurd."[28] In part, the Brazilian legal system reflects a characteristic of Brazilian culture known as *jeitinho*, which refers to an admired quality in individuals to work around rules in any way possible.

Of course, financial openness in Mexico also has a cost, which is the increased possibility of financial instability. The extensive financial integration between Mexico and the United States coupled with their high level of trade integration (exports constitute 33 percent of Mexican GDP, 80 percent of which goes to the United States) meant that Mexico suffered much more than Brazil during the global financial crisis. Neither country suffered their own financial crisis, thanks in large part to their much stronger financial fundamentals, lower leverage, better macroeconomic policy management, and prudential regulation. Output growth in Brazil during the crisis was strong except for a mild recession during 2009 (GDP fell by 0.6 percent). Mexico, on the other hand, saw its GDP decline by a total of 11 percent during the crisis. The two primary drivers of this recession were a decline in Mexican exports to the United States and a precipitous decline in credit. Because US banks play such a large role in the Mexican banking system, the crisis north of the border led to credit contractions south of the border as declines in capital and increases in perceived risk increased credit rationing. Credit growth in Mexico went from more than 30 percent a year in 2005–2007 to below zero in the fourth quarter of 2009. While credit growth slowed throughout the rest of Latin America, it still grew at more than 10 percent a year in Brazil, with much of the growth in credit supported by its large state-owned banks.[29]

When comparing Brazil to Mexico, we see an apparent tradeoff that emerging market economies often have to face: between faster financial development and economic growth on one hand, and the dangers of financial volatility on the other. But examined in another light, there is no tradeoff. The facts that both countries have liberalized, both countries have experienced one of their fastest decades of growth, and that both countries have recently broken the cycle of recurring financial crises suggests that liberalization—when it is done right and in conjunction with prudential regulation and a focus on sound fundamentals—can allow countries to achieve the best of both worlds, even in the face of large obstacles.

Remittances to Latin America

Over 19 million Latin Americans have migrated to work in other countries, often sending wage earnings back to their family and friends. Three-fourths of Latin American migrants work in the United States. Before the global financial crisis, remittances in Latin America were growing at 30 to 40 percent a year and rose to 1.5 percent of GDP in 2008. Total remittances to Latin America are as large a source of foreign capital inflows as foreign direct investment, twice as large as foreign portfolio investment, and ten times the amount of official assistance to the region.[30]

For specific Latin American countries, particularly in Central America and the Caribbean, remittances are much more important than they are for the region in general. Table 1.2 in Chapter 1 lists the 15 largest remittance recipients among emerging economies. Six of these countries are from Latin America when ranked by percentage of GDP, all of which receive remittances of greater than 10 percent of GDP, while the third-largest recipient in total amount of remittances is Mexico.

Remittance growth has been highly variable recently as employment opportunities in the developed world have become scarcer as a result of the global financial crisis. After rapid growth in the early 2000s, remittance growth was –15 percent in the region in 2009, only 2 percent in 2010, and remained below pre-crisis levels (in terms of growth and levels) in 2012. Mexico has been particularly hard hit by the decline in remittances. Mexico has more than eight million migrant workers, 99 percent of whom work in the United States. Before the crisis, remittances made up 34 percent of income for the 1.8 million Mexicans receiving payments from abroad. During the crisis, these remittance inflows fell by more than 20 percent, significantly contributing to the size of the economic downturn in Mexico.[31]

As discussed in Chapter 1, remittances serve many purposes for households in developing countries: enhancing consumption, funding education and capital investments, and providing insurance against negative shocks being the most important. Specifically in Latin America, remittances have been shown empirically to have a number of important positive effects. To briefly name a few, Ramirez and Sharma (2009) find that the impact of remittances on growth is positive and stronger in countries with more developed financial systems, likely because it involves lower transactions costs and has the largest impact on improving financial access. Acosta *et al.* (2008) find that a 1 percent increase in remittances as a fraction of GDP reduces poverty in Latin America by 0.4 percent. Fajnzylber and López (2007) find that remittances reduce country risk in Latin America and are positively correlated with higher sovereign ratings, which in turn reduce borrowing costs in a country. Giuliano and Ruiz-Arranz (2005) find that remittances increase both financial development and access to banking services in Latin America more than in any other emerging region. However, they also find that higher access does not necessarily lead to increases in credit for many households, which are still likely to be credit rationed because of weaker institutions and a lack of information and collateral.

Of course, remittance inflows also present challenges for the region. At a microeconomic level, remittances are still expensive. Remittance fees in the region average 7.3 percent of the amount transferred despite advances in electronic payment systems in the region.[32] This is in large part because only 5 to 10 percent of remittances between North America and Latin America are handled by banks.[33] This is despite the fact that many countries have adopted programs to reduce costs by channeling more remittances through formal financial systems, such as Mexico's Calculadora de Remesas program begun in 2006. Remittances also present macroeconomic challenges. In addition to potentially magnifying external demand shocks from developed countries, the capital inflows generated by remittances can lead to appreciations of the domestic currency that can reduce the competitiveness of export industries and facilitate "Dutch disease." Governments can try to fight this by sterilizing these inflows. In addition, governments faced with large remittances inflows have to prevent remittance-fueled booms in aggregate demand through strict prudential regulation of credit growth, restrictive fiscal policies, and consumption taxes.

Financial disaster: Argentina

In the 1930s Argentina was one of the ten richest countries in the world. Today, the IMF ranks Argentina as having only the 51st-highest level of per-capita GDP in the world despite remarkable endowments in energy, raw materials, agriculture, and a highly educated population. The constraints that have held Argentina back have been largely self-imposed; the ways that Argentina self-immolated its financial system account for many of the most important factors in this relative decline.

In Chapter 7 we discussed the details of the financial crisis in Argentina between 2001 and 2002 which was associated with the failure of its currency board system. In the aftermath of this crisis, unlike in many other Latin American countries such as Mexico and Brazil, Argentina did not reform but further deformed. It recapitalized banks primarily on the backs of depositors when the government froze dollar-denominated deposits in the country and transformed them into pesos at significantly depreciated exchange rates. Bank privatization took place under a corrupt process that created little new bank capital. The government forcibly settled with banks and other holders of its domestic debt at terms highly favorable to the government, causing most foreign banks to flee the country. And the government continued a long, messy, and destabilizing fight with its external creditors, the holders of $155 billion of sovereign debt that Argentina defaulted on.[34]

Today, the Argentinean banking system is dominated by a small number of state-owned banks that provide little long-term lending and almost no consumer or commercial credit, always at high costs. The ratio of total credit-to-GDP in Argentina is less than 15 percent. The government sets interest rate ceilings that are above the official rate of inflation but well below the actual rate of inflation, leading to negative real interest rates that discouraged financial intermediation. Directed lending is pervasive and highly variable, the objectives of which fluctuate with the nature of the political objectives of those in government at the time. All in all, Argentina is a perfect example of how financial repression and uncertainty can kill financial systems.

Recent examples of how the Argentinean government has weakened institutions and eliminated incentives to engage in finance are endless, but four are worth highlighting here. First, the government seized $30 billion in private pension funds in 2008 and folded them into its public pension plan in an effort to raise money to meet its sovereign debt payments. Second, in 2012 the government nationalized the share of the state oil company, Repsol, held by foreign investors. Third, Argentina's president fired the head of the central bank in 2010 when he refused to turn over $6.4 billion of the bank's foreign exchange reserves to the government to finance the government's settlement with foreign bondholders. Since that time, the central bank's reserves have been regularly siphoned by the government, the independence of the central bank has been reduced, and its responsibilities toward financing government deficits have been legally enshrined.[35]

The fourth example is maybe the most egregious. The Argentine government has been manipulating its official inflation rate data in an effort to help the central bank meet its targeted inflation rate, in order to reduce its real payments to the holders of its indexed bonds, and to limit spending on indexed government payment programs. At one point, the chief official in the government's statistical agency was fired for refusing to go along with this manipulation. In 2011, the government reported that inflation was 9.7 percent while private measures of inflation based on prices reported on the Internet indicate that inflation was over 25 percent in both 2010 and 2011.[36] The government has even punished private-sector economists in Argentina for releasing alternative inflation estimates, fining many economists and imposing at least one criminal charge for "publishing false information about inflation data."[37]

These examples lie at the heart of what ails Argentina. Institutions are only good to the extent that they encourage people, particularly entrepreneurs, to engage in productive behavior. As any Argentinean knows, the institutions that are currently in place make engaging in all sorts of otherwise productive behavior unprofitable. At any time, the government is likely to change the rules to benefit some individuals over others, increasing credit risk and the incentives to

credit ration to extremely high levels. Instead of saving, borrowing, and investing, most Argentineans find it much more profitable to spend their considerable
energies "gaming the system," meaning figuring out ways that they can take
advantage of the convoluted system of political power and patronage. It is for
this reason that in Argentinean Spanish the word *empresario* (literally translated
as businessman) is often used as a synonym for a criminal.

By any quantitative measure, Argentina's institutions are poor. According to
Transparency International, Argentina ranks 105 out of 178 countries in perceived corruption.[38] The Heritage Foundation ranks Argentina 27 out of 29 Latin
American countries (and 158 out of 179 overall) in an index of economic
freedom and liberalized economic markets, primarily due to corruption, a lack of
judicial independence, and regulatory encroachment on business.[39] In the World
Bank's Ease of Doing Business rankings, Argentina scores 115 out of 183 countries, scoring worst in starting/closing a business, business regulation, and protecting investors' rights. Amazingly, the World Bank reports that the effective
maximum tax rate in Argentina is 108 percent![40] This explains why income tax
evasion in Argentina is estimated to be above 60 percent.[41]

How do we understand why Argentina's institutions are as dysfunctional as
they are? This is a question that has challenged economists, political scientists,
and historians for decades. In brief, many of the explanations focus on three
important factors. First, elites have traditionally had few checks on their power.
During the colonial phase of Argentinean history, a small number of large hacienda owners dominated the economy and workers were tied to specific plots of
land without property rights in what is known as the *encomiendas* system. As a
result, landowner rights dominated squatters' rights, while concentrated production was favored over the rights of households. This served to significantly
reduce property rights in a process that played out to a greater or lesser extent
throughout Latin America. Second, immigration to Argentina tended to be later
than to North America and was heavily weighted toward single men. As a result,
most immigration was temporary and, in a process similar to that described by
Acemoglu *et al.* (2001a) (see Chapter 3), encouraged exploitive rather than productive policies and laws. Finally, because of vast inequality in the country, populist policies that encouraged redistribution rather than production have
dominated Argentinean politics and public policy. The Perón dictatorship in the
1940s (Argentina's current president is a Peronist) marked the beginning of an
elaborate patronage system that moved the country away from markets and
toward state control.[42] It also led to the disbanding of an independent judiciary
that limited private property rights and weakened the rule of law.

While the country has averaged an incredible 7 percent growth a year between
2003 and 2011, the question on every Argentinean's lips is: how long can this
last? Argentineans know full well that a financial crisis takes place in their
country every ten years or so. Despite new controls imposed on foreign exchange
transactions, the peso continues to steadily decline as Argentineans continue to
find ways to move their savings to other countries.[43] More than $60 billion has
left Argentina since 2008.[44] During 2011, capital flight occurred at twice the rate

it had in 2010 and the central bank saw its foreign reserves fall by roughly $10 billion (from $56.2 billion to $46.2 billion).[45] This disintermediation has been driven by many factors, including negative real interest rates, a black market exchange rate for the peso that is far above the official exchange rate, and the fear of another currency conversion like what happened in 2002. Coupled with a history of monetary mismanagement, debt-to-GDP levels of above 50 percent (remarkably high for a debt intolerant country with a history of default), a lack of transparency, and endemic corruption, the current trends suggest another financial crisis in the near future and deeper cynicism among Argentineans.

Dollarization in Latin America

As discussed in Chapter 4, financial dollarization has become an established fact of life in many emerging market economies, particularly in Latin America. In part this has been necessitated by Latin America's small domestic financial systems and their dependence on foreign trade and finance. But the most important driver of informal dollarization (as opposed to that legislated by the government) has been a long history of high inflation and financial crises in the region. Households and firms that were forced to watch helplessly as their savings were wiped out by inflation, the failure of their bank, a rapid depreciation of their domestic currency, or a sovereign default are likely to have very long memories and be reluctant to resume their trust in the domestic currency for a very long time.

Table 12.3 presents data on four highly dollarized economies in Latin America, in terms of both deposits and loans denominated in dollars. Between 2001 and 2010, de-dollarization has been significant in all of these countries, falling by an average of 25 percent. Despite this, however, dollarization remains significant and is between 40 and 50 percent of deposits and credit for most of

Table 12.3 De-dollarization in Latin America, 2001–2010 (%)

| | | Dollarization | | De-dollarization |
		2001	*2010*	*2001–2010*
Uruguay	deposits	87.0	76.6	−10.4
	credit	75.1	52.5	−22.6
Peru	deposits	78.5	49.5	−28.7
	credit	78.9	52.1	−26.8
Paraguay	deposits	69.7	43.5	−26.1
	credit	53.3	38.6	−14.7
Bolivia	credit	93.2	51.4	−41.8
	deposits	94.4	53.8	−40.7
Average	deposits	82.1	55.3	−26.8
	credit	75.4	49.2	−26.2

Source: García-Escribano and Sosa (2010).

these countries. Likewise, for the seven largest Latin American economies, credit dollarization fell from 45 percent of all loans to 33 percent in 2010, but remains high.[46]

The domestic costs of informal dollarization are significant. First, increased dollarization brings with it the potential risks associated with currency mismatch. During many of the financial crises we have discussed, most obviously during the Argentinean currency board crisis, banks had mismatches between their dollar-denominated liabilities and assets. Even when the bank's levels of dollar assets and liabilities matched, many borrowers still earned their revenues in a domestic currency. As a result, dollar-denominated loans to these firms exposed the bank to exchange rate risk by increasing the chances of default by the borrower.

Second, dollarization makes both external debt accumulation and capital outflows easier, increasing the possibility of capital booms, capital flight, and currency crises.

Dollarization also contributes to financial risk by limiting the power of monetary policy. More dollarized economies mean that the central bank has less control over domestic inflation, interest rates, and exchange rate volatility. Maybe most importantly, because no central bank has an unlimited supply of foreign reserves, its ability to serve as a lender of last resort is severely limited.

The final cost of dollarization is that it discourages financial development. In dollarized financial systems, banks have to put their primary emphasis on managing liquidity, holding capital, and limiting currency mismatch. Most highly dollarized banks operate under high reserve requirement ratios and keep leverage low. As a result, financial depth is limited, credit rationing is rampant, and financial access is restricted.

A good example of the constraints that dollarization imposes on a country is Uruguay, a small, highly open economy squeezed between two giant neighbors, Argentina and Brazil. Uruguay has been referred to as the Switzerland of South America because of its small size, good institutions, and attractiveness to foreign savers. In fact, 23 percent of all deposits in the country are held by foreigners, primarily Argentineans worried about the risk of saving their wealth in Argentina. Foreign savers are also attracted by the ease of saving in dollars; as a result, 77 percent of deposits in Uruguay are denominated in dollars (see Table 12.3).

These attributes have made finance an important sector of the Uruguayan economy. But it has not contributed much to domestic lending within the country. Private credit is only 22 percent of GDP in Uruguay, well below average not only for emerging market economies but for a country of its relatively high income level ($13,700 of per-capita GDP in 2010 (PPP)).

The danger of dollarization is future financial instability, something that Uruguay is all too familiar with. The Argentinean crisis spread to Uruguay in 2002 to disastrous effect as Argentinean depositors panicked and quickly withdrew their dollar holdings from Uruguay after dollar accounts were frozen in Argentina. Uruguay suffered a costly banking crisis and a decline in real GDP of 20 percent. The fact that many of the same conditions still exist today—and the fact that the Central Bank of Uruguay cannot adequately serve as a lender of last resort despite large foreign reserve holdings (more than seven times the amount of short-term external debt)—remains the primary reason why Uruguayans fear holding too much of their wealth in domestic pesos and why Uruguay is still a highly dollarized economy despite having a superficially strong banking system.

In regard to monetary policy, the Central Bank of Uruguay has adopted an inflation target of between 4 and 6 percent, but within this band tries to stabilize short-run fluctuations in its exchange rate around a crawling peg to the dollar. Recently, the Uruguayan peso has been strongly appreciating by more than 6 percent a year against the dollar. The Central Bank of Uruguay has tried to slow this appreciation by increasing their holdings of foreign reserves (in 2010 foreign reserves increased by more than 10 percent of GDP), but this has also put upward pressure on inflation, which has recently been at or above the upper range of its target. In many ways, Uruguay represents the conundrum many emerging market economies face as a result of strong recent growth and increasing openness; trying to balance exchange rate stability versus inflation, and encouraging growth versus worrying about financial stability. Dollarization makes balancing these tradeoffs even more difficult.

How can countries de-dollarize? As we saw in Table 12.3, while informal dollarization remains large, most Latin American countries have de-dollarized over the last decade. Increased financial, economic, and political stability has reduced domestic currency risk and greatly contributed to de-dollarization. Empirically, many factors have been found to be important in explaining de-dollarization in Latin America, including improved macroeconomic policy, increased exchange rate volatility as a result of abandoning rigid exchange rate pegs, and sustained appreciation of exchange rates against the dollar. Higher reserve requirements and capital requirements placed on dollar deposits has increased the costs of dollar deposits and encouraged more domestic currency deposits. Finally, empirical studies have found that larger domestic bond and stock markets as well as more long-term lending in domestic currencies have encouraged more domestic savings and limited the need for dollar holdings.[47] Overall, these results are consistent with a basic rule of finance: domestic finance cannot thrive when uncertainty and risk are rampant.

Conclusions

William Faulkner said: "The past is never dead. It's not even past." Latin Americans know this all too well. The long history of dysfunctional institutions and financial crises in the region has created many obstacles to financial development today. This includes higher perceived risk and uncertainty, low leverage, weak legal systems, a lack of protection for property rights, high perceived credit risk, limited financial access, domestic financial repression, a heavy reliance on foreign finance, and the substantial dollarization of domestic finance.

This said, substantial progress has been made in Latin America over the last decade or more. Financial repression has been loosened, markets liberalized, and macroeconomic policy vastly improved, the political environment is generally more stable, and the region's exposure to external shocks and currency mismatch is much lower. The best evidence of improved fundamentals in the region was Latin America's relative stability during the global financial crisis. However, these positive developments have not yet been sufficient to overcome the vast weight of Latin America's historical legacy of instability. But there certainly is hope that the pessimism and cynicism that have smothered financial and economic development is lessening in most of the region as a more stable macroeconomic environment gradually becomes the "new normal."

Latin America's recent experience directly contradicts the widespread belief that there is a tradeoff between liberalization and financial volatility, between greater financial development and an increased chance of financial crises. For example, no one would trade the financial development of Brazil for Argentina's, nor Brazil's financial stability for that of Argentina's. This is precisely because Brazil has reformed its institutions in ways that encourage appropriate risk taking and productive finance, while Argentina's institutions continue to reward patronage and political influence. The recent history of Latin America offers a distinctly optimistic picture of future financial development where countries can have the best of both worlds if they continue to put institutions and policies in place that encourage productive, and not redistributive, financial activities.

Part V

Conclusions

13 Ten takeaways for understanding finance in emerging market economies

Faith, hope, and money—only a saint could have the first two without the third.

George Orwell (1936)

The above quotation strikes at the heart of a basic truism about economic development. All of the ambition, energy, intelligence, and ideas in the world will not lead to improved standards of living without the resources to implement and support them. And first among these resources is money, because money can be used to purchase the things—human capital, physical capital, and technology—that turn ideas and initiative into income. So how do people with all of these attributes other than money get money? This is what finance is all about: the process of trading money across time; in other words, trading money today for money tomorrow. The word finance is, as noted by Robert Shiller (2012), translatable into the word "goal." Because finance facilitates all of the transactions that drive economic activity, it is absolutely crucial to the ultimate economic goal of widespread development, growth, and improved quality of life.

Financial systems in emerging market economies are incredibly varied and complex; this book is a testament to this fact. Having worked through this complexity, it is valuable to now take a step back and summarize the most crucial points examined in this book. Let's briefly review ten of the most important insights about finance in emerging market economies.

(1) *Financial development is a key to increasing standards of living and, when done right, disproportionally benefits those living in poverty.* Finance contributes to economic development in numerous ways. Greater financial depth facilitates the accumulation of physical and human capital. Efficient financial systems funnel resources to those with the most productive uses for them, increasing aggregate productivity. Finance also provides a means for households and firms to smooth their spending, reducing risk which also encourages more entrepreneurship and productivity. Finance also reduces the risk of saving and borrowing by encouraging the hedging and diversification of risk. Finally, financial development reduces the transaction costs associated with financial transactions, which also increases efficiency and improves standards of living. Many empirical studies cited throughout this book have

supported the conclusion that financial development is a crucial determinant of overall economic development.

Just as importantly, finance does not just benefit the richest individuals. When access to finance is broad and deep it actually benefits the poorest the most because they are the ones who are exposed to the most risk, have the most volatile incomes, are the most credit constrained, and have the most unexploited entrepreneurial initiative. As a result, when the poor gain access to money today it is most likely to increase their welfare and incomes tomorrow. When finance is repressed, it is always the poorest that bear the greatest burden.

(2) *However, financial development is only certain to contribute to overall economic development when it is accompanied by broad financial access.* An often-voiced complaint about finance is that only those who have money can borrow it. The most important—and worrisome—similarity among emerging market financial systems is that while overall financial depth has grown dramatically over the last two decades, its benefits have often not been shared by those living at the lower ends of the income distribution because they do not have access to the formal financial system. This is crucial because in regions such as Sub-Saharan Africa roughly 60 percent of the population lives on less than $2.50 a day. Without access to formal finance, the vast majority of those living in poverty within emerging market economies are forced to rely on informal finance. As a result, their savings earn low returns and are not funneled into productive activities; their borrowing is rationed, short term, and much more costly than it needs to be; their lives are riskier and less productive than they should be. A lack of access to formal finance sets up a vicious cycle in which the poor cannot gain access to the same resources that the rich have, keeping them poor.

The most important financial development goal in emerging market economies in the future is not to increase the depth and size of their financial systems, but to make sure that a greater percentage of their population can participate in these systems. To this end, the development of both microfinance and Islamic finance holds a great deal of promise in helping the financially under-served.

(3) *Information is the most important input to finance.* Finance takes place over time and, in words attributed to the baseball player Yogi Berra, "it is tough to make predictions, especially about the future." As a result, finance always involves an element of risk. Financial transactions are always an act of faith guided by judgment. However, the risk that lenders face is magnified in any financial transaction because of the adverse selection and moral hazard incentives created by asymmetric information. Knowing this, lenders have strong incentives to increase the costs of credit intermediation as well as to credit ration potential borrowers. This is most likely to happen to two groups of borrowers: those households and firms without collateral and those that cannot provide enough financial information to the lender to convince them that they are an acceptable credit risk. These two groups are likely to have the same members: small firms, newer firms, and poorer households. As a result, these are the borrowers that are most likely to find it difficult to obtain formal finance at a reasonable price. Finding ways for these groups to accumulate more and higher-quality

financial information and to obtain more collateral—such as developing accounting structures, creating credit information bureaus, and building legal systems that can help assign property rights—is absolutely crucial to solving the problem of limited formal financial access in emerging market economies.

(4) *Institutions!* The reason people in many emerging economies do not engage in mutually beneficial finance is that the risk is often too great and they have little incentive to do so. Institutions determine the environment that finance evolves within, and as in the biological world, environment shapes structure. When governments and societies create positive incentives to engage in productive behavior by providing legal systems to establish property rights and enforce contracts, distribute information through accounting systems and credit bureaus, limit theft and conflict, reduce uncertainty, and regulate risk, then finance will thrive. But when corruption is more profitable than production, when the rules are uncertain and weighted in the favor of elites, and when property rights are not well defined so that a person's assets cannot be used as collateral for a loan, then finance will only be a means of redistributing income, not creating it.

Three things are important to keep in mind about institutions. First, there is not just one set of institutions that work or will not work everywhere. Instead, institutions have to be consistent with the culture, society, government policies, and history of the country in which they operate. Second, it is de facto (actual) institutions, and not *de jure* (on paper) institutions, that matter. Third, various aspects of quality institutions are interrelated. It is difficult to limit corruption without adequate legal systems, just as it is difficult to improve legal systems without eliminating a culture of corruption.

(5) *Balancing liberalization with prudential regulation is absolutely crucial, but there is no simple formula for doing it.* The weakening of financial repression policies (high reserve and bond holding requirements, interest rate controls, barriers to entry, state-owned banks, capital controls, directed lending, high inflation, exchange rate controls) has greatly increased the depth and efficiency of finance within emerging market economies over the last three decades. Liberalization has also contributed to improving financial access for the poor, who suffer the most from financial repression policies and state-dominated financial systems. But financial markets are not perfectly competitive, primarily because asymmetric information creates risk externalities that magnify financial volatility and are hugely costly for everyone within an economy. Specifically, because most every financial transaction involves borrowing or lending someone else's money, moral hazard can fuel excessive risk taking when there are no limits on behavior imposed by regulators. Because of this, liberalized financial systems must also have prudential regulation and monitoring systems in place that limit systemic risk and discourage this excessive risk taking. Prudential regulation in the form of capital adequacy requirements, accounting standards, information transparency conditions, asset diversification requirements, loan safety standards, limits on exchange rate risk exposure, deposit insurance, the elimination of barriers to entry, and procedures for minimizing corruption can reduce risky financial behavior and prevent costly financial crises from occurring.

However, some forms of prudential regulation (for example, a requirement aimed at reducing bank risk by requiring banks to hold a certain percentage of their assets in low-risk government bonds) can also be financial repression in another context (a government requiring banks to hold sovereign bonds in order to finance their budget deficits). As a result, there is no simple recipe for a unique set of policies that balance the efficiency gains of liberalization against the safety needs of prudential regulation. However, understanding the goal that prudential regulation must achieve in any economy is more important—and more realistic—than delineating simple solutions. Picking the proper balance between regulation and liberalization must be more of a process than a single policy and requires constant adjustment as the financial system evolves. The balance in each country will differ depending upon its unique cultural, societal, structural, and historical environment.

Asia is a region where the difficulty of maintaining this balance is most easily observed. The Asian Model of development, which today is best exemplified by China, has emphasized government control and financial repression in an effort to maximize financial depth, increase investment, and protect the stability of the system. But it has also created a financial system in which markets and prices play a limited role in decision making. As a result, there is no reason to think that finance is going to where it will be used most efficiently. In addition, because risk is not being priced appropriately and prudential regulation is biased by political interference, there are good reasons to think that grave threats of future financial crises lurk within the Chinese financial system.

At the same time, India is an example of a country that has adopted many market reforms and has a system of prudential regulation in place *de jure*. But in practice, endemic corruption and a lingering adherence to some forms of financial repression undermine all of its institutions, including its ability to enforce prudential regulation, and also severely reduce financial access, limiting the contribution that the financial system can make to Indian growth.

(6) *There does not have to be a tradeoff between financial liberalization and financial volatility.* A common fallacy is the belief that financial liberalization may bring faster economic growth but at the cost of increased financial volatility and more frequent financial crises. The fact of the matter is that when quality institutions and prudential regulation are in place, financial liberalization can increase growth while at the same time expanding financial services that can be a means of providing households and firms with insurance against shocks to their income, stabilizing spending and the overall economy. The inherent fallacy of this tradeoff between growth and stability is evident when comparing the recent historical experience of those countries that have deregulated versus those that have continued to have financial systems dominated by repression and state control. In Latin America, no one would trade either the recent growth or stability record of Brazil for that of Argentina. The same could be said of Botswana for Nigeria in Africa, Jordan for Iran in the Middle East, or Malaysia for Indonesia in Asia.

While liberalized markets are not perfect, there is a great deal of evidence that over the long run they outperform financial systems driven by patronage and influence, both in terms of efficiency and in terms of limiting the frequency of financial crises. Once the idea is abandoned that there has to be a tradeoff between growth and stability, a distinctly optimistic picture of future financial development emerges where emerging economies can have the best of both worlds if they can continue to put institutions and policies in place that encourage productive financial activity.

(7) *There has been a vast improvement in macroeconomic policy in most emerging market economies over the last two decades.* For many years, emerging market economies were synonymous with financial crises. A lack of restraint on government spending and a lack of a tax base led to periodic cycles of excessive government borrowing and regular sovereign debt crises. In countries that did not have independent central banks, fiscal dominance created pressure to monetize government debt, often leading to hyperinflation. Sovereign debt crises and hyperinflation contributed to frequent banking crises. This happened repeatedly throughout Latin America and Sub-Saharan Africa in the 1980s and 1990s.

While 20 years is not a long enough period from which to confidently predict the future, it clearly has been a remarkable period in terms of macroeconomic policy within emerging market economies. On average, inflation has been much lower and steadier, fiscal restraint has been much greater, and policymakers have been much more flexible than in previous eras. This likely is the result of policymakers learning from past mistakes, particularly mistakes made preceding the Latin American debt crisis and the East Asian financial crisis. But the globalization of finance has also contributed by imposing external constraints on emerging economies and encouraging greater monetary and fiscal discipline. Open financial markets and steady growth in foreign capital inflows have increased the benefits of macroeconomic policy restraint while also increasing the costs of losing market confidence.

(8) *Both macroeconomic and microeconomic policy mistakes have played an important role in financial crises.* Asset bubbles, banking crises, sovereign debt crises, and currency crises are all very costly. This is true at the time of the crisis in terms of lost output and the costs of bailouts. But financial crises are also costly well after a crisis is over, leaving behind a historical legacy of higher perceived risk, reduced debt tolerance, and limited monetary policy effectiveness because of dollarization. Financial crises do not happen by accident but are the result of short-sighted economic policy. At a macroeconomic level, excessive debt and hyperinflations have certainly contributed to asset bubbles, sovereign debt crises, and banking crises. Also, the rigid reliance on fixed exchange rate policies has often encouraged speculative capital inflow booms and currency mismatch that lead to costly currency crises, particularly in conjunction with other forms of financial crisis.

But macroeconomic policy is not only to blame. In every modern financial crisis in emerging economies, indiscriminate financial liberalization took place before the crisis occurred without first having the appropriate prudential regulation in place. This contributed to speculation fueled by moral hazard, domestic credit booms, foreign capital inflow booms, and currency mismatch. At some point, financial fundamentals deteriorated to the point that a loss of confidence triggered belief-based panic selling that weakened already fragile fundamentals beyond the breaking point. This toxic brew of risky financial fundamentals at the microeconomic level coupled with imbalances created at the macroeconomic level has led to the conditions under which extremely costly financial crises have taken place. The lesson to be learned here is that a whole range of complex factors contribute to financial crises. This is the primary reason why it has been so difficult for many countries to learn from past crises and also why, in the words of Charles Kindleberger (1989), financial crises are "a hardy perennial."

(9) *Foreign capital inflows are great, but it is possible to have too much of a good thing.* Foreign capital offers emerging market economies increased resources for investment without having to limit their domestic consumption. It also provides these economies with a way to diversify their wealth and their financial systems while gaining access to international expertise and institutions. The attractiveness of foreign capital has led many countries to overindulge by enacting policies to attract foreign inflows without a proper respect for its potential dangers.

Three particular policy mistakes have been most costly. First, capital accounts have been opened without first making sure that domestic financial markets have sufficiently liberalized and are mature enough to be able to efficiently distribute the resources and risks these flows bring. Second, capital flows have been liberalized without first having the appropriate prudential regulation in place. Most importantly, limits on foreign-denominated short-term debt (hot money) are needed to reduce the risk of sudden capital flight. Third, many central banks adopted rigid pegs to foreign currencies, particularly the dollar, in order to make their country more attractive to foreign investors. These pegs encouraged both foreign investors and domestic financial systems to treat the dangers of currency mismatch as if it were not there, fueling moral hazard behavior that has greatly contributed to currency crises and which, in turn, contributed to other forms of financial crisis as well.

(10) *For emerging market economies, there are no simple rules to guide monetary policy—only tradeoffs.* There is a long list of factors that influence the costs and benefits of fixing versus floating an exchange rate, making it simply impossible to choose a one-size-fits-all monetary policy for emerging market economies. This is one of the reasons why intermediate exchange rate strategies—such as target zones and inflation targets—are becoming more popular, because these strategies allow countries to tailor their monetary policy to their specific needs. For example, inflation targeting is likely to be particularly attractive to countries with a lack of credibility in regard to maintaining low inflation or suffering from fiscal dominance. Likewise, a crawling peg is an attractive option for countries when their financial systems are too fragile to handle the risk of a fixed exchange rate, but that are also worried about the impact of volatile exchange rates on their exports.

Another trend in monetary policy among emerging market economies is the adoption of undervalued exchange rates in an effort to accumulate foreign reserves and promote exports. China, of course, has been the most prominent adopter of this strategy. While the potential benefits are obvious, the costs of undervalued exchange rates are less obvious, but no less significant because of this. An undervalued exchange rate discourages consumption, keeping standards of living low, and distorts production (toward volatile exports and investment) and financial risk (toward excessive savings and cheap credit) in ways that threaten economic stability. There are good reasons to believe that countries that are purposely adopting undervalued exchange rates now will regret this decision with the perspective of time. Certainly, their citizens are already suffering from much lower standards of living than are possible given their level of income. Too often some of these countries seem to have forgotten that it is higher standards of living, and not just economic growth for growth's sake, that is the ultimate goal of development.

Regardless of the exchange rate regime that emerging market central banks choose, one paramount fact remains: the choice of an exchange rate policy is of second-order importance relative to the premium that must be placed on monitoring and maintaining sound financial fundamentals. Monetary policy contributes to strong fundamentals by encouraging quality institutions through providing a stable and credible macroeconomic policy environment as well as monitoring and regulating systemic risk in the banking system. These are the big-picture goals that must remain paramount in any successful monetary policy strategy.

In conclusion, many emerging market economies across the globe have reached, or will soon reach, levels of economic development where all of the simple avenues to growth have been exhausted. One of the paradoxical results of a country becoming richer is that future growth will necessarily slow. As emerging economies become richer and as growth slows, structural constraints on growth will be harder to overcome and also to dismiss. Is the financial system going to be growth drag or a driver of future economic development? Will finance be a source of stability by smoothing spending or a source of instability by generating financial crises? These questions are important for every economy, but particularly for emerging market economies given their relative poverty and underdevelopment. Better financial systems can be the bridge that helps emerging economies span the development gap between them and developed economies. Economics, and hopefully this book, helps us to understand how to design this bridge. But is there the political will to build it and who is going to do it? The answer to this question will determine which countries will no longer be emerging economies in the future, but will become emerged economies.

Notes

Preface

1 The term "emerging market" is used in this book to refer to both emerging and less developed economies, although these groups are often separated, with the term "emerging market economies" referring to those that are growing rapidly while "less developed countries" are those that are not. Unfortunately, there is no generally accepted term to denote economies outside of the developed world. Thus, the term "emerging market economies" as it is used in this book incorporates Latin America (Central and South America), the Middle East (including North Africa), central and eastern Europe, and the whole of Asia apart from Japan, Hong Kong, Singapore, Australia, and New Zealand.
2 Throughout this text, cross-country GDP comparisons will typically be made based on purchasing power parity estimates of exchange rates (which accounts for the fact that lower prices in most poorer countries boost real spending power) and not based on market exchange rates, unless otherwise noted.
3 Hawksworth (2006).
4 IMF (2011g).
5 CGAP/World Bank (2010).

1 Finance and development

1 Schumpeter (1949).
2 The "rule of 72" says that something growing at x percent a year will double in size every 72/x years. This is a useful rule of thumb for highlighting the power of compounded growth.
3 For a full survey of this literature, see Levine (1997) and Demirgüç-Kunt (2010).
4 See Aghion *et al.* (2005) and Levine *et al.* (2000), among others.
5 See Banerjee and Duflo (2007), Rosenzweig and Wolpin (1993), and Demirgüç-Kunt and Levine (2008).
6 For a more detailed discussion of how the FinDI is calculated, see www.weforum.org/issues/financial-development.
7 These results are consistent with the empirical work of Demirgüç-Kunt and Levine (2001), who find that countries that are richer have more developed and more efficient banks and stock and bond markets.
8 World Bank (2012).
9 See Megginson (2010) for a more complete discussion of the impact of privatization on financial markets.
10 Yang (2011).
11 Yang (2011).
12 Overall, the empirical evidence on the relationship between remittances and economic growth is unclear. See Yang (2011) for a more complete review of the literature.

13 See Aggarwal *et al.* (2006) and Yang (2011) for a full review of the literature.
14 For example, M-Via, a US company, allows customers to add electronic money to their virtual accounts (or a formal bank account) and text these balances to other members.
15 Yang (2011) and *The Economist*, May 19, 2012.

2 Information and finance

1 Throughout most of history, the primary collateral used for most loans was your life or your freedom. The word *draconian* comes from the Greek judge Draco who made laws approving the enslavement of borrowers in default. Debtors' prisons were common in Europe, as any fan of Charles Dickens and William Shakespeare knows, and were not abolished in the Western world until the 1820s in the United States and 1860s in Europe.
2 These regulations in the Philippines have recently been reformed and reduced to the level of onerous, not impossible.
3 See Knoop (2008) for a more comprehensive look at these studies.
4 For example, Beck, Demirgüç-Kunt, and Levine (2007), Demirgüç-Kunt and Levine (2008), Beck, Demirgüç-Kunt, and Peria (2008), and Collins *et al.* (2009).
5 See Bond *et al.* (2008), Banerjee and Duflo (2008), and Paulson and Townsend (2004).
6 See Pham and Lensink (2008), Bond *et al.* (2008), and Hurst and Lusardi (2004).
7 Interestingly, the return on the second $250 from these grants was *negligible*, primarily because resources above the first $250 were consumed. This suggests that many small entrepreneurs are constrained not just in their investment patterns, but also in their consumption.
8 See de Mel *et al.* (2008) and McKenzie and Woodruff (2008).
9 Detragiache *et al.* (2005) find similar results.
10 Yunus (1995).
11 CGAP/World Bank (2010).
12 Giné and Karlan (2009), Hermes and Lensink (2007), Karlan (2007), and Cassar *et al.* (2007) are a few of the studies that find that group-based lending increases monitoring and reduces adverse selection and moral hazard, particularly when these groups have close social or family ties.
13 Cull *et al.* (2007) find empirical evidence that microfinance organizations that rely on group lending instead of individual lending have higher profits and lower risk, but also charge higher interest rates and grant smaller loans. This is consistent with the fact that group-based lending is most likely to be attractive to poorer, credit rationed borrowers.
14 Cull *et al.* (2009) report that delinquency rates for the largest microfinance organizations are between 2 and 3 percent, on average.
15 Hossain (1988).
16 Zohir (2010).
17 See Banerjee and Duflo (2011) and Daley-Harris (2007).
18 See Banerjee and Duflo (2011) for an excellent discussion of the limitations of microfinance.
19 See Armendáriz de Aghion and Morduch (2005) and the World Bank (2007) for examples of such studies and a more detailed review of the literature on this question.
20 Gonzalez and Meyer (2009).
21 Sengupta and Aubuchon (2008).
22 See Collins *et al.* (2009) for case studies of poor households and the financing decisions they make.
23 Cull *et al.* (2009).

24 Dupas and Robinson (2012) found that moving local women in rural Kenya from informal savings associations to more formal savings accounts increased investment and stabilized consumption and education expenditures.
25 *The Economist*, December 11, 2011.
26 The growth in power of microfinance organizations such as Grameen has also invited more government intervention, often repressive. Mohammad Yunus resigned in 2011 as a result of Bangladeshi government pressure to take a mandatory retirement. Many of Yunus' supporters claim that the government is really interested in removing Yunus as a political threat and in gaining more control over the bank's assets, worth roughly $1.6 billion.
27 *The Economist*, April 28, 2012.
28 *The Economist*, April 28, 2012.
29 Beck, Demirgüç-Kunt, and Peria (2008).
30 *The Economist*, March 11, 2010.

3 Institutions and financial systems

1 World Bank (2011).
2 Svensson (2005).
3 An excellent example of this is the Belgian Congo, grippingly portrayed in *King Leopold's Ghost* by Adam Hochschild (1998).
4 Banerjee and Iyer (2005).
5 See La Porta *et al.* (2008) for a complete review of this literature.
6 For example, see Beck *et al.* (2005) and Demirgüç-Kunt *et al.* (2004).
7 Ayyagari *et al.* (2008) find the same relationship between political instability, crime, and financial development.
8 Haber (2004).
9 For example, Barth *et al.* (2006) and Demirgüç-Kunt and Levine (2009).
10 See Barro and McCleary (2003) for a similar study with similar results. Also see Barro and McCleary (2006) for a summary of the literature on the relationship between religion and growth.
11 See Easterly and Levine (2003) and Alesina and La Ferrara (2005).
12 In a similar study, Haslag and Koo (1999) find that the impact of higher reserve ratios on financial development and growth is actually larger than that of higher inflation. Their results indicate that higher inflation only negatively impacts financial development past a threshold level (40 percent).
13 Banerjee and Duflo (2011).
14 La Porta *et al.* (2003), Caprio and Honohan (2001), and Barth *et al.* (2002) find similar results.
15 A great deal of additional empirical work has been done on the effects of liberalizing foreign capital flows, which will be discussed in more detail in Chapter 6.
16 World Bank (2003).
17 Arestis and Demetriades (1997).
18 This underground lending market in large part is financed by recipients of formal loans, primarily state-owned enterprises, that re-lend these funds to the private sector. The underground lending market in China is examined more closely in Chapter 11.
19 Rotating savings and credit associations, or ROSCAs, are small, informal savings groups where people regularly make payments into a pool and periodically receive the entire pool of funds either on a rotating or sometimes on a lottery basis. These are described in more detail in Chapter 9.
20 Shiller (2012).
21 Allen *et al.* (2008).
22 McGregor (2005: 97).

23 The Fitch financial rating agency warned in 2011 that a financial crisis in China could cost as much as 30 percent of its GDP.
24 See Allen *et al.* (2009) for the full results of their survey of Indian businesses.
25 For an excellent source of bribery stories, and for an example of how private citizens can increase transparency about bribery in an effort to fight it, visit the Indian website www.ipaidabribe.com.
26 This data is reported by Allen *et al.* (2009).
27 World Bank (2011).
28 See Chapter 11 and Allen, Chakrabarti, and De (2007) for a more detailed structural analysis of the Indian financial system.

4 Fiscal policy and sovereign debt

1 Tanzi and Zee (2000).
2 Tanzi (1987).
3 See Haggarty and Shirley (1997) and Megginson (2005) for more detailed examinations of the inefficiencies of SOEs.
4 See Kikeri and Nellis (2002) and Megginson (2005, 2010) for more complete reviews of the economic impact of privatization.
5 Reinhart and Rogoff (2009).
6 Sovereignty laws protect most state-owned assets abroad, such as embassies or reserves held at central banks. Typically, the only assets subject to seizure are those deemed to be used for strictly commercial purposes.
7 Reinhart and Rogoff (2011) find that domestic debt booms typically are larger and precede external debt booms.
8 Some sovereign bonds are issued with "collective-action" clauses that force all bond-holders to participate in a debt restructuring if a threshold percentage of bondholders agree to it. Such clauses are becoming more common among new sovereign bond issuances.
9 See Kopits (2000) and Agénor and Montiel (1999) for studies identifying the specific macroeconomic impact of debt crises.
10 Quite a few empirical studies have attempted to quantify the costs of inflation. For example, Barro (1998) finds that a 10 percent increase in inflation reduces growth by 0.025%, and it is the level of inflation, not its variability, that Barro finds is most costly. Bruno and Easterly (1998) find no significant evidence that inflation of less than 40 percent negatively impacts growth, but inflation above this level reduces growth by 2.4 percent on average.
11 In another study, Zoli (2005) finds that between 1995 and 2003 Argentina and Brazil appeared to have had monetary policies driven by fiscal dominance policies, while other emerging market countries such as Columbia, Mexico, Thailand, and Poland behaved in a way completely consistent with neither fiscal dominance nor monetary dominance.
12 Arnone *et al.* (2009).
13 There are plans for the Southern African Development Community to adopt a dollar-based currency union by 2018.

5 Asset bubbles and banking crises

1 Shiller (2005) identifies five weaknesses in the brain's decision-making process—identified from modern psychological and neuroscience research—that contribute to manias and panics. These include (1) the tendency to focus on facts that support pre-conceived beliefs, (2) the tendency to be excessively reliant on story-telling and narratives as opposed to facts, (3) overconfidence and a need to enhance the ego, (4) an inability to conceive of and thus discount all hypothetical events that could occur in the future, and (5) a tendency to be overly influenced by the beliefs of others in the same social group.

2 See Allen and Gale (1998) for such a model of rational asset bubbles.
3 *The Economist*, August 6, 2009.
4 *Wall Street Journal*, June 9, 2011.
5 Chovanec (2010).
6 *Washington Post*, January 11, 2010.
7 *The Economist* blog, April 28, 2011, available at: www.economist.com/blogs/button-wood/2011/04/chinese_property_and_investment.
8 *The Business Insider*, January 13, 2010.
9 *Reuters*, June 13, 2011.
10 The PBOC subsequently reversed itself and lowered interest rates in 2012 in response to worries about a macroeconomic slowdown.
11 *Bloomberg*, March 18, 2012.
12 See the discussion on institutions in the Chinese financial system in Chapter 3 and a more detailed review of the Chinese financial system in Chapter 11.
13 *China Daily*, December 10, 2011.
14 Note that this table does not include banking crises from the 2007 global financial crisis, which are still being accumulated and calculated. The costs from many of these bailouts, particularly in Ireland and Iceland, are sure to exceed some of those in this table.
15 See Mitchell (1941) and Allen and Gale (1998, 2000) for examples of fundamentals-based models of banking crises.
16 See Calvo (1988) for a model of how sovereign debt crises ignite banking crises.
17 Reinhart and Reinhart (2009) and Mendoza and Terrones (2008) similarly find that credit booms and high levels of foreign capital inflows commonly proceed banking crises.
18 See Reinhart and Rogoff (2009) for a discussion of the technical problems in calculating the costs of a banking crisis.
19 These growth costs are roughly similar to those estimated by Demirgüç-Kunt *et al.* (2006) and Hutchison and Noy (2006), but larger than those estimated by Barro (2001) who found that banking crises reduce economic growth by only 0.6 percent.
20 Haber (2005).
21 La Porta *et al.* (2003).
22 Gil-Díaz (1998).
23 Desmet (2000).
24 The causes and mechanics of currency crises are discussed in more detail in Chapter 8.
25 Caprio and Klingebiel (2003).
26 Financial Stability Board (2010).
27 See Özatay and Sak (2002) for a more complete description of the Turkish financial crisis. See Feldstein (2002) and Chapter 4 of this book for a more complete description of the Argentinean crisis.
28 *The Economist*, December 11, 2008.

6 Financial liberalization and capital flows

1 The term "capital account" refers to transactions that involve the transfer of capital and financial assets in a country's balance of payments account. Balance of payment accounting between countries is discussed in more detail in Chapter 8.
2 The Chinn–Ito Index is a *de jure* measure of capital account openness based upon IMF information on the extent of controls on capital within individual countries.
3 Reinhart (2005).
4 See Reinhart (2005), Mody *et al.* (2001), and Taylor and Sarno (1997) for examples of empirical studies attempting to identify the determinants of capital inflows and outflows.
5 See Chapter 4 for a discussion of the Latin American debt crisis.

6 *Institute of International Finance Research Note*, September 25, 2011.
7 Reinhart and Reinhart (2009) present empirical evidence that increased capital inflows are associated with increased incidences of asset bubbles, sovereign debt crises, currency crises, and banking crises.
8 See Kaminsky and Reinhart (1999) and Glick *et al.* (2006).
9 See Glick and Hutchison (2005) and Edwards (2007).
10 Also see Edwards (2001) and De Gregorio *et al.* (2000).
11 IMF (2011b).
12 Also refer to Eichengreen, Arteta, and Wyplosz (2003), Prasad and Rajan (2008), and Williamson (1991) who advocate similar staged-liberalization proposals.
13 See Ahmed and Islam (2009), Henry (2007), and Galindo *et al.* (2002).
14 See Kose, Prasad, and Terrones (2009), Kose, Prasad, Rogoff, and Wei (2009), Eichengreen, Arteta, and Wyplosz (2003), and Eichengreen (2001).
15 Similar results are found in Kose, Prasad, Rogoff, and Wei (2009).
16 Also see Levine and Zervos (1998) and Ito (2006).
17 Also see Claessens *et al.* (2001).
18 See the earlier discussion in Chapter 2 about the financial repression policies followed in Asia in its early stages of economic development.
19 *Institute for International Finance Research Note*, September 25, 2011.
20 *Institute for International Finance Research Note*, June 1, 2011.
21 Similar results are found by Pill and Pradhan (1997), Turtelboom (1991), and Reinhart and Tokatlidis (2003).
22 McGregor (2010: 40).

7 Monetary policy and exchange rate management

1 In Chapter 8 we will consider alternative, non-classical goals for exchange rate management and the reasons why some emerging market economies try to maintain overvalued or undervalued exchange rates over extended periods.
2 This equation assumes that all goods in the basket are internationally tradable. If they are not, an alternative method of calculating a real exchange rate would be to use the ratio of the price of non-tradable goods relative to tradable goods instead of the ratio of the domestic price level to the foreign price level.
3 There are many practical questions associated with calculating a real exchange rate that are not discussed in detail here. What goods should be included in the basket? Should the basket reflect things such as different consumption patterns across countries? What if there is more than one foreign currency other than dollars? How do you treat goods that are not traded internationally (such as real estate)? See Chinn (2006) for a more complete discussion of the applied issues related to estimating real exchange rates.
4 However, purchasing power parity may come closer to holding in emerging economies for specific goods that can be traded at near zero cost. *The Economist* has long reported the "Big Mac Index" that looks at the real exchange rate across countries as measured only in the price of Big Mac sandwiches. A study by Clements *et al.* (2010) suggests that purchasing power parity in Big Macs is a good predictor of nominal exchange rate movements between countries over extended periods.
5 For example, economic data suggests that nominal exchange rates can be as much as three to four times more volatile than relative prices. See Sarno and Taylor (2002) for a review of the empirical literature on exchange rate volatility.
6 This equation is often referred to as *uncovered interest rate parity. Covered interest rate parity* occurs when futures markets exist and traders can lock in a forward exchange rate, removing all uncertainty from the interest rate parity equation. However, for most emerging economies future exchange markets are not sufficiently developed for covered interest rate parity to be possible.

7 Fischer (1982) estimates that dollarization costs small emerging market economies between 0.3 percent and 1.8 percent of GDP in lost seigniorage revenue per year, which is substantial.

8 See Frankel and Rose (2002) and Rose (2005).

9 Another option between pegging to the dollar or to a trading partner's currency would be to peg to a country with a low inflation rate. This option would be most attractive to countries that have had high inflation histories and would be similar to inflation targeting, which is discussed later in this chapter.

10 The arguments here were first developed in the international macroeconomic models developed by Mundell (1961) and Poole (1970).

11 This outcome is similar in structure to the well-known "Prisoner's Dilemma" problem, where a suboptimal outcome occurs (in this case higher inflation) because of an inability to credibly commit to the optimal outcome (in this case, low inflation).

12 For more on this topic, see the discussion of contagion in the next chapter.

13 Countries that are less credible will also find themselves more likely to experience sudden capital flight that could threaten their pegged exchange rates. More on capital flight and currency crises in the next chapter.

14 For example, in 2011 China holds more than $2 trillion in dollar reserves. However, it is unlikely that all of these reserves are held solely as a precautionary measure to protect their exchange rate peg. We will return to this issue in the next chapter.

15 An additional reason why fixed exchange rates make sense for less developed financial systems is that independent monetary policy is unlikely to have a strong impact on the domestic economy through its influence on interest rates and changes in credit in countries with weak financial systems. Instead, monetary policy may have its biggest impact through its influence on the exchange rate, meaning that a fixed exchange rate system may be a means of increasing, not decreasing, the impact of monetary policy on the domestic economy. Bhattacharya *et al.* (2010) test this hypothesis for India and find empirical evidence that the impact of monetary policy on exchange rates played a much bigger role in influencing economic activity than its impact on interest rates.

16 See Frankel (2010) for a complete review of this debate, in which he concludes that empirical studies do not provide clear support that either fixed or floating exchange rate policies consistently outperforms the other across countries.

17 "Fear of floating" is an expression used by Calvo and Reinhart (2002). They find empirical evidence that many emerging countries that claim to float actually have exhibited more volatility in their real exchange rate than their nominal exchange rate, indicating that nominal exchange rates are still being tightly managed.

18 In this figure, inflation targeting is classified as either managed float or pure float, depending upon the country.

19 IMF (2008).

20 There is some evidence that this is exactly what happened in many emerging economies that adopted inflation targets during the 2008–2010 global financial crisis. See Frankel (2010).

21 See Gonçalves and Salles (2008) and Fraga *et al.* (2004).

22 See Mishkin (2006a).

23 See de la Torre (2003).

24 The Argentinean government violated property rights in other ways during this time by changing bankruptcy laws to help favored borrowers, changing the terms of some loan contracts, and breaking utilities contracts with foreign firms.

25 In 2005, the Argentinean government agreed to a debt swap with roughly three-fourths of its private creditors in which they would receive new bonds worth 30 percent of the old bonds in default. Argentina fully repaid the IMF and World Bank by the end of 2008.

8 International financial crises: currency and twin crises

1 See Frankel and Rose (1996), Kaminsky *et al.* (2005), and Reinhart and Rogoff (2009).

2 Kaminsky and Reinhart (2000) also find empirical evidence that financial linkages play a larger role than trade linkages in the spread of contagion. As the number of countries in crisis increases, they find that the probability of contagion spreading to additional countries increases sharply.

3 Others have argued that beliefs do play a large role in twin crises. Goldstein (2005) presents a model in which banking crises occur because investors fear speculative attacks on the currency, while currency crises occur because investors fear bank runs and banking crises. The key link between these two crises is the existence of currency mismatch.

4 Barro (2001) does not attempt to measure the interaction between the banking and currency crises and estimates that the five-year average cost of twin crises is a reduction in growth of roughly 2.2 percent, 1.6 percent of which is attributable to the currency crisis and 0.6 percent of which is attributable to the banking crisis.

5 Hutchison and Noy (2006) examine the costs of currency crises and capital flight alone in 24 emerging economies. They find that over a three-year period, these crises led to reductions in GDP of between 13 and 15 percent. These levels of output losses are similar to those found in Hutchison and Noy (2005) but without examining banking crises. The only conclusion to draw from these studies is that there is considerable uncertainty associated with any of these cost estimates.

6 Corsetti *et al.* (1999).

7 Krueger (2002).

8 Krueger (2002).

9 An interesting example of the importance of having strong prudential regulation can be found in the Philippines. While they had the highest levels of non-performing loans in the region in 1996, the Philippines actually enacted a program of strengthening prudential regulation and recapitalizing weak banks before the crisis took place. As a result, despite having the weakest macroeconomic fundamentals in the region, the Philippines was able to avoid the worst of the crisis. Despite having weak banks, China also avoided a currency crisis and a banking crisis because of the strict foreign capital controls it had in place.

10 For the four large crisis countries, capital accounts moved from net inflows of greater than 10 percent of GDP to net outflows of 11 percent of GDP on average, a net reversal of more than 20 percent of GDP.

11 Hahm and Mishkin (2000).

12 Corsetti *et al.* (1999).

13 Malaysian Prime Minister Mahathir Mohamad famously blamed the crisis on Jewish speculators and George Soros, head of the Quantum Hedge Fund.

14 See Eichengreen, Rose, and Wyplosz (2003b), Williamson (2004), and Eichengreen (2003b).

15 Goldstein (1998).

16 See Hahm and Lim (2006) for a review of the bailout and restructuring of the South Korean banking system.

17 Jeanne (2007).

18 See Bernanke's March 10, 2005 speech, "The Global Savings Glut and the US Current Account Deficit," available at: www.federalreserve.gov/boarddocs/speeches/2005/200503102.

19 These comments particularly apply to China. The structure and dangers of the Chinese financial system, as well as other Asian financial systems, are discussed in more detail in Chapter 11.

20 See Dreher (2009) for a review of the empirical evidence and new empirical work on the growth impacts of IMF conditional lending.
21 The US congress authorized a congressional commission headed by economist Alan Meltzer to examine this issue. This commission concluded that IMF lending has funded moral hazard and makes the case that the Mexican crisis in 1994 was a precursor to the East Asian crisis in 1997. This report is available at: www.house.gov/jec/imf/meltzer.htm.
22 Many of these same arguments are made by conservative critics of debt relief programs as well. See this discussion in Chapter 4.
23 Vasquez (1999).

9 Financial systems in Sub-Saharan Africa

1 Allen, Otchere, and Senbet (2010).
2 IMF (2010a). The eight are Angola (1), Ethiopia (3), Uganda (6), Rwanda (9), Sudan (10), Mozambique (15), Tanzania (16), and Malawi (20).
3 See Demirgüç-Kunt *et al.* (2008).
4 The costs of these informal loans also tend to be inflated when they are expressed in percentage terms. This is because many informal loans are priced on a flat fee, not a percentage, basis. This seems appropriate given that there are significant transaction costs associated with each loan that the lender must recover. However, these flat fees are significantly magnified when put on a percentage basis for small, short-term loans.
5 Some ROSCAs are also associated with "social funds" that can serve as microinsurance. In these social funds, members make regular contributions to a fund that makes payments to members who suffer sudden misfortunes. These social funds are similar to burial funds discussed earlier.
6 See Sacerdoti (2005) for a review of the empirical evidence regarding the credit rationing of SMEs in Africa.
7 Honohan and Beck (2007).
8 Sacerdoti (2005).
9 *The Banker*, January 3, 2012.
10 United Nations (2006).
11 Allen, Carletti *et al.* (2010) find empirical evidence that population density, along with the number of roads and the number of branch banks, plays a large role in explaining the gap in financial development between SSA and other emerging market regions of the world.
12 Honohan and Beck (2007).
13 Beck, Demirgüç-Kunt, and Peria (2008).
14 Honohan and Beck (2007).
15 Beck and Demirgüç-Kunt (2009).
16 Allen, Otchere, and Senbet (2010).
17 Honohan and Beck (2007).
18 Christensen (2004).
19 Allen, Otchere, and Senbet (2010).
20 See Levine (2005) and Armour *et al.* (2009) for a more detailed discussion of the institutional differences between common law and civil code systems.
21 Allen, Otchere, and Senbet (2010).
22 *The Economist*, September 10, 2011.
23 See Allen, Carletti *et al.* (2010), Ahmed and Islam (2009), Serieux (2008), and Pill and Pradhan (1997).
24 IMF (2010a).
25 The countries are Niger, Benin, Côte d'Ivoire, Mali, Senegal, Togo, Burkina Faso, and the non-francophone Guinea-Bissau.

26 The countries are Cameroon, Central African Republic, Chad, Equatorial Guinea, Republic of the Congo, and Gabon.
27 Mishra *et al.* (2010).
28 IMF (2010a).
29 See IMF (2010a) for empirical work on the transmission of monetary policy in SSA.
30 Allen, Otchere, and Senbet (2010).
31 Demirgüç-Kunt *et al.* (2008).
32 IMF (2010a).
33 Central Bank of Nigeria (2007).
34 *The Economist*, May 28, 2011.
35 Nigeria scores poorly in other similar rankings, such as the World Bank's (2011) Ease of Doing Business ranking, where in 2010 it ranked 134 out of 183 countries.
36 The website www.bribenigeria.com is an entertaining and informative collection of stories of bribery submitted by Nigerians.
37 Alawode *et al.* (2000).
38 *The Economist*, December 3, 2011.
39 *The Economist*, July 10, 2010.
40 Isern *et al.* (2009).
41 See Nzotta and Okereke (2009) and Ayadi *et al.* (2008).
42 *The Economist*, May 28, 2011.
43 Acemoglu *et al.* (2001b).
44 Bank of Botswana Financial Statistics, available at: www.bankofbotswana.bw/assets/uploaded/bfsjuly2011.xls.
45 IMF (2011d).
46 The story is more completely told in *King Leopold's Ghost* by Adam Hochschild (1998).
47 Much of this discussion is based upon Michela Wrong's (2001) entertaining book *In the Footsteps of Mr. Kurtz: Living on the Brink of Disaster in Mobutu's Congo.*
48 World Bank (2009).
49 Allen, Otchere, and Senbet (2010).
50 IMF (2011d).
51 Arieff *et al.* (2010).
52 See Berman and Martin (2010). These authors present econometric evidence that SSA is particularly sensitive to changes in the output of developed countries because of trade linkages. They find that economic downturns typically reduce SSA exports by 23 percent and that this contraction in exports lasts from four to seven years.
53 Barajas *et al.* (2010).
54 IMF (2011d).

10 Financial systems in the Middle East and North Africa

1 Countries typically included as part of the MENA region include Afghanistan, Algeria, Bahrain, Djibouti, Egypt, Iran, Iraq, Jordan, Kuwait, Lebanon, Libya, Mauritania, Morocco, Oman, Qatar, Tunisia, Saudi Arabia, Sudan, Syria, the United Arab Emirates, and Yemen.
2 The oil-importing countries in MENA are Afghanistan, Djibouti, Egypt, Jordan, Lebanon, Mauritania, Morocco, Pakistan, Syria, and Tunisia.
3 IMF (2011e).
4 The GCC comprises Bahrain, Kuwait, Oman, Qatar, Saudi Arabia, and the United Arab Emirates.
5 IMF (2011e).
6 De la Campa (2011).
7 CGAP/World Bank (2010).

 8 IMF (2011e). However, it is important to once again note that measures of financial development differ significantly across countries in the region. For example, the credit-to-GDP ratio in Yemen is only 8 percent.
 9 IMF (2011e).
10 See Anzoategui *et al.* (2010) for a more detailed discussion of the structure of MENA banking systems.
11 *The Banker's Top 1,000 World Banks*, at www.thebanker.com/Top-1000-World-Banks/Top-1000-World-Banks-2011.
12 Rocha *et al.* (2011).
13 Creane *et al.* (2007).
14 Pearce (2011).
15 Pearce (2011).
16 IMF (2011e).
17 Madeddu (2010).
18 De la Campa (2011).
19 Creane *et al.* (2007).
20 IMF (2011e).
21 De la Campa (2011) presents empirical evidence in support of this point.
22 Nasr (2006).
23 Nasr (2006).
24 Pearce (2011).
25 Nasr (2006).
26 Nasr (2006).
27 Pearce (2011).
28 *The Banker*, January 3, 2012.
29 See Chapter 11 for more discussion of the *sukuks* and *takaful* industries in Malaysia, a burgeoning global center for Islamic finance.
30 Pearce (2011).
31 See Kuran (2004, 2005) and Landes (1999), among others, for a more in-depth discussion of the history of Islam and its role in influencing modern economic institutions.
32 At the root of Islamic inheritance law is an egalitarian requirement that two-thirds of every inheritance must be distributed to an extensive list of relatives. This often requires the dissolution of concentrated firm ownership upon death that may threaten the existence of firms, or at least dilutes control.
33 Guillaume and Sensenbrenner (2011).
34 Guillaume and Sensenbrenner (2011).
35 Creane *et al.* (2007).
36 Transparency International (2011).
37 The charge is that letters of credit were falsified to gain access to funds that were later embezzled. Many of those charged have alleged ties to the Iranian president. See the *New York Times*, October 10, 2011.
38 *Al Arabiya News*, August 9, 2011.
39 The *hawala* system has come under increased scrutiny recently as it is often suspected of being used to finance terrorism, money laundering, and other illegal activities, in part because of its informal and opaque nature.
40 Hashmi (2007).
41 According to TWacademy.com, available at: www.twacademy.co.uk/news/unspne62942-19-0/news_surge_in_dubai_s_accommodation_fuels_increase_in_visitor_demand/index.html.
42 *The Economist*, November 27, 2008.
43 SWF Institute (available at: www.swfinstitute.org/fund-rankings) and the *New York Times*, October 10, 2011.
44 IMF (2011e).

45 The assets of SWFs do not include (1) the foreign exchange holdings of central banks (unless they have been transferred to an SWF) and (2) pension holdings by governments for citizens or employees.
46 Both the United States and Germany have discussed initiatives for their governments to review foreign investments that "endanger national interests" in the words of a recent German law. However, how such laws or procedures would be enforced is currently unclear.

11 Financial systems in Asia

1 In our discussion here, references to Asia will not include the developed countries/regions of Japan, Singapore, Hong Kong, New Zealand, and Australia, nor will it include North Korea and Papua New Guinea.
2 Here, East Asia includes China, South Korea, and the countries of South East Asia: Cambodia, Indonesia, Laos, Malaysia, Thailand, the Philippines, and Vietnam. South Asia includes India and its neighboring countries: Bangladesh, Bhutan, Myanmar, Nepal, and Sri Lanka.
3 See Adams (2008) and Estrada *et al.* (2010).
4 CGAP/World Bank (2010).
5 IMF (2010c).
6 Bank of International Settlements (2009).
7 *Institute of International Finance Research Note*, September 25, 2011.
8 *Institute of International Finance Research Note*, June 1, 2011.
9 IMF (2011c).
10 As an example of the restrictions on hot money, in 2006 Thailand imposed a restriction that 30 percent of capital inflows must be held on reserve in a Thai account for a least one year.
11 Shimada and Yang (2010).
12 McGregor (2010: xii).
13 The Big Four, in order of size, are the Industrial and Commercial Bank of China (ICBC), the China Construction Bank (CCB), the Agricultural Bank of China (ABC), and the Bank of China (BOC). The ICBC was originally spun off from China's central bank, the People's Bank of China, and today is primarily devoted to FDI investments in Asia and Africa. The CCB is the development bank of China focused on public investment projects. ABC focuses on commercial as well as household lending. The BOC is the oldest bank in China, dating back to 1912, and emphasizes foreign exchange and international trade financing, along with being the Chinese bank with the largest international presence.
14 Shiller (2012).
15 *Global Finance*, September 13, 2010.
16 *The Economist*, November 5, 2011.
17 According to Tsai (2002), there are many reasons why state-owned banks primarily lend to SOEs. SOEs have large workforces that need to be maintained in order to prevent increases in unemployment. Also, most SOEs operate in industries that are perceived by the government to be strategically important. Finally, many banking officials have little experience lending to the private sector and lending to SOEs is perceived to be safe because of their government backing. As a result, many private firms often register as SOEs or pay to use the name of an SOE in order to get a formal loan.
18 These statistics come from Dorn (2006). However, there are huge difficulties in separating private from public firms in China given the myriad ties and obfuscations in the way firms are structured in the Chinese economy to gain access to political influence or finance. According to Huang (2008), the "pure" private sector in China may be no more than 20 percent of GDP.

19 Transparency International publishes an annual survey evaluating the transparency of the 105 largest firms in the world. Chinese banks earned three of the bottom four spots in the survey. The results are available at: www.transparency.org/whatwedo/pub/transparency_in_corporate_reporting_assessing_the_worlds_largest_companies.

20 Chinese banks have government regulators that attend board meetings and have party officials as senior management, even when the bank is not explicitly run by government officials.

21 McGregor (2010).

22 Ferri and Liu (2010).

23 *Also Sprach Analyst*, October 13, 2011.

24 Walter and Howie (2011).

25 Walter and Howie (2011).

26 Ayyagari *et al.* (2010).

27 Tsai (2002) finds that there is a great deal of local variation regarding the permissiveness of local officials to underground lending, which explains why it is widely available in some areas of China but actively prosecuted as illegal in others. Tsai finds that these regional differences depend upon the specific history of each region, including whether it was an early adopter of economic reforms.

28 *Asia Times*, August 26, 2011.

29 *National Public Radio*, October 25, 2011.

30 In 1986, an asset bubble in Wenzhou's underground ROSCA burst. At its peak, it is estimated that 95 percent of Wenzhou's residents were engaged in at least one ROSCA (Tsai 2002). Unfortunately for Wenzhou's residents, a lack of oversight led to corruption and numerous Ponzi-like financing arrangements. While the economic impact of the collapse in the bubble was largely hushed up by the Chinese government, the bankruptcies and losses in wealth sparked numerous suicides and social unrest in the city.

31 *The Economist*, May 5, 2012.

32 As an example of the uncertain risk of underground loans, during the second half of 2011 more than 80 factory bosses and their families disappeared after failing to repay their debts and, most likely, absconding (*National Public Radio*, October 25, 2011).

33 *The Economist*, April 23, 2011.

34 China maintains strict controls on the ability of foreigners to buy their sovereign debt, currently limiting the ability to do so to a small number of central banks, such as in Japan and Malaysia.

35 McGregor (2010).

36 See Durnev *et al.* (2004) for a more complete discussion of the problems with Chinese financial institutions.

37 In March 2012 the Chinese government did announce a pilot program to make the underground lending market in Wenzhou more transparent by allowing underground moneylenders to register as private lenders, granting them legal recognition in return for disclosing their lending activities. Under this program the citizens of Wenzhou would be allowed to save up to $3 million outside China without the government's approval. However, these reforms were only enacted on a pilot basis and only in Wenzhou.

38 In response to this disintermediation, the Chinese government has allowed banks to offer alternative financial products that offer savers higher returns, such as "wealth-management products" that are backed by a mix of financial assets (somewhat like a money market savings account in Western countries). However, these products do not provide deposit insurance as regulated deposits do.

39 China has begun to make some minor moves to make the RMB more attractive as an international currency. For example, it has begun to issue "Dim Sum" bonds that are denominated in RMB but sold in Hong Kong. However, in an effort to limit destabilizing capital inflows, it still remains the case that government approval is needed to

bring RMB into China. As a result, few international assets are denominated in RMB and only 7 percent of China's international trade actually takes place in RMB (see *The Economist*, August 20, 2011).

40 *The Economist*, March 3, 2012.
41 From McGregor (2010).
42 Farrell and Lund (2006).
43 Pension funds in India are similarly repressed and are required to hold 50 percent of their assets in government bonds.
44 Allen, Chakrabarti, De *et al.* (2007).
45 *Financial Times*, August 23, 2011.
46 Farrell and Lund (2006).
47 Jadhav and Raj (2009).
48 IMF (2011c).
49 Shimada and Yang (2010).
50 Shimada and Yang (2010).
51 Transparency International (2010).
52 For a more detailed discussion of cronyism in Indonesia's prudential regulation system, see IMF (2010d).
53 World Bank (2012).
54 Chew (2011).
55 *Arab News*, September 25, 2011.
56 *Business Times*, August 8, 2010.

12 Financial systems in Latin America

1 These generalizations are not true of every Latin American banking system. Two Latin American economies—Chile and Brazil—do have relatively developed banking systems where bank assets are greater than 75 percent of GDP. These countries are also the two highest-ranked economies in Latin America in terms of the World Economic Forum's ranking of financial development (see Figure 1.1). On the other hand, credit-to-GDP is less than 20 percent in Argentina.
2 IMF (2011f).
3 IMF (2010e).
4 Jiménez and Manuelito (2011).
5 De la Torre *et al.* (2012).
6 Moreno (2007).
7 Jiménez and Manuelito (2011).
8 The rate of foreign ownership is lowest in Brazil at only 6 percent. See de la Torre *et al.* (2012).
9 Interestingly, one-third of Latin American exports go to other emerging market economies, half of which goes to China.
10 IMF (2010e).
11 Another benefit of more flexible exchange rate regimes in Latin America is that it has allowed exchange rate movements to serve as an automatic stabilizer of aggregate demand as exchange rates are typically procyclical, making net exports countercyclical. See IMF (2011f) for empirical support for this assertion.
12 IMF (2011f).
13 IMF (2011f).
14 Caruana (2009).
15 Transparency International (2010).
16 See IMF (2010e) for a more complete review of prudential regulation in the region.
17 A recent of example of this that has been in the news is the 2012 conviction of Allen Stanford for financial fraud within the United States after running a Ponzi scheme out of his Antigua-based financial group. See *The Economist*, March 10, 2012.

18 González *et al.* (forthcoming).
19 IMF (2011f).
20 González *et al.* (forthcoming).
21 IMF (2011f).
22 González *et al.* (forthcoming).
23 World Bank (2008).
24 See Mexico's country report from the Financial Stability Board (2010) for a more detailed review of Mexican bank performance.
25 Urdapilleta and Stephanou (2009).
26 Urdapilleta and Stephanou (2009).
27 Shiller (2012).
28 Castor (2002: 65).
29 IMF (2011f).
30 OECD (2010).
31 Fajnzylber and López (2007).
32 World Bank (2010).
33 *The Economist*, May 19, 2012.
34 By the end of 2010, Argentina had settled with the bondholders of 93 percent of its debt, leaving $6 billion in debt still in default.
35 *The Economist*, March 31, 2012.
36 See Cavallo (2012) for a description of how such inflation estimates can be obtained.
37 *Washington Post*, October 31, 2011.
38 Transparency International (2010).
39 Available at: www.heritage.org/index/ranking.
40 World Bank (2011).
41 Bergman (2009).
42 See Beattie (2009) for a more detailed discussion of Argentinean history and its lagging development.
43 For example, the Argentinean government has cracked down on informal money changers and recently declared that citizens must declare any foreign holidays to Argentinean tax authorities in a blatant effort to curb capital flight.
44 Moody's (2011).
45 *Business Week*, December 12, 2011.
46 De la Torre *et al.* (2012).
47 See Kokenyne *et al.* (2010) for a literature review and empirical evidence on de-dollarization.

Bibliography

Abiad, A., Detragiache, E., and Tressel, T. (2008) "A New Database of Financial Reform," IMF Working Paper No. 08/266.

Acemoglu, D., Johnson, S., and Robinson, J. (2001a) "The Colonial Origins of Comparative Development: An Empirical Investigation," *American Economic Review*, 91, 1369–401.

Acemoglu, D., Johnson, S., and Robinson, J. (2001b) "An African Success Story: Botswana," MIT Working Paper No. 01–37.

Acosta, P., Calderon, C., Fajnzylber, P., and Lopez, H. (2008) "What Is the Impact of International Remittances on Poverty and Inequality in Latin America?," *World Development*, 36, 89–114.

Adams, C. (2008) "Emerging East Asian Banking Systems: Ten Years after the 1997/1998 Crisis," Asian Development Bank Working Paper Series on Regional Economic Integration No. 16.

Adams, R. and Page, J. (2005) "Do International Migration and Remittances Reduce Poverty in Developing Countries?," *World Development*, 33, 1645–69.

Adelman, I. and Taylor, J. E. (1990) "Is Structural Adjustment with a Human Face Possible? The Case of Mexico," *Journal of Development Studies*, 26, 387–407.

Agénor, P. R. and Monticl, P. (1999) *Development Macroeconomics*, 2nd edn., Princeton, NJ: Princeton University Press.

Aggarwal, R., Demirgüç-Kunt, A., and Peria, M. S. M. (2006) "Do Workers' Remittances Promote Financial Development?," World Bank Working Paper No. 3957.

Aghion, P., Howitt, P., and Mayer-Foulkes, D. (2005) "The Effect of Financial Development on Convergence: Theory and Evidence," *The Quarterly Journal of Economics*, 120, 173–222.

Ahmed, A. and Islam, S. M. N. (2009) *Financial Liberalisation in Developing Countries: Issues, Theories, Time Series Econometric Analyses and Policy Making*, Heidelberg: Springer.

Aizenman, J. (2007) "Large Hoarding of International Reserves and the Emerging Global Architecture," IMF Working Paper No. 13277.

Alawode, A., Murgatroyd, P., Samen, S., McIsaac, D., Cuevas, C., Laurin, A., Wane, F. I., Chiquier, L., and Navarro-Martin, M. (2000) "Nigeria: Financial Sector Review," *Economic Sector Report No. 29941*, Washington, DC: World Bank.

Alesina, A. and La Ferrara, E. (2005) "Ethnic Diversity Economic Performance," *Journal of Economic Literature*, 43, 762–800.

Algan, Y. and Cahuc, P. (2010) "Inherited Trust and Growth," *American Economic Review*, 100, 2060–92.

Ali, S. S. (2011) "Islamic Banking in the MENA Region," World Bank Financial Flagship Report. Online. Available at: http://siteresources.worldbank.org/INTMNAREG-TOPPOVRED/Resources/MENAFlagshipIslamicFinance2_24_11.pdf (accessed October 24, 2011).

Allen, F. and Gale, D. (2000) "Bubbles and Crises," *Economic Journal*, 53, 236–55.

Allen, F. and Gale, D. (1998) "Optimal Financial Crises," *Journal of Finance*, 52, 1245–84.

Allen, F., Carletti, E., Cull, R., Qian, J., and Senbet, L. W. (2010) "The African Financial Development 'Gap'," Wharton Financial Institutions Working Paper No. 10–18.

Allen, F., Chakrabarti, R., and De, S. (2007) "India's Financial System," working paper. Online. Available at: http://ssrn.com/abstract=1261244 (accessed April 11, 2012).

Allen, F., Chakrabarti, R., De, S., Qian, J., and Qian, M. (2009) "Law, Institutions, and Finance in India and China," in B. Eichengreen, P. Gupta, and R. Kumar (eds.) *Emerging Giants: China and India in the World Economy*, New York: Oxford University Press.

Allen, F., Chakrabarti, R., De, S., Qian, J., and Qian, M. (2007) "Financing Firms in India," paper presented at EFA Meetings, Zurich, August 2006. Online. Available at: http://fic.wharton.upenn.edu/fic/india/10%20allen%20qj.pdf (January 13, 2012).

Allen, F., Otchere, I. K., and Senbet, L. W. (2010) "African Financial Systems: A Review," working paper. Online. Available at: http://ssrn.com/abstract=1569613 (accessed August 25, 2011).

Allen, F., Qian, J., and Qian, M. (2008) "China's Financial System: Past, Present, and Future," in L. Brandt and T. G. Rawski (eds.) *China's Great Economic Transformation*, Cambridge: Cambridge University Press.

Anderson, J. (2006) "Five Persistent Myths about China's Banking System," *Cato Journal*, 26, 243–50.

Anzoategui, D., Peria, M. S. M., and Rocha, R. (2010) "Bank Competition in the Middle East and North Africa Region," World Bank Policy Research Working Paper No. 5363.

Arestis, P. and Demetriades, P. O. (1997) "Financial Development and Economic Growth: Assessing the Evidence," *Economic Journal*, 107, 783–99.

Arieff, A., Weiss, M. A., and Jones, V. C. (2010) "The Global Economic Crisis: Impact on Sub-Saharan Africa and Global Policy Responses," Congressional Research Services Report for Congress. Online. Available at: www.fas.org/sgp/crs/row/R40778.pdf (September 23, 2011).

Armendáriz de Aghion, B. and Morduch, J. (2005) *The Economics of Microfinance*, Cambridge, MA: MIT Press.

Armour, J., Deakin, S., Lele, P., and Siems, M. M. (2009) "How Do Legal Rules Evolve? Evidence from a Cross-Country Comparison of Shareholder, Creditor, and Worker Protection," *American Journal of Comparative Law*, 57, 579–629.

Arnone, M., Laurens, B. J., Segalotto, J. F., and M. Sommer (2009) "Central Bank Autonomy: Lessons from Global Trends," IMF Staff Papers No. 56.

Arrow, K. J. (1972) "Gifts and Exchanges," *Philosophy and Public Affairs*, 1, 343–62.

Ayadi, F. O., Adegbite, E. O., and Ayadi, F. S. (2008) "Structural Adjustment, Financial Sector Development and Economic Prosperity in Nigeria," *International Research Journal of Finance and Economics*, 15, 318–31.

Ayyagari, M., Demirgüc-Kunt, A., and Maksimovic, V. (2010) "Formal versus Informal Finance: Evidence from China," *Review of Financial Studies*, 23, 3048–97.

Ayyagari, M., Demirgüc-Kunt, A., and Maksimovic, V. (2008) "How Well Do Institutional Theories Explain Firms' Perceptions of Property Rights?," *Review of Financial Studies*, 21, 1833–71.

Bagehot, W. (1873 [1991]) *Lombard Street: A Description of the Money Market*, Philadelphia, PA: Orion Editions.

Banerjee, A. and Duflo, E. (2011) *Poor Economics: A Radical Rethinking of the Way to Fight Global Poverty*, New York: Public Affairs.

Banerjee, A. and Duflo, E. (2008) "Do Firms Want to Borrow More? Testing Credit Constraints Using a Directed Lending Program," working paper. Online. Available at: http://econ-www.mit.edu/files/2706 (accessed September 13, 2011).

Banerjee, A. and Duflo, E. (2007) "The Economic Lives of the Poor," *Journal of Economic Perspectives*, 21, 141–68.

Banerjee, A. and Iyer, L. (2005) "History, Institutions, and Economic Performance: The Legacy of Colonial Land Tenure Systems in India," *American Economic Review*, 95, 1190–213.

Banerjee, A., Duflo, E., Glennerster, R., and Kinnan, C. (2009) "The Miracle of Microfinance? Evidence from a Randomized Evaluation," MIT mimeo. Online. Available at: http://econ-www.mit.edu/files/5993 (accessed April 15, 2011).

Bank of International Settlements (2009) "Capital Flows and Emerging Market Economies," Committee on the Global Financial System Working Paper No. 33.

Barajas, A., Chami, R., Fullenkamp, C., and Garg, A. (2010) "The Global Financial Crisis and Worker's Remittances to Africa: What's the Damage?," IMF Working Paper No. 10/24.

Barbosa-Fiho, N. H. (2008) "Inflation Targeting in Brazil: 1999–2006," *International Review of Applied Economics*, 22, 187–200.

Barnett, B. J. and Mahul, O. (2007) "Weather Index Insurance for Agriculture and Rural Areas in Lower-Income Countries," *American Journal of Agricultural Economics*, 5, 1241–7.

Barro, R. (2001) "Economic Growth in East Asia Before and After the Financial Crisis," NBER Working Paper No. 8330.

Barro, R. (1998) "Inflation and Growth," in *Determinants of Economic Growth: A Cross-Country Empirical Study*, Cambridge, MA: MIT Press.

Barro, R. and Gordon, D. B. (1983) "Rules, Discretion and Reputation in a Model of Monetary Policy," *Journal of Monetary Economics*, 12, 101–21.

Barro, R. and McCleary, R. M. (2006) "Religion and Economy," *Journal of Economic Perspectives*, 20, 49–72.

Barro, R. and McCleary, R. M. (2003) "Religion and Economic Growth," *American Sociological Review*, 68, 760–81.

Barth, J., Caprio, G., and Levine, R. (2006) *Rethinking Bank Regulation: 'Till Angels Govern*, Cambridge: Cambridge University Press.

Barth, J., Caprio, G., and Levine, R. (2002) "Financial Regulation and Performance: Cross-Country Evidence," in L. Hernández, K. Schmidt-Hebbel, and N. Loayza (eds.) *Banking, Financial Integration, and International Crises*, Santiago: Central Bank of Chile.

Beattie, A. (2009) *False Economy: A Surprising Economic History of the World*, New York, NY: Riverhead Hardcover.

Beck, T. and Demirgüç-Kunt, A. (2009) "Financial Institutions and Markets across Countries and over Time," World Bank Working Paper No. 4943.

Beck, T., Demirgüç-Kunt, A., Laeven, L., and Levine, R. (2008) "Finance, Firm Size, and Growth," *Journal of Money, Credit, and Banking*, 40, 1379–405.

Beck, T., Demirgüç-Kunt, A., and Levine, R. (2010) "Financial Institutions and Markets across Countries and over Time: The Updated Financial Development and Structure Database," *World Bank Economic Review*, 24, 77–92.

Beck, T., Demirgüç-Kunt, A., and Levine, R. (2007) "Finance, Inequality, and the Poor," *Journal of Economic Growth*, 12, 27–49.

Beck, T., Demirgüç-Kunt, A., and Maksimovic, V. (2008) "Financing Patterns around the World: Are Small Firms Different?," *Journal of Financial Economics*, 89, 467–87.

Beck, T., Demirgüç-Kunt, A., and Maksimovic, V. (2005) "Financial and Legal Constraints to Firm Growth: Does Firm Size Matter?," *Journal of Finance*, 60, 137–77.

Beck, T., Demirgüç-Kunt, A., and Merroche, O. (2010) "Islamic vs. Conventional Banking: Business Model, Efficiency, and Stability," World Bank Policy Research Paper No. 5446.

Beck, T., Demirgüç-Kunt, A., and Peria, M. S. M. (2008) "Banking Services for Everyone? Barriers to Bank Access and Use Around the World," *World Bank Economic Review*, 22, 397–430.

Beck, T., Demirgüç-Kunt, A., and Peria, M. S. M. (2007) "Reaching Out: Access to and Use of Banking Services across Countries," *Journal of Financial Economics*, 85, 234–66.

Beegle, K., Dehejia, R. H., and Gatti, R. (2004) "The Education, Labour Market and Health Consequences of Child Labour," Center for Economic Policy Research Discussion Papers No. 4443.

Berg, A. and Pattillo, C. (1999) "Predicting Currency Crises: The Indicators Approach and an Alternative," *Journal of International Money and Finance*, 18, 561–86.

Bergman, M. (2009) *Tax Evasion and the Rule of Law in Latin America: The Political Culture of Cheating and Compliance in Argentina and Chile*, State College, PA: Pennsylvania State University Press.

Berman, N. and Martin, P. (2010) "The Vulnerability of Sub-Saharan Africa to the Financial Crisis: The Case of Trade," CEPR Discussion Paper No. 7765.

Baliño, T. and Sundararajan, V. (1991) *Banking Crises: Cases and Issues*, Washington, DC: International Monetary Fund.

Beegle, K., Dehejia, R. H., and Gatti, R. (2005) "Child Labour, Crop Shocks and Credit Constraints," CEPR Discussion Papers No. 4881.

Bekaert, G., Campbell, H., and Lundblad, C. (2005) "Does Financial Liberalization Spur Growth?," *Journal of Financial Economics*, 77, 3–55.

Bellas, D., Papaioannou, M. G., and Petrova, I. (2010) "Determinants of Emerging Market Sovereign Bond Spreads: Fundamentals vs Financial Stress," IMF Working Paper No. 281.

Bernanke, B. S. (2002) "Asset Price 'Bubbles' and Monetary Policy," speech given to the New York chapter of the National Association for Business Economics, New York, October 15, 2002. Online. Available at: www.federalreserve.gov/boarddocs/speeches/2002/20021015/default.htm (accessed April 13, 2012).

Bernanke, B. S. and Gertler, M. (1990) "Financial Fragility and Economic Performance," *Quarterly Journal of Economics*, 105, 87–114.

Bernanke, B. S. and Gertler, M. (1989) "Agency Costs, Net Worth, and Business Fluctuations," *American Economic Review*, 79, 14–31.

Bernanke, B. S. and Gertler, M. (1987) "Banking and Macroeconomic Equilibrium," in W. A. Barnett and K. J. Singleton (eds.) *New Approaches to Monetary Economics*, Cambridge: Cambridge University Press.

Bhattacharya, R., Patnaik, I., and Shah, A. (2010) "Monetary Policy Transmission in an Emerging Market Setting," IMF Working Paper No. 11/5.

Bond, E., Tybout, J. R., and Utar, H. (2008) "Credit Rationing, Risk Aversion and Industrial Evolution in Developing Countries," NBER Working Paper No. 14116.

Bordo, M., Eichengreen, B., Klingebiel, D., and Peria, M. S. M. (2001) "Is the Crisis Problem Growing More Severe?," *Economic Policy*, 24, 51–82.

Boyd, J. C., Kwak, S., and Smith, B. (2005) "Real Output Losses Associated with Modern Banking Crises," *Journal of Money, Credit, and Banking*, 37, 977–99.

Broner, F., Didier, T., Erce, A., and Schmukler, S. L. (2010) "Gross Capital Flows: Dynamics and Crises," Bank of Spain Working Paper No. 1039.

Bruno, M. and Easterly, W. (1998) "Inflation Crises and Long-Run Growth," *Journal of Monetary Economics*, 41, 3–26.

Buera, F. J., Kaboski, J. P., and Shin, Y. (2011) "Finance and Development: A Tile of Two Sectors," *American Economic Review*, 101, 1964–2002.

Calvo, G. A. (1988) "Servicing the Public Debt: The Role of Expectations," *American Economic Review*, 78, 647–61.

Calvo, G. and Reinhart, C. M. (2002) "Fear of Floating," *Quarterly Journal of Economics*, 107, 379–408.

Caprio, G. and Honohan, P. (2001) *Finance for Growth: Policy Choices in a Volatile World*, Washington, DC: World Bank.

Caprio, G. and Klingebiel, D. (2003) "Episodes of Systemic and Borderline Financial Crises," mimeo, World Bank Database. Online. Available at: http://siteresources. worldbank.org/INTRES/Resources/469232-1107449512766/648083-1108140788422/ 23456_Table_on_systemic_and_non-systemic_banking_crises_January_21_2003.pdf (accessed June 19, 2011).

Caprio, G., Reinhart, C. M., Laewen, L., and Noguera, G. (2003) *Banking Crises Database*. Online. Available HTTP: http://www1.worldbank.org/finance/html/database_sfd. html (accessed April 14, 2011).

Carrasco, C. A. and Ferreiro, J. (2011) "Inflation Targeting and Economic Performance: The Case of Mexico," *Panoeconomicus*, 5, 675–92.

Caruana, J. (2009) "Financial Globalization, the Crisis, and Latin America," speech given to Central Bank Governors of Latin America and Spain, Punta Cana, Dominican Republic, May 14, 2009. Online. Available at: www.bis.org/speeches/sp090519.htm (accessed April 13, 2012).

Cassar, A., Crowley, L., and Wydick, W. (2007) "The Effect of Social Capital on Group Loan Repayment: Evidence from Field Experiments," *Economic Journal*, 117, F85–F106.

Castor, B. V. J. (2002) *Brazil Is Not for Amateurs: Patterns of Governance in the Land of "Jeitinho,"* Bloomington, IN: Xlibris.

Cavallo, A. (2012) "Online and Official Price Indexes: Measuring Argentina's Inflation," MIT Working Paper. Online. Available HTTP: www.mit.edu/~afc/papers/Cavallo-Argentina.pdf (accessed January 29, 2012).

Central Bank of Nigeria (2007) *Annual Report*. Online. Available at: www.cenbank.org/ OUT/PUBLICATIONS/REPORTS/RSD/2009/CBN%20ANNUAL%20REPORT%20 FOR%20THE%20YEAR%20ENDED%2031ST%20DECEMBER%202007%20-%20 EXECUTIVE%20SUMMARY.PDF (accessed August 8, 2011).

CGAP/World Bank (2010) "Financial Access 2010: The State of Financial Access Through the Crisis," report. Online. Available at: www.cgap.org/gm/document-1.9.46570/FA_2010_Financial_Access_2010_Rev.pdf (accessed January 28, 2012).

Chew, J. (2011) "The Malaysian Financial System," Bank Negara Malaysia report. Online. Available at: www.fstep.org.my/media/File/Overview%20Week%20Notes/

FSTEP%20presentation%20%28JC%29%20-%20The%20Malaysian%20Finan-
cial%20System.pdf (accessed January 21, 2012).

Chinn, M. D. (2006) "A Primer on Real Effective Exchange Rates: Determinants, Over-
valuation, Trade Flows and Competitive Devaluation," *Open Economies Review*, 17,
115–43.

Chovanec, P. (2009) "China's Real Estate Riddle," *Far East Economic Review*, 172, June
8, 2009. Online. Available at: www.feer.com/economics/2009/june53/Chinas-Real-
Estate-Riddle (accessed June 30, 2011).

Christensen, J. (2004) "Domestic Debt Markets in Sub-Saharan Africa," IMF Working
Paper No. 04/46.

Claessens, S. and Van Horen, N. (2008) "Location Decisions of Foreign Banks and Institutional Competitive Advantage," DNB Working Paper No. 172.

Claessens, S., Demirgüç-Kunt, A., and Huizinga, H. (2001) "How Does Foreign Entry
Affect Domestic Banking Markets?," *Journal of Banking and Finance*, 25, 891–911.

Clarke, G., Cull, R., and Peria, M. S. M. (2006) "Foreign Bank Participation and Access
to Credit across Firms in Developing Countries," *Journal of Comparative Economic*,
34, 774–95.

Clements, K. W., Lan, Y., and Seah, S. P. (2010) "The Big Mac Index Two Decades on:
An Evaluation of Burgernomics," University of Western Australia Discussion Paper
No. 10.14.

Collins, D., Morduch, J., Rutherford, S., and Ruthven, O. (2009) *Portfolios of the Poor:
How the Poor Live on $2 a Day*, Princeton, NJ: Princeton University Press.

Corsetti, G., Pesenti, P., and Roubini, N. (1999) "What Caused the Asian Currency and
Financial Crisis?," *Japan and the World Economy*, 11, 305–73.

Creane, S., Goyal, R., Mobarak, A. M., and Sab, R. (2007) "Measuring Financial Development in the Middle East and North Africa: A New Database," *IMF Staff Papers*, 53,
479–511.

Cukierman, A., Webb, S., and Neyapti, B. (1992) "Measuring the Independence of
Central Banks and Its Effect on Policy Outcomes," *World Bank Economic Review*, 6,
353–98.

Cull, R. and Peria, M. S. M. (2010) "Foreign Bank Participation in Developing Countries:
What Do We Know about the Drivers and Consequences of This Phenomenon?,"
World Bank Policy Research Working Paper Series 5398.

Cull, R., Demirgüç-Kunt, A., and Morduch, J. (2009) "Microfinance Meets the Market,"
Journal of Economic Perspectives, 23, 167–92.

Cull, R., Demirgüç-Kunt, A., and Morduch, J. (2007) "Financial Performance and Outreach:
A Global Analysis of Leading Microbanks," *Economic Journal*, 117, F107–F133.

Daley-Harris, S. (2007) "State of the Microcredit Summit Campaign Report 2007,"
Microcredit Summit report. Online. Available at: http://microcreditsummit.org/pubs/
reports/socr/EngSOCR2007.pdf (accessed April 13, 2012).

De Gregorio, J., Edwards, S., and Valdes, R. O. (2000) "Controls on Capital Inflows: Do
They Work?," *Journal of Development Economics*, 61, 59–83.

de la Campa, A. A. (2011) "Increasing Access to Credit through Reforming Secured
Transactions in the MENA region," World Bank Policy Research Working Paper No.
5613.

de la Torre, A. (2003) "Living and Dying With Hard Pegs: The Rise and Fall of Argentina's Currency Board," *Economia*, 3, 43–107.

de la Torre, A., Feyen, E., and Ize, A. (2011) "Financial Development: Structure and
Dynamics," World Bank Policy Research Working Paper No. 5854.

de la Torre, A., Ize, A., and Schmukler, S. L. (2012) *Financial Development in Latin America and the Caribbean*, Washington, DC: World Bank.

de Mel, S., McKenzie, D., and Woodruff, C. (2008) "Returns to Capital in Microenterprises: Evidence from a Field Experiment," *Quarterly Journal of Economics*, 123, 1329–72.

Demirgüç-Kunt, A. (2010) "Finance and Economic Development: The Role of Government," in A. Berger, P. Molyneux, and J. Wilson (eds.) *The Oxford Handbook of Banking*, Oxford: Oxford University Press.

Demirgüç-Kunt, A., and Detragiache, E. (1999) "Financial Liberalization and Financial Fragility," World Bank Policy Research Working Paper No. 1917.

Demirgüç-Kunt, A. and Detragiache, E. (1998) "The Determinants of Banking Crises in Developing and Developed Countries," *IMF Staff Papers*, 45, 81–109.

Demirgüç-Kunt, A. and Levine, R. (2009) "Finance, Financial Sector Policies, and Long-Run Growth," World Bank Working Paper No. 4469.

Demirgüç-Kunt, A. and Levine, R. (2008) "Finance and Economic Opportunity," World Bank Policy Research Paper No. 4468.

Demirgüç-Kunt, A. and Levine, R. (2001) "Bank-Based and Market-Based Financial Systems: Cross-Country Comparisons," in *Financial Structure and Economic Growth*, Cambridge, MA: MIT Press.

Demirgüç-Kunt, A., Beck, T., and Honohan, P. (2008) *Finance for All? Policies and Pitfalls in Expanding Access*, Washington, DC: World Bank.

Demirgüç-Kunt, A., Detragiache, E., and Gupta, P. (2006) "Inside the Crisis: An Empirical Analysis of Banking Systems in Distress," *Journal of International Money and Finance*, 25, 702–18.

Demirgüç-Kunt, A., Laeven, L., and Levine, R. (2004) "Regulations, Market Structure, Institutions, and the Cost of Financial Intermediation," *Journal of Money, Credit and Banking*, 36, 593–622.

Demirgüç-Kunt, A., Levine, R., and Min, H. G. (1998) "Opening to Foreign Banks: Issues of Efficiency, Stability, and Growth," in S. Lee (ed.) *The Implications of Globalization of World Financial Markets*, Seoul: The Bank of Korea.

Desmet, K. (2000) "Accounting for the Mexican Banking Crisis," *Emerging Markets Review*, 1, 165–81.

Desormeaux, J., Fernández, K., and García, P. (2008) "Financial Implications of Capital Outflows in Chile: 1998–2008," Bank of International Settlements Papers No. 44.

de Soto, H. (2000) *The Mystery of Capital: Why Capitalism Triumphs in the West and Fails Everywhere Else*, New York: Basic Books.

Detragiache, E., Gupta, P., and Tressel, T. (2005) "Finance in Lower-Income Countries: An Empirical Exploration," IMF Working Paper No. 167.

de Wet, W. A. (2004) "The Role of Asymmetric Information on Investments in Emerging Markets," *Economic Modeling*, 21, 621–30.

Diamond, D. W. and Dybvig, P. H. (1983) "Bank Runs, Deposit Insurance, and Liquidity," *Journal of Political Economy*, 91, 401–19.

Didier, T., Hevia, C., and Schmukler, S. L. (2011) "How Resilient Were Emerging Economies to the Global Crisis?," World Bank Policy Research Working Paper No. 5637.

Djankov, S., McLeish, C., and Shleifer, A. (2007) "Private Credit in 129 Countries," *Journal of Financial Economics*, 84, 299–329.

Dominguez, K. M. E. (2010) "International Reserves and Underdeveloped Capital Markets," in L. Reichlin and K. West (eds.) *NBER International Seminar on Macroeconomics 2009*, Chicago: University of Chicago Press.

Dorn, J. A. (2006) "Ending Financial Repression in China," Cato Economic Development Bulletin No. 5.

Dreher, A. (2009) "IMF Conditionality: Theory and Evidence," *Public Choice*, 141, 233–67.

Dupas, P. and Robinson, J. (2012) "Savings Constraints and Microenterprise Development: Evidence from a Field Experiment in Kenya," *American Economic Journal: Applied Economics*, forthcoming.

Durnev, A., Li, K., Morck, R., and Yeung, B. (2004) "Capital Markets and Capital Allocation: Implications for Economies in Transition," *Economics of Transition*, 12, 593–634.

Easterly, W. (2007) *The White Man's Burden: Why the West's Efforts to Aid the Rest Have Done So Much Ill and So Little Good*, New York: Penguin.

Easterly, W. and Levine, R. (2003) "Tropics, Germs, and Crops: How Endowments Influence Economic Development," *Journal of Monetary Economics*, 50, 3–39.

Easterly, W., Islam, R., and Stiglitz, J. E. (2001) "Volatility and Macroeconomic Paradigms for Rich and Poor Countries," in J. Dreze (ed.) *Advances in Macroeconomic Theory*, New York: Palgrave.

Edison, H., Klein, M., Ricci, L., and Sløk, T. (2004) "Capital Account Liberalization, and Economic Performance: Synthesis and Survey," *IMF Staff Papers*, 51, 220–56.

Edwards, S. (2007) "Capital Controls, Sudden Stops and Current Account Reversals," in S. Edwards (ed.) *Capital Controls and Capital Flows in Emerging Economies: Policies, Practices and Consequences*, Chicago: University of Chicago Press.

Edwards, S. (2001) "Capital Mobility and Economic Performance: Are Emerging Economies Different?," NBER Working Paper No. 8076.

Eichengreen, B. (2003a) "A Century of Capital Flows," in B. Eichengreen (ed.) *Capital Flows and Crisis*, Cambridge, MA: MIT Press.

Eichengreen, B. (2003b) "Understanding Asia's Crisis," in B. Eichengreen (ed.) *Capital Flows and Crisis*, Cambridge, MA: MIT Press.

Eichengreen, B. (2001) "Capital Account Liberalization: What Do Cross-Country Studies Tell Us?," *World Bank Economic Review*, 16, 341–65.

Eichengreen, B. (1999) *Toward a New International Architecture*, Washington, DC: Institute of International Economics.

Eichengreen, B. and Arteta, C. (2002) "Banking Crises in Emerging Markets: Presumptions and Evidence," in M. Blejer and M. Skreb (eds.) *Financial Policies in Emerging Markets*, Cambridge, MA: MIT Press.

Eichengreen, B. and Razo-Garcia, R. (2006) "The International Monetary System in the Last and Next 20 Years," *Economic Policy*, 21, 393–442.

Eichengreen, B., Arteta, C., and Wyplosz, C. (2003) "When Does Capital Account Liberalization Help More Than It Hurts?," in B. Eichengreen (ed.) *Capital Flows and Crisis*, Cambridge, MA: MIT Press.

Eichengreen, B., Gullapalli, R., and Panizza, U. (2009) "Capital Account Liberalization, Financial Development and Industry Growth: A Synthetic View," *Journal of International Money and Finance*, 30, 1090–106.

Eichengreen, B., Rose, A., and Wyplosz, C. (2003a) "Exchange Market Mayhem: The Antecedents and Aftermath of Speculative Attacks," in B. Eichengreen (ed.) *Capital Flows and Crisis*, Cambridge, MA: MIT Press.

Eichengreen, B., Rose, A., and Wyplosz, C. (2003b) "Contagious Currency Crises," in B. Eichengreen (ed.) *Capital Flows and Crisis*, Cambridge, MA: MIT Press.

Estrada, G., Park, D., and Ramayandi, A. (2010) "Financial Development and Economic Growth in Developing Asia," Asian Development Bank Economics Working Paper Series No. 233.

Fajnzylber, P. and López, J. H. (2007) *Close to Home: The Development Impact of Remittances in Latin America*, Washington, DC: World Bank.

Farrell, D. and Lund, S. (2006) "China's and India's Financial Systems: A Barrier to Growth," *McKinsey Quarterly*, November. Online. Available at: www.mckinseyquarterly.com/Chinas_and_Indias_financial_systems_A_barrier_to_growth_1878 (accessed January 18, 2012).

Fazari, S., Feyen, E., and Rocha, R. (2011) "Bank Ownership and Performance in the Middle East and North Africa Region," World Bank Policy Research Working Paper No. 5620.

Feigenberg, E., Field, E., and Pande, R. (2010) "Building Social Capital through Microfinance," NBER Working Paper No. 16018.

Feldstein, M. (2002) "Argentina's Fall: Lessons from the Latest Financial Crisis," *Foreign Affairs*, 81, 8–15.

Ferguson, N. (2008) *The Ascent of Money: A Financial History of the World*, New York: Penguin.

Ferri, G. and Liu, L. (2010) "Honor Thy Creditors before Thy Shareholders: Are the Profits of Chinese State-Owned Enterprises Real?," *Asian Economic Papers*, 9, 50–71.

Financial Stability Board (2010) "Country Review of Mexico," report. Online. Available at: www.financialstabilityboard.org/publications/r_100927.pdf (accessed January 24, 2012).

Fischer, B. and Reisen, H. (1993) "Financial Opening in Developing Countries," *Intereconomics: Review of European Economic Policy*, 28, 44–8.

Fischer, S. (1982) "Seigniorage and the Case for a National Money," *Journal of Political Economy*, 90, 295–313.

Fisher, I. (1933) "The Debt-Deflation Theory of Great Depressions," *Econometrica*, 1, 337–57.

Fraga, A. Goldfajn, I., and Minella, A. (2004) "Inflation Targeting in Emerging Market Economies," *NBER Macroeconomics Annual 2003*, 18, 365–416.

Frankel, J. (2010) "Monetary Policy in Emerging Markets: A Survey," NBER Working Paper No. 16125.

Frankel, J. and Rose, A. (2002) "An Estimate of the Effect of Common Currencies on Trade and Income," *Quarterly Journal of Economics*, 117, 437–66.

Frankel, J. and Rose, A. (1996) "Currency Crashes in Emerging Markets: An Empirical Treatment," *Journal of International Economics*, 41, 351–66.

Froot, K. A., O'Connell, P. G. J., and Seasholes, M. S. (2001) "The Portfolio Flows of International Investors," *Journal of Financial Economics*, 69, 151–93.

Galindo, A., Micco, A., and Ordoñez, G. (2002) "Financial Liberalization: Does It Pay to Join the Party?," *Economia*, 3, 231–61.

García-Escribano, M. and Sosa, S. (2010) "What Is Driving Financial De-Dollarization in Latin America?," IMF Working Paper No. 11/10.

Giannetti, M., and Ongena, S. (2009) "Financial Integration and Firm Performance: Evidence from Foreign Bank Entry in Emerging Markets," *Review of Finance*, 13, 181–223.

Gil-Díaz, F. (1998) "The Origin of Mexico's 1994 Financial Crisis," *Cato Journal*, 17, 303–13.

Giné, X. and Karlan, D. (2009) "Group Versus Individual Liability: Long Term Evidence from Philippine Microcredit Lending Groups," Yale University Working Paper No. 970.

Giuliano, P. and Ruiz-Arranz, M. (2005) "Remittances, Financial Development, and Growth," IMF Working Paper No. 05/234.

Glick, R. and Hutchison, M. (2005) "Capital Controls and Exchange Rate Instability in Developing Countries," *Journal of International Money and Finance*, 24, 387–412.

Glick, R. and Hutchison, M. (2001) "Banking and Currency Crises: How Common Are Twins?," in R. Glick, R. Moreno, and M. Spiegel (eds.) *Financial Crises in Emerging Markets*, New York: Cambridge University Press.

Glick, R., Guo, X., and Hutchison, M. (2006) "Currency Crises, Capital-Account Liberalization, and Selection Bias," *Review of Economics and Statistics*, 88, 698–714.

Goldstein, I. (2005) "Strategic Complementarities and the Twin Crises," *Economic Journal*, 115, 368–90.

Goldstein, M. (1998) *The Asian Financial Crisis: Causes, Cures, and Systemic Implications*, Washington, DC: Institute of International Economics.

Gonçalves, C. E. S. and Salles, J. M. (2008) "Inflation Targeting in Emerging Economies: What Do the Data Say?," *Journal of Development Economics*, 85, 312–18.

Gonzalez, A. and Meyer, R. (2009) "Microfinance and Small Deposit Mobilization," Microfinance Information Exchange Brief No. 2.

González, M., Khosa, U., Liu, P., Schipke, A., and Thacker, N. (forthcoming) "Offshore Financial Centers: Opportunities and Challenges for the Caribbean," IMF Working Paper.

Guillaume, D. and Sensenbrenner, G. (2011) "Islamic Republic of Iran: Selected Issues Paper," IMF Staff Report No. 11/242.

Guiso, L., Sapienza, P., and Zingales, L. (2006) "Does Culture Affect Economic Outcomes?," *Journal of Economic Perspectives*, 20, 23–48.

Guiso, L., Sapienza, P., and Zingales, L. (2004) "The Role of Social Capital in Financial Development," *American Economic Review*, 4, 526–56.

Haber, S. (2005) "Mexico's Experiment With Bank Privatization and Liberalization, 1991–2002," *Journal of Banking and Finance*, 29, 2325–53.

Haber, S. (2004) "Political Competition and Economic Growth: Lessons from the Political Economy of Bank Regulation in the United States and Mexico," Stanford University mimeo. Online. Available at: http://siteresources.worldbank.org/INTPUB-SERV/Resources/haber_political.pdf (accessed January 29, 2012).

Haggarty, L. and Shirley, M. M. (1997) "A New Data Base on State-Owned Enterprises," *World Bank Economic Review*, 11, 491–513.

Hahm, J. and Lim, W. (2006) "Turning a Crisis into Opportunity: The Political Economy of Korea's Financial Sector Reform," in J. Mo and D. I. Okimoto (eds.) *From Crisis to Opportunity: Financial Globalization and East Asian Capitalism*, Washington, DC: Brookings Institute Press.

Hahm, J. and Mishkin, F. S. (2000) "The Korean Financial Crisis: An Asymmetric Information Perspective," *Emerging Markets Review*, 1, 172–93.

Hashmi, M. A. (2007) "An Analysis of the United Arab Emirates Banking Sector," *International Business and Economics Research Journal*, 6, 77–88.

Haslag, J. H. and Koo, J. (1999) "Financial Repression, Financial Development and Economic Growth," Federal Reserve Bank of Dallas Working Paper No. 9902.

Hawksworth, J. (2006) "The World in 2050: How Big Will the Major Emerging Market Economies Get and How Can the OECD Compete?," PricewaterhouseCoopers report. Online. Available at: www.pwc.com/gx/en/world-2050/growth-in-emerging-economies-oportunity-or-threat.jhtml (accessed March 2, 2011).

Hellmann, T. and Stiglitz, J. E. (2000) "Credit and Equity Rationing in Markets With Adverse Selection," *European Economic Review*, 44, 281–304.

Henry, P. B. (2007) "Capital Account Liberalization: Theory, Evidence, and Speculation," *Journal of Economic Literature*, 45, 887–935.

Henry, P. B. (2003) "Capital-Account Liberalization, the Cost of Capital, and Economic Growth," *American Economic Review*, 93, 91–6.

Heritage Foundation (2011) *Index of Economic Freedom*. Online. Available at: www.heritage.org/index (accessed February 23, 2012).

Hermes, N. and Lensink, R. (2007) "The Empirics of Microfinance: What Do We Know?," *Economic Journal*, 117, F1–F10.

Higgins, M. and Osler, C. (1997) "Asset Market Hangovers and Economic Growth: The OECD during 1984–93," *Oxford Review of Economic Policy*, 13, 110–34.

Hochschild, A. (1998) *King Leopold's Ghost: A Story of Greed, Terror, and Heroism in Colonial Africa*, New York: Mariner Books.

Honohan, P. (2004) "Financial Development, Growth, and Poverty: How Close Are the Links?," World Bank Policy Research Working Paper No. 3203.

Honohan, P. and Beck, T. (2007) *Making Finance Work for Africa*, Washington, DC: World Bank.

Honohan, P. and Klingebiel, D. (2003) "The Fiscal Cost Implications of an Accommodating Approach to Banking Crises," *Journal of Banking and Finance*, 27, 1539–60.

Hossain, M. (1988) *Credit for Alleviation of Rural Poverty: The Grameen Bank in Bangladesh*, Washington, DC: International Food Policy Research Institute.

Huang, Y. (2008) "Just How Capitalist Is China?," MIT Sloan School of Management Working Paper No. 4699–08.

Hurst, E. and Lusardi, A. (2004) "Liquidity Constraints, Household Wealth, and Entrepreneurship," *Journal of Political Economy*, 112, 319–47.

Hutchison, M. M. and Noy, I. (2006) "Sudden Stops and the Mexican Wave: Currency Crises, Capital Flow Reversals and Output Loss in Emerging Markets," *Journal of Development Economics*, 79, 225–48.

Hutchison, M. M. and Noy, I. (2005) "How Bad Are Twins? Output Costs of Currency and Banking Crises," *Journal of Money, Credit, and Banking*, 37, 699–724.

International Monetary Fund (IMF) (2011a) *World Economic Outlook Database*. Online. Available HTTP: www.lmf.org/external/data.htm#data (accessed April 13, 2012).

IMF (2011b) "Recent Experiences in Managing Capital Inflows: Cross-Cutting Themes and Possible Policy Framework," mimeo. Online. Available at: www.imf.org/external/np/pp/eng/2011/021411a.pdf (accessed October 16, 2011).

IMF (2011c) "Regional Economic Outlook: Asia and Pacific," *World Economic and Financial Surveys*, Washington, DC: IMF Publication Services.

IMF (2011d) "Regional Economic Outlook: Sub-Saharan Africa," *World Economic and Financial Surveys*, Washington, DC: IMF Publication Services.

IMF (2011e) "Regional Economic Outlook: Middle East and Central Asia," *World Economic and Financial Surveys*, Washington, DC: IMF Publication Services.

IMF (2011f) "Regional Economic Outlook: Western Hemisphere," *World Economic and Financial Surveys*, Washington, DC: IMF Publication Services.

IMF (2011g) *International Financial Statistics*. Online. Available at: www.imf.org/external/data.html (accessed April 12, 2012).

IMF (2010a) "Regional Economic Outlook: Sub-Saharan Africa: Resilience and Risks," *World Economic and Financial Surveys*, Washington, DC: IMF Publication Services.

IMF (2010b) "Regional Economic Outlook: Middle East and Central Asia," *World Economic and Financial Surveys*, Washington, DC: IMF Publication Services.

IMF (2010c) "Regional Economic Outlook: Asia and Pacific," *World Economic and Financial Surveys*, Washington, DC: IMF Publication Services.

IMF (2010d) "Indonesia: Financial System Stability Assessment," IMF Country Report No. 10/288.

IMF (2010e) "Regional Economic Outlook: Western Hemisphere," *World Economic and Financial Surveys*, Washington, DC: IMF Publication Services.

IMF (2008) "De Facto Classification of Exchange Rate Regimes and Monetary Policy Frameworks." Online. Available at: www.imf.org/external/np/mfd/er/2008/eng/0408. htm (accessed March 28, 2012).

Isern, J., Agbakoba, A., Fleming, M., Mantilla, J., Pellegrini, G., and Tarazi, M. (2009) "Access to Finance in Nigeria: Microfinance, Branchless Banking, and SME Financing," World Bank Working Paper. Online. Available at: www.microfinancegateway. org/gm/document-1.9.34020/56437.pdf (accessed July 15, 2011).

Ito, H. (2006) "Financial Development and Financial Liberalization in Asia: Thresholds, Institutions and the Sequence of Liberalization," *North American Journal of Economics and Finance*, 17, 303–27.

Ito, H. and Chinn, M. (2012) "Notes on the Chinn–Ito Financial Openness Index 2010 Update," mimeo. Online. Available at: http://web.pdx.edu/~ito/Readme_kaopen2010. pdf (accessed April 14, 2012).

Jadhav, N. and Raj, J. (2009) "Financial Systems in India and China: A Comparative Study," in B. S. Reddy (ed.) *Economic Reforms in India and China: Emerging Issues and Challenges*, Thousand Oaks, CA: SAGE Publications.

Jeanne, O. (2007) "International Reserves in Emerging Market Countries: Too Much of a Good Thing?," *Brookings Papers on Economic Activity*, 1, 1–55.

Jiménez, L. and Manuelito, S. (2011) "Latin America: Financial Systems and Financing of Investment," *CEPAL Review*, 103, 45–71.

Joyce, J. P. (2011) "Financial Globalization and Banking Crises in Emerging Markets," *Open Economies Review*, 22, 875–95.

Kamal, M. (2010) "Inflation Targeting in Brazil, Chile, and South Africa: An Empirical Investigation of Their Monetary Policy Framework," William Davidson Institute Working Paper No. 100.

Kaminsky, G. L. and Reinhart, C. (2000) "On Crises, Contagion, and Confusion," *Journal of International Economics*, 51, 145–68.

Kaminsky, G. L. and Reinhart, C. (1999) "The Twin Crises: The Causes of Banking and Balance-of-Payments Problems," *American Economic Review*, 89, 473–500.

Kaminsky, G. L. and Schmukler, S. (2003) "Short-Run Pain, Long-Run Gain: The Effects of Financial Liberalization," NBER Working Paper No. 9787.

Kaminsky, G. L., Reinhart, C., and Végh, C. A. (2005) "When It Rains, It Pours: Procyclical Capital Flows and Macroeconomic Policies," *NBER Macroeconomics Annual 2004*, 19, 11–82.

Kaminsky, G. L., Reinhart, C., and Végh, C. A. (2003) "The Unholy Trinity of Financial Contagion," *Journal of Economic Perspectives*, 17, 51–74.

Karlan, D. S. (2005) "Using Experimental Economics to Measure Social Capital and Predict Financial Decisions," *American Economic Review*, 95, 1688–99.

Karlan, D. S. (2007) "Social Connections and Group Banking," *Economic Journal*, 117, F52–F84.

Karlan, D. S. and Zinman, J. (2010) "Expanding Credit Access: Using Randomized Supply Decisions to Estimate the Impacts," *Review of Financial Studies*, 23, 433–64.

Karlan, D. S. and Zinman, J. (2009) "Expanding Microenterprise Credit Access: Using Randomized Supply Decisions to Estimate the Impacts in Manila," Economic Growth Center Discussion Papers No. 976.

Keynes, J. M. (1936 [1964]) *The General Theory of Employment, Interest, and Money*, London: Macmillian.

Keynes, J. M. (1933) "National Self-Sufficiency," *The Yale Review*, 22, 760.

Khandker, S. R. (2005) "Microfinance and Poverty: Evidence Using Panel Data from Bangladesh," *World Bank Economic Review*, 19, 263–86.

Kikeri, S. and Nellis, J. (2002) "Privatization in Competitive Sectors: The Record to Date," World Bank Policy Research Working Paper No. 2860.

Kindleberger, C. (1989) *Manias, Panics, and Crashes: A History of Financial Crises*, New York: Basic Books, Inc.

King, R. G. and Levine, R. (1993) "Finance and Growth: Schumpeter Might be Right," *Quarterly Journal of Economics*, 108, 716–37.

Klein, M. W. (2003) "Capital Account Openness and the Varieties of Growth Experience," NBER Working Paper No. 9500.

Knack, S. (2004) "Aid Dependence and the Quality of Governance: Cross-Country Empirical Tests," *Southern Economic Journal*, 68, 310–29.

Knoop, T. (2008) *Modern Financial Macroeconomics: Panics, Crashes, and Crises*, Hoboken, NJ: Wiley-Blackwell.

Kokenyne, A., Ley, J., and Veyrune, R. (2010) "Dedollarization," IMF Working Paper No. 10/188.

Kopits, G. (2000) "How Can Fiscal Policy Help Avert Currency Crises?," IMF Working Paper No. 185.

Kose, M. A., Prasad, E., Rogoff, K., and Wei, S. (2009) "Financial Globalization: A Reappraisal," *IMF Staff Papers*, 56, 8–62.

Kose, M. A., Prasad, E., and Terrones, M. (2009) "Does Openness to International Financial Flows Raise Productivity Growth?," *Journal of International Money and Finance*, 28, 554–80.

Krueger, A. O. (2002) "IMF Stabilization Programs," in M. Feldstein (ed.) *Economic and Financial Crises in Emerging Market Economies*, Chicago: University of Chicago Press.

Krugman, P. (2008) *The Return of Depression Economics and the Crisis of 2008*, New York: W. W. Norton.

Krugman, P. (1979) "A Model of Balance-of-Payments Crises," *Journal of Money, Credit, and Banking*, 11, 311–25.

Krugman, P., Obstfeld, M., and Melitz, M. (2011) *International Economics*, 9th edn., Upper Saddle River, NJ: Prentice Hall.

Kuran, T. (2005) "The Logic of Financial Westernization in the Middle East," *Journal of Economic Behavior & Organization*, 56, 593–615.

Kuran, T. (2004) "Why the Middle East Is Economically Underdeveloped: Historical Mechanisms of Institutional Stagnation," *Journal of Economic Perspectives*, 18, 71–90.

Laeven, L. and Valencia, F. (2008) "Systemic Banking Crises: A New Database," IMF Working Paper No. 08/224.

Landes, D. S. (1999) *The Wealth and Poverty of Nations*, New York: W. W. Norton.

La Porta, R., Lopez-de-Silanes, F., and Shleifer, A. (2008) "The Economic Consequences of Legal Origins," *Journal of Economic Literature*, 46, 285–332.

La Porta, R., Lopez-de-Silanes, F., and Shleifer, A. (2002) "Government Ownership of Banks," *Journal of Finance*, 57, 265–301.

La Porta, R., Lopez-de-Silanes, F., and Zamarippa, G. (2003) "Related Lending," *Quarterly Journal of Economics*, 118, 231–68.

Levine, R. (2005) "Law, Endowments, and Property Rights," *Journal of Economic Perspectives*, 19, 61–88.

Levine, R. (1997) "Financial Development and Economic Growth: Views and Agenda," *Journal of Economic Literature*, 35, 688–726.

Levine, R. and Zervos, S. (1998) "Capital Control Liberalization and Stock Market Development," *World Development*, 26, 1169–83.

Levine, R., Loayza, N., and Beck, T. (2000) "Financial Intermediation and Growth: Causality and Causes," *Journal of Monetary Economics*, 46, 31–77.

Lucas, R. E. (1988) "On the Mechanics of Economic Development," *Journal of Monetary Economics*, 22, 3–42.

McGregor, J. (2005) *One Billion Customers: Lessons from the Front Lines of Doing Business in China*, New York: Simon and Schuster.

McGregor, R. (2010) *The Party: The Secret World of China's Communist Rulers*, New York: Harper.

McKenzie, D. and Woodruff, C. (2008) "Experimental Evidence of Returns to Capital and Access to Finance in Mexico," *World Bank Economic Review*, 22, 457–82.

McKinnon, R. I. (1992) *The Order of Economic Liberalization*, Baltimore, MD: Johns Hopkins University Press.

Madeddu, O. (2010) "The Status of Information Sharing and Credit Reporting Infrastructure in the Middle East and North Africa Region," World Bank Financial Flagship Report. Online. Available at: http://siteresources.worldbank.org/INTMNAREGTOP-POVRED/Resources/MENAFlagshipCreditReporting12_20_10.pdf (accessed October 11, 2011).

Megginson, W. L. (2010) "Privatization and Finance," *Annual Review of Financial Economics*, 2, 145–74.

Megginson, W. L. (2005) *The Financial Economics of Privatization*, New York: Oxford University Press.

Mendoza, E. G. and Terrones, M. (2008) "An Anatomy of Credit Booms: Evidence from the Marcro Aggregates and Micro Data," NBER Working Paper 14049.

Mihaljek, D. (2010) "Domestic Bank Intermediation in Emerging Market Economies During the Crisis: Locally Owned Versus Foreign-Owned Banks," Bank of International Settlements Papers No. 54.

Minsky, H. P. (1982) *Can It Happen Again? Essays on Instability and Finance*, Armonk, NY: M. E. Sharpe.

Mishkin, F. S. (2006a) *The Next Great Globalization: How Disadvantaged Nations Can Harness Their Financial Systems to Get Rich*, Princeton, NJ: Princeton University Press.

Mishkin, F. S. (2006b) "Globalization: A Force for Good?," speech given for Weissman Center Distinguished Lecture Series, New York, October 12, 2006. Online. Available at: www.federalreserve.gov/newsevents/speech/Mishkin20061012a.htm   (accessed April 14, 2012).

Mishkin, F. S. (1999) "Global Financial Instability: Framework, Events, Issues," *Journal of Economic Perspectives*, 13, 3–20.

Mishra, P. (2005) "Macroeconomic Impact of Remittances in the Caribbean," unpublished IMF working paper.

Mishra, P., Montiel, P. J., and Spilimbergo, A. (2010) "Monetary Transmission in Low Income Countries," CEPR Discussion Paper No. DP7951.

Mitchell, W. C. (1941) *Business Cycles and Their Causes*, Berkeley, CA: University of California Press.

Mody, A., Taylor, M. P., and Kim, J. Y. (2001) "Modeling Fundamentals for Forecasting Capital Flows to Emerging Markets," *International Journal of Finance and Economics*, 6, 201–16.

Montiel, P. J. and Reinhart, C. M. (1999) "Do Capital Controls and Macroeconomic Policies Influence the Volume and Composition of Capital Flows? Evidence from the 1990s," *Journal of International Money and Finance*, 18, 619–35.

Moody's (2011) "Banking System Outlook: Argentina," report. Online. Available at: www.ambito.com/diario/aw_documentos/archivospdf/2005/id_doc_5736.pdf (accessed January 11, 2012).

Morduch, J. (1999) "The Microfinance Promise," *Journal of Economic Literature*, 37, 1569–614.

Moreno, L. A. (2007) "Extended Financial Services to Latin America's Poor," *McKinsey Quarterly*, March, 83–91.

Mundell, R. A. (1961) "A Theory of Optimum Currency Areas," *American Economic Review*, 51, 657–65.

Nasr, S. (2006) "Access to Finance and Economic Growth in Egypt," World Bank Report. Online. Available at: http://siteresources.worldbank.org/INTEGYPT/Resources/Access_to_Finance.pdf (accessed October 13, 2011).

Naudé, W. (1996) "Financial Liberalisation and Interest Rate Risk Management in Sub-Saharan Africa," CSAE Working Paper Series 1996–2012.

Nzotta, S. and Okereke, E. J. (2009) "Financial Deepening and Economic Development of Nigeria: An Empirical Investigation," *African Journal of Accounting, Economics, Finance and Banking Research*, 5, 52–66.

Obstfeld, M. (1996) "Models of Currency Crises with Self-Fulfilling Features," *European Economic Review*, 40, 1037–47.

OECD (2010) *Latin American Economic Outlook 2010*, Paris: OECD Publications.

Orwell, G. (1936 [1969]) *Keep the Aspidistra Flying*, New York: Mariner.

Özatay, F. and Sak, G. (2002) "The 2000–2001 Financial Crisis in Turkey," Central Bank of the Republic of Turkey Working Paper No. 0308.

Paulson, A. and Townsend, R. (2004) "Entrepreneurship and Financial Constraints in Thailand," *Journal of Corporate Finance*, 10, 229–62.

Pearce, D. (2011) "Financial Inclusion in the Middle East and North Africa," World Bank Policy Research Working Paper No. 5610.

Pham, T. T. T. and Lensink, R. (2008) "Household Borrowing in Vietnam: A Comparative Study of Default Risks of Formal, Informal and Semi-formal Credit," *Journal of Emerging Market Finance*, 7, 237–61.

Pill, H. and Pradhan, M. (1997) "Financial Liberalization in Africa and Asia," *Finance and Development*, 34, 7–10.

Poole, W. (1970) "Optimal Choice of Monetary Policy Instruments in a Simple Stochastic Macro Model," *Quarterly Journal of Economics*, 84, 197–216.

Prasad, E. (2009) "Some New Perspectives on India's Approach to Capital Account Liberalization," NBER Working Paper Series No. 14658.

Prasad, E. and Rajan, R. (2008) "A Pragmatic Approach to Capital Account Liberalization," *Journal of Economic Perspectives*, 22, 149–72.

Rajan, R. G. and Zingales, L. (2003) "The Great Reversals: The Politics of Financial Development in the Twentieth Century," *Journal of Financial Economics*, 69, 5–50.

Ramirez, M. D. and Sharma, H. (2009) "Remittances and Growth in Latin America: A Panel Unit Root and Panel Cointegration Analysis," *Estudios Economicos de Desarrollo Internacional*, 9.

Reinhart, C. M. (2005) "Some Perspectives on Capital Flows to Emerging Market Economies," *National Bureau of Economic Research Reporter*, Summer. Online. Available at: www.nber.org/reporter/summer05/reinhart.html (accessed June 24, 2011).

Reinhart, C. M. and Reinhart, V. R. (2009) "Capital Flow Bonanzas: An Encompassing View of the Past and Present," in J. Frankel and F. Giavazzi (eds.) *NBER International Seminar in Macroeconomics 2008*, Chicago: Chicago University Press.

Reinhart, C. M. and Rogoff, K. S. (2011) "From Financial Crash to Debt Crisis," *American Economic Review*, 101, 1676–706.

Reinhart, C. M. and Rogoff, K. S. (2009) *This Time Is Different: Eight Centuries of Financial Folly*, Princeton, NJ: Princeton University Press.

Reinhart, C. M. and Tokatlidis, I. (2003) "Financial Liberalisation: The African Experience," *Journal of African Economies*, 12, 53–88.

Robinson, J. (1952) *The Rate of Interest and Other Essays*, London: Macmillan.

Rocha, R., Farazi, S., Khouri, R., and Pearce, P. (2011) "The Status of Bank Lending to SMEs in the Middle East and North Africa Region," World Bank Policy Research Working Paper No. 5607.

Rodrik, D. (2007) *One Economics, Many Recipes*, Princeton, NJ: Princeton University Press.

Rose, A. K. (2011) "Exchange Rate Regimes in the Modern Era: Fixed, Floating, and Flaky," *Journal of Economic Literature*, 49, 652–72.

Rose, A. K. (2005) "Which International Institutions Promote International Trade?," *Review of International Economics*, 13, 682–98.

Rosenzweig, M. R. and Wolpin, K. (1993) "Credit Market Constraints, Consumption Smoothing, and the Accumulation of Durable Production Assets in Low-Income Countries: Investment in Bullocks in India," *Journal of Political Economy*, 101, 223–44.

Roubini, N. and Sala-i-Martin, X. (1992) "Financial Repression and Economic Growth," *Journal of Development Economics*, 39, 5–30.

Sacerdoti, E. (2005) "Access to Bank Credit in Sub-Saharan Africa: Key Issues and Reform Strategies," IMF Working Paper Series No. 05/166.

Sachs, J. (2005) *The End of Poverty: Economic Possibilities for Our Time*, New York: Penguin.

Sargent, T. and Wallace, N. (1981) "Some Unpleasant Monetarist Arithmetic," *Federal Reserve Bank of Minneapolis Quarterly Review*, Fall, 1–17.

Sarno, L. and Taylor, M. P. (2002) *The Economics of Exchange Rates*, Cambridge: Cambridge University Press.

Schumpeter, J. (1949) "The Communist Manifesto in Sociology and Economics," *Journal of Political Economy*, 57, 199–212.

Schumpeter, J. (1912 [1934]) *The Theory of Economic Development*, Cambridge, MA: Harvard University Press.

Sengupta, R. and Aubuchon, C. P. (2008) "The Microfinance Revolution: An Overview," *Federal Reserve Bank of St. Louis Review*, 90, 9–30.

Serieux, J. (2008) "Financial Liberalization and Domestic Resource Mobilization in Africa: An Assessment," International Poverty Centre Working Paper No. 45.

Shah, A. and Patnaik, I. (2011) "Reforming the Indian Financial System," National Institute of Public Finance and Policy Working Paper No. 2011–80.

Shiller, R. J. (2012) *Finance and the Good Society*, Princeton, NJ: Princeton University Press.

Shiller, R. J. (2005) *Irrational Exuberance*, 2nd edn., Princeton, NJ: Princeton University Press.

Shimada, T. and Yang, T. (2010) "Challenges and Developments in the Financial Systems of the Southeast Asian Economies," *OECB Journal: Financial Market Trends*, 10, 137–59.

Sidaoui, J. (2008) "The Impact of International Financial Integration on Mexican Financial Markets," Bank of International Settlements Papers No. 44, pp. 341–62.

Stiglitz, J. E. (2002) *Globalization and Its Discontents*, New York: W. W. Norton.

Stiglitz, J. E. (2000) "Capital Market Liberalization, Economic Growth, and Instability," *World Development*, 28, 1075–86.

Stiglitz, J. E. (1990) "Symposium on Bubbles," *Journal of Economic Perspectives*, 4, 13–18.

Stiglitz, J. E. and Greenwald, B. (2003) *Towards a New Paradigm in Monetary Economics*, Cambridge: Cambridge University Press.

Stiglitz, J. E. and Weiss, A. (1981) "Credit Rationing in Markets With Imperfect Information," *American Economic Review*, 71, 333–421.

Stiglitz, J. E., Jaramillo-Vallejo, J., and Park, Y. C. (1993) "The Role of the State in Financial Markets," *World Bank Research Observer*, Annual Conference on Development Economics Supplement, pp. 19–61.

Svensson, J. (2005) "Eight Questions about Corruption," *Journal of Economic Perspectives*, 19, 19–42.

Tanzi, V. (1987) "Quantitative Characteristics of the Tax Systems of Developing Countries," in D. Newbery and N. Stern (eds.) *The Theory of Taxation for Developing Countries*, Oxford: Oxford University Press.

Tanzi, V. and Zee, H. H. (2000) "Tax Policy for Emerging Markets: Developing Countries," IMF Working Paper No. 35.

Taylor, M. P. and Sarno, L. (1997) "Capital Flows to Developing Countries: Long- and Short-Term Determinants," *World Bank Economic Review*, 11, 451–70.

Tornell, A., Westermann, F., and Martinez, L. (2003) "Liberalization, Growth and Financial Crises: Lessons from Mexico and the Developing World," *Brookings Papers on Economic Activity*, 2, 1–88.

Transparency International (2011) "Perceptions of Corruption," report. Online. Available at: www.transparency.org (accessed April 15, 2012).

Tsai, K. E. (2002) *Back-Alley Banking: Private Entrepreneurs in China*, Ithaca, NY: Cornell University Press.

Turtelboom, B. (1991) "Interest Rate Liberalization: Some Lessons from Africa," IMF Working Paper No. 91/121.

Udry, C. (1994) "Risk and Insurance in a Rural Credit Market: An Empirical Investigation in Northern Nigeria," *Review of Economic Studies*, 61, 495–526.

United Nations (2006) *World Urbanization Prospects: The 2005 Revision*, New York: United Nations.

Urdapilleta, E. and Stephanou, C. (2009) "Banking in Brazil: Structure, Performance, Drivers, and Policy Implications," World Bank Policy Research Working Paper No. 4809.

Vasquez, I. (1999) "The International Monetary Fund: Challenges and Contradictions," paper presented to the International Financial Advisory Commission, Washington, DC, September 28, 1999.

Walter, C. E. and Howie, F. J. T. (2011) *Red Capitalism: The Fragile Financial Foundation of China's Extraordinary Rise*, Singapore: John Wiley & Sons Publishing.

Weber, M. (1905 [2002]) *The Protestant Ethic and the Spirit of Capitalism*, London: Penguin Classics.

Williamson, J. (2004) "The Years of Emerging Market Crises: A Review of Feldstein," *Journal of Economic Literature*, 42, 822–37.

Williamson, J. (1991) "On Liberalizing the Capital Account," in R. O'Brien (ed.) *Finance and the International Economy*, Oxford: Oxford University Press.

World Bank (2012) *World Development Indicators*. Online. Available at: http://data.worldbank.org/indicator (accessed April 14, 2012).

World Bank (2011) *Doing Business 2011*, Washington, DC: World Bank.

World Bank (2010) "Issue Briefs: Migration and Remittances," September. Online. Available at: http://siteresources.worldbank.org/INTPROSPECTS/Resources/334934-1110315015165/MigrationAndDevelopmentBrief12.pdf (accessed April 15, 2012).

World Bank (2009) *Doing Business 2009*, Washington, DC: World Bank.

World Bank (2008) *Finance for All? Policies and Pitfalls in Expanding Access*, Washington, DC: World Bank.

World Bank (2007) "Impact Evaluation for Microfinance: Review of Methodological Issues," Doing Impact Evaluation No. 7.

World Bank (2003) *The East Asian Miracle: Economic Growth and Public Policy*, Washington, DC: World Bank.

Wrong, M. (2001) *In the Footsteps of Mr. Kurtz: Living on the Brink of Disaster in Mobutu's Congo*, New York, NY: HarperCollins.

Yang, D. (2011) "Migrant Remittances," *Journal of Economic Perspectives*, 25, 129–52.

Yunus, M. (1995) Speech and interview at World Bank, Washington, DC, October 4, 1995.

Zak, P. J. and Knack, S. (2001) "Trust and Growth," *Economic Journal*, 111, 295–321.

Zohir, S. (2010) "Number of Microcredit Clients Crossing the US $1.25 a Day Threshold During 1990–2009," Microcredit Summit campaign report. Online. Available at: www.microcreditsummit.org/uploads/files/Bangladesh_Report_FINAL.pdf (accessed April 14, 2012).

Zoli, E. (2005) "How Does Fiscal Policy Affect Monetary Policy in Emerging Market Economies," Bank of International Settlements Working Paper No. 174.

Zoli, E. (2004) "Credit Rationing in Emerging Economies' Access to Global Capital Markets," IMF Working Paper No. WP/04/70.

Index

Page numbers in *italics* denote tables, those in **bold** denote figures.